The indispensable
Internet Directory
to
World Wide Sport

You can use this directory to:

follow your favourite sport from your computer

check the latest sports news

visit sports fan sites

chat online with other fans around the world

place bets on sports events

buy tickets, sports equipment and other goods and

arrange travel to sports tournaments and locations online.

Happy Surfing!

rainbowdirectories

WORLD WIDE SPORT

First published in the United Kingdom in 2000
by

Dragon Publications Limited
PO Box 24076
LONDON
NW4 3ZR

Other titles in this series:
WORLD WIDE TRAVEL
WORLD WIDE SHOPPING

Printed and bound in Finland by
WS Bookwell

.

All manufacturing processes conform to the environmental regulations of the
country of origin. Nordic Environmental Label, Licence no. 444.004.

This book has been printed with the pages laid cross-weave, which means that it stays open
when laid down. We think that this is a useful feature in a directory

© **Dragon Publications Ltd. 2000**
dragonpublications.com

ISBN 1-903524-02-4

Contents

Staff and Contributors

Editor	Moshé Elias
Researchers	Alan Duffy
	Gary Gardner
	Petra Hausknecht
	Fei Kwok
	Maciek Lozinski
	Michael Parkinson
	Daniel Weinberg
Design & Layout	Gee-Design
Illustrations	Neil Webb

Introduction

Everyone enjoys some form of sport either as player or spectator or both. Sport, aside from the few hooligans who spoil the game, brings people together in a spirit of friendly competition where winning is stupendous but only part of the fun.

The old idea that it is more fulfilling to participate than to win may have tarnished a little now that sport commands so much media attention and controls such enormous sums of money. But just the same, some of that basic spirit lives on and guides the world of sport.

Countries that are not the best of friends, often enough come out through the same gate onto the same playing field and though the atmosphere may be a little tense before kick off, the game is all that matters once the whistle is blown. And when the match is over, opposing players shake hands and exchange shirts no matter which side wins.

TV has brought historic competitions into our homes where they can be shared with friends, eating crisps and drinking beer. We cheer with joy when the shot does its work and sigh with pain when it misses its target. That's all tremendous and spiritually bonding. But something's still missing; we can only watch what the TV producers, in their infinite wisdom, present us and what's worse, we cannot interact. Scream with pride or hurl abuse, the TV screen remains impassive.

Then along comes the World Wide Web to give us entertainment unlimited. We can choose what we want when we want. Chat rooms, notice boards and the tantalising prospect of virtually talking direct with our all-time heroes becomes real life experience. We can tell them how we feel, what we think, beg an autograph and vow undying loyalty. We can e-mail them knowing they will answer and communicate with fellow fans anywhere in the world to share mutual enjoyment.

Some sites give audio and video clips we can play over and over again. We can research players, teams and tournaments in our own time; buy tickets, make travel arrangements and kit up all at one source. And if that is not enough, we can follow our hunches and place bets online. Nothing can be easier nor have we had it so good before.

Because of the vast number of sites, the enormous quantity of information and the overlap of subject material, you can spend a good deal of time and money searching the Internet before finding the exact nugget of information you want. Search engines of Internet Service Providers give you so many references you can end up in a maze from which the only way out is to switch off.

rainbowdirectories are designed as friendly guides to take you directly to the web site you want to access for information, to transact or simply for entertainment.

This guide provides a directory of the best spectator sports sites we have found on the World Wide Web. As it is impossible to include every site, we chose only those we believe are the best currently available. We hope that our choice will give you endless fun and enjoyment.

Some of the sites in this directory allow you to purchase tickets, goods and services online. Please heed all warnings before purchasing and communicating your personal or financial details over the Internet. Most sites allow you to make payment in a variety of ways. If you are in doubt about the organisation represented in the web site, then take whatever steps are necessary to clear those doubts before placing an order.

What is the Internet?
The Internet is a giant network of computers spanning the globe.
It connects anyone with a computer and a modem to anyone else with a computer and a modem.

What started in the 1980's as a project to collect and securely save and disseminate information within the US Defence Organisation, came into the public domain with the ending of the Cold War. The network received a boost after 1990, when private organisations offered services to process information for general use.

The commercial potential of the Internet was recognised once telecommunications technology had improved sufficiently to allow fast data transmission at reasonable cost. The first commercial web site joined the Internet in 1991. The phenomenal growth of the network coupled with competition between service providers has driven down prices, making the Internet accessible to home users. There are now more than 2,000,000 web sites and the number is growing daily.

How do I access the Internet?

You need a computer with a modem attached to it and connected to a telephone line. You also need to subscribe to any of the Internet Service Providers and have one of the Internet browser programs installed on the hard drive of your computer. You connect to the Internet via your Service Provider, then use the browser software to find and view the particular web site you want.

What will I find at a Web Site?

A World Wide Web document, or web site, is like a file in a filing cabinet except that it stores its information in a variety of visual and sometimes aural forms. You may read text, see images as well as hear sound.

The best web sites are crammed with useful information on every conceivable topic, much of which you can act upon. Many sites are interactive and may even allow you to play games on them, joining other players from anywhere in the world. The data on most sites can be downloaded to your computer so that you can make a hard copy of the information.

Your security on the line

Your major concern if you intend to purchase on the Internet is credit card security. How well founded are people's fears about handing over their credit card details online? Despite the recent expansion in online buying, there have been very few reported cases of credit card details being intercepted online. You are more likely to have your wallet or purse lifted at a crowded match than your credit card details lifted online. The majority of online shops will authenticate all transactions before debiting card accounts. In the very unlikely event that your card details are intercepted online, all credit card companies will compensate for unauthorised transactions as long as they are reported promptly.

In this directory, most of the sites that allow you to buy online are official sites; it is therefore unlikely that you will meet an unscrupulous dealer. But just the same, take a few simple precautions and bear in mind that UK consumer protection laws do not apply to overseas traders. If you are at all unsure of buying from an overseas site it would be better to leave well alone.

Online Betting

Probably the best piece of advice to start this section is never to bet more than you can afford. Many companies limit the size of your bet; this should be a good guide. Even when you get the tip from the horse's mouth it is prudent to remember that no horse ever bet on a man.

You are always better off working with an organisation you know than one you don't. If you do place your bet with a company you have never used before, then keep your wager small to begin with. It does not matter with whom you bet if you lose, only when you win.

It is essential that all your transactions remain confidential. Make sure that there is a statement on the site that assures this confidentiality. At the same time check that a secure server is in place as this usually guarantees that your personal details cannot be easily accessed. You will find more about this and other useful precautions in the sections How Secure Payment Servers Work and Online Shopping Tips below. Much of what is said there also applies to betting online.

Online Auctions and how they work

Online auctions are much the same as real world auctions except that they are conducted electronically and a time to start and end is stated. Normally you are asked to register before you can bid; this is usually free and requires your credit card details. Registration gets you a password which you use to certify a bid. Most auction sites help you with procedures and you soon get the hang of them.

Responsible auction sites require private sellers to register as members. They monitor their members and maintain a member rating system based on the seller's past performance. You should check this rating. If in doubt, don't deal with that member. If any member does not provide the service you expect, e-mail the auction site with your complaint. Their rating may then be reduced.

Never send cash for an auction purchase. Many online auction sites offer an independent service to hold payment until you receive your goods. Make use of this service whenever possible.

But always bear in mind that ultimately you have to take the same care in cyberspace as you would when betting in the real world.

How Secure Payment Servers Work

Interacting with the Web means that information passes between computers; each time this happens, there is the possibility that the message can be intercepted unless there is some form of security in place. Most sites with online shops have a secure server for transactions.

In simple terms, a secure server encrypts or scrambles your order and payment information and sends it to the online shop. This encryption process is very sophisticated and almost impossible to crack. The one most commonly used to safeguard your online transactions is the SSL system.

You will know that you are in a secure server environment if
● you are advised that you have requested a secure document;
● there is a small locked padlock icon at the bottom of your browser window;
● the web address at the top of the browser changes to https://.

Like everything else you should be cautious. Never reveal anything you wish to keep confidential unless a secure connection has been made and take note when your browser warns you that something is amiss.

Tax and Import Duties
If you are buying from an overseas site, be sure to check if you are liable for any import duties on the goods you are ordering. You may find this information on the retailer's site. The importing of some items may also be restricted in your home country. If in doubt, check with the appropriate authorities first.

Buying Online
If you haven't bought anything online before, here is our simple guide on how to do it.

1. Connect to the Internet and enter the address of the web site you want in your web browser.

2. Once the site has been loaded on your browser, find the item. Most sites have lists of categories of products as well as a search engine to help you find what you want quickly. Generally search engines will work even if the information you give is incomplete. Just give it your best shot.

3. When you have found what you want, check any picture or details to make sure it is the right thing.

4. If you are satisfied that it is what you are looking for and the price is right, order it. Most sites have some form of virtual shopping basket or cart for you to drop items into, which then automatically adds them to

your order. Don't worry, you haven't committed yourself to buying anything yet. That comes later.

5. Do the same for any other items you want to buy from the site.

6. Once you have chosen everything you want, go to the virtual checkout and check the contents of your basket. Be careful about the quantity of each item as it is easy to add an extra number by mistake and end up ordering more than you intended. If you change your mind about an item then take it out of the basket.

7. At the checkout you will need to provide some personal details such as your e-mail address and password if you have an existing account with that retailer.

8. Generally at this point you will pass into the secure shopping server if the site uses one. You have to click your agreement to do this. If the site does not offer a secure payment server, you may want to pay by another method, such as telephoning your credit card details or posting a cheque.

9. Once you are in a secure environment, complete the order form by filling in your personal details, credit card number and the delivery address, which may be different from your own. You should also be able to confirm delivery options and charges at this stage.

10. If it is your first purchase from the site you may need to register and choose a password. This serves both to welcome you and put in place security features to safeguard mutual interests. The password is per sonal to you and can be used whenever you visit the site. Once registered, normally free of charge, you will find an array of services you can use.

11. You will have the opportunity to check all your details and the items you have ordered. Be sure to do this very carefully before finally confirming your order.

12. All done. The online retailer will reconfirm your order by e-mail. Sit back, relax and look forward to delivery. Easy, isn't it?

Online Shopping Tips

● Check for delivery options, costs and minimum order conditions. Delivery costs may vary enormously. Courier services are usually more expensive than regular post, but they are faster with the items normally insured in transit.

● Check the retailer's returns policy before you buy.

● Take account of local tax and import duties in your calculations if you are buying from and overseas site.

● Buy in bulk if you can or try to qualify for group discounts.

● When buying gifts, check if the site offers a gift wrapping service.

● Place small orders with an unfamiliar retailer until you are satisfied with their service

● Check the local compatibility of electrical goods.

● Check if the site has secure online payment facilities. We have focused on those that do; however make sure you are happy to pay by another method if there are no secure facilities. Most ordering screens on secure servers are prefixed https:// and often display a closed padlock symbol on your web browser.

● Never give your personal or credit card details to an insecure site. Never fax your complete personal or credit card details to any company. Always black out part of the information to prevent its being intercepted and misused. Never send these details by e-mail, as this is very insecure.

● Print or take a screenshot of the order confirmation screen after paying with your credit card as your proof of purchase.

● Ask for an e-mail confirmation of your order. You can also print this and keep it as your record.

● Note the retailers' contact details where possible in case of any problems. We have listed e-mail addresses where available, but you may also want to note their telephone and fax numbers.

● Give a delivery address where you know you will be during daytime to receive it.

● If a courier is delivering your purchase, get a tracking number when you complete your order. You can use this to check the progress of your delivery on the courier's own web site.

● Check if your orders are insured in transit – some credit card companies insure all purchases made with their card, but it is always worth making sure.

● When an item is delivered, check the packaging carefully before signing for it. If it has been damaged in any way, do not accept delivery.

● If the goods are priced in foreign currency make sure you are getting a fair exchange rate. Some sites have currency converters so ensure that what you are paying converts correctly into your own currency.

How to use your rainbowdirectories WORLD WIDE SPORT book.
The Contents page lists the categories. The web sites are arranged alphabetically within each category.

Each web site entry is set out so that it contains:
its name
its Internet address (URL)
a review of the web site (in most cases)
an e-mail address if available.

Many commercial web sites allow you to buy and pay for products and services via the Internet. These facilities are noted in the reviews where appropriate.

If you like this book and find it useful, look out for our other Internet directories on

World Wide Travel and

World Wide Shopping

online at Amazon.com, Bol.com or in your local bookshop.

With a little help from our friends . . .

The Internet is changing very quickly and trying to keep up with those changes is a never-ending exercise. Although all the Internet addresses in this directory were correct at the time of printing, don't be alarmed if you find a few do not work or have changed when you try to access them. The problem may only be temporary so it may be worth trying again later. If you do find that an address has changed or if you know of other useful sports sites, please let us know at:

email@rainbowdirectories.com

We'll try to include them in our next edition.

So, now you are ready to use the Directory join the cheering crowd....

American Football

The Sport

ABC Monday Night Football

abcmnf.go.com

This online offspring of the famous TV show is as entertaining and informative as its original. Packed to bursting with news, results and schedules, the site also covers the game with terrific columns and articles. A photo gallery, video and audio clips and interviews with star players make a visit to this site an absolute must.
e-mail: askmnf@abc.com

American Football UK

www.americanfootball.org.uk

Valuable news and information resource covering the game in Britain with much detail. While the form could be better, the content is top rate – news and views, in-depth articles and links to British clubs.
e-mail: contact@americanfootball.org.uk

British American Football Coaches Association

www.geocities.com/Colosseum/9242/
Very useful for coaches of American Football in Britain. Information on how to join the Association comes with news of coaching conferences, transcripts of interviews with coaches and detailed explanations of various coaching routines, techniques and talking points. Links go to other relevant sites.
e-mail: damon.kirby@avis-europe.com

British Collegiate American Football League

www.bcafl.org
The student American Football scene in Britain on a site that could do with sprucing up. Just the same, the news and information, league tables, all-star lists and tips on recruiting new players are fairly well covered.
e-mail: bsafapres@netscapeonline.co.uk

Dick Butkus Football Network

www.dickbutkus.com

The legendary player and sports commentator Dick Butkus presents his own American Football web site. NFL, CFL, college and high-school football are all featured in terrific detail and you'll find lots of good stuff, all-time great players and columns worth a read. Although the design is a little clumsy, the site more than warrants a visit.

e-mail: info@dickbutkus.com

Draft Notebook

www.draftnotebook.com

This refers to the annual NFL draft. The prospects page details more than 300 of the top senior positions; if you pay for an Online Premium Service you get a tome of information on draft prospects which is updated throughout the year.

e-mail: Brian@DraftNotebook.com

European Federation of American Football

www.efaf.org

Not an inspiring site but it tells you something about the Federation and sets the scene for the game in Europe. All major competitions are covered with listings of the most successful teams in Europe.

e-mail: schneidermsafv@bluewin.ch

Football Central

www.footballcentral.net

A very useful directory with loads of links to American Football sites world wide. It guides you to everything from jobs for coaching staff to American Football sites in Europe and the more regular US sites. A classifieds page lists job vacancies, job seekers and buy and sell features.

e-mail: via online form

Football.com

www.football.com

From this informative and entertaining site you get as good a view of American football as a US fan. The news service is up-to-date with enough quality articles to keep you reading for a while. A truck-load of statistics comes with a very helpful database of players. Thoroughly good overall.

e-mail: Kick@football.com

Football Insider

footballinsider.com

All the latest American Football news and rumours. Each team has a page of rosters, drafts and behind-the-scenes goings-on; there are good sections on betting and fantasy football.

e-mail: contact@footballinsider.com

Footballfix.com

www.footballfix.com

Handy resource providing a huge range of links to American Football sites of every description, from news and statistics to official team sites and online shops. Football fans who visit should watch the clock and not forget to switch off when they leave.

e-mail: 2 joe@footballfix.com

Gridiron Grumblings

www.gridirongrumblings.com

The name says it and the site confirms that you are about to take an irreverent look at the world of American Football. The columnists are an opinionated bunch who don't pull any punches;

therefore the material is likely to be honest, informative and highly entertaining. If you have something you're dying to say, scratch it up on the message board.
e-mail: staff@gridirongrumblings.com

GridironUK.com

www.gridironuk.com
League tables, results, and match reports are all very detailed and informative, but fall short of giving a useful overview of the game in the UK because there are no stories and articles. The directory of British clubs goes some way to help.
e-mail: via online form

Maxfootball.com

www.maxfootball.com
NFL and NCAA news site of high order with a range of information matched only by the brilliant design. Top features include a fine video show hosted by former NFL coach Jerry Glanville and gory clips of sports surgery! Each team has its own page packed with news, results, schedules and injuries, so whoever you support in the NFL, you're bound to find enough material to keep you happy.
e-mail: producer@maxfootball.com

NCAA Football.net

www.ncaafootball.net
The US college football scene comes under the spotlight on this chatty site filled with news, results and articles. You get a glimpse of those players on the verge of hitting the big-time of the NFL. And if you really enjoy college football, then log on and see live as-it-happens descriptions of top college games.
e-mail: feedback@ncaafootball.net

NFL.com

www.nfl.com
As good as you'll get. They use all their official clout and produce a fabulous American Football site. Everything's here, news, results, players, polls and some truly superior columns. You'll also find video clips, online shopping, links to other well-chosen sites and regular live chats with star players.
e-mail: via online form

NFL Europe

www.nfleurope.com
Europe may not have totally warmed to the game yet, but you can't fault this site for not trying. Informative and neatly constructed, the site follows the style of its transatlantic big brother and brings you loads of good stuff - video clips, live chat and news but the cheerleaders seem to have missed the boat.
e-mail: nfleurope@sports.com

NFL High School Football

www.nflhs.com
The stars of tomorrow are brought into focus on this slick site. News, results and player profiles take their place beside information on scholarships,

safety and health. Some of the kids on the site look too mature for schoolboys; maybe it's their diet or they take longer to graduate.
e-mail: nflhs@nfl.com

NFL History

www.nflhistory.com
Fascinating and incredibly detailed history of American Football. Every Superbowl championship and play-off has been catalogued and analysed. You get information on players and teams through the years and first rate articles on the history of the game. The design of the site is basic, but the features, content and huge number of links to other sites make this an invaluable American Football resource.
e-mail: not available

NFL Players.com

www.nflplayers.com
The Player's Association gets its very own web site and very nice it is. Slick to the hilt with well-presented news, player profiles and analyses. Links take you to other player sites and there's a mammoth merchandising section.
e-mail: not available

NFLTalk

www.nfltalk.com
Keep abreast of the rumours and breaking stories from the world of American Football. You'll find it all in the columns and articles, interviews, bulletin boards and stats. The list of features is almost endless with the rumour page in particular a must-see for football fans.
e-mail: comments@sportstalk.com

Pro Football Hall Of Fame

www.profootballhof.com
While the real Pro Hall of Fame is far away in Canton, Ohio, this virtual version does a super job reeling out loads of material on the history of football. Players, teams, milestones and memories are all lovingly presented and you can tune in to the induction process and forthcoming events.
e-mail: via online form

Pro Football Weekly

www.profootballweekly.com
An online football magazine, Pro Football Weekly has lively, readable articles and columns. News and statistics take their place beside detailed coaching tips. The Whispers section brings to the surface all the latest rumours from the NFL.
e-mail: editors@pfwa.com

Quarterbacks and Coaches Chalkboard

www.li.net/~football/index.htm
Here's your chance to learn the technical aspects of the game if you don't already know them. Useful to coaches, players and fans alike, the role of the quarterback is examined in the closest

detail with explanations, examples and diagrams. This site is all concentration and well worth the effort if you're a serious fan of the game. There are links to other sites.
e-mail: football@li.net

Robert's American Professional Football Page

www.geocities.com/Colosseum/ Sideline/6352/
Robert gives us an American Football site full of illuminating stuff, most notably a full list of NFL end-of-season league standing, play-offs and Super Bowls. A fascinating section deals with American Football art where you will see logos and helmet art, past and present, for NFL, CFL, NFL Europe and World league teams. Robert also gives us his theories on how the sport should progress in the future!
e-mail: robsfb@swbell.net

Superbowl.com

www.nfl.com/sb34/
The biggest game of the year gets the big treatment on this big site. The two competing teams are examined almost under the microscope and then the experts dissect them in a series of articles. Fun touches come from video clips and photos of past Super Bowl clashes, a daily radio show and live webcam shots from the stadium and competing cities.
e-mail: via online form

The Official Site Of The Canadian Football League

www.cfl.ca
Their football may not reach the standard of their southern neighbours,

but their official site certainly matches up with anything Stateside. Stacked with news, player biographies, results and statistics, the site tells you everything you want to know about Canadian Football. Enjoyable articles, video clips, a photo gallery and an online shop complete the picture.
e-mail: slam@canoe.ca

Two Minute Warning.com

www.twominutewarning.com
Those who enjoy statistics will get a real kick out of this site. You get facts and analyses by the bus-load on teams, players and head-to-heads, for a valuable insight into America's number one game. Not a site to visit if you're looking for pure entertainment.
e-mail: feedback@twominutewarning.com

XFL.com

www.xfl.com
The new professional football league set up by the WWF introduces itself with a very snazzy web site. A stylish intro is followed by video clips of press releases and interviews relating to this bold new venture. Information extends to coaches and teams.
e-mail: Lucas@xfl.com

Yahoo Broadcast – NFL

www.broadcast.com/sports/football/nfl/
Links galore to audio and video coverage of all the NFL teams on this totally useful site. Live radio coverage, video news and radio talk shows are all accessible via Yahoo Broadcast and should keep the most fervent football fan fully entertained. Any plug-ins you may need are available for download via links.
e-mail: via online form

The Teams

Aarhus Tigers

www.tigers.dk
One of Europe's top American Football teams has a good site with all the usual info but lacks the multimedia features so common on US sites. If you register as a member, you can chat live, enter quizzes and shop online. Worth a visit.
e-mail: info@tigers.dk

Bristol Aztecs

www.aztecs.co.uk
This easy-to-use site tells you all you could ever wish to know about Bristol's finest American Football team and provides a lesson in economical web design. It's all there with a bit of general news from the football world.
e-mail: tim.dewson@aztecs.co.uk

Bristol Aztecs - Bristol Aztecs American Football Club

hometown.aol.com/~paulyd54/index.html
e-mail: PaulyD54@aol.com

Dallas Cowboys

www.dallascowboys.com
The official cyber-home of the Dallas Cowboys is a superior site with some very cool multimedia features. From the moment the rock soundtrack greets you to the daily video reports and Cowboys TV section, you get a highly entertaining site. News, schedules and results appear as usual, the online shop has lots to sell and a section shows off the team's cheerleaders.
e-mail: not available

Dallas Cowboys - Mary's Dallas Cowboys Page

www.geocities.com/Colosseum/7458/Cowboys/index.html
e-mail: shsusr@hotmail.com

Dallas Cowboys - The Ultimate Dallas Cowboys Fan Page

www.profootballworld.com
e-mail: UltimateDallasFan@profootballworld.com

Denver Broncos

www.denverbroncos.com
Nice to look at but slightly awkward to navigate, this official site has all the usual features like news, results and statistics. Press releases and a look behind the scenes increase your knowledge of the club and you can buy tickets if you're planning a jaunt over.
e-mail: tickets@broncos.nfl.com

Denver Broncos - Denver Broncos Fan Palace

www.personal.psu.edu/users/l/j/ljo106/broncos/bindex.htm
e-mail: Imperium21@hotmail.com

Denver Broncos - The Denver Broncos Page

members.aol.com/BroncoPage/index.html
e-mail: MillerTroy@msn.com

Glasgow Tigers

www.gla.ac.uk/Clubs/Tigers
A little lack-lustre but all the same the site updates you on all the latest news, results and forthcoming events from the Scottish club. A useful site for fans north of the border.
e-mail: tigers@silentstorm.co.uk

Green Bay Packers

www.packers.com
Nice, very nice and it does everything you'd expect it to. A visit will bring you up to speed with all things Green Bay and as a bonus you get to enter several competitions. Fans might check out the history of Lambeau Field; non-fans can look elsewhere for diversion.
e-mail: via online form

Green Bay Packers - Packer Palace

www.packerpalace.com
e-mail: beerkid@packerpalace.com

Green Bay Packers - The Green Bay Packers

members.xoom.com/kingpack/index.html
e-mail: via online form

Indianapolis Colts

www.colts.com
Good quality official site to make any Colts fan happy. The cyber-Colts section is packed with audio and video interview clips and while some sections remain unfinished, new features are being added all the time.
e-mail: Info@Colts.NFL.com

Indianapolis Colts - Ben's Stampede

php.iupui.edu/~bbunn/colts.html
e-mail: via online form

Indianapolis Colts - Tony's Colts Page

www.kimbanet.com/~hutchead/Colts.htm
e-mail: tonyhutchens@kimbanet.com

Jacksonville Jaguars

www.jaguarsnfl.com
Jaguar fans get a daily ration of news and information on this top quality official site. The history section charts the Jacksonville team's NFL journey from gaining a franchise in 1989 to the present day. The virtual tour of the Alltel stadium is worth downloading with a free plug-in for merchandising and cheerleader sections.
e-mail: fanmail@jaguars.com

Jacksonville Jaguars - Jaguars Universe

www.geocities.com/jaguarsuniverse/index2.htm
e-mail: bcb1999@hotmail.com

Jacksonville Jaguars - The Jacksonville Jaguars Unofficial Website

www.geocities.com/Colosseum/Bleachers/1282/
e-mail: cburgess@mail3.newnanutilities.org

Kansas City Chiefs

www.kcchiefs.com
Invaluable site if you're a fan of the team. The huge selection of features gives all the information you could ever need. A virtual tour of the stadium and chat rooms come online.
e-mail: via online form

Kansas City Chiefs - KC Chiefs Fanatics Page

www.geocities.com/Colosseum/Sideline/5096/
e-mail: KCChiefsFanatic@home.com

Kansas City Chiefs - Wild Bill's Chiefs Page

www.teknetwork.com/~bkrumel/
e-mail: wildbill@wildbillschiefs.com

Miami Dolphins

dolphinsendzone.com
You get everything you'd expect from an official US site - player and coaching staff info, photographs, press releases, live match reports and of course a pro shop. If you feel lonely write to a cheerleader!
e-mail: via online form

Miami Dolphins - Dolphinman.net

www.dolphinman.net
e-mail: comments@dolphinman.net

Miami Dolphins - Phins.com

www.phins.com
e-mail: curt@phins.com

New England Patriots

www.patriots.com
One of the best NFL sites. Video and audio news features are impressive and taken together with all the other stuff like downloadable digital memorabilia, chat rooms and live video broadcasts of press conferences, the site outshines most of its rivals.
e-mail: via online form

New England Patriots - Go Pats.com

www.gopats.com
e-mail: patriots@monehp.com

New England Patriots - Zip's Patriots Page

home.sprynet.com/~alarico2/patriots.htm
e-mail: alarico2@sprynet.com

New York Giants

www.giants.com
Video highlights from every game appear weekly, bolstered by audio clips of interviews and press conferences. If you join the Giant's global fan register, you receive the latest news and also hook up with fellow fans all over the world.
e-mail: not available

New York Giants - Big Blue Interactive.com

www.bigblueinteractive.com
e-mail: bigblue@webway.com

New York Giants - New York Giants Central

homepage.dave-world.net/~giants
e-mail: via online form

Oakland Raiders

www.raiders.com
A very fluent site from L A's finest, which covers all aspects of the club, results, schedules and player biographies with

a few extras thrown in to increase the measure – screensavers, live chats with players, merchandising and delectable cheerleaders.
e-mail: feedback@raiders.com

Oakland Raiders - Oakland Raiders Rap

www.raidersrap.com
e-mail: jdeloach@raidersrap.com

Oakland Raiders - Outlaw Raider Nation

www.raidernation.com
e-mail: Raidernation@usa.net

San Francisco 49ers

www.sf49ers.com
Aside from news and statistics stuff, fans get a range of fun games, trivia and downloads. The virtual tour of 3-Com Park is worth a look around and true fans can comb through the facts page.
e-mail: via online form

San Francisco 49ers - 49ers Frontline

www.49ersfrontline.com
e-mail: llcoolm99@yahoo.com

San Francisco 49ers - 49ers Report

www.49ersreport.com
e-mail: via online form

Scottish Claymores

www.claymores.co.uk
Well-designed, fun to use and filled with news and information. The youth side of the sport in Scotland is covered and the team mascot, Shuggie, a strange looking bear-like creature, who has his own page. If you feel the urge, e-mail him or her from the site!
e-mail: info@claymores.co.uk

Scottish Claymores - TouchdownClaymores.com

www.touchdownclaymores.com
e-mail: via online form

Seattle Seahawks

www.seahawks.com
Packed top to toe with great stuff. When you've checked out the news and other bits about the Seattle club, take your time with the multimedia features and 360-degree views of the stadium, video and audio clips and some brilliant photos. The chat rooms and message boards invite you be nice or spit fire if you prefer.
e-mail: teamldrapply@fan.seahawks.com

Seattle Seahawks - DaHawkMan's Seahawks Page

www.geocities.com/Colosseum/7436/
e-mail: lovedoc27@hotmail.com

Seattle Seahawks - The Seahawks Nest

home.earthlink.net/~seatownjay/
e-mail: satownjay@earthlink.net

St. Louis Rams

www.stlouisrams.com
This official site for the winners of Superbowl 2000 maintains the high standards of design, easy use and quality of news and information. Press releases and reports of injuries and player transactions keep you in touch. You can join the Rams fan club online.
e-mail: not available

St. Louis Rams - Rams Football.com

www.ramsfootball.com
e-mail: via online form

St. Louis Rams – Ramsworld

www.ramsworld.com
e-mail: via online form

Sussex Thunder

www.sussexthunder.co.uk
Clunky and simple, this official site
offers fans little more than forthcoming
games, results and a little club history.
There are links to other British clubs.
e-mail: not available

Tennessee Titans

www.titansonline.com
The team formerly known as the
Houston Oilers delivers one of the best
American Football sites around. The
attention to detail beggars belief with
post-match quotes, photos, injury
reports and statistics for the latest
games. You can take a virtual tour of
the stadium, tune in to the Titans'
radio station, read excellent columns
and shop.
e-mail: via online form

Tennessee Titans - Mike's Titanic Tennessee Titans Fanpage

www.homestead.com/we4myers/
Titans.html
e-mail: mikelob@hotmail.com

Tennessee Titans - Tennessee Titans Fan Page

www.tennessee-titanfans.com
e-mail: tnoilers@mailcity.com

Washington Redskins Official Website

www.redskins.com/index.asp
The fan photo gallery, which displays fan
snapshots of games, is a particularly
good feature. News and information
sections are well presented and you
can learn the lyrics of the team song -
Run or pass and score, We want a lot
more – Beatles, cry your hearts out!
e-mail: via online form

Washington Redskins - Skins Net

www.geocities.com/Colosseum/Field/
2887/redskins.html
e-mail: jannam@geocities.com

Washington Redskins – Webskins

www.webskins.org
e-mail: csuh@pobox.com

Athletics

The Sport

10k Truth

www.10ktruth.com

Compendium where runners describe their experiences and observations about the sport. The site is loaded with tips on how to improve performance and avoid injury and you can send in questions on the subject by mailing the Q&A section.

e-mail: therage@10ktruth.com

ADAMAS Athletics Club

www.adamas.org.za

South African athletics club based in Kimberley. All the usual club news, results, and competition schedules enhance a number of articles on athletics. Running Free Magazine, mentioned online, is South Africa's athletics voice.

e-mail: not available

Advantage Athletics

www.advantageathletics.com

A popular track and field training and coaching site. A notable feature is the selection of sequence pictures of pole vaulting, javelin, high jump and shot put to help competitors work on their technique. Pole-vaulters can order a video that analyses their technique frame by frame against that of a champion.

e-mail: tim@advantageathletics.com

AIMS

www.aims-association.org

The Association of International Marathons and Road Races promotes road running throughout the world. They have set the standards of course measurement now adopted by the IAAF. A calendar of races comes by e-mail while the directory of members' events and statistics are online.

Membership application forms can be downloaded in MS Word and PDF format.
e-mail: aimssec@aol.com

Amateur Athletic Federation of India

www.aafindia.com
Their official web site tells you a little about the history of athletics in India, details of the Federation board, their affiliates, a schedule of forthcoming events, results and records from Indian athletics and contact details.
e-mail: board@aafindia.com

Athletic Federation of Yugoslavia

www.asj.org.yu/english/index.html
Yugoslav authority responsible for athletics in the country. The web site has English text and sports an unusual and impressive design. There are brief profiles of top Yugoslav athletes, club listings and forthcoming events, results, news and statistics.
e-mail: asj@eunet.yu

Athletic WeekWatch Online

members.xoom.com/WeekWatch/ index.htm
An online newsletter addressed to all athletics enthusiasts. It gives a weekly summary of athletic events around the globe from road races in Albania to track competitions in Zaire, spiced with comments. If you prefer to receive the newsletter direct, sign up online and have it delivered free by e-mail each week.
e-mail: athleticWW@iname.com

Athletics Australia

www.athletics.org.au
Formerly known as the Australian Athletic Union, the site gives detailed coverage of the sport in the country with lashings of news and results for all age and competition levels from major international events to clubs and schools. There are profiles of Australian athletes and coaching details. Ticket and contact information is posted on the home page. You'll need Acrobat Reader for some of this.
e-mail: athletics@athletics.org.au

Athletics Canada

www.athleticscanada.com
Biographies on this official site relate to prominent Canadian athletes with some notes on national and international fixtures and competition

results. The news covers speed, power and endurance events. Paralympic programmes and a records book are also available.
e-mail: athcan@athletics.ca

Athletics Home Page

www.hkkk.fi/~niininen/athl.html
If you're interested in athletics records, this site is a good place to start. World records for men and women, indoor and outdoor, adult and junior. Also available are area records for Asia, Africa, Europe and South America plus a large selection of links to pages with national records from countries around the globe.
e-mail: not available

Athletics New Zealand

www.athletics.org.nz
Affiliated to the IAAF, this is the national athletics body in New Zealand. The site tells you about the organisation and its members, covers all athletics nationwide, presents profiles, news, an events calendar and records. Merchandise can be ordered using the online form.
e-mail: athnz@netlink.co.nz

Athletics Performance

www.rdg.ac.uk/~snsgrubb/athletics
Howard Grubb asks, Which is the best world record? By looking at a range of statistical models he attempts to compare top athletic performances to provide an answer. If you want to check up on your own performance there are several online tools provided for your use.
e-mail: H.J.Grubb@reading.ac.uk

Athletics South Africa

www.athletics.org.za
Coverage of track and field in South Africa from the official web site of this IAAF affiliated organisation. Records are listed for senior, junior and school levels including road-running events. You can log-in and chat in the M-Web supported Chat Zone.
e-mail: asa@athleticssa.co.za

Atletica Leggera

www.atleticaleggera.com
Italian web site with a pile of national and world wide statistics, all-time records, a photo gallery and biographies of some athletes. Text is in English and Italian.
e-mail: posta@atleticaleggera.com

Austrian Decathlon

members.chello.at/katzenbeisser/
Austrian fan site by Robert Katzenbeißer dedicated to the Decathlon. The text deals with results and forthcoming meetings. The best Austrian decathletes get a mention together with the latest news and statistical data.
e-mail: deca@chello.at

Bulgarian Track and Field Athletics Federation

www.athletics.netbg.com
The site covers athletics from a Bulgarian perspective. A history of the Federation, athletics news archives, national team details and achievements, records and competition results come in a package. The site is home to the bi-monthly Atletika Magazine, which has online profiles and photographs.
e-mail: athletics@olympic.bg

Canadian Speed and Power Group Pole Vault

speedandpower.com/vault/
Pole Vaulting in Canada with news, results, competitor biographies, training, coaching and ranking. A photo gallery and e-mail directory of all Canadian pole-vaulters concludes the site.
e-mail: ross@hg.uleth.ca

CanThrow.Com

canthrow.com
Canadian site devoted to field throwing events with training tips on discus, javelin, hammer, shot put and general throwing. There are interviews with throwers and coaches in Canada who share their insight and knowledge, artiocles on training for these events, guides to basic throwing principles and discipline specific guides. You can post classified ads on the site or take part in the chat on the discussion board. Merchandise is available from the CanThrow online store using a secure server.
e-mail: steinke@hg.uleth.ca

DECA

www.decathlonusa.org/contact.html
A resource for decathlon information, news, competitions and results, an illustrated guide to the sport's history, a database and athletes' records. The DECA newsletter is published online.
e-mail: zarnowsk@msmary.edu

eGroups highjump

www.egroups.com/group/highjump
Primarily a series of discussion sites for enthusiasts. This one deals with the High Jump. You can discuss problems with your approach and get advice from fellow jumpers. Messages are archived

for twelve months so you can easily check the status of your question.
e-mail: via online form

Endure Plus

www.endureplus.com
Online magazine for athletes competing in endurance events. Nutrition, training and health are thoroughly discussed and news updated regularly. Whole sections are devoted to issues about diet, medicine, doping and psychology and there is an Olympics page.
e-mail: info@endureplus.com

European Athletic Association

www.eaa-athletics.ch
One of the six Continental groups of the International Amateur Athletic Federation. The official web site keeps you up-to-date with the operation and events of the EAA. A calendar of competitions, results and statistics are set down for easy reading. Their monthly circular is published online with documents available for download, some of which require Acrobat Reader.
e-mail: eaa.office@t-online.de

FLA

www.fla.lu
Official site of the Fédération Luxembourgeoise d'Athlétisme. You get a history of athletics in Luxembourg, contact details of member clubs, news, records, and an events calendar. The online guest book welcomes comments.
e-mail: fla@fla.lu

Golden Girls

homepages.go.com/~oztrack/oztrack.html
Highly praised web site dedicated to women's track and field athletics in

Australia. Heaps of information include a potted history, athlete profiles and ranking. The site author Graham Thomas provides up-to-date news and five chapters of text.
e-mail: graham.thomas@dewrsb.gov.au

High Jump Coach
www.stonemicrodesigns.com/ HighJumpCoach.htm
If you need a leg up with your high jump this site may help. There is an article on the mechanics of the sport, the theory of the curved approach and how to customise it to suit yourself. You can download a free demo version of High Jump Coach 2000 software aimed at improving your performance.
e-mail: sales@stonemicrodesigns.com

Hong Kong Amateur Athletic Association
www.hkaaa.com
In both English and Chinese, this is the official home on the web of athletics in Hong Kong. Information is directed at competitors and fans alike. News, results of local meets and championships,

a calendar of forthcoming events with contact details, documents of the association and HKAA ranking are nicely laid out. Some documents on this site require Acrobat Reader.
e-mail: hkaaa@hksdb.org.hk

IAAF International Amateur Athletic Federation
www.iaaf.org
The International Amateur Athletic Federation is the world governing body for track and field events. All major events are covered, and where possible, with live web-based feeds. The multimedia section has audio and video clips of athletes in action. A good site for fans.
e-mail: not available

ISTAF
www.istaf.de
In both English and German this is the site for the Berlin leg of the IAAF Golden League event. Lots of details and statistics about events and competitors come with ticket information and location particulars.
e-mail: mailbox@istaf.de

Javelin Discussion Forum II

discserver.snap.com/Indices/109718.html
Busy online discussion forum dedicated
to the javelin. You can post articles
and comments online and respond to
others. A search facility enables you
to check if topics have been discussed
previously. You'll find a bunch of
related links worth checking out.
e-mail: Jabalina_2y@yahoo.com

JavelinNET

www.saunalahti.fi/tonirah/index.html
This Finnish web site has a remarkable
set of images of javelin throwers in
action. Static photographs and animated
images of throwers going through the
motions add to the sheer visual pleasure
of the site. In addition there are links
to videos of competitors in the field in
AVI and MOV format.
e-mail: tr@ren.to

Lithuanian Athletic Federation

www.laf.lt
Athletics in Lithuania with contact
particulars for the Federation, a list of
the best male and female Lithuanian
Athletes of the century, results, news
and statistics. Text is in English and
Lithuanian.
e-mail: info@laf.lt

Long and Strong

www.longandstrong.com
Throwing events are the central feature
of the site. Interviews with top discus,
shot put and highland games athletes
and throwing coaches shed some light
on what it takes to be a world class
thrower. The Coaches Corner has brief
biographies of a number of coaches
who will answer your questions by e-mail.
e-mail: Thrower60@aol.com

Meeting Gaz de France Paris Saint-Denis

www.gazdefrance.com/meeting/
One of the IAAF Golden League events
held at the Stade de France. News,
photos, information and an events
calendar put you in the picture. A nice
feature is the facility to write a message
to a competing athlete, which the
organisers promise to forward. Ticket
information comes with a link to the
online box office.
e-mail: not available

Meeting Herculis Zepter

www.herculis.com/index_us.html
This is the Monaco leg of the IAAF
Golden League. The schedule of the
event, results and start list are all
recorded. News, interviews, photographs
and a video section of highlights in
RealVideo format take up the rest of
the site.
e-mail: fma@fma.mc

Memorial Van Damme

www.memorialvandamme.be
One of the track and field grand prix meetings which make up the IAAF Golden League. This event is held in Brussels and the web site tells you everything about the event. Tickets can be purchased online.
e-mail: gp@bbs-apbjs.be

Nikaia 2000

www.nikaia.org
Beautifully designed official web site of the international athletics meeting held in France and chosen by the IAFF to take part in the Grand Prix I circuit. The event and its history, a photo gallery and video clips of highlights are available in RealVideo and MPEG format. You can post messages on the board. Text is in English and French.
e-mail: contact@nikaia.org

Onrunning For Every Runner

www.onrunning.com
Latest news from across the globe for fans and competitors. Many of these items are available to listen to online using RealAudio. Peter Elliot's Training camp provides a training schedule, stretching and exercise tips for several distance running disciplines including the half marathon. To promote your own event by listing it on the site, fill out an online form. Download screensavers and wallpaper or browse the online store for accessories and running equipment. BUPA's Great North Run, the world's biggest half marathon, is shown in focus.
e-mail: enquiries@onrunning.com

Portuguese Athletics Federation

www.fpatletismo.pt
With text in both English and Portuguese this official site has a changing focus in its coverage. Presently it is the forthcoming IAAF World Cross Country Championships to be held in Vilamoura in 2000.
e-mail: fpatletismo@ip.it

Rachel's Women Throwers

www.geocities.com/Colosseum/Stadium/4283/index.html
US women's throwing events described online with schedules of forthcoming meets, TV coverage and updated results. The site takes a look at the four major throwing events – shot put, discus, hammer and javelin and finishes off with articles, features and book reviews.
e-mail: rt_thrower@hotmail.com

Ricoh Tour 2000

www.ricohtour.com
Tour held in Ghent in Belgium, Lievin in France, Stockholm in Sweden and Birmingham in England for prize money. The site gives you the results and performances of current and past years. You will need RealVideo format for the video highlights.
e-mail: not available

Rieti 2000

www.rietimeeting.com
IAAF Grand Prix II event held annually in Italy. The web site previews the forthcoming meet and archives those of previous years. Records achieved by athletes at Rieti are detailed. Some parts of the site use Shockwave Flash and require the Flash plug-in. Text is in English and Italian.
e-mail: info@rietimeeting.com

Rockingham Athletics

bolian.upnaway.com/~abd/
These district centres in Western
Australia hold weekly athletics
competitions for children from
neighbouring clubs. This is a thoroughly
heart-warming site as it records children's
achievements in age categories and the
results from the Satte Relay and
Championships.
e-mail: abd@rock.upnaway.com

Runner's World

www.runnersworld.com
Being the online companion to
Runner's World Magazine makes this
a massive and popular site. News
coverage is superb with topical articles,
training tips, nutritional advice and a
lot more to encourage competitive and
social runners alike. If you need advice
on the right shoes, treadmills or
stopwatches to buy, you will almost
certainly find the answers online. The
message board is crammed with topics
to discuss with other enthusiasts. You
can subscribe to the magazine online.
e-mail: not available

Singapore Amateur Athletic Association

home1.pacific.net.sg/~saaa/
The official site keeps results of some
of the competitions organised by the
Association and national records for
senior and junior men and women,
forthcoming attractions and scheduled
events. There are notes about the
Association and its activities and a
mention for Adrenaline, the official
magazine.
e-mail: saaa@pacific.net.sg

Sportscreen

**www.athletics-online.co.uk/
running.htm**
Dedicated to collecting news of
competitions and athletes world wide,
this site presents information about
recent events and archived items.
Interviews with competitors are featured
as are illustrations. You can interact
online with other enthusiasts by
posting messages on the board or
taking part in regular chat sessions.
e-mail: paul_halford@bigfoot.com

The Athletic Association of Ireland

www.athleticsireland.ie
A rundown on the organisation and a
fixture list of both international and
domestic events at regional, county
and club level. National indoor and
outdoor records, a guide to AAI coaching
and an archive of national competition
results complete this official web site.
e-mail: admin@athleticsireland.ie

The Athletics Site

www.eexi.gr/athletix/
Popular, well-constructed and
comprehensive web site bringing
together Greek and World athletics
records. The latest news from track
and field events and day-by-day
summaries of international competitions are held in archives online.
There are biographies of Greek athletes
and a picture gallery.
e-mail: athletix@eexi.gr

The Century's 100 Greatest Competitions

www.michtrack.org/century.htm
Sportswriter Jeff Hollobaugh has
assembled his choice of The Century's

100 Greatest Competitions. His collection is not necessarily of great performances, though many are; he focuses rather on great engagements, which he thinks were exciting and historically significant. So here you get to re-live great athletic battles of the past with illustrated summaries of the events.
e-mail: not available

The Prefontaine Classic
www.preclassic.com
Prestigious meet ranked first among all annual track and field competitions in the USA by the IAAF. Previews of forthcoming meets and details for previous years, records and competition results take up several web pages. Posters and T-shirts can be previewed on site.
e-mail: tjordan@dnsi.net

The Triple Jump Site
media2.cs.berkeley.edu/webvideo/ people/jleng/welcome.htm
First rate web site devoted to the Triple Jump. The discipline is broken down into constituent parts and analysed. The mechanics of the hop, skip and jump phases are looked at in detail with photographs and QuickTime video clips. The history and development of the triple jump are discussed in an international context.
e-mail: jerleng@aol.com

ThrowFarther.Com
www.throwfarther.com
Resource for all throwers - hammer, shot put, discus, javelin, and highland games events. There are performance lists for several national and international

athletic associations. A photo gallery, training tips and techniques are fully documented with video clips. Visitors can submit content or join the mailing list using the online forms. Video clips are in MPEG format and require Windows Media Player.
e-mail: not available

Track and Field Media
www.tnfmedia.com
Online magazine giving running fans a behind-the-scenes look at the sport. There is a lot served up online - results, meeting reports, interviews, photographs, and regular columnists. The message boards and chat room are for interaction with other fans. You can sign up to join the mailing list.
e-mail: schief@rungroteschief.com

Track & field all-time performances homepage
www.algonet.se/~pela2/
Peter Larsson has assembled an incredible set of records here. He lists not only the current world records but the fastest all-time records. For example he gives a whole line up of the fastest 100-metre runs in history with details of wind assistance, hand timing, rolling starts and whatever else goes to make a record. All athletics events are covered for both male and female competitors.
e-mail: pela2@algonet.se

TrackAndField.com
www.trackandfield.com/content/home/
Claims to be the ultimate source for track and field athletics on the Internet. The US-based resource includes results and stats from top-level meets, US high

schools and NCAA colleges. News, previews of forthcoming events, regularly featured columnists and interviews get space online.
e-mail: Info@TrackAndField.com

UK Athletics
www.ukathletics.org
The national governing body covering all aspects of athletics in the UK. News, stats, records, articles, press releases and an archive make up a good portion of the site. Use the search facility to bring out the biographies of athletes.
e-mail: information@ukathletics.org.uk

United Kingdom Track and Field All-Time Lists
members.aol.com/martinrixx/
Fully comprehensive UK track and field athletics and all-time statistics put together on this site by Martin Rix. Age ranges start under 15 and go up to seniors; events include sprints, distance running, hurdles, decathlon, heptathlon, walks, relays, indoor and outdoor events and more. Other UK, international, and miscellaneous stats are also recorded. This is a great place to start research.
e-mail: MartinRixx@aol.com

UK Running Track Directory
www.runtrackdir.com
Here is a directory of imposing dimensions - comprehensive details of virtually all the more than 550 tracks in the UK. There are summaries of facilities, photographs, contact information and sections on proposed new tracks and tracks under construction. Researchers need look no further.
e-mail: tim@runtrackdir.com

USA Pole Vault Academy
www.speed-fitness.com/uspva/index.shtml
The club is dedicated to the pole vault and works with athletes of all ages. This US web site gives an overview of the discipline, explains safety-related issues, documents the key stages of the sport for basic and advanced levels and then some more.
e-mail: jkeys@erols.com

USA Racewalking

www.geocities.com/Colosseum/Loge/7503/

Site dedicated to the sport of racewalking. The event itself may need some describing to the unfamiliar and certainly the basic rules and technique require explanation. The photo gallery shows walkers on track; there are details of forthcoming events and current US ranking.

e-mail: michellekirk@usa.net

USATF On The Web

www.usatf.org

US governing body covering all track and field competition, road racing and race walking. The site gives a good round up of general athletics and contact information to the 57 member associations, membership details and an e-mail directory of its officers and staff. Take a look at the selection of sports clothing in the merchandise section or use one of the busy boards to post your messages.

e-mail: usatfprogs@aol.com

VaultWorld

www.polevault.com

The Pole Vault event at all levels of the sport. News, results, a calendar of forthcoming meets and events and a packed picture gallery take up a large part of the site. The online store sells related material and several bulletin boards provide an arena for discussion and posting local news and results.

e-mail: askeddie1@aol.com

Vertical Assault

www.verticalassault.net

Their primary purpose is to develop and improve the pole vault skills of athletes of all ages. Programmes are explained in detail and reinforced with past successes. They are based in Florida and tell you how to contact them on the site.

e-mail: wproc41@gate.net

Waterford Athletic Club

members.tripod.com/waterford.ac/

The Irish club discloses its activities, history and place in the record books. A range of articles covers related topics, profiles of Irish athletes and a schedule of forthcoming events.

e-mail: not available

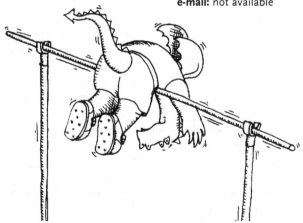

The Athletes

Ato2000

www.atoboldon.com

Impressive official web site of Trinidad born champion sprinter Ato Bolden. The latest version of the site is constructed entirely with Shockwave Flash and requires the Flash plug-in. Here you'll find heaps of information about Ato from early life to date, with photographs. His career record and achievements including fastest times are listed and you can use the Ask Ato section to quiz the man and read his responses to questions posted via the web site. There are video clips of several of Ato's races, audio clips and a message board.

e-mail: via online form

Bruny Surin

brunysurin.infinit.net

The Canadian sprinter's site comes in English and French and has a personal message on the home page. His career, hobbies and forthcoming races are recorded with an account from his coach of his training schedule, outlining the changes at each stage required to produce peak performance. Fans can post questions and comments direct to the man using an online form.

e-mail: via online form

Donovan Bailey

www.donovanbailey.com

The Canadian sprinter fills his web site with great all round coverage of his life, track results, schedules and press releases. Photographs show his performance to advantage and you can interact with others on the message board and chat facilities.

e-mail: donovanbailey@donovanbailey.com

Gail Devers

www.gaildevers.com

US sprinter and gold medal winner writes her own biography which she illustrates with photographs of herself growing up. The official site covers Gail Force Inc, which runs the Gail Devers Foundation and Club Force, her Fan Club. You need the Flash plug-in to hear Gail welcoming you to her web site.

e-mail: via Online form

Irène Dimwaogdo Tiendrebeogo

www.geocities.com/Colosseum/4879/ tiendrebeogo

Web site of Irène Dimwaogdo Tiendrebeogo which means - think about tomorrow. The high jump competitor from Burkina Faso in Africa participated in Atlanta in 1996. She illustrates her career with photographs, has a message board and encourages visitors to e-mail her.

e-mail: itiendrebeogo@yahoo.fr

Marko Koers

www.markokoers.nl

Dutch born middle distance runner Marko Koers has an official web site where you can browse a photo gallery, read his biography, career development and achievements. Send a message if you wish, direct to the athlete via the webmaster.

e-mail: markoers@hotmail.com

Marla Runyan

www.marlarunyan.com

Marla Runyan is a successful and highly ranked middle distance runner with a difference. At the age of nine her vision had begun to deteriorate and she has been legally blind since. On this site you can read her description of her visual impairment and articles from newspapers about her and her track and field successes.

e-mail: not available

Maurice Greene - The Worlds Fastest Human

kckansas.com/kckmauricegreene.htm
Unofficial fan site for the top sprinter with a photo gallery of Maurice on the track and a video of his world record breaking 100 Metre dash. You can post comments and questions on the message board.

e-mail: webmaster@kckansas.com

Niki Bakogianni

www.niki-bakogianni.gr
In English and Greek, the official web site of the Atlanta women's high jump silver medallist gives her biography, competition successes, race results and a photo gallery of her in action. You can contact Niki directly by e-mail. A video of her performance in Atlanta can be viewed in AVI format.

e-mail: bakogianni@otenet.gr

Randy Barnes

www.randybarnes.com
Official home page of 1996 Olympic shot put gold medallist Randy Barnes. This site has his biography, personal details and career achievements. There is a photo gallery of Randy in action from 1996 to the present. You can purchase an instructional video guide to the sport and autographed photos online.

e-mail: not available

Steve Prefontaine

www.prefontainerun.com
The late American distance runner Steve Prefontaine, subject of two major motion pictures, held most US distance running records at the time of his death in 1975 at the age of 24. On this site you can read more about his life and achievements and download results of the Prefontaine Memorial Run in Adobe Acrobat or Microsoft Word format.

e-mail: gopre@prefontainerun.com

Suzy Favor Hamilton

www.suzyfavorhamilton.com
The US runner tells you her story, her hobbies and interests; gives you training tips and a running diary. The Ask Suzy feature is for Q & A – You ask by e-mail, Suzy answers online.

e-mail: deedeeruns@aol.com

Tatiana Grigorieva

www.tatiana.com.au
Australian-based pole-vaulter details her training program, exercises and biographical information online. She also has a part-time job as a model and you can check out photographs of both sides of her career in the gallery. You can e-mail her direct using an online form.

e-mail: via online form

The Carl Lewis myth and legend

www.angelfire.com/celeb/carllewis/frame.htm
Carlton Frederick Lewis won 20 gold medals in four classes of events. Now you can read a full biography with links to many of his major achievements. You'll enjoy following his progress year

by year from 1979 to 1996, viewing the photographs and complete statistics covering his career.

e-mail: not available

The Unofficial Denise Lewis Home Page

www.btinternet.com/~m.holland/ home.html

British heptathlete Denise Lewis gets her fan site here. The site explains the disciplines that make up a heptathlon and looks at record holders in the sport. A biography of Denise, news, highlights from her career and a good selection of photographs are all available online. Denise is clearly thrilled as she thanks Mark Holland in a letter for this unofficial site. You can leave a message in the online guest book.

e-mail: mark@holland.nederlands.com

The Unofficial Michael Johnson Page

www.baylor.edu/~Todd_Copeland/ Johnson/Johnson.html

Legendary US sprinter Michael Johnson won 58 consecutive 400-metres races and here Todd Copeland compiles an impressive resource based on his career. His 58 consecutive wins, brought to an end in 1997, are listed online.

e-mail: Todd_Copeland@baylor.edu

Viktor Tchistiakov

www.viktor.com.au

Australia-based 1994 World Junior Pole Vault champion has an official web site with a biography, photo gallery of the athlete in competition and relaxing with family, transcripts of several newspaper and magazine articles.

e-mail: via online form

Aussie Rules Football

The Sport

AFANA

www.afana.com
The Australian Football Association of North America is the body that actively develops this unique sport in the USA. This official site covers the sport in Australia and the USA, adds a bulletin board, chat facility and something about itself.
e-mail: via online form

AFL

www.afl.com.au
The Official Australian Football League site is certainly the best place for fans to start. You get news and information on every club and match with loads of photographs. The Netcast section presents live audio commentary for selected games; members of the Premiers Club receive live broadcasts of every AFL Premiership match including the Finals. You require RealPlayer to enjoy this. A chat room, online shop and other facilities put you where the action is.
e-mail: general@afl.com.au

AFL Web Ring

www.eisa.net.au/~ogrady/AFLRing/
This is the main Australian Football League Web Ring which links up with 174 fan sites devoted to AFL clubs, players and stories.
e-mail: via online form

BARFL

www.barfl.co.uk
British Australian Rules Football League. This is the home of the sport in the UK with links to the top British

clubs. Fixtures and results, a photo gallery and how to become a match umpire come online.
e-mail: info@barfl.co.uk

CAFA

www.aussierulescanada.net
The Canadian Australian Football Association was established in May 1989 and ten years later, membership topped 500. This newsy official site writes up the league tables and fixtures, links up with sites of leading clubs and supplies a chat facility and message board.
e-mail: via online form

FootyForum

forums.f2.com.au
The F2 Network brings you a general Aussie football forum and others dedicated to AFL clubs Carlton, Collingwood, Hawthorns and Western Eagles. You can read messages as a guest but must log-in to post.
e-mail: forums@dispatcher.fairfax.com.au

International Australian Football Council

www.iafc.org.au
As a counterpart to the AFL this Council covers Aussie football around the world. If you are looking for international web sites for this sport, look no further. Online links go to federations and leading clubs world wide. Interaction takes place on the message board and in the chat room.
e-mail: clarkey@onthenet.com.au

OzRules

www.ozrules.com
AFL news and information site. Forums for each match where fans can have their say somehow confirm the site's billing as the only footy site where you can say what you want. To balance fan opinions with fact you get real news, fixtures, league tables and stats.
e-mail: via online form

realfooty.com

realfooty.com.au
All round coverage of the AFL with fixtures, results and related audio-video clips in RealPlayer format. Get your AFL match updates while they are in progress with instant feedback and graphics. Leading columnists write regular features on the game.
e-mail: not available

W.A. Women's Football League

www.wawfl.org.au
Formed in 1987, the League had four teams and when night games were introduced in 1999 it grew to seven. On this official site you'll find all the usual news and events listing, match fixtures and results, league tables and player profiles.
e-mail: wawfl@excite.com

The Teams

Adelaide Crows

www.afc.com.au
You need RealAudio to receive the full-blooded rendition of the squad singing the club song, which you can also download. The site gives you the latest club and team news, fixtures, results and player profiles. You can view and buy club merchandise online in the Crowmania shop.
e-mail: pbiglands@afc.com.au

ADELAIDE CROWS

Adelaide Crows -Crows Supporters Group

home.iprimus.com.au/crows_sg/
e-mail: not available

Adelaide Crows - Football Club accommodation in Ballarat

www.ballarat.com/footycrows.htm
e-mail: not available

BRISBANE LIONS FOOTBALL CLUB

Brisbane Lions Football Club

www.lions.com.au
Aside from a bit of club history, an online store and a photo gallery looking over the past two seasons, this official site has an Ask the Boss section. E-mail your questions and the appropriate club officer will be sure to answer. A message board and chat room give you some interaction with a promise to forward messages to players.
e-mail: email@lions.com.au

Brisbane Lions Football Club - The Lions' Den

www.geocities.com/Colosseum/ Stadium/7147/
e-mail: not available

CARLTON FOOTBALL CLUB

Carlton Football Club

www.carltonfc.com.au
You can listen to comments straight from the Blues Locker room in WAVE format, send a Carlton postcard by filling out an online form and have your picture hung up in the Blues Fans Gallery, so long as you are fully decked out in Blues gear. Statistics, club news and an online shop are also in place.
e-mail: blues@sportsview.com.au

Carlton Football Club - Aaron Hamill Fan Club

clubs.yahoo.com/clubs/aaronhamill
e-mail: not available

Carlton Football Club - Canberra Carlton Blues

www.arrive.at/CanberraCarltonBlues/
e-mail: not available

Carlton Football Club - Lowey's Unofficial Carlton Football Club

users.interact.net.au/~psle/index.htm
e-mail: not available

COLLINGWOOD FOOTBALL CLUB

Collingwood Football Club

www.collingwoodfc.com.au
Subtitled Home of the Mighty Pies, this official web site keeps scores, fixtures, match reports, league tables and latest club news. The club song and interviews

can be heard online with video footage of press conferences. Player profiles, a photo gallery and a club shop round off the site.

e-mail: magpies@sportsview.com.au

Collingwood Football Club - Buckley Surfers

www.geocities.com/buckleysurfers/
e-mail: not available

Collingwood Football Club - Extreme Black And White

www.alphalink.com.au/%7Ehotrod/extreme.html
e-mail: not available

Collingwood Football Club -From The Outer

www.fromtheouter.com
e-mail: not available

Collingwood Football Club - Magpies.org

www.magpies.org.au
e-mail: not available

Collingwood Football - ClubHot Pies

www.magpies.org.au/hotpies/
e-mail: not available

ESSENDON FOOTBALL CLUB

Essendon Football Club

www.essendonfc.com.au
Multimedia clips bring you interviews with players and coaches and audio interviews with Kevin Sheedy each week after the game. These last are conducted throughout the year and can be downloaded. Latest club and team news, results and match reports keep

you up to speed while the online club shop is stocked with goodies.
e-mail: via online form

Essendon Football Club - Coach Kevin Sheedy

www.sheedyvision.com.au/home.htm
e-mail: not available

Essendon Football Club - James Hird Shrine

www.fortunecity.com/skyscraper/solomon/210/james.html
e-mail: not available

FREMANTLE FOOTBALL CLUB

Fremantle Football Club

www.fremantlefc.com.au
Who are playing, who are hurt, where and when is it happening and what happened when it did? If you have RealPlayer you can hear and watch post match interviews that can be downloaded or streamed online with a karaoke version of the Fremantle Football Club victory song. The online store will sell you club merchandise.
e-mail: via online form

Fremantle Football Club - Shane's Fremantle Dockers Page

users.wantree.com.au/~richmond/doc.htm
e-mail: not available

Fremantle Football Club - The Mighty Dockers

thedocker.homepage.com
e-mail: not available

GEELONG FOOTBALL CLUB

Geelong Football Club

www.gfc.com.au
Although a major site re-design is in
the pipeline these official pages give
you a whole lot of good stuff. Latest
results and match reports, stats on all
your favourite cats players in the Our
Team section and club news from Billy's
Banter. Player profiles and photographs
put the finishing touches.
e-mail: via online form

Geelong Football Club – Catland

www.alphalink.com.au/~stac/
e-mail: not available

Geelong Football Club – GFC

www.superhwy.com.au/gnus/gfc.html
e-mail: not available

Geelong Football Club - Go Cats

www.geelongfc.homestead.com
e-mail: not available

HAWTHORN FOOTBALL CLUB

Hawthorn Football Club

www.hawthornfc.com.au
Features include match reports and
analyses, fixtures, stats and league
tables, club news and an online shop to
buy club merchandise. To view video
footage you need to sign up first.
e-mail: hawks@sportsview.com.au

Hawthorn Football Club - Hawk Headquaters

www.comcen.com.au/~suemark/
hawkhome.htm
e-mail: not available

Hawthorn Football Club – Hawks

www.fortunecity.com/olympia/atlanta/
265/index.htm
e-mail: not available

Hawthorn Football Club - History of the Hawthorn Football Club

www.labyrinth.net.au/~slug/hawks/
index.html
e-mail: not available

KANGAROOS FOOTBALL CLUB

Kangaroos Football Club

www.kangaroosfc.com.au
You can become a Net Member online
for free, which allows you to visit the
Fans Forum, Webmail and Chat, Send
A Postcard and take part in the Footy
Tipping Competition. You can also
read The Quit Campaign and join a
group of Kangaroos players who act as
key ambassadors for the Smoke Free
Message. That's a lot just for filling a
form. All the latest news, fixtures,
results and statistics come online and
latest scores appear while matches are
in progress.
e-mail: via online form

Kangaroos Football Club - Ilan's Kangas Homepage
www.ozemail.com.au/%7Eikatz/
e-mail: not available

Kangaroos Football Club - Inside The Roos
home.primus.com.au/jrobertson/
e-mail: not available

Kangaroos Football Club - The Mighty Roo Boys
www.webpotato.com.au/kangas/
e-mail: not available

MELBOURNE FOOTBALL CLUB

Melbourne Football Club
www.demons.com.au
Aside from the usual features of fixtures and match reports, club and team news, a training schedule and online shop, this official site has a Player of the Week spot. This focuses on a particular squad member and gives him a big boost with a career profile and photographs.
e-mail: melbfc@demons.com.au

Melbourne Football Club – Demonology
www.effect.net.au/vm/index.html
e-mail: not available

Melbourne Football Club - Epa's Demon Page sit back and relax
www.angelfire.com/sk/epa/index.html
e-mail: not available

Melbourne Football Club - Melbourne FC discussion board!
welcome.to/headliner
e-mail: not available

Richmond Football Club
www.richmondfc.com.au
The Club Museum is highlighted online with marvellous squad photographs that run over the years from 1920. Click on a thumbnail photograph and you get a full size captioned picture with all the players named and profiled.
e-mail: not available

ST. KILDA FOOTBALL CLUB

St. Kilda Football Club
www.stkilda.afl.com.au
The club coach writes regular columns on the progress of the team. Match accounts, scorecards and photographs, weekly training schedules and injury reports lead up to club membership details and fees. You can join online.
e-mail: not available

St. Kilda Football Club - Cyber Moorabbin
www.geocities.com/Colosseum/Stadium/7473/
e-mail: not available

St. Kilda Football Club - Go Saints
www.geocities.com/Colosseum/Sideline/1140/welcome.htm
e-mail: not available

St. Kilda Football Club - The Canberra St Kilda Supporters' Club
www.tip.net.au/~mos/actstkfc.htm
e-mail: not available

SYDNEY SWANS FOOTBALL CLUB

Sydney Swans Football Club
www.sydneyswans.com.au
After a Flash intro page you get to the

club's community projects, a photo gallery, downloadable screensavers and wallpaper and entry to the club store. If you join the Swans Netclub you automatically have access to video highlights of matches including coach Rodney Eade previewing the forthcoming game.
e-mail: swansmembership@ sydneyswans.com.au

Sydney Swans Football Club - Go Swannies

www.angelfire.com/hi/julzzz/swans.html
e-mail: not available

Sydney Swans Football Club - Swans Talk

sportsonly.com/a/7596/
e-mail: not available

WEST COAST EAGLES FOOTBALL CLUB

West Coast Eagles Football Club

www.westcoasteagles.com.au
The site is about to launch the club on web radio. Hear the latest news, views and interviews, information and entertainment in the style of a conventional radio station. Music blends in with the content, players request tracks and tell you why. The Internet Radio feature requires Windows Media Player.
e-mail: membership@ westcoasteagles.com.au

West Coast Eagles Football Club - Benjamin's West Coast Eagles Page

www.geocities.com/Colosseum/Rink/4432/
e-mail: not available

WESTERN BULLDOGS FOOTBALL CLUB

Western Bulldogs Football Club

www.westernbulldogs.com.au
Become a net member for free and gain access to exclusive content on the site including the Video Archive. Fixtures, match reports, photographs, club and team news can be accessed directly.
e-mail: not available

Western Bulldogs Football Club - Western Bulldogs

pages.hotbot.com/sports/thecopps/index.html
e-mail: not available

Baseball

Anaheim Angels

www.anaheimangels.com

Listen live or join the chat room at this Californian team site. Whenever the Angels have a game coming up you get a notice to tell you where and when to watch and listen. Inside Pitch is a free e-mail service that keeps you posted with game notes, press releases and so much more.

e-mail: halobaseball@aol.com

Anaheim Angels - The Angels Bullpen

clubs.yahoo.com/clubs/
theangelsbullpen

Anaheim Angels -
The Angels Dugout

clubs.yahoo.com/clubs/
theangelsdugout

ATLANTA BRAVES

Atlanta Braves

www.atlantabraves.com

More than just a baseball site. You can win prizes at the Cyber Skipper, listen to radio broadcasts through the mlb radio link, buy Braves merchandise online and when you're done, check out local attractions through Atlanta links to places of interest.

e-mail: braves.web@turner.com

Atlanta Braves -
The Atlanta Braves 4 ever

clubs.yahoo.com/clubs/
atlantabraves4ever

Atlanta Braves - The Atlanta
Braves Tomahawk Chop

clubs.yahoo.com/clubs/
theatlantabravestomahawkchop

BALTIMORE ORIOLES

Baltimore Orioles

www.theorioles.com
Good site that keeps you on your toes.
Lots of regularly updated team news
and links to related sites. Good
readable feature stories.
e-mail: fanservi@opacy.com

Baltimore Orioles - Baltimore Oriole UK Fan Club

clubs.yahoo.com/clubs/
baltimoreoriolesukfanclub

Baltimore Orioles - Orioles Clubhouse

clubs.yahoo.com/clubs/
oriolesclubhouse

BOSTON RED SOX

Boston Red Sox

www.redsox.com
A bright red site for Boston's finest,
with links to game coverage, the year's
schedule, tickets, a plan of the famous
ballpark and the obligatory online store
for souveniers. The Yesteryear link has
Quicktime movies of special moments
in the club's past games to download.

Boston Red Sox - Boston Red Sox Fan Club

clubs.yahoo.com/clubs/bostonredsox-
fanclub

Boston Red Sox - Fenway Frank

clubs.yahoo.com/clubs/
fenwayfranksredsoxclub

Boston Red Sox - Red Sox Baseball

clubs.yahoo.com/clubs/
thebostonredsox

CHICAGO CUBS

Chicago Cubs

www.cubs.com
Get 10 per cent off a Cubs wall clock,
if you want one, vote in the poll to
choose the best player, tune in to the
radio broadcast with mlb and enjoy
yourself in the Interactive Fun section.
There are several absorbing features
worth reading.
e-mail: comments@mail.cubs.com

Chicago Cubs - Chicago Cubs Loyal Fans

clubs.yahoo.com/clubs/
chicagocubsloyalfans

Chicago Cubs - Cubs Coven

clubs.yahoo.com/clubs/cubscoven

CHICAGO WHITE SOX

Chicago White Sox

www.chisox.com
Frank Thomas doubles and Ray
Durham beats the throw home, comes
from the multimedia shot accessible
from the home page. Open the media
viewer and see it for yourself.
A wonderful site, user-friendly and full
of hyper-links. If you want to know
what it's like to be enrolled in a training
camp, you have a 10-year-old camper's
diary to tell you. Aside from the usual
stuff like buying tickets online, there is
a lot to keep you entertained.
e-mail: webhost@chisox.com

Chicago White Sox - Fans of the White Sox

clubs.yahoo.com/clubs/
fansofthewhitesox

Chicago White Sox - Unofficial White Sox Club

clubs.yahoo.com/clubs/
chicagowhitesoxofficalclub

CINCINNATI REDS

Cincinnati Reds

www.cincinnatireds.com
If you subscribe to the official club newsletter Redlegs Monthly, you can keep up-to-date with what's happening Cincinnati-wise. The team comes live on the multimedia page. Player profiles and details of the new ballpark are well presented on the site.
e-mail: commintern@cincyreds.com

Cincinnati Reds - Cincinnati Reds Super Fan Club

clubs.yahoo.com/clubs/
cincinnatiredssuperfanclub

Cincinnati Reds - The Cinergized Reds Fans

clubs.yahoo.com/clubs/
thecinergizedredsfans

CLEVELAND INDIANS

Cleveland Indians

www.indians.com
You can catch video highlights from the games or take a tour of the Indians home ground and Jacobs Field. Visit the CyberTribe page to chat to other fans, the players, play online games and enter contests.

Cleveland Indians - Chief Wahoo's Indian Fan Club

clubs.yahoo.com/clubs/
clevelandindianswahooofans

Cleveland Indians - Cleveland Indians Web Fan Club

clubs.yahoo.com/clubs/
clevelandindianswebfanclub

DETROIT TIGERS

Detroit Tigers

www.detroittigers.com
What is Tony Clark's slugging percentage? Find out by visiting Gameday at this site. Buy your tickets online and follow quick links to statistics, schedules and an online store.
e-mail: feedback@detroittigers.com

Detroit Tigers - Detroit Tigers Club

clubs.yahoo.com/clubs/
detroittigersclub

Detroit Tigers - The Tigers Domain

clubs.yahoo.com/clubs/thetigerdomain

FLORIDA MARLINS

Florida Marlins

www.floridamarlins.com
Families and children hold centre stage at this site with the Family Sundays feature. Just click the panel on the home page for a full display of the photos. The Team Store offers all the Marlins gear you could ever want and the Multimedia section has video clips of the stars in action and audio clips of the club theme songs.

Florida Marlins - The Marlins Diamond

clubs.yahoo.com/clubs/
themarlinsdiamond

HOUSTON ASTROS

Houston Astros

www.astros.com

Slow loading and complicated site. The online seating plans help you choose your tickets and the search engine gets you what you're after. Follow the link to MLB radio network broadcasts and take time out to read the team and stadium history.

Houston Astros - The Astro Dugout

clubs.yahoo.com/clubs/theastrodugout

Japanorama

www.japanorama.com/baseball.html

Horace Wilson, an American teacher, introduced Japan's modern national sport into the country in 1872. The first formal baseball team was organised in 1878 by a railroad company. This site has an index of all Japanese teams with contact addresses and phone numbers and a glossary of Japanese baseball terms. But unfortunately, Japanese baseball web sites do not seem to exist in English.

KANSAS CITY ROYALS

Kansas City Royals

www.kcroyals.com

Ask nicely and they'll send you free e-mail @theroyals.com. Take a look at the spring training programme, find a job or go into the front office next to the ticket booth.

Kansas City Royals - KC Royals Dugout

clubs.yahoo.com/clubs/kcroyalsdugout

LOS ANGELES DODGERS

Los Angeles Dodgers

www.dodgers.com

An excellent site if you have Flash. The Dodgers, in conjunction with the History Channel, present This Day in Dodger History, which takes a look at the people and events that shaped the Dodgers' rich and colourful history. At their fantasy camp you can live out your dreams and play baseball with some of the greats.

Los Angeles Dodgers - Fans of the Dodgers

clubs.yahoo.com/clubs/fansofdodgers

Los Angeles Dodgers - LA Dodgers Best Fans

clubs.yahoo.com/clubs/
ladodgersbestfans

MILWAUKEE BREWERS

Milwaukee Brewers

www.milwaukeebrewers.com
Find out what's brewing by signing up for the new e-mail service. You can also pick up the news at the Press Box and see some action on the multimedia page. The Brewers online store has a lot on offer.

Milwaukee Brewers - Brewers Dugout 2000

clubs.yahoo.com/clubs/brewers

Milwaukee Brewers - Milwaukee Brewers Y2k

clubs.yahoo.com/clubs/
milwaukeebrewersy2k

MINNESOTA TWINS

Minnesota Twins

www.mntwins.com
There's a lot of good readable stuff and recorded audio clips of games on the site and you can also buy tickets for upcoming games. Lots of other goodies can be had at this site, including the Twins' bobblehead doll. That is, if you haven't already got one.
e-mail: twins@twinsbaseball.com

Minnesota Twins - John's Minnesota Twins Page

members.aol.com/puck71/twins.html
e-mail: puck71@aol.com

Minnesota Twins - Save the Minnesota Twins

www.wcug.wwu.edu/~johnb/twins/
e-mail: soulpilgrim@go.com

MONTREAL EXPOS

Montreal Expos

www.montrealexpos.com
You can read the full story of Costas Guerrero, one of the most gifted players ever, in English or French. If you feel up to it, sign up for one of their club camps. Place your vote online if you think you know where the Expos will finish the 2000 campaign.
e-mail: info-e@fans.montrealexpos.com

MONTREAL EXPOS

Montreal Expos - Martin's Expos Fan Page

clubs.yahoo.com/clubs/
martinsexposfanpage

Montreal Expos - Montreal Expos Fan Club

clubs.yahoo.com/clubs/
montrealexposfanclub

NEW YORK METS

New York Mets

www.mets.com
The Met Man is here. He's the animated icon of the club. If you don't have Flash you can download it before you set off to enjoy the site. The history

page holds the archives, which also asks you to vote on your favourite moments from the history books.

New York Mets - The New York Mets Fan Club

clubs.yahoo.com/clubs/
thenewyorkmetsfanclub

New York Mets - The New York Mets Fan Forum

clubs.yahoo.com/clubs/
newyorkmetsfanforum

New York Yankees - The New York Yankees Fan Club

clubs.yahoo.com/clubs/
thenewyorkyankeesfanclub

New York Yankees - The Yankee Clubhouse

clubs.yahoo.com/clubs/
theyankeeclubhouse

New York Yankees - Yankee Fan hangout

clubs.yahoo.com/clubs/
yankeefanhangout

NEW YORK YANKEES

New York Yankees

www.yankees.com

Probably baseball's most famous team has a packed web site. Take your pick from the ruler menu - the forum, stat zone or online shop, then run across to the Extreme page for a free trial membership of the fan club, with e-mail address and web space.

OAKLAND ATHLETICS

Oakland Athletics

www.oaklandathletics.com

A very busy site but easy to navigate. You can download wallpaper to change the look of your computer, chat online and post a message, visit the kids corner at Stomper's home page, go down on the Farm to check out the minor league and get your gear from the online store.

Oakland Athletics - Oakland Athletics fan Club

clubs.yahoo.com/clubs/
oaklandathleticsfanclub

Oakland Athletics - The Oakland A's

clubs.yahoo.com/clubs/oaklandas

PHILADELPHIA PHILLIES

Philadelphia Phillies

www.phillies.com
Sign up for a free e-mail account or
have your favourite Phillies links and
player photo right on your home page!
Visit the veteran's stadium and find out
the state of development at the new
arena.
e-mail: phans@phillies.com

Philadelphia Phillies - Philadelphia Phillies Dugout

clubs.yahoo.com/clubs/
philadelphiaphilliesdugout

Philadelphia Phillies - The Philadelphia Phillies Official Club

clubs.yahoo.com/clubs/
philadelphiaphilliesofficialc

PITTSBURGH PIRATES

Pittsburgh Pirates

www.pirateball.com
PNC Park construction is moving fast
and you can follow the progress on this
site. The countdown clock is ticking
away as you read. To be a part of history, click a brick to get it personalised at
the new Park. The Glory Days section
has a history of the club.

Pittsburgh Pirates - Demention's Pirates Bullpen

clubs.yahoo.com/clubs/
dementionspiratesbullpen

Pittsburgh Pirates - Pirates Baseball Dugout

clubs.yahoo.com/clubs/
piratesbaseballdugout

Robs Japanese Cards

robsjapanesecards.com
Japanese baseball cards in English
for collectors. The site explains the
different types of cards, gives
biographies of great Japanese players
and sells cards from all years. Fellow
collectors' want lists are posted with
what they have to trade for them.
An interesting curiosity.
e-mail: ochia@mindspring.com

San Diego Padres

www.padres.com
View the Padres live through a video
feed or the progress of the new ballpark
through a web cam. The online auction
is where you get yourself a certified
authentic piece of memorabilia. If you
want to enter the Steal-A-Meal contest
or maybe Pitch to the 76, then check
out the special promotions.

SAN FRANCISCO GIANTS

San Francisco Giants

www.sfgiants.com/home
Get to the head of the line for season
tickets by becoming an On Deck Seat
holder; a deposit gets you on the
waiting list. Quick links lead to the
store, rewards club, tickets and
statistics to name a few features.

San Francisco Giants - Giants Rock

clubs.yahoo.com/clubs/giantsrock

San Francisco Giants - San Francisco Giants Club

clubs.yahoo.com/clubs/
sanfranciscogiantsclub

SEATTLE MARINERS

Seattle Mariners

www.mariners.org
Through the live camera link you can
see the Safeco and the Mariners Home
Fields. Click the A-Z to find the
answers to your questions about the
ballpark. Check out forthcoming
games, visit the clubhouse and the kid
zone or buy tickets online.
e-mail: mariners@digital-sherpas.com

Seattle Mariners – Mariners

clubs.yahoo.com/clubs/mariners

Seattle Mariners - Seattle Mariners' Dugout

clubs.yahoo.com/clubs/
seattlemarinersdugout

ST LOUIS CARDINALS

St Louis Cardinals

www.stlcardinals.com
The Cardinals will become part of your
daily life when you download the free
screensaver. If you are planning a trip
to the club take advantage of the great
give-aways coming up this season. You
get free e-mail when your name's on
the list so keep up-to-the-minute with
official news from the club.

St Louis Cardinals - Cardinals Country

clubs.yahoo.com/clubs/
cardinalscountry

St Louis Cardinals - St Louis Cardinals Dugout

clubs.yahoo.com/clubs/
stlouiscardinalsdugout

TAMPA BAY DEVILS

Tampa Bay Devils

www.devilray.com
Winning an autographed jersey or
visiting the archives are two attractions

on this enjoyable site. Check out the video highlights or get yourself a devilish e-mail address.

Tampa Bay Devils - Devil Rays Place
clubs.yahoo.com/clubs/devilraysplace

Tampa Bay Devils - Rays Dogout
clubs.yahoo.com/clubs/raysdogout

TEXAS RANGERS

Texas Rangers
www.texasrangers.com
Attitude is everything is the catch phrase of this team site. As you run your cursor over the menu bar, a dialogue balloon opens up to tell you what's in store on those pages. The live audio game link will keep you busy for a while.

Texas Rangers - The Texas Rangers
clubs.yahoo.com/clubs/thetexasrangers

Texas Rangers - The Texas Rangers Club
clubs.yahoo.com/clubs/atexasrangersclub

TORONTO BLUE JAYS

Toronto Blue Jays
www.bluejays.ca
Downbeat site compared to the other baseball offerings made up mainly of lists. Buy official Blue Jays gear or check the latest news on the day's game in the Game Center.
e-mail: bluejays@bluejays.ca

Toronto Blue Jays -Adeel's Toronto Blue Jays
clubs.yahoo.com/clubs/adeelstorontobluejayscl

Toronto Blue Jays - Blue Jays Baseball
clubs.yahoo.com/clubs/bluejaysbaseball

Basketball

FIBA - International Basketball Federation

www.fiba.com

You get good coverage of all the latest news from the basketball world, info on national teams, clubs and loads of players. The history of international competitions and tournaments is well documented with accompanying photos and videos. A general section deals with the rules of the sport and forthcoming tournaments.

e-mail: via online form

NBA.com

www.nba.com

You can spend hours on this site, probably the best on basketball events played by the world's greatest and most celebrated teams. It's all here - the rules and regs, the very latest news, scores and tables; live broadcasts and after-match commentaries by players, coaches, press reporters and avid fans. An immense archive holds the facts, the pictures and the videos from previous years with statistics and player profiles. The site hosts official pages for all league teams, with results, player profiles, an online shop to buy kit and club gifts and a box office to book tickets for NBA matches. Each club guides you through their arena, pins up photos from past and present and links up to a women's team.

e-mail: via online form

Telebasket

www.telebasket.com

Since most national and league servers are outdated, this seems to be the most reliable source of news on European basketball with information galore for fans all over the world, from both professional and amateur teams, sorted by country, league and tournament. There's a gigantic database of national teams, clubs, players and coaches who play or have played basketball. Additional attractions include live broadcasts, a schedule of fixtures and a few items to buy online.

e-mail: telebasket@telebasket.com

Turkish Basketball

www.turkishbasketball.com/eng

Though unofficial, this site brings you

the best and most thorough information you are likely to get on Turkish basketball - the whole range of news and league results, tournaments and national team matches. There are details of teams and players, chat rooms, a video gallery and guest book.
e-mail: webmaster@turkishbasketball.com

NBA Teams

ATLANTA HAWKS
Atlanta Hawks Resource
www.spydersempire.com/sports/nba/atla.htm
e-mail: via online form

The Atlanta Hawks
www.nando.net/SportServer/basketball/nba/atl.html
e-mail: via online form

Unofficial Atlanta Hawks Page
members.xoom.com/uahp/hawks.htm
e-mail: via online form

BOSTON CELTICS
Boston Celtics HQ
www.geocities.com/celtics_11
e-mail: martin@int-usa.net

Boston Celtics Mystique Page
www.the-spa.com/fbb
e-mail: celticsfan@iname.com

Celtic Web!
people2.clemson.edu/~rprasha/celtics/celts.htm
e-mail: rprasha@clemson.edu

CHARLOTTE HORNETS
HornetsWeb.com
www.hornetsweb.com
e-mail: via online form

CHICAGO BULLS
Bull6.com
bulls6.com
e-mail: webmaster@bulls6.com

Chicago Bulls!!
members.aol.com/tmescan/welcome.html
e-mail: Sccovell@AOL.com

Chicago Bulls - A Look from the Stands
www.geocities.com/Colosseum/Field/2962
e-mail: mikeyb1998@hotmail.com

Chicago Bulls Chat
www.geocities.com/Colosseum/Lodge/3044/BullsChat.html
e-mail: via online form

Chicago Bulls Fans
www.angelfire.com/ct/yvonne9/index.html
e-mail: not available

Chicago Bulls Gallery
members.aol.com/jumpman45/Bulls-artgallery.html
e-mail: jumpman45@aol.com

Chicago Bulls Picture Gallery
www.acoolplace.freeserve.co.uk/Gallery.html
e-mail: RichieBabyls@acoolplace.freeserve.co.uk

Chicago Bulls Sporting Den

www.geocities.com/Colosseum/Lodge/
3044/BullsDen.html
e-mail: not available

da Bulls

www.essex1.com/people/jmiller/bulls.htm
e-mail: jem@bullsfan.com

Michael Jordan

www.unc.edu/~lbrooks2/jordan.html
e-mail: lbrooks2@email.unc.edu

Michael Jordan's Official Website

jordan.sportsline.com
e-mail: via online form

Portrait of an era

www.thebullsbook.com
e-mail: info@thebullsbook.com

The Chicago Bulls Locker Room

www.geocities.com/Colosseum/
Field/5842
e-mail: not available

DALLAS MAVERICKS

Dallas Mavericks Courtside

www.smu.edu/~myers
e-mail: dallasmavs@hotmail.com

Dallas Mavericks Fan Central

www.star-telegram.com/sports/mavericks
e-mail: via online form

Dallas Mavericks Fan Page

www.allsports.com/nba/mavericks
e-mail: not available

Dallas Wheelchair Mavericks

home.flash.net/~wheelmav
e-mail: not available

The Dallas Mavericks Unofficial Homepage

www.geocities.com/Colosseum/Loge/
4905
e-mail: not available

The Lone Mavs Fan

web2.airmail.net/jdport
e-mail: jdport@mail.airmail.net

DENVER NUGGETS

Alan Switzer's Denver Nuggets Fan Page

www.mindspring.com/~aswitzer/
nuggets.html
e-mail: not available

Nugz Online

nugzonline.com/nugz.html
e-mail: nugzfan@yahoo.com

DETROIT PISTONS

Detroit Pistons Assembly Line

pistons.rivals.com
e-mail: via online form

Detroit Pistons Press Box

www.aa-design.com/pistons
e-mail: not available

PistonsWeb

www.geocities.com/pistonsweb2k/
pw.html
e-mail: tomtessin@yahoo.com

GOLDEN STATE WARRIORS

Golden State Warriors

free.prohosting.com/~gsw
e-mail: via online form

HOUSTON ROCKETS

Clutch City Online

www.clutchcity.net
e-mail: clutch@clutchcity.net

Houston Rockets Space Center

www.geocities.com/Colosseum/
Pressbox/6544
e-mail: clutchtown@hotmail.com

INDIANA PACERS

Pacerfanzone

www.nbafanzone.com
e-mail: not available

Remember the ABA: Indiana Pacers

www.geocities.com/Colosseum/5290/
Indiana-Pacers.html
e-mail: not available

Unofficial Indiana Pacers Homepage

fly.to/indianapolis
e-mail: not available

LA LAKERS

LakerBasketball.com

www.lakerbasketball.com
e-mail: not available

Lakers Webring

www.webring.org/cgi-bin/
webring?ring=lalakers;list
e-mail: not available

Mel and Will's Awesome LA Lakers Website

www.geocities.com/Colosseum/
Arena/1735
e-mail: not available

The Lake Show

www.armory.com/~lew/sports/
basketball
e-mail: lew@armory.com

NEW YORK KNICKS

Knicks Courtside

www.nykcourtside.com
e-mail: not available

ORLANDO MAGIC

Adam's Orlando Magic Web Site

members.aol.com/damagicfan
e-mail: damagicfan@aol.com

Ben Gad's Orlando Magic Site

www.geocities.com/Colosseum/
Track/3043
e-mail: not available

My Orlando Magic Page

www.dclink.com/rusty/kevin/magic.htm
e-mail: not available

O-Zone Orlando Magic Fan Forum

magic.arecool.net
e-mail: not available

Orlando Magic Jam

members.tripod.com/ZopopOnline
e-mail: not available

Orlando Magic Resource

www.senet.com.au/~gioiosa/magic.htm
e-mail: not available

Orlando Magic - The Web Site

www.geocities.com/Colosseum/Stadium/
6008
e-mail: plateau@mailexcite.com

Phil's Phat Orland Magic Page

**shoga.wwa.com/~wutang/basketball/
orlando/magic.html**
e-mail: not available

The Penny Hardaway Palace

**www.geocities.com/Colosseum/5913/
index.html**
e-mail: romyvco@ix.netcom.com

PHOENIX SUNS

Phoenix Suns Back Court

suns.rivals.com
e-mail: not available

PORTLAND TRAIL BLAZERS

BlazerWeb

trailblazers.rivals.com
e-mail: mail@rockitland.com

Blazing Stoudamire

**members.tripod.com/
DamonStoudamire**
e-mail: blazingstoudamire@
hotmail.com

Oregon Live - Portland Trail Blazers

www.oregonlive.com/blazers
e-mail: otalkback@oregonlive.com

Portland Trail Blazers

www.teleport.com/~mbn/blazers.html
e-mail: not available

Rose Quarter Online

www.rosequarter.com
e-mail: webmaster@ripcity.com

SAN ANTONIO SPURS

CAP3's San Antonio Spurs Fanpage

home.talkcity.com/ArenaBlvd/pac10
e-mail: SpursWorldChamps99@
yahoo.com

Dan's San Antonio Spurs Page

tdb.tripod.com/spurs
e-mail: tdb007@email.com

Spurs Basketball Homepage

www.geocities.com/carlosmtz/index.html
e-mail: spurs@basketball.com

Spurs Central

**olympia.fortunecity.com/ronaldo/81/
rhs.htm**
e-mail: spurscentral@hotmail.com

Spurs City

members.tripod.com/SpursCity
e-mail: jatdrago@earthling.net

Spurs Mania!

members.tripod.com/~Spurmania
e-mail: spursmania_1999@yahoo.com

Spurs Report

spursreport.com
e-mail: via online form

Spurschat

www.spurschat.com
e-mail: not available

UTAH JAZZ

Adam's Unofficial Utah Jazz Homepage

jazz.cscweb.net
e-mail: magicbox@bestweb.net

Jensky's Utah Jazz Homepage

oeonline.oeonline.com/~jensen/
jenskyutahjazz.html/jenskyutahjazz.html
e-mail: jensen@oeonline.com

The Utah Jazz Rule

utahjazz.iwarp.com
e-mail: utahjazzfan@utahjazz.iwarp.com

Utah Jazz Fan Page

www.allsports.com/nba/jazz
e-mail: via online form

Utah Jazz Fans Ring

www.geocities.com/ujjs/jazzring.htm
e-mail: via online form

Utah Jazz News

www.utjazz.com
e-mail: via online form

Utah Jazz Page

www.xmission.com/~odie/jazz.html
e-mail: odie@xmission.com

Betting

Online Sportsbook

www.osportsbook.com
You get real time betting in Las Vegas but no financial transactions actually take place within the USA as the site is licensed in Antigua. You don't have to place a minimum deposit and personal data is strictly confidential. There are many ways to make payment and bets can be placed on all major international sports competitions and league matches.
e-mail: osportsbook@osportsbook.com

007 Online Sports Betting

www.007sportsbetting.com
Offshore betting site licensed by the government of Antigua. They provide instant access to real time betting lines in Las Vegas and let you bet on any sport. Members, who join absolutely free and pay no deposit, also have access to real time sports news and an online casino. Your personal data and gaming status are kept strictly confidential. You get a 10% discount when you sign up.
e-mail: via online form

1 Online Sportsbook

www.numberonesportsbook.com
Multi-lingual betting site for all major US and international sport. All transactions are legal and bonded by the government of Antigua and no deals take place within the USA. Anyone who opens an account and submits cheque, money order or credit card details can bet on this site. No minimum charges apply and all information is confidential. The sports line-up includes American football, basketball, baseball, boxing, golf, motor sports, football, cricket, rugby, tennis and others listed on the site. Specific rules apply to each sport and are worth noting. Once you are registered you are given access to an online casino.
e-mail: via online form

1-800 Online Sports

www.1-800-online-sportsbook.com
Online sports betting and gambling services licensed by the government of Costa Rica. All members have access

to Las Vegas real time betting lines but no financial transactions take place in US territory. Members' personal data and gaming status remain confidential. You don't pay an initial deposit; discounts are given to first-time users or for introducing other members and you can even insure against losses. All major North American and European sports are covered. There are betting tutorials online and they organise gambling for fun for those under the legal age or living in countries where betting is illegal.
e-mail: info@2betdsi.com

Eurobet

www.eurobet.com
UK online sports betting service with up-to-date information on the 15 most popular world sports plus all major international tournaments. The site gives a complete guide to sports betting including financial rules and special regulations for each sport. Betting online is tax-free and confidential. They accept major credit cards and offer a secure payment server.
e-mail: via online form

IG Index Sport

www.igsport.com
This is the Sports section of the IG Index spread betting online service. The rules are described in great detail with many examples provided on how to go about it. You'll also find a manual of rules applicable to each sport. Membership is free and brings with it many special offers.
e-mail: helpdesk@igsport.com

InterBet International

www.inter-bet.com
Online tax-free betting service based in Guernsey. They specialise in UK horse racing and provide live programs and early prices. You can also bet on European football and other major international sports events. There are membership rules and restrictions that should be noted. All personal data is kept confidential.
e-mail: via online form

Interwetten Wien

www.interwetten.com
Austrian online betting site serving more than 50,000 customers world wide. They don't require membership fees or a minimum deposit and maintain confidentiality. The minimum stake is $5 and maximum payout $10,000. Bets can be placed on European and North American sport.
e-mail: service@interwetten.com

Ladbrokes

www.ladbrokes.co.uk
Britain's largest and popular bookmaker whose online site guarantees tax-free betting. Their secure server accepts the four major credit cards used in the UK. You can bet on horseracing, greyhounds, football, golf, tennis, motor racing and rugby. Additionally, they offer packages within each sport for various competitions. The site has an up-to-date sports results server. Betting is only available to members and registration is free.
e-mail: care@ladbrokes.co.uk

Majestic Sportsbook

www.1bet.com
Online betting facility and casino licensed in Costa Rica. Betting is restricted to those over 18 who register. Members' personal data and gaming activities remain strictly confidential. You don't have to place an initial deposit but there are limits on the size of bets. All major international sports are fair game and payment methods are flexible.
e-mail: info@1bet.com

MegaSports

megasports.com.au
Australian online betting facility available for those who are over 18 and not residents of the USA. The site gives an undertaking not to reveal details of your transactions. You'll find a guide to betting rules and regulations as they apply to each sport. Bets can be placed online using the secure credit card system or by phone.
e-mail: sports@megasports.com.au

Olympic Sports

www.thegreek.com
The blurb says that this is the most advanced online sports book on the Internet. It has a very good section on Olympics events for viewing and betting. First you need to register and this requires a minimum initial deposit of $100. If you sign up over the web, the deposit drops to $50. You pay the money so you decide.
e-mail: support@thegreek.com

SportsInsite@Bowman International

209.5.35.52
This US sports betting site has up-to-date news on a wide range of international sports as well as all the odds and handicapping for US team sports like American football, basketball and ice hockey.
e-mail: info@bowmans.com

SSP International Sports Betting

www.ssp.co.uk
Multilingual UK offshore online betting service. They cover major North American and European team sport, motor racing, tennis, athletics and a list of others, with the main focus on football.
e-mail: webmaster@ssp.co.uk

The New Zealand TAB

www.tab.co.nz
Online sports betting site based in New Zealand with the emphasis on horseracing and rugby but you can also bet on major present-time sports events. There's a complete guide to sports betting with an explanation of the rules of the game. They keep your betting record completely confidential. An information server brings you up to speed with the latest sports results.
e-mail: via online form

William Hill International

www.willhill.com
William Hill is well known in the British betting market. They offer permanent tax-free betting online, cash-backs and a minimum stake of one penny. You can bet on most British leagues, horse racing, motor racing and US sports. The site is very well constructed and you get the latest results online.
e-mail: questions@willhill.com

The following betting sites are generally licensed and bonded by the government of a Caribbean or Central American State. They waive all membership fees and give members access to real time betting in Las Vegas but no financial transactions take place in US territory. All personal details and gaming information are held in strict confidence. With one or two exceptions, deposits are not required but some restrict minimum and maximum bets to $10 and $1,000 respectively. Online payments by credit card go through encryption by secure server or if you prefer, you can use cheques or money orders. You can bet on most spectator sport, in particular NFL American Football, NBA and college asketball, NHL and college ice hockey, baseball, boxing, golf, motor sports, NASCAR, football, cricket, rugby and tennis. Members also have access to casinos. Also see the specific notes on some sites.

7 Seas Sports Betting

www.7seassportsbetting.com
e-mail:
support@7seassportsbetting.com

A Bookie Joint

www.abookiejoint.com
e-mail: info@abookiejoint.com

Action Bets

www.actionbets.com
e-mail: not available

All Mayan Sportsbook

www.mayansports.com
Takes bets on US sports only.
e-mail: info@mayansports.com

All Sports Casino

www.allsportscasino.com
The minimum deposit is $20.
e-mail: support@allsportscasino.com

All Star Gaming

www.allstargaming.com
e-mail: via online form

At HomeSportsBook

www.athomesportsbook.com
They take bets up to $5000.
e-mail:
support@athomesportsbook.com

Bet2Day

www.bet2day.com
e-mail: info@bet2day.com

British Caribbean Gaming

www.bcbet.com
e-mail: nigel@bcsports.net

Casablanca Sportsbook and Casino

www.wagerweb.com
The minimum deposit is $100.
e-mail: questions@wagerweb.com

Centrebet

www2.centrebet.com.au
Not available to US residents. Text is
in English, Danish, Swedish,
Norwegian and Finnish.
e-mail: info@centrebet.com

Cyber Sports Betting

www.cybersportsbet.com
e-mail: via online form

Desert Palace Casino

desertpalace.com/sportsbook
e-mail: via online form

Diamond Sportsbook International

www.amigoscasino.com
e-mail: not available

EasyBets

www.easybets.com
Text is in 20 languages and you get the
latest results online.
e-mail: info@easybets.com

Fair Deal

www.fairdealsports.com
The minimum deposit is $100;
minimum bet $1 maximum $5,000.
e-mail: memberservices@
fairdealsports.com

Game Day Sportsbook

www.gamedaysportsbook.com
e-mail: playerinfo@gamedaycasino.com

Grand Central Sports

www.gcsports.com
e-mail: linemaker@gcsports.com

Grand Prix Sportsbook and Casino

www.grandprixsports.com
e-mail: support@grandprixsports.com

i-Sportsbook

www.i-sportsbook.com
e-mail: via online form

Intertops

www.intertops.com
They accept bets on a wider range of
sport, politics, cinema and the stock
market.
e-mail: Bet@Intertops.com

MySportsbook

www.mysportsbook.com
e-mail: via online form

Place My Bet

www.placemybet.com
There are no fees for deposits over
$100.
e-mail: support@PlaceMyBet.com

Players Sportsbook and Casino

www.playersonly.com
e-mail: not available

Post Time Sports

www.post-time.com
e-mail: not available

Premierleague

www.premiereleague.com
e-mail: premierleague@candw.ag

Pyramid Sportsbook

www.pyramidcasino.net
e-mail: service@pyramiddownload.com

SPLBET

www.splbet.co.uk
e-mail: enquiries@surreysports.com

Sportfanatik

www.sportfanatik.com
You also get the latest sports news.
e-mail:
webmaster@SPORTFANATIK.com

SportingbetUSA

www.sportingbetUSA.com
e-mail: via online form

Sports Betting Games

www.sportsbettinggames.com
e-mail: support@softecsystems.com

Sports Interaction

www3.sportsinteraction.com
e-mail: support@sportsinteraction.com

Sportsbetting.com

www.sportsbetting.com
e-mail: help@sportsbetting.com

! Sportsbook Betting

www.exclamation-sportsbook-
betting.com
e-mail: via online form

SportsBookPro

www.sportsbookpro.com
e-mail: not available

Sterling Sports and Race Book

www.wagepage.com
e-mail: sterling@wagepage.com

Superbet

www.superbet.com
e-mail: support@superbet.com

SuperBowlBet

www.superbowlbet.com
Dedicated to the main event, but other
sports are available.
e-mail: not available

The Big Book

www.thebigbook.com
e-mail: service@thebigbook.com

VIP Global Gaming

www.vipglobalgaming.com
e-mail: not available

World Games Sportsbook

www.worldgamescasino.com
e-mail: not available

World Soccer Betting

www.worldsoccerbetting.com
Betting on major football tournaments,
international matches and top leagues
only. You get information on results
and injuries.
e-mail: via online form

Worldgaming Sportsbook

sportsbook.worldgaming.com
e-mail: via online form

Boxing

3615 Boxing Avenue

www.boxing-records.com

The web site holds the fight records of more than 20,000 boxers with records, news and lists of champions thrown in as an extra. Some features of the site require subscription. Text is in English, French and Spanish.

e-mail: gfax@boxing-records.com

About.com Boxing

boxing.about.com/sports/boxing/mbody.htm

One of many similar web sites offering expert guides to particular subjects, which make up into a very impressive resource. News and information are of a sustained high standard and there is a large handful of good and varied boxing related links. The Discussion Board, Chat Room and site newsletter keep you constantly in touch.

e-mail: boxing.guide@about.com

BCN

www.boxingcollectors.com

Internet version of Boxing Collectors' Newsmagazine which you can subscribe to by using the online form. If you collect boxing memorabilia you will find the site very instructive. Several articles explain the fake market and show you how to avoid getting gulled into believing what your instincts tell you are not what they seem to be. The Collector-to-Collector page puts you right into the marketplace where you can advertise what you want to buy, sell or trade.

e-mail: askbcn@boxingcollectors.com

Berliner Klitschko Bros. Fanpage

www.east-berlin.de

Witali and Vladimir Klitschko are boxing brothers from the Ukraine. This is their fan site filled with photos, reports and statistics. Videos of the boys in the ring come in MPEG Video format and you can use the forum, chat room or leave messages in the guest book.

e-mail: via online form

Big George Foreman's Place

www.georgeforeman.com
George Foreman was Mohammed Ali's opponent in the legendary Rumble in the Jungle clash. Foreman retired in the late 1970s to become a preacher. He returned to the ring, in part to fund a youth centre he had built with his own money, and won a version of the World Title at the age of 43. The different threads of Big George's life are recounted here. His favourite religious scripts sit alongside his boxing record and family photographs. You can buy merchandise and join a fan club online.
e-mail: ladygf@aol.com

Boxing Mania

www.boxingmania.com
Louisville boxing promoters have launched a mission to revive boxing in Muhummad Ali's birthplace. The message board gets an awful lot of traffic.
e-mail: editor@boxingmania.com

Boxing Monthly

www.boxing-monthly.co.uk
UK online companion to Boxing Monthly magazine. The site brings together articles from current and past issues. A selection of clothing can be bought online using a secure server facility and, naturally, you can also subscribe to the magazine. A great feature is the interactive guest book which doubles as a message board and attracts a large number of postings on all aspects of the fight game.
e-mail: jo@boxing-monthly.demon.co.uk

Boxing News

www.fightnews.com
If you want or need up-to-the-minute news about boxing this is a good place to start since they aim to be the first with boxing breaking news on the Internet. Fighter world ranking is listed and forthcoming scheduled fights with TV show times are also published.
e-mail: editor@fightnews.com

Boxing OJ

www.eonline.com/Fun/Games/Boxing/
If you want to climb into the ring with O J Simpson, slug it out, and see who remains standing at the end, get your gloves on. You can play Boxing OJ online so long as you have, or download, the Shockwave plugin. Dance around and throw left and right jabs but watch out for the counter blows as he pulls no punches. It's free and it's fun.
e-mail: games@eonline.com

Boxing On The Web

www.ipcress.com/writer/boxing.html
Entertaining, illuminating and wide open boxing site. There are hundreds of biographies and career records of fighters, male and female. This is not just historical record as present day

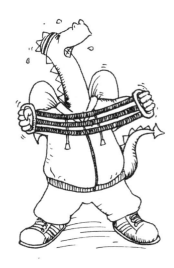

boxers get exciting coverage from the ringside - bout results, world rankings and forthcoming fixtures. A winning page details the World Champions of the numerous boxing organisations.
e-mail: boxing@ipcress.com

Boxing Photos From the 80s

www.crl.com/~jshenry/dokes.html
Respected American photographer Scott Henry has assembled a first-rate album of his boxing pictures for site visitors to browse online. The high quality pictures with captions of greats like Ali, Hearns, Hagler, Sugar Ray Leonard, and Joe Louis make this a very satisfying site.
e-mail: jshenry@crl.com

Boxing Trivia and Fun Stories

members.tripod.com/~jeffsboxing/trivia.html
Why does Tyson wear black trunks? Which boxer has held a world title for the shortest time? What are the records for the longest and shortest fights in history? The answers are here. You get three pages of short stories and boxing trivia on this fan site.
e-mail: jeffsboxing@deathsdoor.com

Boxinginsider

www.boxinginsider.com
Omnibus site giving the latest boxing headlines from the news hotline, archives for reference, fight odds and schedule, ranking and more. Or sign up for a free, web based e-mail service and get your own @Boxinginsider.com address. Or again shop for boxing merchandise and purchase online or visit the gallery of Ring Girls photographs.
e-mail: larry@boxinginsider.com

boxingonline.com

www.boxingonline.com
Magazine style boxing web site brings you fight schedules, results and reviews and profiles of boxers, many well known and others who will be. A classy audio/video section - requires Microsoft Windows Media Player – brings you face to face with interviews and other material from the noble sport. Boxing Online also hosts regular live webcam broadcasts.
e-mail: not available

Boxingpress.com

www.boxingpress.com
Another comprehensive boxing site brings you match schedules, results, rankings and news. Fans will enjoy the very busy online Message Board; you get continuous contact with other enthusiasts to praise your heroes and slander the other guys, rerun fights that didn't go the way you wanted and decide who would beat whom in a fantasy boxing match. Java enabled browsers can use the Chat Room. There are so many articles, interviews and letters to read, you will be hard put to get it all in at one sitting; then when you return there's a lot more new stuff to get to grips with. Text is in English, German and Italian.
e-mail: admin@boxingpress.com

boxingtimes.com

www.boxingtimes.com
North American online boxing magazine with a TV guide that lists boxing related programmes for the week ahead. Regular writers fill the columns with all manner of boxing news and analyses of recent matches. The Classified Ads

section helps you buy and sell collectors' items and find a sparring or training partner if you are so inclined.
e-mail: via online form

Danish Prime Fighters

home5.inet.tele.dk/nielsm/start_uk.html
Absolutely everything you ever wanted to know about Danish Boxing is here. You will find all the retired and active Danish fighters with their photos, personal statistics, promoters and fight records all up-to-date, with news and world ranking from WBA, WBC, IBF and other bodies. A lot of hard work went into this site.
e-mail: danish_boxing@hotmail.com

Don King Productions

www.donking.com
The official web site of the flamboyant boxing promoter Don King tells his life story and gives details of the fighters he manages. Fight cards for forthcoming Don King events are detailed online with regular boxing news updates.
e-mail: donking1@bellsouth.net

Evander Holyfield

www.evanderholyfield.com/index1.html
Evander Holyfield, the man who had his ear bitten by Mike Tyson has his life story told online with photographs. Video clips need Windows Media Player format. You can join his fan club online, read about the Holyfield Foundation and his restaurant. An online store sells merchandise and memorabilia.
e-mail: info@evanderholyfield.com

Gene Tunney

bally.fortunecity.com/mayo/239/
Gene Tunney was World Heavyweight Boxing Champion from 1926 to 1928. The site exhibits his boxing cards, fights records, photographs and book extracts. Even his birth certificate and Social Security application are displayed online.
e-mail: not available

Harry Greb

www.harrygreb.com
The author has brought together a welter of rare information, film footage, articles, books, comics and images from a variety of private sources and produced a truly excellent example of a boxing fan site. Dedicated mainly to the 1923 World Champion Harry Grebb it also serves other Old Timers who ended their careers before 1960. And what is so very good is that it comes online for free.
e-mail: harrygreb@harrygreb.com

HBO Boxing

www.hbo.com/boxing/
This Home Box Office site previews fights and announces schedules and results world wide. Scoring big fights online round by round and playing the judge is only one of the interactive activities available. You can ask questions of a panel of experts, sound off using the hectic Bulletin Board and chat yourself dry in the room set aside for that purpose.
e-mail: not available

Heavyweights.co.uk

www.heavyweights.co.uk
Web magazine all about heavyweights, presented in four sections – British,

German, European and American.
Articles and features include news,
fight results, ratings and a photo
gallery.
e-mail: editor@heavyweights.co.uk

Houseofboxing.com

www.houseofboxing.com
Michael Katz writes a daily column for
this online publication which has heaps
of prize quality boxing journalism and
video clips of interviews for which you
need RealPlayer. You get an opportunity
to sign up for their own free web-based
e-mail and a bi-weekly newsletter. Text
is in English, French, Spanish and
German.
e-mail: MikeKatz@wwes.net

Hurricane

www.the-hurricane.com
Web site of the film Hurricane, which
was based on the life of boxer Rubin
Carter starring Denzil Washington. You
get a behind the scenes glimpse of the
movie in the making. A sample of each
song in the film soundtrack is available
for download. Read how Carter's story
inspired the filmmakers and actors and
download his speech to the United
Nations if you wish. You require
RealPlayer to enjoy the audio-video
sequences.
e-mail: not available

Hurricane Watch

hurricanepetermcneeley.com
Peter McNeeley, the Boston
Heavyweight, tells his life story in
words, pictures and fight statistics.
e-mail: peter@hurricanepeter
mcneeley.com

IBHOF.com

www.ibhof.com/ibhfhome.htm
Fighters from the early pioneers of the
sport to the present have their stories
told online, some with sound clips and
photographs. You can buy autographed
gloves and trunks by mail order.
e-mail: publisher@ibhof.com

Irish Boxing News

**home.talkcity.com/libertyst/
boxinginireland**
The focus is on Irish boxing. You will
find career records of all currently
active Irish born boxers; you can test
your knowledge in the Quiz Section or
leave a comment in the Guest Book.
Use the club directory to find the
address and telephone number of your
local boxing club.
e-mail: gerry.callan@the-start.ie

Joe Louis Official Web Site

**www.cmgww.com/sports/louis/
louis.html**
Official web site of the Brown Bomber,
idol of the forties. If you remember the
era you will recognise the photographs;
if you don't then you will see the
gentleman who was also the World
Heavyweight Champion. The story of
his life recounts in summary his career
as a boxer and quotes from the man
himself.
e-mail: sportsinfo@cmgww.com

Joyce Carol Oates: On Mike Tyson

**www.usfca.edu/fac-staff/
southerr/ontyson.html**
Talented and award winning author
Joyce Carol Oates turns her pen to
writing a series of high quality articles
on the key points of Mike Tyson's life.

Five lengthy and detailed pieces cover Iron Mike's troubled career from the early days of 1986 to date.
e-mail: randy@davidbowie.com

Lennox Lewis

www.lennox-lewis.com
Everything you ever wanted to know about Lennox Lewis is here on this well-designed site. The biography abounds with photographs and the online shop will sell you any of its merchandise if you order by e-mail. You can read the fan mail and join the Fan Club using the online form. Some sections of the site require a Flash plugin.
e-mail: mailbox@mediamac. demon.co.uk

Mike Tyson Ate My Balls

www.geocities.com/SoHo/Lofts/6436/
Stumpy Joe's original page dedicated to the famous Tyson ear-chewing incident during his fight with Evander Holyfield. It takes a humorous photo comic-strip approach to the story that will surely go down into the archives and has spawned several copycat web sites.
e-mail: not available

Mohammad Ali

www.geocities.com/Colosseum/Park/ 5703/
Nice little site dedicated to Mohammad Ali with twenty high quality thumbnail images of the champ in action in the ring. You get in addition his fight record and links to other Ali related web sites on the Internet.
e-mail: erikinsf@ix.netcom.com

Mohammad Ali: Definition Of a Champ

www.definitionofchamp.com
Unofficial and tasteful fan site of Donald L. Crawford Jr. dedicated, in his opinion, to the greatest boxer of all time. A detailed biography is supported by more than fifty photographs and a forum for visitors to discuss, or idolise, the great man. You can write your views about the man and opinions of the site in the Guest Book and Message Board pages.
e-mail: webmaster@thegreatest.cjb.net

Mr. Boxing

users.pandora.be/mrboxing/
Daniel Van de Wiele's Belgian web site. Although he hands out a fair amount of world boxing news and information, his main purpose is to give serious coverage to the European boxing scene. The guest book invites you to leave your comments about his regularly updated site.
e-mail: mrboxing@pandora.be

Oscar De La Hoya

www.oscardelahoya.com
A very cool site for the boxer Oscar de la Hoya includes video clips, merchandise, photos and a chat room with extensive usage of Shockwave Flash and sound. Video clips require RealPlayer or Windows Media Player.
e-mail: not available

Otis G. Grant

otisgrant.com
Grant, the former world middleweight boxing champion, takes his web site seriously enough to write up forthcoming major boxing bouts himself then

analyse them after the event.
He merchandises his goods online
and aside from the usual information,
features an Ask Otis page that
apparently produces a personal
response from the man himself.
e-mail: via online form

Pat's Boxing Page

www.boxingweb.com
Pat Mulcahy is a big boxing fan both as
observer and participant and he wants
you to enjoy it too. He gushes with
tips and tricks on how to get started in
the sport like an illustrated guide on
How To Wrap Your Hands. You can
interact with the site by viewing and
signing the Guest Book and contact the
author by ICQ or the e-mail form. Pat
does not address only youngsters
either; he has information on boxing
for older people as well. Easy on the
eye the site makes a good impression.
e-mail: pat@boxingweb.com

Prince Naseem Hamed

www.princenaseem.com
This is the Prince's official homepage.
It's all been worked out for you –buy

Naz clothes, posters and badges online
from the Naz Merchandise page where
you can also join the official Fan Club.
Analyses of his fights and a gallery of
photographs show him in action. Post
your views on the busy Prince Naseem
Discussion Forum or leave a message
in the Guest Book.
e-mail: via online form

Prince Naseem Hamed USA Invasion

**www.insidetheweb.com/
messageboard/mbs.cgi/mb105121**
A Message Board for the Prince.
e-mail: not available

Ringside.com

www.ringside.com
They sell boxing equipment off an
online catalogue. You can purchase
gloves, jump ropes, punch bags and
the like. For good measure they have
added a selection of very readable
articles and entertaining features.
e-mail: mailto:boxing@ringside.com

Rocky Marciano

www.rockymarciano.com
Former World Heavyweight Champion

Rocky Marciano has a web site. The gallery page contains a moving slideshow of black and white images from his fighting career. A biography of this boxing legend makes good reading and includes his complete fight record.
e-mail: not available

Scott Husband Boxing and Sportsmen Prints

scotthusband.freeservers.com
UK artist Scott Husband invites you to preview and purchase prints of his original drawings of sports personalities among whom you will find Ali, Tyson, McGuigan, Naz, Rocky Marciano and a whole portrait gallery of others.
e-mail: scottghusband@ tinyonline.co.uk

Sky Sports Boxing

www.sky.com/sports/boxing/
Part of Sky TV Sports coverage with up-to-the-minute boxing headlines from around the world and several in-depth features. Try to catch the live chat events with sports stars including boxers or read the transcripts online after the event. There is always a full listing of forthcoming boxing stories appearing on Sky TV.
e-mail: ringside@skysports.co.uk

Smokin' Joe Frazier

www.joefraziersgym.com/html/ index.html
Official site of Joe Frazier, the former World Heavyweight Champion. His ring record comes with a biography and photographs.
e-mail: not available

Sporting Life

www.sporting-life.com/boxing/news/
Sporting Life is a UK weekly sports newspaper. This site is its online version. The boxing section of the site has the latest news about the fight game.
e-mail: feedback@sportinglife.com

Sports Autographs and Memorabilia

dspace.dial.pipex.com/town/terrace/ od12/sports.htm
This site sells sports memorabilia, autographs and photographs of athletes from various sports including boxing, tennis, football, and cricket. Based in Yorkshire, the site is regularly updated but payment cannot be made online; you have to pay in the traditional way. There is a money back guarantee on all items.
e-mail: od12@dial.pipex.com

Sportslive

www.sportlive.net
UK site maintained by the sports section of the Express newspaper, which reports on a multitude of sports events including boxing. A search on the site for boxing brings up over 2,000 findings. Flash 4 is required if you want to play the Mohammad Ali Sportslive Slider game where your task is to make the photograph of Ali display correctly.
e-mail: via online form

Square Deal Boxing

www.squaredealboxing.com/index.html
Boxing memorabilia for collectors including autographs, boxing gloves and T-shirts. All purchasing procedures

are explained on this UK site. 10% of all proceeds go to a deserving childrens' charity.
e-mail: not available

The Boxing Wise Website

members.tripod.com/~fivedogs/
No frills web site with first rate content and truckloads of opinions, a message board that never lows down and the most complete list of fights anywhere on the Net, they say. All great stuff packed with punchy information.
e-mail: fivedogss@msn.com

The Cyber Boxing Zone

cyberboxingzone.com/boxing/ pastchp.htm
Online boxing magazine that covers current news and information and keeps boxing records. Every boxing champion from 1885 to the present day is listed on the site with apparently none missed out. The Cyber Boxing Journal, written by experts and fans alike, is published monthly online on this site. In addition to the bare-knuckle champs of the Queensbury era, forthcoming scheduled fights are also included.
e-mail: research@cyberboxingzone.com

The Ferocious Fernando Vargas Web Site

www.fernandovargas.com
Get the low-down on Fernando Vargas, his fight statistics, biographical information and a large selection of photographs on this official site. Interact with the site by e-mailing Fernando direct or sign the guest book. Online merchandise is coming soon.
e-mail: Ferocious@FernandoVargas.com

The Fight Page from Total Action

www.totalaction.com/fightpage/ fightpage.htm
Boxing news from sites all over the Internet is gathered here in one place with links archived for at least six months. Altogether this is an ideal place to catch up on what you missed. World boxing ratings for all weights are listed.
e-mail: fightpage@totalaction.com

The Guvnor Lenny Mclean

www.geocities.com/Pipeline/Slope/7003/
Lenny Mclean was a British bare-knuckle fighter who went on to star in the British gangster film Lock, Stock and Two Smoking Barrels. The site has many articles and newspaper clippings about the Guvnor and photographs of him in action. A video of Lenny in the ring is available for download and requires WinZip to unzip and RealPlayer to play it.
e-mail: mailto:athomas43@hotmail.com

The People's Boxing Organization

www.peoplesboxing.org
Official web site of the People's Boxing Organisation Founded in 1999. The PBO certifies bouts for its own boxing titles and claims to be the only professional boxing sanctioning body operated and controlled by the fans.
e-mail: not available

The Shrine To Naseem Hamed

home.clara.net/wildlife/naz/
Matt Winchester's fan site has a news section, fight reports, statistics on the Prince's height and weight and a fight by fight career record. The Guest Book is open for both friendly and unfriendly messages. The site requires some

updating it seems.
e-mail: winchester@imtoosexy.com

The Smoking Gun: Archive

www.thesmokinggun.com/archive/
tysonpsychev1.shtml

This site has the ten-page psychiatric
report on Mike Tyson prepared by the
Nevada Athletic Commission. Tyson
tried, unsuccessfully, to prevent this
report being published. The Commission
concluded that Tyson was fit to return
to the ring and you can read all about it.
e-mail: editor@thesmokinggun.com

The World Boxing Association

www.wbaonline.com

With text in English and Spanish a
good deal of content lies buried in this
site and needs more than a few links to
get to it. This is the official site of the
WBA and you can read press releases,
interviews, ranking, fight results and
a lot else. Contact details for the
executive committee, including e-mail
addresses, come to light without too
much trouble.
e-mail: wbaven@telcel.net.ve

Title Boxing - Boxing Equipment

www.titleboxing.com

All your boxing equipment needs, from
boots to headgear, available for purchase
at this online store. Alternatively ask
for a printed catalogue and have your
orders delivered to your door.
e-mail: info@titleboxing.com

TKO Boxing

www.geocities.com/Colosseum/Field/
3523/index.html

Boxing simulation game played by
e-mail. Sign up for the newsletter and

create up to three fighters to do battle
on your behalf. Best of all it's
completely free.
e-mail: wesley@casscomm.com

WBC Home

www.wbcboxing.com

The World Boxing Council officially
on the Internet. The history of the
Council, its rules and constitution are
highlighted together with a Hall of
Fame. You can take advantage of their
regular newsletter.
e-mail: wbc@wbcboxing.com

Women's Boxing

www.womenboxing.com

Whether you do or don't think women
have a place in the ring, this site gives
you all the news and views. You can
start with the history of women's boxing
then go on to read the fight schedules,
results and rankings or any which way
you wish. There are photographs and
special features like Women Cops Who
Box and Mixed Matches between male
and female fighters. A Guest Book and
free newsletter come online.
e-mail: fox@womenboxing.com

Women's Boxing on the Web

www.femboxer.com

Dedicated to both amateur and professional women's boxing this site has articles, profiles and fight reports. Audio interviews can be streamed from here in RealAudio format. You can leave a message in the Guest Book.

e-mail: not available

Women's Boxing Page

www.geocities.com/Colosseum/Field/6251/

Promises serious coverage of women's amateur and professional boxing and it delivers what it says. Features include biographies, scheduled fights, match results and a heavily posted forum. A great and extensive gallery of photographs finishes off a very good site.

e-mail: ringrrrlz@geocities.com

Women's Boxing – UK

www.ladyboxer.co.uk

This is the home of women's boxing in the UK. You get biographies, forthcoming fights, match results and a list of gyms that welcome and train women boxers. You are encouraged to have your say via e-mail and don't pull your punches if you think women don't look their best in the ring.

e-mail: fempunch@ladyboxer.co.uk

World Boxing Organisation

www.wbo-int.com

If you want to know about the WBO, one of the governing bodies of boxing, get with this site. Documents online include the constitution, regulations and bye-laws. Forthcoming bouts take the edge off the officialese.

e-mail: via online form

World Heavyweight Scene

www.geocities.com/Colosseum/Bleachers/5737/index.html

The focus of this fan site is the big men of boxing and Oliver Fennell. They have been gathered together in a wealth of material and profiles of the top fighters. The End of the Decade Awards look back at heavyweight boxing in the 1990s and hand out laurels in categories such as Upset of the Decade and KO of the Decade. You can take your seat at ringside and make your own decisions.

e-mail: heavyscene@hotmail.com

World of Boxing News & Software

www.boxing.clara.net/index.htm

Aside from two years worth of news archives easily accessed on this well-designed site, there are write-ups on boxing related computer games. You can download demos and, by filling out the online form, opt to receive all the latest boxing news via e-mail.

e-mail: via online form

www.world-boxing.com

www.world-boxing.com/shtml/index.shtml

World Boxing is produced in association with UK boxing promoter Frank Warren. You get the news, results and press releases. Columnists include Warren himself and former champ Barry McGuigan. There are some wonderful video clips where you see the likes of Mike Tyson, Joe Calzhage and Julius Francis being interviewed and in the ring. For this you must have a QuickTime 4 player.

e-mail: via online form

Cricket

Amul World Cricket Rankings

cricket.amul.com
It does what it says on the label.
e-mail: listserv@amul.com

Ananova.com

www.ananova.com/sport/cricket
The Press Association cricket news and
results - a quick way to check the latest
sports news.
e-mail: inquiries@ananova.com

AskMe.com

**www.askme.com/SearchResults.asp?id
=35307333&query=cricket –**
Free cricket advice.
e-mail: feedback@AskMe.com

Ceat World Cup Ratings

www.ceatcricketrating.com
The first live source of cricket rating
world wide.
e-mail: rbhalu@yahoo.com

Cricinfo

www-uk.cricket.org
A major cricketing site. It is the most
comprehensive and informative
resource of cricket on the Internet.
Use the Global Navigation scrollbar to
access the official sites of all full ICC
member countries. From here you can
also access the International Cricket
Council and European Cricket Council
pages. CricInfo Extras's links take you
to the Random Database Picks:
Pictures, Statistics, Ratings,
Scorecards, Player Profiles and What
happened Today in Cricket History.
Live coverage of both domestic and
international matches can be found for
each country on the left hand menu
bar. CricInfo also features in-depth
analyses and articles from the Cricketer
International magazine. In the CricInfo
Interactive section, you can check the
coaching tips, audio, video and more in
the Carnival of Cricket. Cricket chat,
polls, online cricket games and
classified advertisements can be found
in this section as well. There are also
random writings and original
outburst on the cricket game.
e-mail: help@cricket.org

Crick Nasha

www.crick.nasha.com
One of the largest single-sport databases on the Web. Scores and other information on all international cricket, interactive events, player profiles, first-class cricket and stacks more.
e-mail: shashank_nigam@hotmail.com

CrickBase.8m.com

emitra.hypermart.net
Database of all matches, a score card, news and then lots more.
e-mail: vdabke@hotpop.com

Cricket Base

www.cricketbase.com/cgi-bin/ webdriver?MIval=home
Probably the most comprehensive and up-to-date source of international cricket statistics on the Internet.
e-mail: desk@cricketbase.com

Cricket Crazy

www.cricketcrazy.co.uk
Player profiles, scoreboards, events 2000, women's cricket and more
e-mail: via online form

Cricket - Hey Guys I'm Nishant

members.tripod.com/Nishant8/ cricket.htm
Links to clubs around the world
e-mail: coolguy_98_99@hotmail.com

Cricket World

www.cricketworld.com
International cricket
e-mail: via online form

Cricketfever.com

www.cricketfever.com/main.htm
Records, billeting boards, archives, chat room, history and player profiles. A funky site but slow loading. Only webmaster's e-mail available.
e-mail: not available

Cricketline.com

www.cricketline.com
World's ultimate cricket resource.
e-mail: via online form

CricketLover.com

www.cricketlover.com
Sports database on the Internet for scores and other information on

international cricket matches, player profiles, first-class cricket, cricket rating and much more. There is an online store.
e-mail: webmaster@cricketlover.com

CricketUnlimited

www.cricketunlimited.co.uk/Articles/ 0,5217,78434,00.html
Articles on cricket and links to international teams. E-mail not available, but you can login and chat.
e-mail: not available

CricketView

www.cricketview.com
Views from cricket fans.
e-mail: info@cricketview.com

Cricketzone.com

www.cricketzone.com
e-mail: not available

Cricmania

www.cricmania.com
Player statistics, cricket database, rating and scorecards
e-mail: not available

Cricmaniac

www.cricmaniac.com
Official e-mail for cricket fans. You can sign-up for a free you@cricmaniac.com address.
e-mail: via online form

CyberCricket

www.cybercricket.com
Cricket calendar, facts and figures, team and player profiles, chat, news and more.
e-mail: mail@magiccricket.com

Danish Cricket Association

www.cricket.dk
e-mail: mailto: dcf@cricket.dk

dreamcricket.com

www.dreamcricket.com
Online fantasy game site. Fans all over the world can create their own dream teams by choosing players from any teams.
e-mail: feedback@dreamcricket.com

Ecricketer.com

www.ecricketer.com
Very good site with many links, well constructed and easy to navigate. This Week in Cricket, Spotlight this week, Today in History, Ecricketer Dream Team make good reading. Teams, grounds, players, polls, events calendar and more.
e-mail: live@ecricketer.com

English Cricket Web Site

englishcricket.8m.com
Latest scores and facts from the English team.
e-mail: Williscool.donbavand@ learnfree.co.uk

European Cricket Council

www-ind.cricket.org/link_to_database/ NATIONAL/ICC/ECC/
Here you will find details of forthcoming tournaments, a media gallery, development programs, news, reports and coaching links.
e-mail: help@cricinfo.com

Federazione Cricket Italiana

www.crickitalia.org
e-mail: mailto:info@crickitalia.org

France Cricket

www.ffbsc.org
e-mail: via online form

Goldwire Cricket.com

www.goldwirecricket.com
All the news about cricket.
e-mail: via online form

Green'un Evening Post – Sport

www.epost.co.uk/standards/
cricketindex.html
Links to UK cricket sites and
scorecards.
e-mail: mail@epost.co.uk

Icricketer.com

www.icricketer.com
Cricket news.
e-mail: not available

Imran's Cricket Guidance

www.cricketer.homepad.com
A little history then a discussion about
developing skills in all cricket
disciplines -batting, bowling, fielding,
wicket-keeping with tips, chat and an
online book store.
e-mail: not available

International Cricket Council

www-ind.cricket.org/link_to_database/
NATIONAL/ICC/
The site is hosted by Cricinfo, home of
cricket on the Internet. The main part
deals with the ICC Annual conference
2000, carries a statement from Saber
H Chowdhury MP, President of the
Bangladesh Cricket Board and the
Development program of the ICC. The
site goes on to define the Rules and
Regulations of International Cricket,
lists all ICC members, international

umpires and referees. There is a link to
the World Cup site. The ICC does not
have the resources at the moment to
respond to email queries, but you can
e-mail CricInfo at : help@cricinfo.com.
e-mail: help@cricinfo.com

Irish Cricket Union

www.theicu.org
e-mail: info@ulsterweb.com

Khel.Com - World Cricket

www.khel.com/cricket/WI/index.html
Aside from a vast number of links,
you get all the usual coverage of players,
statistics, records of team performance,
batting, bowling and fielding. Test
matches and one-day Internationals get
good write-ups.
e-mail: feedback@khel.com.

Lardy's Club Cricket Links Page

www.geocities.com/Colosseum/
Bleachers/1492/uklinks.html
155 Links to second rank UK Clubs.
e-mail: not available

Lord's

www.lords.org
The original Lord's cricket web site has
been recently replaced. It is the official
online voice of the England and Wales
Cricket Board. The site is easy to
navigate and carries the main menu on
the home page. Each section connects
with a group of topics. You get
up-to-date news, live scores for home
and international matches and an index
of all tours. The home page also has
links to all county cricket clubs as well
as a club directory that gives you contact
details and a list of web sites hosted by
CricInfo. It's all here - Associations

and Societies, first-class Counties, minor Counties, Leagues and Clubs. County links give brief notes on each club and a hypertext link to that club's official web site. The 2000 Season has its own links to fixtures, team progress, statistics, history, tables, rain rules, an events diary and more. The Fan Centre has live chat and a message board, ticket status and facilities to mail the team. Other links lead to the Scorebook, Archives, Player Profiles and Grounds.
e-mail: info@lords.org

Magic Cricket

www.cybercricket.com
Chat, archives, picture gallery and a cricket calendar.
e-mail: etcmail@magiccricket.com

PriceWaterhouseCoopers

www.pwcglobal.com/uk/eng/ins-sol/spec-int/cricket/index.html
Ratings of international cricketers. You will find the latest One Day Ratings and Test Ratings together with details of how Ratings are calculated and the difference between the two types of Rating.
e-mail: contact.uk@pwcglobal.com

Queens Park Cricket Club

www.qpcc.com
A good and informative web site with international cricket news, details of forthcoming events and several wonderful links. Supporters and site visitors will find lots to read about the club, its history and cricket records. Use the chat room to unburden yourself. The home page tells you about membership, services and facilities and there is a link to CricInfo.
e-mail: admin@qpcc.com

Sportinglife – Cricket

www.sporting-life.com/cricket/news/index.html
Cricket News.
e-mail: enquiries@sportinglife.com

Test Cricket Ratings Service

www.geocities.com/Colosseum/Stands/8832/index.html
e-mail: test_cricket_ratings_service@yahoo.com

The Cricket Collection

www.cricketcollection.bigstep.com
Shopping site with lots of cricket-related products.
e-mail: duncanmac56@hotmail.com

The Fixture List

www.thefixturelist.org.uk/cricketlinks-clubs.html
This is the definitive listing of UK Cricket Clubs, showing English Clubs by county; Scottish, Welsh and Irish Clubs by country.
e-mail: thefixturelist@spinneret.net

ThePavilion.com.au

www.thepavilion.com.au
Cricket's mega site.
e-mail: bdiamond@theage.fairfax.com.au

This is Cricket

www.thisiscricket.com
Unique and enjoyable web site on cricket. Statistics, ranking, live scores, online polls, schedules, history, quizzes, jokes, chat, picture galleries, quotations, interviews, autographs, contests, coaching, tournaments and the latest news will keep you busy for a while.
e-mail: via online form

Trenowden's Cricketana

www.cricketana.demon.co.uk
Cricket memorabilia and autographs online
e-mail: trendy1@cricketana.demon.co.uk

UK Local Cricket Forum

website.lineone.net/~alan.rowley/cricket.html
UK local cricket forum, a message board for results and information on all non-county level cricket.
e-mail: karone@bigfoot.com

Welcome to Cricket Fan Email

cricketfan.zzn.com/e-mail/login/login.asp
Free e-mail addresses for cricket fans all around the world.
e-mail: webmaster@cricketfan.zzn.com

Welcome to Cricketfan Mail

cricketfan.zzn.com/email/login/login.asp
Get yourself a free e-mail address.
e-mail: webmaster@cricketfan.zzn.com

Wisden

www.wisden.com
They record scores and statistics and provide authoritative comment on all aspects of cricket.
e-mail: asksteven@guardian.co.uk/beamer@guardian.co.uk

AUSTRALIA

Australian cricket is mainly State or City centred. The sites reviewed represent major clubs and legendary cricketers.

Adam Craig Gilchrist

www.angelfire.com/mi/Gilly/index.html
e-mail: not available

Allan Border

www.q-net.net.au/~gihan/border/
e-mail: gihan@pobox.com

An Unofficial Tasmanian Tigers Homepage

www.ra.phys.utas.edu.au/~dr_legge/tastiger/tastiger.html
e-mail: dr_legge@postoffice.utas.edu.au

Anjohn Barua's Cricket Page

www.geocities.com/CollegePark/Center/7725/AnjCricket/index.htm
The page is all about Shane Warne, showing all the latest pictures in the Gallery and analysing and viewing stats.
e-mail: cj147@city.ac.uk

Applecross Cricket Club Webpage

members.iinet.net.au/~vinka/main.html
They believe they may be the first sub-urban Cricket club with a homepage.
e-mail: not available

Aussies Cricket Heroes - A place to worship Aussie Cricket Heroes

clubs.yahoo.com/clubs/aussiescricketheroes
Online chat site for Australian cricket fans.
e-mail: not available

Australian Cricket Board

www.aus.cricket.org/link_to_database/NATIONAL/AUS/
As a more or less mother site the Cricket Board pages leave little uncovered. They keep you abreast of current matches, international and domestic series and of course, views and news. A large section deals with the rules of cricket while the Stats Guru search engine on the home page and

the vast database combine to give researchers every imaginable fact and figure on the subject. What's On lists all current or scheduled matches while the Hall of Fame and the Players links are a goldmine for supporters. The shop is loaded with memorabilia of the immortal Australian legends - Bradman, Border, Waugh, Taylor, Trumper and Walters as well as gifts, videos, books, games and top quality equipment. Alternatively, visit eBay, the world's leading and largest person-to-person online trading community, for your entire cricket needs, or if you wish, sell sporting items you no longer want. Then you get highlights from the latest matches, sights and sounds, fun, games and feedback. Several links take you to masses of information about the Board.
e-mail: acb@cricinfo.com

Australian Cricket Page

www.ozsports.com.au/cricket
This page is mostly about Australian and New Zealand cricket, a bit of general cricket stuff and links to other places.
e-mail: cricket@ozsports.com.au

Bee's Mark Vaugh page

www.geocities.com/Colosseum/Ring/7978
e-mail: belbee@oze-mail.com.au

Bradman Pages

www.cricket.org/link_to_database/PLAYERS/AUS/B/BRADMAN_DG_020 00492/ARTICLES/
Personal contribution by Dave Liverman about Don Bradman
e-mail: not available

Bradman's page

www.bradman.sa.com.au
e-mail: not available

Brett Lee

www.geocities.com/Colosseum/Turf/2704/
e-mail: kbleeze@hotmail.com

Con's cricket page

con.clan.tf/cricket/
Details of the current Australian cricket season.
e-mail: con@pobox.com.NOSPAM

Eastern Suburbs Cricket Association

home.vicnet.net.au/~esca/
e-mail: easterncricket@primus.com.au

Esther's Ponting Shrine

www.angelfire.com/ms/ponting/
Esther's Ricky Ponting site.
e-mail: beeblebrox14@hotmail.com

Guide to Bradman's collection

dino.slsa.sa.gov.au/library/collres/bradman/guide.htm
e-mail: research@slsa.sa.gov.au

Heidelberg Cricket Associationof Melbourne

home.vicnet.net.au/~hdca/
e-mail: not available

Howazzat!

members.tripod.com/~cricket9/
All in one cricket web site with downloads (games, wallpapers, screensavers etc.), quizzes, player of the month, links, trivia, coaching tips, current events
e-mail: ranjit@antisocial.com

JL: Legend

www.angelfire.com/mt/JustinLanger/index.html
A site dedicated to Justin Langer
e-mail: maize@mpx.com.au

Melbourne Cricket Club

www.mcc.org.au
This skilfully designed site blends pictures from club history and its emblem with the text. Links from the home page take you to the scoreboard, a news section, the museum of Melbourne cricket and a library of cricket books. The site also has links to other sports, like soccer and golf. Membership details come within a large hypertext link that tells you what

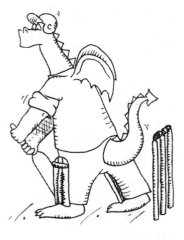

they offer - dining rooms, bars, squash courts, a library and of course membership categories, waiting lists, lady's cards and so on.. On match days you are told where and when to enter the grounds, ticket status and seat reservation. The ticketing page is a masterpiece of linkages that tell you everything and leave you in doubt about nothing.
e-mail: membership@mcc.org.au

Melbourne University Cricket Club

ariel.unimelb.edu.au/~cricketm/main.htm
e-mail: cricketm@ariel.its.unimelb.edu.au

Michael Scott Kasparowics

www.angelfire.com/biz4/kasper/kasper.html
A site about Michael Scott Kasparowicz.
e-mail: not available

Monash University Cricket Club

www-personal.monash.edu.au/~mspencer/cricket/
e-mail: marcus.spencer@adm.monash.edu.au

Moreland & Moonee Valley Cricket Association

avoca.vicnet.net.au/~mmvca/
e-mail: mmvca@vicnet.net.au

My Aussie Cricket Page

www.homestead.com/ej8/ponting.html
Pictures and a profile of Ricky Ponting, pics of other players and links.
e-mail: crazy_chicken@chickmail.com

New South Wales Blues

www-aus2.cricket.org/link_to_database/NATIONAL/AUS/FC_TEAMS/NSW
Interactive web site with a lot of Cricket Chat, presented in conjunction with Cricinfo. You get live ball-by-ball commentary on international and domestic cricket, take part in interviews with players and cricket celebrities or simply talk to other CricInfo visitors. You can listen to commentaries but if you wish to chat follow the online instructions. On the other hand you can leave messages on the Forum. Statistics are given in depth in alphabetical order and every which way. Player profiles and snapshots, living legends, forthcoming tournaments, club history and weather forecasts are all in place. Merchandise from the shop can be purchased by mail order or the online order form.
e-mail: nswca@cricket.org

Nick's Aussie Cricket Page

www.oze-mail.com.au/~nickbr
All the latest news on Aussie Cricket, discussion on a topical issue in Australian Cricket, the averages of all current Aussie players.
e-mail: cricketman@geocities.com

North Melbourne Cricket Club

www.geocities.com/Colosseum/Stadium/7576/index.html
e-mail: panda@hotkey.net.au

North West Cricket Association

home.vicnet.net.au/~nwca/
e-mail: not available

Queensland Bulls

www.qldcricket.com.au
Good interactive site with an entry page that carries the latest cricket headlines. Major links include sections on fixtures, supporters, coaching and development,

players, the administration, tickets and merchandise. The shop has a handsome range of Bull cricket equipment and a new collection of supporter polo shirts, t-shirts, caps and broad-brimmed cricket hats. Online ordering is not available and tickets must be purchased from their agents.
e-mail: qldc@qldcricket.com.au

Sale Maffra Cricket Association

www.locallink.com.au/vic/saleregion/
sport/cricket/smca.htm
e-mail: maffrasec@locallink.com.au

Sanasi's Steve Waugh page

www.geocities.com/Colosseum/
Midfield/9132
e-mail: sanasi@yahoo.com

South Australian Cricket Association

www.saca.com.au
Site under reconstruction
e-mail: not available

Southern Districts & Churches Cricket League

members.tripod.com/Horizon/southern
e-mail: billweeden@aol.com

Southern Reedback

www.redbacks.sa.com.au
The website is currently under recon-struction.
e-mail: not available

Steve Waugh's page

www.geocities.com/Colosseum/Turf/1694/
e-mail: scasman@hotmail.com

Suzy's Page

members.tripod.com/~sttis/index.html
Supporter of the Queensland Bulls.
e-mail: sttis@hotmail.com

Talk City

talkcity.com/calendar/events/
event2090.htmpl
Cricket chat.
e-mail: not available

Tasmania University Cricket Club

www.utas.edu.au/docs/sports_council/
cricket/index.html
e-mail: annac@postoffice.utas.edu.au

Tasmanian Cricket Association

www.utas.edu.au/docs/sports_council/
cricket/tca.html
Another unofficial site of Tasmanian cricket. The Tasmanian Cricket Association is the governing body of cricket in Tasmania. It administers both the State team and the southern Tasmanian club competition, in which eight clubs compete. This site is not official, but is maintained with the co-operation of the TCA. The TCA plans an official web site in the future.
e-mail: not available

Tasmanian Tigers

www.aus2.cricket.org/link_to_database/
NATIONAL/AUS/FC_TEAMS/TAS/
CricInfo hosts this web site which has very little information when compared with other State sites. The Pura Milk Cup and Mercantile Cup are discussed with statistics, points tables and summaries. Squad and Players links are in pretty good shape and give all their personal performance data. Archives cover all seasons from 1850 to the present.
e-mail: aus@cricket.org

The Aussie Cricket Fans Page !!!

members.xoom.com/ozziecricket/
welcome.htm
For fans of cricket in Australia and all
over the world. There's even a page to
bag the umpires!
e-mail: ozziecricket@xoommail.com

The Australasian Cricket Zone

www.cricket.simplenet.com
Everything you may want to know
about Australasian Cricket.
e-mail: not available

The University Cricket Club

www.ee.uwa.edu.au/~aips/uccold.html
A page with club history and match
results.
e-mail: not available

Tim's cricket page

tim.freeservers.com/cricket/index.html
e-mail: webmaster@tim.freeservers.com

Tim's Mark Vaugh page

tim.freeservers.com/cricket/
markwaugh/index.html
e-mail: webmaster@tim.freeservers.com

Traralgon District Cricket Association

www.netspace.net.au/~iceman/tdca/
tdca.html
e-mail: iceman@netspace.net.au

Ultimate Tubby

members.tripod.com/~tubbyhubby/
tubby.html
Dedicated to the former Australian
captain, and joint holder of Australia's
highest Test innings score.
e-mail: ultimate_tubby@yahoo.com

Victoria Bushrangers

www.bushrangers.com.au
Lots of graphics make this a most
attractive web site. From the home
page you get to meet the team, read
the news, learn about women's cricket,
coaching and development and VCA
Premier Cricket. The Get Involved
section invites juniors to sign on and
offers new opportunities to members
and budding umpires. All the usual
club news, match results, fixtures and
competitions are well laid out and the
shop will sell you cricket apparel,
equipment and memorabilia.
The home page has the order form.
You will need Adobe Acrobat Reader,
which can be downloaded online.
e-mail: info@bushrangers.com.au

Victoria Cricket Association

www.viccricket.asn.au
e-mail: not available

Victorian Blind Cricket Association

www.vbca.org.au
e-mail: scott.peucker@dsto.defence.
gov.au /jimp@rvib2.rvib.org.au

Waugh Brothers site

waughs.tripod.com
e-mail: shawcross@e-mail.com

Welcome Fans

members.tripod.com/waughrev/
index-2.html
Website for cricket lovers and Steve
Waugh worshippers from around the
world.
e-mail: find_me_35@hotmail.com

Welcome to my page on Adam Craig Gilchrist

www.angelfire.com/mi/Gilly/index.html
e-mail: not available

Welcome to the Steve Waugh Fan Club

www.geocities.com/Colosseum/ Midfield/3398/index3.html
e-mail: stevewaughclub@hotmail.com

Western Warriors

www.waca.com.au
Graphics, photographs and animated news headlines make this a great web site, but a little slow on the draw. The main menu bar on the left has major links to fixtures, a museum, club history, signage opportunities, sponsors, western fury, warriors merchandise and other cricket sites. Apart from the main menu, graphical icons signpost more links to match results, weekly warriors coach updates, membership, news and the next game in the season 2000-1. The membership page lists all the benefits of joining the club and if you are moved to do this, download the application form. You can interact by voting on whatever subject is current or choose your favourite Australian cricketer and check out his profile in the Team section. There is no e-mail facility so use the online contact forms. Club |history since 1835, corporate entertainment, membership details and a catalogue of goods for purchase and an auction are all online.
e-mail: not available

ENGLAND & WALES

A Salute to Women's Cricket

www.webbsoc.demon.co.uk
e-mail: don@webbsoc.demon.co.uk

Berkshire Cricket League

www.berkshirecricketleague.org.uk
e-mail: martin.bishop@bt.com

Derbyshire CCC

www.dccc.org.uk
Well-presented pages with the club crest on the entry page. You navigate the site using the main menu buttons - Club Shop, Corporate Area, Junior Area, Players' Area and Supporters' area. The last tells you about the Supporters' Club Committee, lists all members and has a feedback button for your comments. You can also find out about membership details and in particular the benefits it brings, one of which is a free Season Ticket. You can apply for membership online. Apart from news regarding forthcoming matches and sponsorship there are individual records for each member of the squad in the Player Records and Results section. The Junior Area gives all young supporters and members their very own page with regular features, competitions and the opportunity to write in with comments and suggestions. The Corporate area is more or less concerned with advertising, sponsorship and promoting the hospitality of the club.
e-mail: post@dccc.org.uk

Durham CCC

www.durham-ccc.org.uk
The presentation of this home page is admirable. There is a battery of subject

links which help you find your way around the site - Players, Internationals, Fixtures, Membership, Hospitality, Conferences, What's New, Online Shop, Club Links and Club Location. The Players area has a feature - Team Talk. This is for you to send your name, address and e-mail information with or without your comments about matches or anything else you fancy. At the top of this page you will find a scroll bar with names of all team players. Select the one you want to talk to. The club is in the process of developing online shopping and soon you will be able to purchase goods on the site. Until this is available, you can use the club's real world shop. For more information and a brochure, click on the More Information button. The Executive hospitality boxes provide luxury and style, overlooking the cricket ground where you can have your own private seating area and entertain guests. Details of what you pay and what you get are spelled out with no unpleasant surprises.

Links: http://www-uk.cricket.org/
e-mail: marketing@durham-ccc.org.uk

England's Barmy Army

www.barmy-army.com
The England Team fan pages
e-mail: contact@barmy-army.com

Essex CCC

www.essexcricket.org.uk
The home page offers the possibility of enrolling for membership online, a brief summary of news and details of forthcoming events. The Results link takes you where you would expect, scores from matches played over the two last months. The Team page has all the low down on team players and individual hypertext links to the bowling coach, cricket consultant, capped and uncapped staff. The Club was formed in 1876, which is where the history pages start. The Membership link is fully detailed and best seen on site where costs and benefits are listed. To find out about the fully lined and carpeted marquees at all home grounds, visit the Hospitality section.

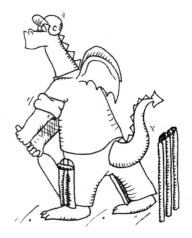

The online shop sells replica shirts, white and coloured, training wear and other Cricketing items.
e-mail: administration.essex@ecb.co.uk

Essex - Cricket - The Greatest Game in the World.....

pitch.phon.ucl.ac.uk/home/gordon/cricket.html
An Essex club supporter.
e-mail: not available

Essex - Unofficial Essex County Cricket Club Website

www.mstaines.freeserve.co.uk
e-mail: mickey@mstaines.freeserve.co.uk

Glamorgan CCC

www-uk.cricket.org/link_to_database/NATIONAL/ENG/FC_TEAMS/GLAM/
The official web site of Glamorgan C.C.C. was launched in conjunction with CricInfo in August 1996 and was the first of its type in the U.K. The site is very well laid out, interactive and easy to navigate. The main menu has ticket and general information, membership details, hospitality facilities,

wonderful training, practice and playing areas, facilities for indoor six-a-side cricket, video cameras and whatever else. Club records give the latest scores and statistics. The Players' section has an alphabetical directory of all players, their profiles, players in test cricket, players in one-day internationals and a lot of photographs in slide shows and a picture gallery. Other links from the home page lead to Historical Archives, Club Information and talk about the grounds. An interesting feature is the Chat Room. A number of Glamorgan supporters are connected to the Internet and have e-mail addresses. Some of these are listed. You can add your name to this directory and then share views and comments. The membership section spells it all out, listing the benefits associated with each class.
e-mail: glam@ecb.co.uk

Gloucestershire CCC

www.glosccc.co.uk
The home page has a simple design with a welcoming message. Then there are details of the 1999 Double

Champions, all the latest English Cricket scores with tables and statistics, a fair number of players' profiles, facilities at Gloucester and the Cheltenham and Gloucester Festival. The five major topics featured are News, Scores, Team, Shop, and Club. The Team section gives you individual hypertext links to all the players with photographs, brief biographies and thumbnail sketches of the men and their professional prowess. The scores link takes you to the Lords' home page, which in turn has links to other county cricket sites. The Club link holds the real database - membership, sponsorship, hospitality, conferencing and banqueting facilities and festivals. Members and the public are urged to become involved with club activities from simply watching the matches to using the sport as the venue for corporate goals and private functions. An online shop selling tickets, membership and merchandise is advertised but not yet available.
e-mail: info@glosccc.co.uk

Gloucestershire - Imraan Mohammed Fan Club

www.chodnet.co.uk
First class cricketer who plays for Gloucestershire.
e-mail: chris@chodnet.co.uk

Gloucestershire - the home page of the Jack Russell Gallery

www.jackrussell.co.uk
e-mail: crimson@crimsontide.co.uk

Hampshire CCC

www.hampshire.cricket.org
Hosted by CricInfo, this web site is very easy to navigate. One link, Club News

has the full report for the 1999 and 2000 seasons. Information about membership and sponsorship comes under Club Information. The same section has details of the new golf facility, booking arrangements, green fees and tuition rates. The Club Shop hypertext link offers books and Club ties, clothing items, Club shirts, sweatshirts and T-shirts, hats, prints and tea towels all appropriately emblazoned. Mail orders are welcome and most sizes are available. You can also order by e-mail. The range of information on the home page is wide, well structured and presented. Club statistics, scorecard archive and the club history are listed as main topics. Supporters will enjoy the Photo Album with images of the 2000 season, Captain's Gallery, Celebrations, Action Pictures, Team Photos and a whole lot else. There is a Players' link with an alphabetical directory of all players between1864 and 1999, current players' profiles, test players and one-day International players.
e-mail: enquiries.hants@ecb.co.uk

Highland CC

www/highlandcc.freeserve.co.uk/ Links.htm
Links to all the world's cricket clubs; century and half century cricket sites.
e-mail:
secretary@highlandcc.freeserve.co.uk

Kent CCC

www.kentcountycricket.co.uk
The home page has a very simple design and a few pictures, but information is plentiful and the site is easy to navigate. Several major links located at the top of the page lead you to news, fixtures,

players, marketing, club hospitality and facilities, an online shop, coaching, membership, records and other links. The Players area features profiles of current and past players with their photographs. The Membership section is divided for juniors, students, members and friends and life members each class enjoying benefits and privileges. The records link takes you into the history of the club and publishes the best performances in batting, bowling and all the other records a club would keep. Click appropriately on the menu on the left and you get details of corporate hospitality facilities - marquees, boxes, match hosts, picnic, the Harris room and more. You can download a hospitality booking form to make reservations; this requires Adobe Acrobat Reader which can be downloaded free online. The club shop sells tickets, membership, posters, gear, ties, clothing, books, hats, caps and souvenirs. Use the shopping cart and pay by credit card encrypted for security. If you buy from the online shop, check out their shop policy and use the size guide just to be sure.
e-mail: via online form

Kent - Sean's Cricket Page

www-star.qmw.ac.uk/~scg/cricket.html
Kent County Cricket supporter.
e-mail: S.C.Greaves@qmw.ac.uk

Lancashire CCC

www.lccc.co.uk
The site is informative, easy to navigate and has animated cricket news headlines on the entry page. The main links cover the latest news, features, team, club, tickets, hospitality,

conferences and banqueting, Old Trafford lodge, membership and merchandise. The team section is very rich in club and general cricket information. It has profiles of all team players with their season scores in every match played in the two last years with links to each scorecard. The same section also contains statistics, all current tables, player averages and career figures, all Second XI matches, venues and start times. Links on the club page take you to honours, a history of Lancashire CCC, maps of Old Trafford, the museum, officers of the club and the indoor cricket centre. The rich history of Lancashire cricket is exhibited in the club museum at Old Trafford. The ticket section lays out the ground and seating plan, with admission prices to games for adults, juniors and families. There are several classes of membership and you can contact the club by telephone, fax, mail or e-mail. The whole site could do with a little livening up.
e-mail: sales.lancs@ecb.co.uk

Lancashire - The unofficial Andrew Flintoff website

fly.to/flintoff
e-mail: karen_stretch@hotmail.com

Leicestershire CCC

www.leicestershireccc.co.uk
The first page has the club logo with animated figures of cricketers. Clicking on this logo takes you to the colourful home page and their mascot - Charlie Fox. The main links on the left and right of the page are for news and reports, fixtures, membership, feedback and the home of the LCCC. To join,

complete the online application form. Membership comes in several classes, each with benefits, details of which are on the home page. As a member you may well bookmark this site. The aim is to provide all the latest news and information to keep you up-to-date with the club. The home of the LCCC section has a little about the club's history and its unusual museum. Statistics and records date back several years and star players get their stories featured. If you are unsure where the club is, the How to Find Us section has a five stage zoom-in map. Shortly the Grace Road shop will join the Internet enabling you to order club merchandise and souvenirs online.

e-mail: info@leicestershireccc.co.uk

Middlesex CCC

www.middlesexccc.co.uk
This is a truly grand site both in its layout and the sheer interest of content. The home page features two major topics - The Team and The Club. The Team link tells you about the 1st and 2nd teams, illuminates player profiles - click on the picture to learn more about each player. You get match reports, a merchandising section, forthcoming events and news. For membership information look under the Club section; you can subscribe annually or join for life, either way use the form online. This section also has team cricketer biographies including those of the legendary Mike Gatting, Bill Eldrich and Denis Compton. The Merchandising section has a lot on offer, shirts and caps, sweater and fleece tops and more all of which you can order by e-mail. If you are a member of the Club you get free membership of the Sports Academy which comprises a sports hall, cricket nets, 5 squash courts, a well-equipped fitness centre, aerobic classes and a whole lot else to cater to your body and soul. Outdoor and indoor sports are arranged for players of all ages and ability. An interesting feature is Team Talk. From the scroll bar at the top of the page, you can choose the player you wish to talk to, submit your name and address and wait.

e-mail: enquiries.middx@ecb.co.uk

Minor Counties Cricket Association

www.uk4.cricket.org/link_to_database/ARCHIVE/1999/ENG_LOCAL/MCCA/STATS/MINOR/
Not very attractive, but it has all you need to know about the minor counties and their contests. Check Championship results from most matches, as well as fixtures, scorecards, statistics and tables or read the latest news.

e-mail: help@cricinfo.com

Northamptonshire CCC

www.nccc.co.uk
The first page is very slow loading. The site has player records and results, NCCC links, contacts, junior members' area, Paul Taylor Benefit 2000, supporters and members, the cricket board, a corporate area and the shop. As you follow the links all is revealed. You can apply for membership online in the supporters and members section. Details and privileges for each class of membership are listed. The club shop is situated at the county ground, inside the brand new indoor cricket centre.

The range of merchandise leaves little to be desired as it caters to all ages and tastes. Click on the price list button to view the selection and order using the printable online form. The junior area offers all sorts of opportunities to young members with competitions and great prizes.
e-mail: post@nccc.co.uk

Nottinghamshire

www.nccc.co.uk/nccc.htm
In order to view this fascinating site to advantage your browser must be Java-enabled. The entry page has a news index, cricket pages, a link to the Trent Bridge Cricket Centre, Squash Club hypertext link, online shop and international match details. The shop offers the full range of cricket equipment, posters, memorabilia and the official garb to go. Their merchandising department has done a good job of displaying all products with prices and ordering online is by secure server. You can buy tickets and pay your membership fees online. Or you could choose to join their Squash Club which has six courts, a bar and offers free admission to NCCC matches and competitive discounts on other facilities, like the gymnasium and physiotherapy clinic. The Cricket Pages contain a link to international cricket, player profiles, match reports, scorecards, membership information, a juniors page, club sponsors, club history which dates back to 1841. And the ladies aren't forgotten as a few pages are devoted to their matches. They have a hospitality section and hire out rooms on non-match days with in-house conferencing and banqueting facilities.

The Junior's page hires ball boys and girls for matches at Trent Bridge throughout the season.
e-mail: administration.notts@ecb.co.uk

Nottinghamshire - Ste's cricket page

www.bignet.co.uk/clientwp/dazzler
e-mail: dazza_g@hotmail.com

OxfordshireOnline - Oxfordshire Cricket Board

www.oxfordshire.gov.uk/sh.idc-p=781146020a.htm
e-mail: community.groups@oxfordshire.gov.uk

Saracens Hertfordshire Cricket League

www.hertfordshire-league.org.uk
e-mail: admin@hertfordshire-league.org.uk

Somerset CC

www.lords.org
The main menu holds the links to the squad with player profile, stories, snapshots and statistical records. In fact most of the site deals with records of every type - results, team batting, partnership, bowling, all round, fielding, almost without end. Other links lead to fixtures, results, ground and averages.
e-mail: editor@lords.org

Staffs Cricket

www.staffscricket.co.uk/index2.htm
e-mail: ptravis@thisisstaffordshire.co.uk

Surrey CCC

www.surreyccc.co.uk
Very comprehensive and good quality

page with a broad range of information. Most of the home page is taken up with headlines of the cricket news of the day. Each headline is also a hypertext link that takes you to more on the subject. The left bar has animated welcoming messages and more links to forthcoming matches and league tables. The main menu at the top of the page covers sponsorship, the team, the club, conferencing, membership, contacts and the search engine. The site is expertly designed with pop-up menus for each main link. The membership link explains county, international and junior membership, boundary supporters and how to apply. The team page has player profiles and photographs, fixture lists, county championship and national league tables and match reports. The club section tells you about the club's history and honours, coaching facilities, the club shop, tickets and provides other cricket links. There is no online shopping available as yet but there is a catalogue you can browse. The search engine of this thoroughly good web site will help you find items fast.

e-mail: via online form

Sussex CCC

www.sccc.demon.co.uk

Clicking the club logo on the entry page takes you to the home page. The major links are floodlights, fixtures, hospitality, the club shop, juniors, the squad, membership and contacts. You can enjoy club hospitality by calling the commercial department or by e-mail and choose your menu online. Prices quoted include admission to the marquee or box hire, two or three sessions of play, reserved seating and so on, leaving little to ask for. Every link brings with it an abundance of privileges. Sussex young cricketers can enjoy coaching schemes and summer playing programmes, while their parents investigate affiliated schools and associations. The club shop sells shirts, sweatshirts, caps and ties. Click on the item and it is displayed with full details. They accept American Express,

Visa, MasterCard, Switch and Delta. You can give credit card details over the telephone, as their server doesn't yet support secure ordering. Meet the players on the squad page with their pictures and e-mail addresses although this is not a direct link to them.
e-mail: CorporateHospitality@sccc. demon.co.ukFran@sccc.demon.co.uk

The Internet Home of UK Cricket Clubs

ourworld.compuserve.com/ homepages/wth/linkclub.htm
UK Cricket Club Directory - worth a visit for contact details
e-mail: not available

UK Local Cricket Forum

website.lineone.net/~alan.rowley/ cricket.html
Quite a useful site with a message board to allow cricket fans to communicate with each other. Also has many links to UK clubs, leagues and general cricket information.
e-mail: karone@bigfoot.com

Warwickshire CCC

www.thebears.co.uk
The main menu bar at the top of the home page has links to Bearsnet, the shop, tickets, home, the club, its history, the team, news, matchday and webcall. The last is interactive to post and receive messages and the way to search for messages is explained on the site. Matchday has a two-month timetable of forthcoming matches. You can check the weather forecast and links to the latest scores of other county matches. The team link is all about the squad and has links to each individual player, with his profile and photograph, averages, tables, scorecards and reports. Use the club link for details of membership categories and benefits. You can shop for cricket wear at the online shop where their fashion, replica and souvenir ranges cover Warwickshire CCC, England and general cricket products. They also carry stocks for national teams – Pakistan, India, Australia, South Africa and the West Indies. The bookshop at Edgbaston

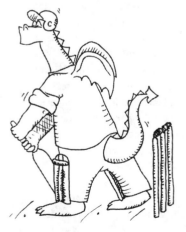

has a massive stock of books, audio and videotapes. The equipment shop is new but already has a great range in stock. You can order by e-mail using the online facility with specified credit cards or print off the order form and pay by cheque or postal order, or fax or phone.

e-mail: info@thebears.co.uk

Welcome to Lincolnshire County Cricket Club

www.btinternet.com/~lincs.cricket/
e-mail: Edward.Brindle@btinternet.com

Worcestershire CCC

www.wccc.co.uk
Click on the logo to enter the home page. This is an informative and easy to navigate site with links to areas, supporters in particular may find interesting. The Junior Black Pears Club offers those 16 or under the opportunity to enjoy watching their favourite players in action. The link to the club shop invites you to browse products like replica kits, leisure wear for adults and children, ties, bags, gifts and souvenirs. All goods are displayed with price tags. To order online use the shopping basket. You can also apply and pay for membership at the shop. Enter your e-mail address to receive their monthly newsletter, packed with the latest on the club, team and forthcoming events. They are creating an online archive documenting 100 years of the club. If you have any material you think could be included, e-mail them. The team link on the main menu bar has player profiles, team photographs, averages and tables. Club records and photo archives can be found in the club

link on the main menu. If you have any comments, suggestions or information simply fill in the feedback form as the club would like to know.

e-mail: mail@newroad1.co.uk

Yorkshire CCC

www.yorkshireccc.org.uk
Uninspiring home page with major links to the team, news, fixtures, membership, admissions, hospitality, match details, latest scores, sponsorship, cricket school, the online shop, credits and other links. The first page of the team link is dedicated to the captain but you can scroll down to select the team player you want. Every player has a picture. The cricket school section discusses courses and facilities, fees and so on. Membership comes in several classes including one for overseas residents. Other links tell you what their names suggest. In the White Rose shop, you can buy authentic Yorkshire County Cricket Club Leisurewear and collectibles by completing an order form and sending it off either by post or online. There are shirts, training tops and pants as worn by players, some smaller items ideal as gifts or souvenirs. Unfortunately the goods are not displayed.

e-mail: cricket@yorkshireccc.org.uk

Yorkshire - unofficial Michael Vaughan and Gavin Hamilton Homepage

www.fortunecity.co.uk/olympia/decathlon/23
e-mail: fosters@globalnet.co.uk

INDIA

123India.com Cricket

cricket.123india.com
Live coverage of all Indian cricket matches.
e-mail: via online form

ACE Sachin Tendulkar

members.tripod.com/~srinivasan_vr/sachintendulkar.html
Real Videos and lots of pictures of the master cricketer; see especially the six-hour long cricket match archives online for free.
e-mail: srinivasan_vr@hotmail.com

Appu Online

www.appuonline.com/websites/Sports_and_Games/Sports/Cricket/Players/index.htm
You would be hard put to find a more comprehensive list of sites for cricketers - batsmen, bowlers, fielders, all-rounders, spinners and everyone else who gets on the pitch.
e-mail: not available

Azharuddin

www.geocities.com/SiliconValley/5903/azhar.html
Pictures, records and enjoyable articles about Mohammed Azharuddin.
e-mail: pawar@giasdlo1.vsnl.net.in

Cricket Fever

www.geocities.com/Colosseum/Stadium/6820/index.html
Great Indian cricketers, past and present, with snapshots and statistics of personal performance. Then come news, surveys of the Indian cricket scene and a lot more to keep you interested.
e-mail: cricket@hotpop.com

Cricket Zone

members.tripod.com/~ADIB_M/
Exhaustive look at cricket with profiles of Indian players, photos, news, an over-the-shoulder look at World Cup 99.
e-mail: cricketzone@earthcorp.com

Cricketzone.com

india.cricketzone.com
Live coverage, cricopinion, cricchat, cricrecords, news, matches and players. Their e-mail newsletter brings you the latest in news, scores, stats and lots more.
e-mail: support@indiaexpress.com

Cyber Hunt Cricket page

members.tripod.com/~pramki/Cricket.htm
Great Cricket pages with all the facts and figures – batting, bowling, team rating and more.
e-mail: rammail@yahoo.com

Domestic Indian Cricket

www.khel.com/cricket/domestic/index.html
Scorecards and statistics from India's domestic cricket tournaments, including the Ranji, Duleep and Irani Trophies.
e-mail: feedback@khel.com

India Go

cricket.bol.net.in/go-india-go.html
It's all here - live coverage, recent matches, World Cup schedules, teams, previous World Cup tournaments and cricket records.
e-mail: not available

Indian Cricket Fan Mailing list

cricket.faithweb.com
Free mail shots for fans with login and chat facilities.
e-mail: not available

Indian Cricket Fans' Meeting Lounge

icfml.virtualave.net/links/pages
Fans can get themselves on the mailing list for regular updates.
e-mail: icfml@icfml.com

Indian Cricket Fever

www.geocities.com/Colosseum/
Stadium/6820/india.html
This vast resource on Indian cricket presents a huge picture gallery, up-to-date news, stats, forthcoming and past series, articles, stories and more.
e-mail: karan_mahajan@hotmail.com

Indian Cricket Mania

members.xoom.com/cricketmania/
Described as a page for fanatics by a fanatic, this site is a tribute to the Indian Cricket Team. Well written and informative, it has profiles of all Indian test cricketers, each of whom has a separate home page. The message board and the chat room invite you to interact. Check the latest cricket news, work your way through cricket rules if you don't already know them and take a backward glance at the last cricket World Cup. The Indian Cricket Mania fan club makes its debut online.
e-mail: via online form

Indian Cricket Paradise

www.geocities.com/Vienna/Strasse/7306/
A site that tells you all you want to

know about Indian cricketers. You get their profiles, snapshots and an interactive survey.
e-mail: madhav_n@india.com

Indian Cricket Zone

come.to/cricket
Good coverage of Indian cricket with lots of photographs, stats, match schedules, news and more.
e-mail: prashgupta@hotmail.com

Kapil Dev's Homepage

www.cstp.umkc.edu/personal/rganesh/
kapildev/kapildev.html
e-mail: not available

KHEL.COM

www.khel.com
Indian Cricket on the Internet. Player profiles, scorecards, questions and answers and live coverage of the Independence Cup.
e-mail: feedback@khel.com

Latest info on Indian Cricket

members.tripod.com/~RitwikK/
cricket.html
Updated after every match means you stay on the ball with the latest stats on teams and players.
e-mail: ritwikk@hotmail.com

Robin Singh

robinsingh.cjb.net
If you know this Indian cricketer you'll want to read about him.
e-mail: logmanish@yahoo.com

Robin Singh's First Exclusive Page on the Web

www.geocities.com/Colosseum/
Midfield/9483/robin.htm

Great pages with the story, stats and achievements of the cricketer from Tamilnadu.
e-mail: rammail@yahoo.com

Stumpman's Indian Cricket page

www.geocities.com/Colosseum/1314/index.html
A big fan of Indian cricket gives you all the low down on the subject.
e-mail: vatz@geocities.com

Sunil Mahohar Gavaskar

www.angelfire.com/tn/nalint/SMG.html
This page on Sunil Gavaskar features his records and comments about him from other great cricketers.
e-mail: nalint@hotmail.com

That's Cricket

www.thatscricket.com
India's colourful premier cricket web site has several interactive features. A Message board, opinion poll, chat forum and e-mail generally seek your views and queries. Scorecards are live, you can sign on for the newsletter and check the latest cricket news. The home page has links to an online shopping area, profiles of players from several countries and two search engines. Well-written and exclusive columns on the Cricket World Cup and Asia Cup come with their links.
e-mail: via online form

The Rahul Dravid Portal

dravid.cjb.net
The largest collection of pictures anywhere, with photo galleries that seem to update themselves, stats, interviews, a chat room, fan club and more.
e-mail: not available

Welcome to Rahul Dravid's Fanpage

members.tripod.com/rdravid/
Packed with facts, figures and pictures of the one and only Rahul Dravid.
e-mail: abhishekr@hotmail.com

Welcome to Rishab's World

rishabh.webjump.com/crickpics.htm
Rishab dedicates his fan pages to Hritik Roshan, Sharukh Khan and links up with World cup 99.
e-mail: rishabh@coolrishabh.com

NEW ZEALAND

Auckland Cricket

www.aucklandcricket.co.nz
Though slow loading, this web site has links to club history, coaching and other matters you should know. The authors tell you how to get involved in New Zealand's greatest summer game, what you get for membership, sponsorship prospects and a list of other ways to get in with the gang. The Events page presents the calendar and takes you to the draws and points table for all grades of club cricket. Check out the opportunities for men and women to participate and compete.
e-mail: via online form

Blind Sport New Zealand Inc

www.blindsport.org.nz/cricket.html
All about cricket for the blind in New Zealand.
e-mail: cricket@blindsport.org.nz

Cairnsey

www.angelfire.com/ms/cairnsey/
Site dedicated to the world's greatest all-round cricketer.
e-mail: dion_nash@hotmail.com

Daniel Luca Vettori

www.angelfire.com/stars/dantheman79/
e-mail: daniel_vettori_fan@yahoo.co.nz

James Veales Unofficial New Zealand Cricket Page

www.voyager.co.nz/~veale/
Unofficial but worth a visit for the news flashes, statistics, graphs and player profiles.
e-mail: veale@voyager.co.nz

Manukau City Cricket Club

www.geocities.com/Colosseum/Stands /4446/
Very simple page of a minor NZ club with team information and statistics
e-mail: jhall@ihug.co.html

New Zealand Cricket

www-uk4.cricket.org/link_to_database/ NATIONAL/NZ/ABOUT/
Another official site hosted by Cricinfo. This one brings together the whole New Zealand cricket scene. Current domestic and international matches are set out with player profiles, pictures and statistics which you can search using the helpful

Stats Guru. The Grounds section shows you around their venues. women's cricket has its own page and the latest news comes with live coverage. The online shop stocks a few items for sale.
e-mail: via online form

NZ Cricket Headquarters

www.geocities.com/Colosseum/Stands /2570
A site designed by a fan gives his e-mail list of more than 35 loyal members. You can visit McMillan Magic, that part of his web site which focuses on the player Craig McMillan. There is also a photo album.
e-mail: maccie_bab@hotmail.com

Sir Richard Hadlee

www.hadlee.co.nz
One of New Zealand's finest cricketers.
e-mail: via online form

Springlands Taverna Celtic Cricket Club

www.geocities.com/Colosseum/Park/ 9975/
This is the home of New Zealand fast bowler Carl Bulfin, rising young star

Jarrod Englefield and the new Central Districts fast bowler, Brent Hefford. It is the largest cricket club in Marlborough and fields 11 teams at all grades. Other links include club history, subscription information, player registration, a hall of fame, statistics and a shopping mart.
e-mail: celticcricket@geocities.com

Stacey's New Zealand Cricket Site

www.geocities.com/Colosseum/Ring/9093/
News, pictures, player profiles, autographs, future tours, photos from a fan's perspective and a guest book.
e-mail: blackcapsite@hotmail.com

The Dion Nash Site

pages.hotbot.com/sports/nzcricket/nash.html
e-mail: dion_nash@hotmail.com

The Mighty Centurions Cricket Club

www.geocities.com/Colosseum/Stadium/9818/index.html
You get access to player profiles, great club moments, humour, quiz and crossword pages.
e-mail: not available

Union Cricket Club

www.zwap.to/union/
This Week in History section, during the season, presents club information and personal achievements for the week. The interaction bit wants your vote and asks you to sign the guest book, leave a message and your e-mail address. A navigation bar takes you to the photographs.
e-mail: cricket@unioncricket.virtualave.net

Wellington Collegians Living Legends AFASF

www.geocities.com/Colosseum/Hoop/3575/LIVING_LEGENDS.html
NZ club site with links to scores, profiles, an archive gallery and a bit of club history.
e-mail: mortonr@m-co.co.nz

PAKISTAN

Akhtar, Shoaib

www.geocities.com/Colosseum/Court/
6627/

Pakistani fast bowler. No stats, just
personal details and pictures.

e-mail: not available

Anwar, Saeed

members.tripod.com/~AnwarClub/

Dedicated to the Pakistan captain who
is also one of their leading batsmen.

e-mail: anwarclub@hotmail.com

Cricket

www.pak.gov.pk/special/cricket/
cricket(frame).htm

A most informative history of Pakistani
cricket, stadiums and scoring. Then
you get schedules and links to other
teams

e-mail: not available

Fan site of Saqlain Mushtaq

hlmughal.paklinks.com

e-mail: hula17@hotmail.com

Imran Khan Nazi

www.geocities.com/UmerPak83/
ImranKhan/Index.htm

If you think you know him, check out
this site.

e-mail: not available

Khel.com - World Cricket – Pakistan

www.khel.com/cricket/PAK/index.html

Current and previous players, recent
matches and One Day Internationals
get some mileage on this site.

e-mail: feedback@khel.com

Legends of Pakistan Cricket

members.tripod.com/~PAKSTAR/
index-2.html

As the name says these are the legends
of Pakistani cricket. The message
forum lets you blow off steam if you
need to or just say something friendly.

e-mail: support@hostboard.com

Pakistan Association Cricket Club

www.cs.ust.hk/faculty/iahmad/pacc

Introduction to the Pakistani Team,
Sunday League with a schedule of
matches, score card and photographs.

e-mail: not available

Pakistan Association of Cricket Statisticians and Scorers

www-aus.cricket.org/link_to_database/
SOCIETIES/PAK/PACSS/

e-mail: naumanb@brain.net.pk

Pakistan Cricket Board

www-uk.cricket.org/link_to_database/
NATIONAL/PAK

Another official web site hosted by
CricInfo with the latest Pakistani and
international news. There are links to
players, news and articles, statistics, a
gallant picture gallery, scorecards and
test match reports. The National Bank
of Pakistan Cup, Coca Cola Cup,
Sharjah tournament and other trophies
get full and lively coverage. Links take
you to other international cricket teams
and the International Cricket Board.

e-mail: pcb@cricket.org

Pakistan Cricket Page

www.zip.com.au/~shaukat/PakPage.htm

First rate site that brings to life matches,
loads of pictures, articles and interviews
Aagib Javed, Basit Ali, Wasim Akram,

Hasan Raza and others. The site certainly has the handle on Pakistani cricket.
e-mail: 7172620@pager.mirabilis.com, shaukat@zip.com.au

Pakistan Cricket Page

shakti.trincoll.edu/~skhan/pakcricket.html
Current scores and matches, domestic tournaments, past and forthcoming tours, a whole album of pictures and player statistics.
e-mail: Shahryar.Khan@mail.trincoll.edu

Pakistan Cricket team picture gallery

maxpages.com/said/Pakistan+Cricket+Team
It is what it says on the label.
e-mail: dhamaka99@usa.net

Pakistan Cricket Web

www.cricket.web.pk
e-mail: not available

Pakistan Player Information

www-usa.cricket.org/link_to_database/PLAYERS/PAK/
e-mail: help@cricinfo.com

Pakistani Cricket team

www.geocities.com/Colosseum/Stands/7466
e-mail: sadia47@hotmail.com

Rediff On the Net – News

www.rediff.com/news/paktour.htm
All the news about cricket in Pakistan.
e-mail: news@rediff.co.in

Saeed Anwar

saeedanwar.paklinks.com
e-mail: Hula17@hotmail.com

Wasim Akram

www2.cs.uwindsor.ca/60-205/99F/sec1/awan/akram.htm
They call him the bowler of the century.
e-mail: not available

Welcome to Ashar Khan's Web Page

www.angelfire.com/ak/asharkhan/
e-mail: ash_kha@yahoo.com

World Cup 99 – Pakistan

bol.net.in/cricket/teams/pakistan.html
The site is hosted by World Cup 99 and has live coverage of matches, schedules, team stories and stacks to say about previous World Cup tournaments.
e-mail: webmaster@indiamart.com

SOUTH AFRICA

Free State Cricket Union

www.fscu.co.za
New site is under construction.
The old version has news headlines, scorecards, statistics, a SuperSport series from the last season and player profiles.
e-mail: fscu@cricket.org

Gauteng Cricket Board

www-aus.cricket.org/link_to_database/NATIONAL/RSA/FC_TEAMS/TVL/
Don't be satisfied just reading about the clubhouse and stadium or following live coverage of the latest matches on the homepage. Go on to the Cricket Chronicle which gives the current headlines, news and articles of current and past seasons. You can access ticket options, prices and seating plans at the Ticket office. The Team page has player profiles and all fixtures for the current

season can be found in the Calendar section.

e-mail: general@cricketgauteng.co.za

Kingsmead Mynahs Club

www.icon.co.za/~mynahs/
One of the smaller SA clubs.
e-mail: mynahs@icon.co.za

Kwazulu-Natal Cricket Union

www-aus.cricket.org/link_to_database/
NATIONAL/RSA/FC_TEAMS/NATAL/
Ordinary but newsy site. The home page links up with fixtures and news, the Kwazulu Natal Cricket Academy and the Player of the Month section. Match tickets cannot be purchased online but can be obtained from any Union office.
e-mail: dolphins@natalcricket.co.za

North West Cricket Board   (North West Dragon)

www-aus.cricket.org/link_to_database/
NATIONAL/RSA/FC_TEAMS/NWEST/
The hyper link from the UCBSA takes you to the North West Dragon provincial team instead of North West Cricket Board. The funky home page has a hard-working icon that takes you to cricket tips, contests, chats, audio-video clips, interviews and a lot more. All the other stories – club history, player profiles, fixtures and match results are in place.
e-mail: nwcb@iafrica.com

Northern's Cricket Union (Northern Titans)

titans.cricket.org
Information is plentiful - seasons, squads, news, fixtures, grounds, conferences, club development and players. The home page has the latest headlines and

other information.
e-mail: titans@ncu.co.za

Shaun Maclean Pollock

www2.one.net.au/~proteapc/
e-mail: pollygirl79@yahoo.com

The Mike Procter Cricket

www.exinet.co.za/sport/procter/
procter.html
e-mail: procter@aztec.co.za

The Shaun Pollock Experience

www.exinet.co.za/sport/procter/
procter.html
e-mail: procter@aztec.co.za

United Cricket Board of South Africa

www-aus.cricket.org/link_to_database/
NATIONAL/RSA/
CricInfo, hosts of this web site, have designed the home page in the country's national colours. Their sites, which cover the world of cricket on the Internet, give in-depth coverage of the sport. This is of the same high standard with news headlines, scorecards and reports, profiles of the nation's players, details of their grounds and a bulky archive section. There are links to connect up with Test matches, one-day Internationals and domestic matches. The obliging Stats Guru dashes around searching for just the statistic you want.
e-mail: ucbsa@cricket.org

Western Province Cricket Association

www.wpca.cricket.org
They hover over the cricket scene in the Cape Town area. The home page carries the latest headlines, all the

details of the next match, an events calendar for the whole year and records for three previous years. You can bone up on the club, check scorecards records and players. The home page gets you right in with cricket tips, contests, chats, audio-video and interviews.
e-mail: info@wpca.co.za

SRI LANKA

Arjuna Ranatunga -The Captain of the World Champions of Cricket

www.ccom.lk/cricket/players/arjuna/
Articles, statistics and photos of Sri Lanka's captain and premier player. Unfortunately the site has not been updated for some time.
e-mail: rifki@ccom.lk

Nalanda Cricket Page

www.infolanka.com/people/nalanda/cricket/
Simply put together site with records, stories from past seasons and profiles of Nalanda Test Cricketers. Roshan Mahanama's World Test Record and live scores of the Ananda-Nalanda 50-overs cricket match in April 97 are lovingly reproduced with a bit of Sri Lanka's Cricket History.
e-mail: not available

Sanath Jayasuriya Tribute Site

www.geocities.com/Colosseum/Loge/4067/
Reliable and up-to-date information on this top Sri Lankan batsman. Articles, interviews, photos, records, statistics and more make this a very complete site.
e-mail: pinch-hitter@geocities.com

Sri Lanka Cricket Board - Official Page of Sri Lanka cricket

www.lanka.net/cricket/
Pretty full web site covering all aspects of the sport in Sri Lanka. News headlines come on the home page with more in-depth coverage when you click on the title. Local and international cricket reports, all match details and a cricket calendar take up several pages. Team profiles and highlights have video clips.
e-mail: cricket@sri.lanka.net

Sri Lanka Cricket Picture Archive

slcpa.home.ml.org
Lots of pictures of Sri Lankan cricket players
e-mail: cricket-fan@usa.net

The Hot & Live Action of Sri Lanka Cricket

www.info.lk/cricket/
Online links take you to well-documented news and current information on Sri Lanka's international and domestic cricket. World cricket news comes from CricInfo.
e-mail: not available

The Official Home of Sri Lankan Cricket - by CricInfo

www-aus.cricket.org/link_to_database/NATIONAL/SL/
Up-to-date news on the home page with headlines backed by scorecards and reports. Live scores, start times, weather forecasts and player profiles are clearly set out. Statistics are jammed packed on every aspect of play - bowling, batting, individual and team records, Test and match results and everything else. Links on the tournaments

page take you to forthcoming international cricket, domestic and recent matches and archives.
e-mail: help@cricinfo.com

WEST INDIES

Anansi Web Works

members.tripod.com/anansiweb/windies.htm
General information site with links on Trinidad and Tobago tourism and a mention of West Indies Cricket.
e-mail: anansiweb@usa.net

Barbados Cricket

www.barbados.org/crick.htm
Very simple site with some words about the history of cricket in Barbados, its significance to the country and a photo album. The online shop has a small range of cricket items and books for sale. A link takes you to tourism in Barbados.
e-mail: not available

Caribbean News Agency

www.cananews.com/cricket.htm
Regularly updated news on West Indies Cricket.
e-mail: via online form

Central page of West Indies cricket

www.caribcentral.com/cricket.htm
This is an unofficial site of West Indies cricket. Comprehensive coverage of all aspects of cricket in the Caribbean - scores, ratings, news, statistics, player profiles and local tournaments.
e-mail: webmaster@caribcentral.com

Courtney Walsh

sites.netscape.net/jackieahewitt/homepage
Site dedicated to Courtney Walsh.
e-mail: itss0031@herald.ox.ac.uk

Trini Posse

www.triniposse.com
Fan association with cricket links and lists of forthcoming events. You can search for photos by date or country.
e-mail: triniposse@usa.net

We Love it!

cricket.toneware.com/indexwi.htm
Player pictures.
e-mail: not available

West Indies Cricket News by CricInfo

www.cricket.org/link_to_database/NATIONAL/WI
The official site of West Indies is hosted by CricInfo – home of cricket on the Internet. Apart from details about players and grounds of West Indies cricket, you can keep up to date with the latest news on the home page. The web site has also all you need to know about the domestic cricket, statistics, scorecards and reports. More articles about cricket can be found in the West Indies Interactive section.
e-mail: Help@cricinfo.com

Windies On-line

boards.rivals.com/default.asp?sid=1191
Kathy-Lynn Ward, a loyal West Indies fan from Barbados runs this unofficial West Indies cricket fan site. If you really want to keep in touch with cricket in this part of the world, join the fan mailing list.
e-mail: info@rivals.com

ZIMBABWE

Africa Online - Discussion Forum

www.africaonline.co.zw/wwwboard/
messages/1144.html
Talk all you want about Zimbabwean
cricket stars and leave your impressions
for others to read.
e-mail: via online form

Cricket Zone – Zimbabwe

members.tripod.com/~ADIB_M/zimb.htm
Very simple web site with some
information about the current team,
grounds and forthcoming tours.
e-mail: not available

David Dyte's Zimbabwean Cricket Page

zikzak.net/~ddyte/
Good run down of Zimbabwean cricket,
their successes with scorecards and
pictures.
e-mail: ddyte@zikzak.net

KHEL.COM - world cricket

www.khel.com/cricket/ZIM/
Another general information site on
Zimbabwean cricket.
e-mail: feedback@khel.com

Zimbabwe Cricket Union

www-usa.cricket.org/link_to_database/
NATIONAL/ZIM/
Another CricInfo site, this one
specifically for Zimbabwean cricket at
international and first class levels. All
their tournaments are fondly reported
with live ball-by-ball coverage reserved
for Test matches and one-day
Internationals. Cricket grounds, youth
development programmes, player
profiles with pictures, statistics,
biographies, domestic matches are
all nicely presented in lively articles.
e-mail: zcu@samara.co.zw

Zimbabwe Home Page

www.criclive.com/htm/Zimbabwe.htm
General information about cricket in
Zimbabwe.
e-mail: not available

Zimbabwe Provincial Cricket News

www.cricinfo.com/link_to_database/
ARCHIVE/CRICKET_NEWS/1999/DEC/
012808_ZCO_16DEC1999.html
Mainly links to players, grounds,
statistics and cricket news.
e-mail: jward@samara.co.zw

Darts

Abbacus

www.abbacus.com/CompanyInfo.html
Web site of the US manufacturers
of electronic plastic tip and NFL
Coin-Operated dart games and a
variety of darts accessories. Order
online, or in the USA use the Toll
Free telephone number.
e-mail: Abbacus@recrooms.com

ABC Dart League

www.cobweb.net/~tganter/abcindex.htm
In 1993 some darts playing inhabitants
of Ambridge, Pennsylvania started a
league. The ABC league is mixed, soft
tipped, single in/single out 301. Today
it has expanded to 21 teams from 14
establishments. League positions,
individual statistics, news and venue
details are on this site as well as an
amusing set of rules.
e-mail: tganter@cobweb.net

Akron Canton Dart Club Community

**anexa.com/akroncantondartclub/
index.lhtml**
Open forum for members of the club
and all darts enthusiasts. You can join
the club and enjoy the private chats,
newsletters and referrals, check out the
events calendar and the classifieds.
Anyone can take part in discussions in
the chat room or debate in the public
discussion section. Before you leave,
visit the guest book to read comments
and if you wish, add your own.
e-mail: akroncantondarts@hotmail.com

American Darts Organization

www.cyberdarts.com/ado/
The home of the US organisation has
a wealth of information about itself, its
activities and its contacts with the
sport in other countries.
e-mail: editor@cyberdarts.com

Andy Jenkins

**www.andyjenkins.mcmail.com/
index2.html**
In you have a Flash plug-in you can see
one of the funniest splash pages of any
darts player. Andy sits on a flying dart
and splats into the board. The whole
site profiles the player, tells you how to

get in touch and to round things off you can play a game of darts online. For best results you require the Flash plug-in and a Java capable browser.
e-mail: andy.jenkins@mcmail.com

Azdarts

azdarts.com
The site of the Arizona Federation of Dart Associations gathers together information from leagues in the AFDA area. There are State Championship statistics and team photos, the Tournament Calendar and darts news.
e-mail: editor@azdarts.com

Bracknell & Binfield Men's Dart League Page

www.georgelavender.fsnet.co.uk
League tables of Divisions One and Two, competition news and results and coverage of the Finals Night. The author of the site welcomes contact by e-mail.
e-mail: georgelavender@ georgelavender.fsnet.co.uk

Bristol's Dart Page

www.brisdet.com/darts.htm
This Boston based site deservedly won an award for its brilliant presentation. You will find a darts FAQ section, tournament schedules world wide and local darts news. The guest book is visited regularly and if you intend building a site of your own, you'll find a variety of darts-related graphics to download in the Darts Vault.
e-mail: darts@brisdet.com

British Darts Organisation

www.bdodarts.com
Official web site of the British Darts Organisation which covers national,

inter-county and youth levels of the sport. You will find player statistics and past tournaments, match reports and hotographs from the Embassy World Championship and tables from the British Grand Prix.
e-mail: 101455.2114@compuserve.com

Buckinghamshire Darts Organisation

www.bucksdarts.co.uk
They are full members of the British Darts Organisation. Their web site gives local darts news, Division 2 Inter-County results, score averages and statistics.
e-mail: gem.67@virgin.net

Bull's Eye News Magazine

www.bullsinet.com
Online magazine for darts players covering the USA and the international arena with a good measure of expert advice on how to improve your game. The coverage of global tournaments with schedules and detailed results is good. If you like what you see, then follow directions online to have the print version of the magazine delivered to your door.
e-mail: ben@BullsEyeNews.com

Bullshooter

www.bullshooter.com
This is the web site of Arachnid Inc, manufacturers of electronic dart games. There are details of their coin operated Black Widow package, tournament news and technical support literature. Downloads require WinZip and Adobe Acrobat Reader.
e-mail: mmccarty@bullshooter.com

Charity Dart Systems

personal.boo.net/~tdi/cds/cds.htm
Here you can read the history of
Charity Dart Systems and view the
hall of fame. Voting procedures and
contact details are also available.
e-mail: not available

Colin Monk Homepage

www.hampshire-darts.mcmail.com/
colin.htm
The darts player Colin Monk gets a
web site to himself. Pages contain
his tournament records, photos and
contact information. The sound track,
if you are so equipped, is The
Monkees' theme song.
e-mail: mo2vmj00@cwcom.net

Crosby and District Amateur Darts League

www.pcweb.liv.ac.uk/davel/darts/
low_bw.html
Based in Liverpool, this league web
site contains a wealth of information.
League tables, match reports, cup draws
and a lot more are neatly set out online.
e-mail: d.g.laybourne@liverpool.ac.uk

Crow's Dart Page - Steel and Soft-Tip Darts

www.crowsdarts.com
Mr. Cronian from Alabama started this
site in 1996 since when it has grown
from a page covering local darts statistics
to become a large and impressive site.
It still covers local league results but
includes tips and tricks for darts
enthusiasts at all levels and a good
list of resources. You can contact the
author using ICQ or by e-mail.
e-mail: crow@crowsdarts.com

Cyber Darts

www.cyberdarts.com
Here you get darts news world wide
and share in the travels and experiences
of Dartoid as he roams the world, from
Amarillo to Zurich, playing darts and
writing entertaining reports of his
experiences for Cyber Darts visitors.
Next time you hit a 180 be sure to
register it online and see your
achievement displayed.
e-mail: editor@cyberdarts.com

Dallas Darts Association

www.dda-darts.org
Steel tipped league of the Dallas Darts
Association formed in 1971. Schedules,
league tables and match results with a
list of DDA Participating Pubs
accompanied by map links. If you want
to enter a tournament in the Dallas area
check out the listings available on this site.
e-mail: news@dda-darts.org

Dartbars.com

www.dartbars.com
If you are looking for a bar to play darts
or a venue for your team this is a good
place to start. Organised on a regional
basis they have created a world wide
database of steel and soft tip darts bars
which currently contains some 3,000
entries, each with contact details.
e-mail: crow@crowsdarts.com

Dartplanet

www.dartplanet.com
A neat and friendly site giving you
up-to-date world news on darts with
an emphasis on activities in The
Netherlands. You can get yourself on
the Dartplanet Newsletter mailing list.
e-mail: not available

Darts Clubs

www.stud.ee.ethz.ch/~mroth/clubs.html
This site is a compilation of links to darts clubs on the web, largely from around Europe. Both steel and soft tipped clubs are included. To add your club simply e-mail the author and ask nicely.
e-mail: mroth@stud.ee.ethz.ch

Darts Federation of Australia

www.dfa.berlyn.net
The home site of the DFA with details of its rules and constitution, contact information and e-mail addresses of the Executive. There are listings of darts tournaments in Australia for the year and players' rankings from organisations across the country. You can also subscribe to the darts magazine Points and Tips.
e-mail: via online form

Darts In The Harrogate District

www.harrogatedarts.freeserve.co.uk
Martin Newton gives top flight coverage to the darts scene in Harrogate, Knaresborough, Nidderdale, Dales, and Boroughbridge. He maintains the site with care and keeps information up-to-date.
e-mail: not available

Darts Information Center

www.darters.com
Tournaments, team listings and league tables right across the USA. In the games section you can play darts or do the online crossword. There is a battery of links to other darts sites and an online shopping guide. You can download a selection of graphics for free. If you have something to say or

a question to ask use the form.
e-mail: twfisher@aol.com

Darts Victoria

www.dartsvictoria.com
Three darts leagues based in Victoria and British Columbia in Canada maintain this site jointly. They give you all the news of past and forthcoming events, team information, match and player statistics for the area.
e-mail: dartsweb@dartsvictoria.com

Darts World Record Register

users.skynet.be/mvp/records/
It does what it says on the label – all the world records and their holders are listed on this site. What is the record for completing 1001 using the fewest number of darts? How long has anyone played darts non-stop? If you want the answers to these and other questions, look no further.
e-mail: swo2@yahoo.com

England Darts

www.englanddarts.f9.co.uk
Official England Darts site. Pages
include details of the England Open
with information on how to enter, the
European Cup and the World Cup.
Results of National Singles matches
and the England male and female
squads are listed. You are encouraged
to communicate by e-mail with squad
members and contact the site authors.
e-mail: peter@englanddarts.f9.co.uk

English Darts Plus

www.englishdartsplus.com
US online darts store with a full catalogue
and probably holding everything in
stock. The search facility makes quick
work of finding what you want. Online
ordering uses SSL encryption.
e-mail: dartplus@execpc.com

Ewa Marie Hallberg

www.geocities.com/Colosseum/Court/
2733/
Homepage for the celebrated women's
darts player Ewa Marie Hallberg. There
are personal and biographical notes
about her.
e-mail: e.hallb@usa.net

Friendly Darts Matches

users.skynet.be/jve/friendly/
If you've ever wanted to organise a
friendly non-competitive game for your
team and not known how to do it, visit
this site. The bulletin board has
messages listed by Country and State
with all the team contact details. You
may find a match to suit but in any
case register your team and practise
while waiting for responses.
e-mail: sw02@yahoo.com

Game On

www.embassydarts.com
The prestigious Embassy World Darts
Championship gets extensive coverage
here with a day by day well-illustrated
account of the year's championship
and brief reviews of previous years.
You can contribute opinions and
comments to the Readers Corner
section by e-mail and request their
newsletter. Sports writer Clive
Downton covers the latest news from
the world of darts.
e-mail: mailto:gameon1@msn.com

Gusty's Homepage of Darts in Luxembourg

www.homepages.lu/gust.mees/
default.html
Gusty welcomes you to the world
of Darts in Luxembourg in this
award-winning site. Luxembourg's
Leagues, player ranking and even
tourist board information come together
with a feature on the Luxembourg
Spring Cup 2000. Check out the guest
book to discover how much praise
visitors across the globe have heaped
on the site.
e-mail: gust.mees@vo.lu

Howard County Dart Association (HCDA)

www.hcdadarts.com
Steel tip darts league based in Howard
County, Maryland. This site contains
information about their history, rules
and directors with e-mail addresses
to contact members.
e-mail: dartinfo@hcdadarts.com

Isle Of Wight County Darts Association

wight2ooo.co.uk
The site has all the darts news for the island with good write-ups about local teams and players. The Isle of Wight Open tournament is amply discussed.
e-mail: isleofwight2ooo@AOL.com

Ivars Peterson's MathLand

www.maa.org/mathland/ mathland_5_19.html
Why are the numbers on the dartboard arranged in that order? You can think about it or ponder Ivars Peterson's mathematical explanations. There are other insights on these pages to fascinate, whether you are a darter or have mathematical leanings.
e-mail: ip@scisvc.org

John Lowe – Professional Darts Player

www.hitandrundarts.com/ AAJOHNLOWE.htm
John Lowe has been playing darts professionally since 1976 and holds the record for winning the most Open matches. He is probably the most popular professional darts player in the world. This site covers his whole career. You are encouraged to contact him and if you wish, call and arrange to meet him.
e-mail: not available

Lancashire Darts Organisation

ourworld.compuserve.com/ homepages/LANCSDARTS/
Darts in the Lancashire area, highlighting inter-county fixtures for the forthcoming Premier Division season and last season's tables, with detailed match by match analyses. The Lancashire Super League, Lancashire Open and Gold Cup fixtures results and averages are also tabled.
e-mail: 113561.3446@compuserve.com

Martin Adams

www.adams18o.freeserve.co.uk
This is the England team captain Martin "Wolfie" Adams. A biography includes his tournament record, an FAQ section, contact information and how to get Wolfie darts and flights.
e-mail: Martin@adams18o. freeserve.co.uk

Minute Man Dart League

www.mmdl.org
Massive and comprehensive site to encompass the Minute Man Dart League which is the largest in the world. You get the whole bit – leagues, rules, schedules, weekly results and more. Use the Guest Book if you wish to leave your comments.
e-mail: cabhome@cabscorner.com

NC Darts Archives

metalab.unc.edu/ncdarts/
Steel tip darts in North Carolina State with league news, statistics and contact details. There are several links to external darts sites.
e-mail: via online form

New Jersey Darts

www.njdarts.com
Darts in the New Jersey area of the USA. Places to play are listed by county and you have information on local leagues and players. If you wish you can get on their mailing list online.
e-mail: not available

New York Dart League

www.geocities.com/Colosseum/
Dugout/3625/

Darts news from the Bronx Tuesday
and the NYC Darts leagues. JC Mac's
Bar makes the competition
announcements.

e-mail: mac235@yahoo.com

Palm Beach County Darting Association

www.gopbi.com/community/groups/
darts/index.html

PBCDA is a member of FDA and ADO
and seeks to promote darts at all levels.
You will find contact details and
information on upcoming events.

e-mail: a17oout@aol.com

Pittsburg Darts Association

www.pdainfo.com

This is a very original site. After a nice
Shockwave Flash introduction, you
get to the real content but this is
only available by downloading Adobe
Acrobat PDF files of league statistics,
fixtures tournaments and so on and
a recommended out shot guide.
To enjoy this site you need Flash 4
plug-in and Adobe Acrobat Reader.

e-mail: darts@pdainfo.com

Planet Darts

www.planetdarts.co.uk/index2.html

The Professional Darts Corporation
have put together a top-flight web site,
very well designed and packed with
darts goodies. The news section is
thorough in content and updated daily.
Player profiles, world ranking, diary and
tournament coverage are all online.
They have added a great games section
and free wallpaper to download onto

your desktop. You can take part in the
discussion on the chat board or e-mail
the UK company to register your opinion.

e-mail: enquries@planetfootball.com

Premier Darts League – Kuwait

www.geocities.com/Colosseum/Loge/
8092/

Kuwait has a thriving Darts League
and all the details can be found on this
humorously written site. The fixtures,
results and team news go back to the
1996/97 season. While you are online
you can find your way around Kuwait
and follow links to other darts-related
sites. Captain Zarras, the author
welcomes your comments, news and
feedback via e-mail.

e-mail: premdarts@geocities.com

Raymond van Barneveld

www.vanbarneveld.berlyn.net

Twice crowned World Champion
and top Dutch player, Raymond van
Barneveld has his own web site. He
sets out, very attractively, photographs,
statistics, world and Netherlands
rankings, out shots and a form to
contact him.

e-mail: via online form

San Francisco Darts Association

www.sfda.net

All about darts in San Francisco.
Local tournaments and leagues,
schedules, fixtures, players' rankings
and statistics are all equally well
covered. There is a thumbnail picture
archive of players in action and taking
a break from the stress of competition.
The Darts Clinic section provides tips
on chalking, etiquette and practice.

e-mail: someone@sfda.net

Savon Darts

www.savondarts.com
An extensive merchandising site with an online illustrated catalogue of darts, flights, shafts, boards, scoreboards, cabinets and everything else except the beer. You can order by phone; in the USA use the toll free number.
e-mail: not available

Scottish Darts Association

www.geocities.com/scotland_darts/
There is a good deal of information about SDA events, past and forthcoming, a diary of matches and other meetings and a bit about the Association itself. Inter-county fixtures, recent results and tables take up the rest of the site.
e-mail: not available

Sheila Handley's Darts Around Essex

web.ukonline.co.uk/sheila.handley/
Shelia has put together a good deal of information on darts played in the Essex region at county, local league and grass roots levels. She gives you up-to-date league tables, Essex competition information, fixtures and results.
e-mail: sheila.handley@ukonline.co.uk

Smile online java darts game

games.smilie.com/darts/darts.html
Yorkshire based Smile Ltd make Java games and you can test your skill at darts online for free. The throwing action is quite natural - just point and click with the mouse - and it all looks so attractive and easy. Make sure you have a Java enabled browser.
e-mail: sales@smilie.com

Spitfire Darts Team

www.the-spitfires.freeserve.co.uk
Latest news and team information from the Cumbrian team in north England. There are league tables, fixtures, recent match and tournament results and an Interactive Darts Quiz.
e-mail: the_spitfires@e-mail.com

Swedish/Scanian Darts Organisation

www.sdd.dart.se/index2.htm
Sven Silow put this site together to cover the Swedish national and local Scanian darts scenes. A particularly useful section, entitled The Historical Archives, stores details of all major tournament statistics. Links to other darts sites are excellent and worth following through as they

include recommended general sites and country by country list.
e-mail: kansli@sdd.dart.se

Swindon Darts

www.soft.net.uk/richell/
With a guide to all the darts news in Swindon, this site contains fixtures and tables making particular reference to Arkells Houses and the Friday Night 4-a-side leagues.
e-mail: darts@swindondarts.net

The American Darters Association

www.adadarters.com
All the information that you require on the American Darts Association and the American Darts League is here on this well presented site. The leagues cater to all levels of play including a system that allows players of different abilities to compete equally called the Neutralizer. The site authors can be contacted using the appropriate e-mail address.
e-mail: adadarts@inlink.com

The Bad Boy's Dart Team

home.ici.net/~jimmcget/badboys/
Home site of an Australian darts team with photos, biographies and statistics of the players. Online you can check the rules of their league - Minute Man Dart League - which is the largest in the world.
e-mail: not available

The Belle Vue Darts Team

www.pubdarts.com
Detailed coverage of a local darts team. Latest news includes match by match reports. Fixtures and statistics come with a picture gallery.
e-mail: giles@badarts.co.uk

The Dart Thrower

www.dartbase.com
Good articles and an FAQ section on technique, equipment and the psychological side of the game. You can interact with other enthusiasts by joining the Dart Thrower's discussion list or by posting your views on the moderated discussion board.
e-mail: via online form

The Darts Page Netherlands

www.xs4all.nl/~dartsnl/
Darts in Holland. Organisations, leagues, cafes and pubs where the game is played are all neatly set out. A handy dart calculator can be downloaded for free. You can buy darts and accessories online and catch up on the Embassy championships while you visit. Text is mainly in Dutch with an English alternative.
e-mail: dartsnl@xs4all.nl

The French Darts Federation

perso.wanadoo.fr/ffd/pages_a/index.htm
The French site welcomes visitors and tells them all about the sport in France. A national map pinpoints the locations of all the clubs and links are provided to their web sites. They explain the rules of the game with good graphics. A history of the Federation, championship details and a schedule of events keep you on target. You can contact the authors by e-mail.
e-mail: f.f.d@wanadoo.fr

The Golden Harvest North American Cup Dart Tournament

www.goldenharvestdarts.com/ghome.htm
The North American Open has a total prize pot of C$305,400, about £150,000,

which makes it the richest darts Open in the world. As a result the tournament attracts the world's best players. This site hosts the official competition and for further information e-mail the author, Willi Heinermann.
e-mail: goldenharvestdarts@home.com

The House of Darts

www.frognet.net/~bbennett/
This award winning web site is a good guide to the game. Rules, definitions and terms are explained, the history of the sport is unfolded and an interesting section defines What makes a Dart. You can participate in the online poll, write in the guest book and e-mail your comments to the author. The site has teamed up with South of Polaris Darts shop to give away equipment to those who sign up.
e-mail: bbennett@frognet.net

The International Dart Players Association

www.idpa.cwc.net
All the European tournament results for the year are posted on this site - German, Finnish, Scottish and Dutch Open competitions and the Embassy World Championship. The WDF and BDO player rankings keep you abreast of the international darters' scene.
e-mail: not available

The Les McDanger Wallace Homepage

www.mcdanger.cwc.net
Page about the Scots darter Les McDanger Wallace – his playing record, photos and how to get in touch. You can read all about him with bagpipe accompaniment if you have sound capabilities on your computer. On the other hand you may

prefer to leave the sound off.
e-mail: Frank.Branscombe@btinternet.com

The Most Complete Collection Of Dart Games On The Web

dartgames.homepage.com
Pool player turned darts fan Rod Mendez has searched high and low to gather together 47 unique games to play on a dartboard. Rules and playing guides for each game are graded according to difficulty with a section on dart etiquette giving advice on how to avoid being a sore loser, among other tips on proper behaviour.
e-mail: rpmendez@yahoo.com

The National Capital Area Darts Page

www.capitalnet.com/~ottadart/
What is going on in the Ottawa darts scene can be gleaned by visitors and locals alike from this site. You will find a detailed guide to venues, trivia, game rules and news from Ontario.
e-mail: ottadart@capitalnet.com

The National Dart Association

www.ndadarts.com
The NDA is the sanctioning body of electronic darts and this is its official site. You get all the tournament information, player and team rankings and the latest news via the Bulletin Board. There are details of how to join the Association.
e-mail: director@ndadarts.com

The Official Sussex Darts Organisation Page

ourworld.compuserve.com/ homepages/biccdiv1/hpsussex.htm
This regularly updated site has all the Sussex area darts information, inter-county league details and match

reports. The calendar includes all forthcoming darts events at county, national and international levels.
e-mail: vicsexton@bdodarts.com

The Polish Darts Organisation

www.pzdarta.nb.com.pl/index_eng.htm
When the darts boom took Poland by storm in the mid-nineties, the authors got to work to construct this site. The first league season and Polish Darts Cup took place in 1998-99. This well-designed site gives an excellent history and account of the sport in the country. There are links to Polish local and international web sites and you can contact the authors by e-mail.
e-mail: artur@arzgalicja.com.pl

The UK's one and only Britannia Club site

www.angelfire.com/ok/resort2/
The Britannia teams, which compete in the Colchester and district premier league, hold centre stage on this site. All the league tables of divisions One

to Five are posted and the photo gallery takes a tongue in cheek look at their activities.
e-mail: prism@talk21.com

Top Flight Darts

topflightdarts.com
Online store for the full range of darts equipment and supplies. Check out the Hot Deals they have put together. Payment by credit or debit card goes via PayPal.com, a secure system and registration gets you additional customer services.
e-mail: via online form

Total Rebound - Human Darts

totalrebound.com/gamepages/Human Darts.html
Human Darts is the name and the game. Players strap on dart flights and points, take aim then jump on to a giant inflatable dartboard to score. Weird or what?
e-mail: info@totalrebound.com

Turkish Darts Pages

members.xoom.com/RattleSenol/
The author has put together several pages of absorbing interest to any darter. The glossary of darts terms explains the nicknames of various scores, like Bag O' Nuts, and other phrases. He also explains the attributes needed for darts beginners and lists rules for many darts games. Text is in English and Turkish.
e-mail: not available

Vicky and Lisa's Place for Dart Stuff

www.geocities.com/Colosseum/Arena/4041/

Vicky and Lisa's lively passion for the game of darts shines through on this site. There are articles on the history of the game through the ages, how dart-boards are made with descriptions of regional variations to the standard board and the rules for 501. They also cover the local darts scene in Washington.

e-mail: dartplayers@geocities.com

Web Darts - an online darts game

homepages.enterprise.net/rglennie/darts/darts.html

You need a Java enabled browser to play online, but be warned it can become addictive. You can play darts online with no downloads, using only your PC. Two clicks of the mouse determine horizontal and vertical directions, then throw at the board. Scoring is computed automatically. Available in single or multi-player format where you can play whoever is logged in. You still have to end on a double though.

e-mail: rglennie@enterprise.net

Welsh Darts Organisation

www.welshdarts.org

Well put together official site with a lot of good information - Welsh player ranking, scores, averages and tournament statistics. Other subjects covered are the men's, women's and youth sections with coverage of the national team and Welsh inter-county meetings.

e-mail: welsh@welshdarts.org

Winmau, The force behind darts

www.winmau.com

The well-known manufacturers of bristle dartboards and other darts related merchandise display all their products in an illustrated online catalogue. They also list forthcoming tournaments.

e-mail: info@winmau.com

World Darts Federation

wdf.hostingcheck.com

Site of the World Darts Federation which keeps you up to date with Tournament fixtures and results, progress of the World and European Cup and the WDF world rankings. There is a history of the Winmau World Masters dating from 1974 to the present. If you are seeking a WDF contact in your country check the listing on the site.

e-mail: not available

WyldBill's Dart Connection

www.geocities.com/SouthBeach/Lights/2981/dart.htm

WyldBill's pages for darts enthusiasts. They explain how to set up a dartboard, rules for the 501 game and the scoring areas on a board. The author invites you to get in touch by e-mail or ICQ.

e-mail: wgerickson@canada.com

Extreme Sports

Adrenalin
www.adrenalin-magazine.com
Dedicated to covering extreme sports, with background music and lots of visuals, so you won't be disappointed. Surfing, skating and snowboarding are featured and a site map in case you get lost. There are some extreme games to get you started.
e-mail: editorial@adrenalin-magazine.com

Adventurelifestyle
www.adventurelifestyle.com
Love Risk Love Life. If that's you, you'll enjoy this site for the adventurous. Well designed, the site shows what their production crew and adventure athletes get up to. They travel the world to bring to you web casts of expeditions, races and international events. The site compliments the Pure Life magazine.
e-mail: feedback@adventurelifestyle.com

Aggressive.com
www.aggressive.com
Great resource for skaters, novices or experienced. Photos, video clips and tips show you how it's done. A bulletin board, chat facility and product reviews give you more input and you get guidance on basic treatment for injuries just in case. You can download skating wallpaper for free.
e-mail: justin@seas.smu.edu

American Barefoot Club
barefoot.org
Official site of the governing body for US barefoot water-skiing with news and schedules of national and regional competitions and results. The author will be happy to receive your comments and questions and you can order videos on barefoot water-skiing from the list online.
e-mail: heeney@ixi.net

Barefoot Central
www.barefootcentral.com
All about barefoot water skiing. The site exchanges ideas on the sport, reviews equipment and lets you meet other footers to share experiences and have some fun. Tournament schedules,

stories and a coach's corner lead up to great video footage of Keith St. Onge flipping about on the water, demonstrating why he's the best around. The guest book is for you to write in or read comments from other fans. You'll need RealPlayer for part of this site.
e-mail: chuck@barefootcentral.com

Big Air Paragliding

www.bigairparagliding.com
Paragliding site with classified ads, details of clubs and shops. You get lots of handy assistance from the weather webcam, a pilot address book and product reviews. The photo and video gallery are well worth a visit. You can say your piece in the paragliding forum.
e-mail: not available

Bluetorch

www.bluetorch.com
This is where you start! Up-to-date on everything in the surfing, snowboarding, BMX and skating communities with a whole lot more on other extreme sports. This is a truly multimedia site bulging with video clips and audio snips. They host their own competitions, follow all the others world wide and accompany a TV programme and sports magazine.
e-mail: support@corpbig.com

BMX AIR

www.bmxair.com
An online magazine bringing you the best in BMX. All the tournaments are described with reviews, results, photos and RealPlayer clips. Join the mailing list, subscribe to the magazine online or send in your own comments and pictures.
e-mail: submit@bmxair.com

Bmxtrix

www.bmxtrix.com
News, competitions, photos and stories on the BMX front with some of the best graphics and sound relays on the web. If you have any stories or photos of your own, don't be shy, send them in as the authors always welcome new input.
e-mail: bmxtrix@bmxtrix.com

Bmxweb.Com

bmxweb.com
A good place to start if you want to get to all the Internet sites carrying information on freestyle BMX bikes. The search engine lets you look specifically, check out the latest additions or see them all. You can e-mail for more information or recommend links you think will improve the site.
e-mail: link@bmxweb.com

Boater Talk

www.boatertalk.com
This is where you get to talk about boating and white water sport. Several message board forums split the discussions so you can stick to the subject – white water boating, equipment and locations.
e-mail: not available

Bungee Zone

www.bungeezone.com/
This is an award winning web site, so it doesn't matter whether you enjoy dropping from a great height at the end of a rubber band or you are too scared to give it a go, enjoy the experience online. And this is bungee jumping world wide - club lists, photos, equipment information, a history of the sport,

bungee cartoons and jokes. E-mail the author if you have something to say or questions to ask.

e-mail: Alex@BungeeZone.com

Eco-Challenge

www.ecochallenge.com

To find out more or just keep in touch with news from the Eco-Challenge Expedition Race, log-in to this official site. It's all there, including a history of the race, some great pictures and details on adventure travel. You can receive daily race reports by e-mail and other worthwhile race-related services.

e-mail: not available

Epic Street Luge

www.teamepic.com/index.html

All about street luge, extreme skateboarding with riders lying flat and flying down steep hills. There are lots of readable articles and a graphic guide to making your own luge board at minimal cost. You can e-mail your questions and comments.

e-mail: mail@teamepic.com

Extreme Sports

www.extreme-sports.com

All the extreme sports from the simplest to the toughest, including the less well known challenges like Skimboarding. There's a report online from ISPO - the largest and most comprehensive sports show. If you have something you want to say in no more than 200 words, send off your e-mail and they may put it online.

e-mail: info@extremesports.com

Extremists

www.awezome.com

This is the extreme sports page. Body boarding, surfing, skiing, mountain biking, motor biking and whatever else takes you to the edge. Read the experiences of others in the X-Files section or submit your own story, the scarier the better.

e-mail: via online form

Footer's Home Page

www.isd.net/footer/

Bare foot water skiing at its best. An essential guide to the sport also explains how you can take part. A guest book, message forum and lots of action photographs round off a very good site.

e-mail: not available

Gravity Games

www.gravitygames.com

The official site of the annual extreme sport competition. Skateboarding, luge, snowboarding and bike riding are the front runners. A great photo gallery and video clips give you the thrill of being there.

e-mail: not available

HardCloud

www.hardcloud.com

Resource for skate, snow and surf sports with stories from wherever the action is. Reports on events and conditions come with a photo gallery and product reviews. If you register you can get your own @hardcloud.com e-mail address and anything else on offer.

e-mail: not available

Mountain Nomad

www.mountainnomad.co.uk

UK resource covering mountaineering, climbing, hiking and skiing. There is a

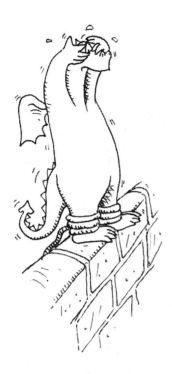

section on climbing in Nepal, news, book reviews, message boards and some very good photographs.
e-mail: editor@mountainnomad.co.uk

Rapid Ferret Racing
home.rmi.net/~rturner/rapid-ferret/
Streetluge is a variation of skateboarding where you head down a steep hill very fast lying flat on your back. If the end of your ride requires a trip to a hospital, check out the best hospitals guide online. Including events calendar, associated companies and a guide to the pilots.
e-mail: not available

Sandboard Magazine
sandboard.com/home.htm
Californian online Internet magazine for sandboarders. Similar to

snowboarding, this sport has the advantage that sand does not normally melt. A photo gallery, videos and events calendar come with tips and tricks from Dr. Dune himself.
e-mail: sandboard@ccis.com

skateboard.com
www.skateboard.com
Good stuff on skateboarding with news and chat, a world wide skate park directory, book reviews, videos you can download and interviews with top skateboarders. Videos are in Windows Media Player and RealVideo formats.
e-mail: info@skateboardinc.com

Skatedork
www.skatedork.org
Skateboarding for everyone with lots of photographs, chatty columns, reports from the scene and a popular and busy message board. Started as a web site, it now has a printed magazine with its own unique content.
e-mail: steve@skatedork.org

SnowboarderReview
www.snowboarderreview.com
This is your web site to write reviews on boards, gear and resorts and read what others have to say. Articles and a directory of resorts back up the MarketPlace, where you can trade in new and second-hand equipment.
e-mail: via online form

sports3
www.sports3.com
Extreme sports videos to view online and download - surfboard, skateboard, bodyboard, snowboard, wakeboard and mountain biking. If you'd like to see

your own videos on the Net, send them in.
e-mail: info@sports3.com

SSI Pro Tour

ssiprotour.com
The official professional skysurfers and freeflyers organisation since 1995. You get a run through all the competitions they monitor with schedules, results and video clips you can download.
e-mail: not available

StreetLuge

www.geocities.com/speedluge/
Canadian web site that takes the mystery out of street luge. They tell you how to build the board, what equipment you'll need, show you the techniques and put it all together with some first-rate pictures. For a bit of

interaction, use the guest book and message board.
e-mail: not available

StreetLuge.com

www.streetluge.com
The online home of professional street luge racing. It covers the X Games and tells you how to qualify for the competition. The Association publishes its events with detailed street luge plans. Photos, an e-mail contact form and links to other web sites complete the story.
e-mail: jlewis@streetluge.com

Treeclimbing.com

www.treeclimbing.com
Using the motto - Get high, Climb a tree! - the organisation promotes tree climbing as a recreation. Anyone can join the school to meet fellow climbers and learn new techniques. There are journals, gear info, a photo gallery and a chat facility.
e-mail: treeman@mindspring.com

ViviSurf

www.vivisurf.ch
Professional skysurfer Viviane Wegrath writes his official web site in English and German. He tells you about himself in words and a gallery of some great photos. There's a section on coaching and you can e-mail him for more information.
e-mail: vivisurf@compuserve.com

WindSurfer

www.windsurfer.com
Wind surfing made easier with reviews of boards, locations, weather reports and a lot of links to related sites. The online shop helps you with an

illustrated catalogue and you can submit your own comments to the site.
e-mail: not available

X-tremesport.net

www.x-tremesport.net
This site features BMX, skateboarding, snowboarding, and soap shoes. Find out the latest news, with pictures and mpeg video clips. If you didn't already know, soap shoes means soaping the soles of your shoes and sliding down poles, banisters and anything scarier.
e-mail: not available

Xtreme Scene

www.xtremescene.com
Fantastic photo gallery sponsored by a Utah Outdoors magazine with big cliffs, huge air, sheer rock walls, neck-deep powder, nasty bike rides and mad skateboarding shots. They want to hear your extreme stories and offer a free T-shirt if they put yours online.
e-mail: not available

XtremeSoul.com

www.xtremesoul.com
For the hottest selection of extreme sports news get stuck into this site. Live webcasts of skateboarding, snowboarding, surfing, motox and BMX come direct to your screen. They review the latest gear on the market and sell it online. You can join the live online discussions in the chat room and pick up free e-mail.
e-mail: not available

Golf

The Sport

19th Hole.com

19thhole.com
Entertaining US online golf magazine provides top class columns and features covering all aspects of the game. You'll also find reviews of golf books and videos, an online shop and a message board.
e-mail: via online form

A Royal and Ancient History

www.foreteevideo.co.uk
What at first seems to be a simple advertisement for a golf video, turns out to be a very informative site that spans the history of the game, results and statistics. You'll also find information on some of the world's top courses, online games, golf humour and various golf links.
e-mail: via online form

Asian Golf Review

www.asiangolf.com
The Review brings you news, results and articles from the world of golf, particularly in Asia. There are interesting features on industry news and golf equipment and you'll find lists of courses in Singapore, Malaysia, Indonesia and Australia. Though these lists are extensive, they would benefit from a little more detail.
e-mail: admin@asiangolf.com

Australian Golf Union

www.agu.org.au
A complete guide to Australian golf, this user-friendly site covers everything from news to tournament schedules. A handy Australian club directory is included along with details of State associations and the rules of the game. A helpful search engine gives you a hand.
e-mail: agu@agu.org.au

Backspin

www.backspin.com
Available in both French and English, Backspin gives you the low-down on the game in France. You'll find huge amounts of detail on courses in France,

golf news and rankings. One of the best looking golf sites around, if a little slow to load.
e-mail: backspin@backspin.com

Bad Golf Monthly

www.badgolfmonthly.com
This witty American site provides a welcome haven for those of us not blessed with the gifts of Tiger Woods. There are lots of fun features including amusing articles, a hall of shame featuring some of the worst scores from around the world, golf jokes and cartoons. An excellent antidote to the many straight-laced golf sites on the web.
e-mail: badgolfer@badgolfmonthly.com

British and International Golf Greenkeepers Association

www.bigga.co.uk
The unsung global green-keeping fraternity gets its very own and very good web site. Aside from industry news, you'll find a fine selection of articles, information on careers in the profession and links to similar organisations all over the world.
e-mail: admin@bigga.co.uk

British Minigolf Association

members.aol.com/MiniGolf98/index.html
If you like your golf with novelty obstacles, concrete greens and miniature everything, then this is the site for you. Run by the UK's governing body for mini-golf, the site is full of news, information and results from the world of golf's smaller and weirder cousin.
e-mail: MiniGolf98@aol.com

Caddiechat.com

www.caddiechat.com
Take a look at the world of golf through the eyes of the oft forgotten caddie on this very entertaining and easy-to-use site. Loads of news and views from the world of caddying come with tournament diaries, live chat and message boards.
e-mail: info@caddiechat.com

Cantour.com

www.cantour.com
Rather basic official site of the Canadian professional golf tour. You get live leader boards, news and player biographies, schedules and links to other sites.
e-mail: cantour@cantour.com

Carnoustie Golf Links

www.carnoustie.org/golf.htm
Carnoustie was the location for the 1999 British Open and its web site has information on the courses, clubs, accommodation and travel in the area. Courses are described in hole-by-hole detail with photographs.
e-mail: admin@carnoustie.org

Clubtest.com

www.clubstest.com
Ideal site for the serious golfer. Full of very detailed reviews, tests and reports on the latest golf clubs. A weekly overview gives you an analysis of what clubs the pros are using. If you join the Virtual Country Club, you can use the hints section to improve your swing and become a club-tester yourself. Leader boards and golf news are also provided.
e-mail: via online form

Dubai Desert Classic

www.dubaidesertclassic.com
The site for this big-money golf event tells you all about the course, lists the players and publishes the press releases. During the event, live scoring and a leader board come online. If you'd like to go yourself, all the golf clubs and resorts in Dubai are highlighted.
e-mail: christine@dwtc.com

Dubai Golf Online

www.dubaigolf.com
You'll find information on two top golf clubs, the Dubai Creek Golf & Yacht Club and Emirates Golf Club, on this nicely presented site. Information on the courses, facilities and golf academies is all provided, although the course descriptions are rather superficial.
e-mail: not available

Eurogolfing.com

www.eurogolfing.com
EuroGolf provides a valuable directory for, not surprisingly, Golf in Europe. A huge list of courses and clubs is provided along with information on hotels, accommodation, restaurants and transport. If you want a more permanent golfing holiday you can check out the properties for sale section.
e-mail: via online form

EuropeanTour.Com

www.europeantour.com
Fabulous design and ease-of-use make exploring this official PGA site a treat. You'll find news on all the latest European tournaments, lots of statistics and interesting articles and a very nifty live scoring feature.
e-mail: via online form

Global Golf Guide

www.globalgolfguide.com
The snazzy video and graphics by themselves are good enough reason to visit this site. You get to go on virtual tours of over 16,000 golf courses world wide, well presented with video clips and photographs. To this are added tee times, contact details for each course and online booking for accommodation and car hire. This is a very special site and you'd do well to bookmark it.
e-mail: info@virtualvisits.com

Golf At Half Price.com

www.golfathalfprice.com
A real treasure of golf stuff, crammed full of features, photographs, screensavers, games, jokes and classified ads. Then take a look at the sections on equipment, free golf software, links to other golf sites and cart loads of discounted golf courses and accommodation. To expect more would be greedy.
e-mail: golf@golfathalfprice.com

Golf.com

www.golf.com
About as comprehensive a golf resource as you'll find, Golf.com has information on every aspect of the golfing world. News, statistics, tournaments, amateur golf, women's golf and even kids golf are all covered in fine detail. Although the site is US based, you'll find plenty of coverage of the European and international game.
e-mail: editor@golf.com

Golf In Europe

www.ecs.net/golf/
On this very extensive site you'll find a list of over 4,000 golf courses and clubs from around Europe. As well as information on clubs, there are listings for golf-related accommodation, publications, businesses and official organisations.
e-mail: infogolf@ecs.net

Golf In Spain

www.golfinspain.com
If playing a leisurely round of golf under the Mediterranean sun is your idea of heaven, then check out Golf In Spain. The list of courses and clubs is extensive, excellently presented with information in great detail and altogether very helpful. You get lots of news and information on Spanish golf.
e-mail: support@golfinspain.com

Golf In Thailand

www.golfinthailand.com
If you get bored of the temples, the beaches and whatever else you might find in Thailand, you could always get in a round of golf. This very basic site has information on the courses, golfing holiday packages and general stuff on Thailand.
e-mail: cookken@usa.net

Golf Links

www.golflinks.co.uk
This UK-based golf resource offers information on courses, clubs, hotels and driving ranges in the UK and Ireland. You can also check lists of golf travel operators, currency rates and travel advice. And if you're more interested in watching than playing, a good selection of information and links for the major tournaments is provided.
e-mail: via online form

Golf Magic

www.golfmagic.co.uk
While you'll find a good range of information and features on the current golf scene, the real power of this UK site is in its very extensive selection of links to golf clubs, associations, courses, course designers, tours, pro sites and retailers to name but a few! Well worth a look.
e-mail: feedback@GOLFmagic.com

Golf Online & iGolf

igolf.golfonline.com
This merger of two good golf sites makes up into an excellent resource on the sport. Features range from player profiles, classified ads, travel information to online games. The history section with a golf timeline and hall of fame is well worth a look.
e-mail: via online form

Golf Review.com

www.golfreview.net
Everything from golf shoes to golf courses come under the spotlight on this site. The reviews written mainly by members of the golfing public are to the point and pull no punches. However, the site is totally US-oriented and according to the authors, every course in the USA is reviewed. Other features include tips and links.
e-mail: george@golfreview.com

Golf South Africa

www.golfingsa.com
Every aspect of South African golf is covered on this generous site.

A course guide, player biographies, tournament news and player standing are set out for easy reference. As a bonus you'll find information on golf resorts, country tours and safaris.
e-mail: via online form

GolfEurope

golfeurope.com
A very extensive guide to European golf including a huge directory of clubs around Europe with reviews by golfers, a concise outline of each country's golf facilities and holiday information. You can also check out player biographies and golf history.
e-mail: not available

Golfing Ireland

www.golfing-ireland.com
With a fine introduction to golf in Ireland, this site gives you the low down on courses, accommodation and forthcoming events. You can book a round at any number of courses and reserve your hotel room and car hire online. A very practical site.
e-mail: via online form

Golfism.net

www.golfism.net
Official site of the sports agents, International Sports Management. They publish news and information on their stable of golfers including Darren Clarke, Lee Westwood and Andrew Coltart. Visually great, the site has golf stories and news and gives you screensavers to download. A number of new features like competitions, auctions, games and shopping are in the process of being added.
e-mail: ism@golfism.net

GolfScotland2000.com

www.golfscotland2000.com
If you're planning a golfing holiday in Scotland, then this is the site for you. Browse the extensive lists of courses and local accommodation and book the whole thing online via the extensive links.
e-mail: info@golfscotland2000.com

Kenya Golf Union

www.kgu.or.ke
Courses and competitions in this beautiful country where you may share a fairway with a wildebeest or two are set out on this simple site. Course information is minimal and no accommodation information is provided.
e-mail: info@kgu.or.ke

Links Of Heaven

www.irishgolf.com
If you're planning a golf trip to Ireland then this US site will tell you everything you need to know. 130 top Irish courses are set out for you with loads of information, travel hints, accommodation, and bags of other golf and holiday

stuff. The site recommends exciting tours and you can even hire a car online.
e-mail: swhitley@myna.com

LPGA.com
www.lpga.com
A feature packed site, LPGA.com covers the women's US golf tour in extensive detail. A very good news service is provided with live scoring during tournaments. Biographies, statistics and a very interesting history of the LPGA make this a very impressive, well-designed site.
e-mail: via online form

Murphy's Irish Open
www.murphysirishopen.ie
Added to the usual news, results and leader board stuff, you get fun features like an interactive 3-D course guide and daily competition video diaries on this very slick site. Ticket information is also provided.
e-mail: feedback@mdimedia.com

Mygolfzone.com
www.golfzone.co.uk
A terrific site, Golfzone is a portal for golf fans into the Web. Full of links, search engines, news and competitions, the site covers the global game excellently.
e-mail: via online form

NedbankGolfChallenge.com
www.milliondollar.co.za
The site of the Sun City Million Dollar tournament has information on the players, the scores, the schedule and the statistics. A nice tour of the Gary Player Country Club course and a selection of press releases complete

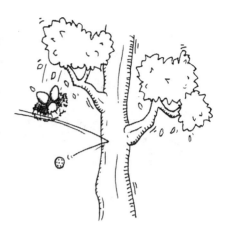

this attractive site.
e-mail: lross@sunint.co.za

New Zealand Open
nzopen.co.nz
This official site of the New Zealand Open covers the event in great detail with news, results and scores all present and correct. A history of the competition, television coverage particulars and a limited course guide complete the site.
e-mail: not available

Pebble Beach
www.pebble-beach.com
An apt site for this world-famous US golf resort. You'll find terrific course tours with fly-by videos and photos to put you in the picture. There are tips, news and statistics on major tournaments held there. The Legend & Lore section is well worth a look as it lovingly recalls the history of Pebble Beach with engrossing anecdotes and lively photographs. Detailed accommodation and booking information is supplied.
e-mail: not available

PGA.com

www.pgaonline.com
On this official site of the US PGA, come news, tournament information, golf history and probably most useful, equipment advice. There is a good industry news section and details of the US PGA itself.
e-mail: via online form

PGA Tour Australia

www.pgatour.com.au
All the news and statistics for the Australia and New Zealand PGA Tour is well-presented. You get the usual material such as player biographies, results and schedules in good measure as well as video and audio clips, a golf quiz and a set of useful links.
e-mail: not available

PGATour.com

www.pgatour.com
The number of features on this excellent site is very impressive. Live scoring, audio and video clips and a very cool virtual tour option which lets you look 360 degrees around some of the USA's best courses, are simply wonderful. News, views and interviews

are also included.
e-mail: comments@mail.pgatour.com

Ryder Cup

www.rydercup.com
Choose from the European or US sections, then find out everything you would want to know about this famous event. The site is full of information on both the latest and future Ryder Cups with schedules, teams, reports, scores and TV coverage. You can also check out video and audio interviews, photographs of the courses and links to other tournaments.
e-mail: not available

ScottishGolf.com

www.scottishgolf.com
A highly impressive site with a good selection of news and features on the sport from the land of its birth, with a bit set aside for the rest of the world. You can check out course guides and travel information and use the online shopping facilities.
e-mail: via online form

Senior Amateur Golf Tour

www.zyworld.com/golftour/ HomePage.htm
This is a basic but useful site dedicated to senior amateurs in the north-west of the UK. Schedules and entry regulations regarding local tournaments are provided as well as results and registration information.
e-mail: Golftour@zyworld.com

St. Andrews Links

www.standrews.org.uk
Find out all you ever wanted to know about the world-famous Scottish golf

course where it all began. In addition to reading a history of the course, you can book a round for yourself via the online service, arrange local accommodation and pick up equipment at the online shop.
e-mail: linkstrust@standrews.org.uk

Swiss Golf Association

www.asg.ch
You'll find a good selection of information on the Swiss golf scene on this simple site. As well as news and information on upcoming tournaments, the site also provides biographies of Swiss players and links to other sites.
e-mail: info@asg.ch

The Belfry

www.thebelfry.com/golf.htm
The famous Belfry golf course forms part of the Devere Belfry leisure centre and hotel. You'll find information on both the hotel and the course on this site. Guides to courses, golf pro services, news on forthcoming tournaments and online shopping take up the rest of the site.
e-mail: enquiries@thebelfry.com

The Golf Channel

www.thegolfchannel.com
A good golf site with an American slant. The online version of the US TV channel is heavy on video and audio feeds, live broadcasts, press conferences, news and golfing tips. The site also has information on the latest tournaments and several good articles.
e-mail: via online form

The Masters

www.themasters.cc
The US major tournament is given the unofficial treatment on this average site. There are leader boards, news, player biographies, a good course guide, photographs and an opportunity to view and purchase golf-related art and books.
e-mail: not available

The Official Site Of The Masters

www.masters.org
This official site of the US Masters provides slick coverage of the golf major. You'll find loads of information on players, schedules and scores, lots of video clips and a virtual course tour.
e-mail: not available

The Old Course

www.theoldcourse.com
Although very detailed and informative, this is an unofficial site for The Old Course at St. Andrews. Material on everything from the history of the game to the major tournaments has been especially well selected. Other features include weather reports and a section on the Dunhill Cup. Details of the course and accommodation available locally are set out for ease of reference.
e-mail: via online form

The Open Championship

www.opengolf.com
First held in 1860, the historic British Open enters the digital age with this slick and informative site. As well as all the usual facts and figures, other interesting features include live scoring and live webcam coverage during the tournament.
e-mail: via online form

The Pinehurst Experience

www.pinehurst.com
As well as being a top class resort, Pinehurst is also one of the most famous golf clubs in the USA, with eight courses to choose from. Information on the courses and other golf facilities is rather limited. There is an online pro-shop, course and accommodation reservation facilities.
e-mail: pinehurst.info@ourclub.com

The Royal Birkdale Golf Club

www.royalbirkdale.com
Simple but informative, the site for this famous links course has photos and a detailed description of each hole, a history of the course and tournament results. Booking information is available, and an online shop is being set up.
e-mail: secretary@royalbirkdale.com

The United States Golf Association

www.usga.org
Loads of information on this site, from the rules of the game and the handicapping system right through to upcoming tournaments. Very comprehensive and informative, it even has a museum of golfing video clips.
e-mail: usga@usga.org

UK-Golf

www.uk-golf.com
Whether you want a round of golf at home or abroad, you should find all the information you need at UK-Golf. Lists of courses and clubs have useful links to more details. Travel and accommodation options come with lists of hotels and car-hire details.
e-mail: via online form

US Amateur Championship

www.usamateur.org
Get a look at the future stars of golf on this official site of the US Amateur Golf Championship. Not quite as slick as the pro tournament sites, it still offers a good standard of information on the players, courses and results.
e-mail: not available

USOpen.com

usopen.lycos.com/home.html
This official site of the US Open is full of information on the course, the players and the history of the competition. Very good articles combine with information on the USPGA, interviews with the players and an online shop.
e-mail: not available

Virtual Golfer

www.golfball.com
The real enjoyment of this quality golf resource is the selection of very well written golfing articles and stories. Now scroll to the golf instruction section for some free lessons, get the tournament news and use the chat room. The new course directory still needs to be completed.
e-mail: not available

Wentworth

www.wentworthclub.com
This golf, tennis and fitness resort is best known for playing host to major golf tournaments like the World Match-Play and PGA championships. The site gives particulars of the courses, tournaments, an absorbing history of the famous club and some more to keep you online a while.
e-mail: via online form

World Golf

www.worldgolf.com
As well as news and articles from the world of golf, you'll find information from major tournaments, a guide to golfing holidays and a very useful listings section with information on a huge range of golf courses world wide.
e-mail: advertising@worldgolf.com

World Golf Championships

www.worldgolfchampionships.com
The site for this relatively new tournament and ranking system has news and information on the current standing and performance of the players. Though slick and well put together, the features on the site are rather limited.
e-mail: not available

The Players

John Daly

www.gripitandripit.com
Fans of the controversial US star will enjoy this user-friendly and comprehensive official site. Crammed full of features, video clips, golf tips and an online shop, the fun site also offers a chatroom and your chance to e-mail the big man a question.
e-mail: via online form

Laura

www.lauradavies.co.uk
Simple and informative official Laura Davies site packed with the career history of the British star. Fine articles from Women & Golf magazine, competitions to enter and an online shop take up the remaining pages.
e-mail: via online form

Nicklaus.com

www.nicklaus.com
The site run by the Great Bear himself, mixes facts and figures, photos and memories of a great career in golf with news and information on his course design and equipment companies as well as affiliated courses. Great to look at with loads of photos and graphics, the site is a fitting tribute to an all-time great.
e-mail: via online form

Phil Mickelson

www.phil-mickelson.com
This is a very well-designed user-friendly site that gives you a good range of facts and figures about this consistent US golfer. It also lets you e-mail Phil questions which he answers himself and fans are given the opportunity to have their articles posted.
e-mail: gaylordsports@attglobal.net.

Raymond Floyd

www.rayfloyd.com
Dodge your way past the cigar humidors, golf umbrellas and magnet therapy sets for sale and you'll find an average site with a relatively good range of information on the veteran player. Golf tips are also included.
e-mail: service@rayfloyd.com

Sergio Garcia

www.geocities.com/Augusta/Fairway/5494/index.html

A well put together fan site for the exciting young Spaniard is badly let down by a lack of current news. Just the same you will still find a brief biography, ranking, results and many good photographs.

e-mail: candy@netrover.com

Shark.com

www.shark.com

As much concerned with Greg Norman's myriad corporate interests as with his golf career, you'll still find plenty of features on the Great White Shark himself, with news, reports, facts and figures. Other features include golf instruction and an archive of Norman's career.

e-mail: via online form

The Fred Couples Homepage

www.earthgolf.com/fred

A top site for a top golfer. Slick, easy-to-use and full of information on the popular US star. News, statistics and an elegant picture gallery are all included with space left over for Freddie's fans to discuss their hero in the chat room and on the message board.

e-mail: fredhomepage@earthgolf.com

The Lee Westwood Official Fan Club

www.lee-westwood.co.uk

Keep up-to-date with the comings and goings of one of Europe's top players on this very ordinary official fan-site, run by Lee Westwood himself, along with his family. Features include news, photos and statistics of the man himself. Listen out for a hideous muzak version of 'Baker Street' in the background.

e-mail: fanclub@westyuk.com

The Master - Nick Faldo

w1.318.telia.com/~u31803624/N.Faldo.html

What this fan-site lacks in presentation it makes up for in detail. You'll find information and statistics on practically every golf ball Nick Faldo has hit in his

illustrious career. How much prize money he has earned, what his ranking was, what tournaments he won and how he won them. It's all on board with his very own autograph!
e-mail: marika.hallen@ molndal.mail.telia.com

The Official Ben Crenshaw Website

www.bencrenshaw.com
Slick and well-presented site, full of information on the veteran player, with a biography, news, golf tips and the inevitable merchandising.
e-mail: sayers@bencrenshaw.com

The Official Ernie Els Website

www.ernieels.com
Dedicated to the South African golfing superstar, the site has his biography, ranking and photographs of the man himself. Somewhat disappointingly, most of the information comes via links to other sites.
e-mail: not available

The Officially Unofficial Davis Love/David Duval Site

mdc.alphalink.com.au
You get two for the price of one on this informative fan site. Choose either Davis Love III or David Duval and then check out the biographies, statistics, results and photographs of these top golfers. Not the slickest of sites, it still rates a visit for fans of either player.
e-mail: mdc@alphalink.com.au

The World Of Gary Player

www.garyplayer.com
The Black Knight's official site is a top quality mix of his career and commercial interests. The entertaining gallery of photographs going all the way back to the 1950's is well worth a look for fans.
e-mail: info@garyplayer.com

Tiger Woods

www.tigerwoods.com
Everything you ever wanted to know about golf's Golden Boy. Tiger's history, Tiger's golf stats, where Tiger's playing next, excerpts from Tiger books, Tiger videos, Tiger's shop and Tiger's foundation. Of course if you don't like Tiger then forget it.
e-mail: not available

Tiger's Den

www.geocities.com/Colosseum/Track/ 6331/index.html
Full of nice features, this unofficial web site has photographs, audio and video clips and screen savers of the golf superstar. All the usual information is backed by a chatroom for Tiger fans to talk Tiger.
e-mail: not available

Horses & Dogs

General Racing Sites

About – Horse Racing

horse racing.about.com/sports/
horse racing/msub52.htm
The last word in horse racing sites
heaped full with everything on the
subject. Racetracks, famous racehorses,
stories about trainers and jockeys, a
database on past performance and that
only scratches the surface. It also has
a very good casino guide around the
world, that is to say, around the world.
e-mail: Horse racing.guide@about.com

Alabama's Premier Training Facility

www.dbarkranch.com/racing.html
Success comes naturally when you have
the ability, equipment and facilities to
train as you race. D Bar K Ranch offers
world class facilities including spacious
stalls, five-eighths mile training track,
six horse walker and more. On its web
pages, you will also find information

such as horses and trailers for sale.
e-mail: Sales@dbarkranch.com

American Greyhound Track Operators Association

www.agtoa.com
Non-profit corporation of owners and
operators of 29 greyhound tracks located all over the USA. You will find a
great deal of information about the
sixth largest spectator sports in the
USA – the dogs, the tracks, history of
the sport, racing terms and newsletters.
e-mail: agtoa@agtoa.com

Arabian Jockey Club

www.arabianracing.org
The Arabian Jockey Club is a national
organisation dedicated to the promotion
and professional management of the
Arabian racing industry in the USA.
Their site sets out rules, regulations and
racing terms and an events calendar
tells you everything about their race
meetings. You will also find the rising

fortunes of Arabian racehorses in
important races around the USA.
e-mail: ajc@arabianracing.org

Arcade Horse Racing

users.skynet.be/zorox/ahr.htm
The first and best horse racing game
on the Internet. If you like what you see
on the screen shots pages, you can
download them or order using the
online form.
e-mail: via online form

Association of Racing Commissioners International

www.arci.com
This Kentucky horse racing association
aims to promote a national license
system for interstate horse racing
owners. At present, it gives a list of
the most updated rulings in relation to
horse racing. Additional information
for the rulings is available for members
only. Check out online how to become
a member.
e-mail: ewaters@arci.com

AusRace

ausrace.com
Comprehensive guide to horse racing
in Australia. It has an Australia Racing
Directory and Archives. It gives tips,
tricks and techniques to bet on the races.
It also has a chat room for you to
exchange information. If you subscribe
online, all the information will be sent
direct to your e-mail address.
e-mail: admin@ausrace.com

Barbados Turf Club

www.barbadosturfclub.com/home.html
The Barbados Turf Club is the governing
body for thoroughbred racing at the

Garrison Savannah racetrack. There
are three racing seasons each year.
Stories about jockeys, horses, trainers
and racing news abound. The photo
gallery is excellent.
e-mail: dhughes@barbadosturfclub.com

Betabuck.com

betabuck.com/horseracing.htm
This sports site provides super links for
horse racing, race-tracks, odds, races
and events. Simply click on the links
on the web pages and you will find
every exciting moment in American
Horse racing updated.
e-mail: via online form

betWest

www.betwest.com.au
Premium ratings, prices, form, markets,
tips, selections and information on
Western Australian thoroughbred horse
racing for punters large or small,
bookmakers and breeders. There are
very good links to other racing sites in
Australia. To enjoy their complete services
on horse racing in Australia, join up.
e-mail: support@betwest.com.au

Bill Straus

www.horseimages.com
A Kentucky photographer has made a
career out of capturing stunning shots
of horse racing, horse farms and
thoroughbred racing. To marvel at the
pictures, click on the subjects at the
bottom of the page. The pictures are
for sale; just fax through your order.
e-mail: Info@horseimages.com

Birmingham Racing Commission

www.mindspring.com/~brc/
The Commission is a public corporation

authorised to license and regulate thoroughbred and greyhound racing and pari-mutuel wagering in Birmingham, Alabama, USA. Online, you will find rules and racing information and a bunch of good links to other US racing-related sites.
e-mail: brc@mindspring.com

BRISnet.com

www.bris.com
This is the Internet's largest US horse racing information service. It offers free a daily handicapping newsletter and thoroughbred industry journal. Other freebies include a live tote with real-time odds and instant race results. Members have access to a vast array of low cost products for punters and horsemen.
e-mail: Brisinfo@brisnet.com

California Tracker - Bet2win Horse Racing

www.bm-dist.com
This site provides handicapping, horse racing results and horse racing discussion at hottakler. It offers Free Trial, California Tracker, horse racing tips. On its web pages, you can also find links to other horse racing sites and betting sites.
e-mail: awinner@webcom.com

Complete Guide to Horse Racing

www.equineinfo.com/horseracing.htm
On this site you get information and links to every racetrack in the USA, racing association and publication, breeding, buying, selling or leasing a horse, handicapping, pedigree research and training. To search on the site, click on the home page topics.
e-mail: info@equineinfo.com.

Daily Racing Form

www.drf2000.com
America's Turf Authority since 1894. For more than a century, this publication has provided handicappers and racing fans with the most comprehensive racing news available. Races, trainers and jockeys are covered in the reports and there are racing links and track information for the whole country.
e-mail: cservcie@drf.com

Direct Racing Horse Racing services

www.horseracing-uk.fsnet.co.uk
Premier online horse racing and tipping service. To benefit from the services you must sign up online. Then you receive free daily racing tips, details of trainers, courses, bets and much more. Racing tips are constantly updated.
e-mail: General@directracing.com

Encyclopedia.com

www.encyclopedia.com/articles/06062.html
This electronic library provides a brief introduction to horse racing and a collection of articles on related topics. There are historic pictures and maps for racing and racecourses. Excellent site for boning up on the subject.
e-mail: via online form

Epsom Downs Racecourse

www.epsomderby.co.uk
Updates on two of the best known race meetings in the UK -the Derby and the Oaks. The Derby is probably the greatest and most famous flat race run anywhere in the world and with prize money totalling £1million it attracts the very best horses. The Oaks Day benefits from the addition of the Vodafone

Coronation Cup which encourages racing of the highest order and makes these two days of racing at Epsom in June the most exciting in the year's calendar. If you want to be there, buy your ticket online.
e-mail: epsom@rht.net

European-Horseracing

www.egroups.com/group/european-horseracing/
They offer a convenient way to connect with others who share the same interests. On the web pages you get to discuss anything relating to horse racing on the flat in Europe, big-race results, assessments of the top horses, trainers, jockeys, racing administration and running and whatever you want to get off your chest.
e-mail: suggestion@egroups.com

Famous Racehorses

www-users.york.ac.uk/~sjp22/
A terrific site dedicated to the great equine champions of both the flat and national hunt. Famous Racehorses provides race statistics, histories and photographs of a huge selection of legendary horses. The site also features excellent articles, a good range of links and even John McCririck! Excellently presented and a joy to use. The site is a must for any fan.
e-mail: steve_parrott_1@email.com

Fast Track Simulcapping

www.simulcapper.com/lastndx.htm
While you sleep, tipsters for major tracks in the California and New York circuits are working to provide you with a list of contenders and speed ratings that will jump-start your handicapping.

Information is posted by 0700 on race days.
e-mail: simulcapper@hotmail.com

Federation Of Horseracing Authorities

www.horseracingintfed.com
This federation was founded jointly by the racing authorities of the USA, France, the UK and Ireland. The aim is to protect the integrity of horse racing and select the best horses to improve breeding standards. You will find information about the authorities, lists of races open to thoroughbreds of any country with and without restrictions. This is an informative site and well worth a visit.
e-mail: ifha@compuserve.com

Florida Thoroughbred Farm Managers

www.flfarmmanagers.com
Directory of Florida thoroughbred farm managers. Information covers thoroughbreds, equine farms, equine identifiers, bloodstock, transportation and auctions. Use the online chat room to talk personally with members who will happily answer your questions.
e-mail: via online form

Foundation Horseman

www.foundationhorseman.com/racing_us.html
This site provides links to thoroughbred horse farms in Canada and the USA. You will also find horses for sale and a stallion directory. The search engines are user-friendly and a few clicks will bring up all the advertisements on the site.
e-mail: rc@foundationhorseman.com

French Horse Racing On Line

www.frol.com

The French are passionate about everything they do and this site makes the point. You will find a whole lot of information on the horse racing scene in France, including today's news and tomorrow's previews, current and past performance results, breeding, statistics and a racing calendar. The real bonus is that you can read it all in English.
email: editor@frol.com

Gambling Link Portal

www.ibetz.com/horserace.htm

Links on this site take you to horse racing directories in North America. Other information includes sports and gambling books, games, casinos and shopping links. A good site to bookmark.
e-mail: Horseracing@ibetz.com

HayNet: Horse Racing

www.haynet.net/Horse_Racing/

Literally hundreds of Internet links to sites related to horse racing, which include blood stock agencies, sales, races, stables and trainers, governing bodies, steeple-chasing, courses, racing software, general information and news. Not to get lost among the links, use the search engine.
e-mail: webmaster@haynet.net

Horse Click

gallop.cc

Database and information centre about horses and races. The home page sets out the topics - world rider ranking, stables, show jumping, racing, horse painting, care and health and just horses. The site is well worth a visit for the sheer bulk of data.
e-mail: stefan@welebny.com

Horse Racing - Suite101.com

www.suite101.com/welcome.cfm/horse_racing

Whether you wager or not, the stories about thoroughbreds, jockeys, trainers, races and the tracks in the USA make for enjoyable reading.
e-mail: Ricco@herald.infi.net

Horsesales, Inc

www.horsesales.com/chaplaincy/index.htm

Internet market site for race and sports horses. Advertising online uses photos and videos on demand. There is a guide to trading in retired racehorses.
e-mail: amys@horesales.com

Horsesites.com

www.horsesites.com

User-friendly site packed with news, race results and sales of racehorses. To search, click on the titles or use the search engine. You can bet online. If you know of links to thoroughbred sites not yet on the site let them know through the online form.
e-mail: via online form

Iowa Quarter Horse Racing Association

www.iqhra.com

Quarter Horse racing originated in North America shortly after the founding of Jamestown in 1607. It is now the largest horse registry in the world. The Association is a non-profit organisation and sponsors a variety of programs to complement all aspects of the Quarter Horse racing industry in Iowa and provides information about breeders, sales and races.
e-mail: not available

Irish Racing

www.irish-racing.com
All the fervour of the Irish love of
horses and racing almost live on this
site. It covers all the race meetings of
the year with a wealth of web pages for
jockeys, trainers, race results, reviews
and statistics. There is a betting page
and a most interesting Whisper page
that puts out information about the
condition of the horses each season.
e-mail: racing@irish-times.com

Jack's Melbourne Racing Tips

**people.enternet.com.au/~philippe/
jack.htm**
Jack gives you all the hot tips for the
Melbourne and Sydney race meetings.
He analyses all the important races in
these two Australian cities and, from
time to time, tips winners in races at
other venues. On the web pages, you
will find links to racing tracks and clubs
all over the country. Jack also warns you
to bet only what you can afford to lose!
e-mail: philippe@enternet.com.au

Jocks and Jockeys

www.jocksandjockeys.com
Racing cards are picked each week for
the Saturday and Sunday meets. Tracks
vary depending upon which are open
and where the best picks can be found.
Analyses of races are focused on these
courses which can be anywhere in the
USA.
e-mail: Photofinish@jocksand
jockeys.com.

Jordan's Horse Farm

**www.bcpl.lib.md.us/~wjordan/
horsehome.htm**
Jordan's Horse Farm is located in

Williamstown New Jersey, USA. It
offers horse stabling and thoroughbred
training facilities. On its web pages,
you will find pictures of horses in the
farm.
e-mail: jordanmc@erols.com

Louisianaracing.com

www.louisianaracing.com
Very specialised information on
thoroughbred racetracks in Louisiana -
New Orleans Fair Grounds, Evangeline
Downs and Louisiana Downs. The
information package includes horse
racing analyses, free selections and
tips. Despite its plain design, it offers
interesting links to thoroughbred sites
and Southern California Sports Books.
e-mail: laracing@eatel.net

Mr. Horse

www.mrhorse.it
This is the world equestrian site with
text in English, French, German, Italian,
Spanish and Portuguese. Topics like
the rainbow horse-show, veterinarian
matters, laws and horses are amply

covered. Then there is horse racing in Italy, an English chat room and links to other topics and sites.
e-mail: not available

National Museum of Racing and Hall of Fame Online

www.racingmuseum.org
This US site unfolds the history of thoroughbred racing in America. Links take you to the past, from the earliest days of the sport to almost yesterday. There are historical photographs of memorable moments.
e-mail: webmaster@racingmuseum.org

New Zealand Thoroughbred Breeders' Association

www.nzthoroughbred.co.nz
Breeding, buying and racing thoroughbreds in New Zealand. This official site is packed with information on studs, stallions, equine health, news, views and articles on the subject of horses.
e-mail: susan@nzthoroughbred.co.nz

North American Pari-Mutuel Regulators Association

www.napraonline.com
This form of betting divides the losers' stake among those who back the first three places. The association promotes the industry and safeguards its integrity in North America. Owners, trainers and jockeys can apply for licenses online and you get to learn the rules, read press releases and follow links to other horse racing sites.
e-mail: leda@mindspring.com

One Stop Tip Sheet Shop!

www.tipshop.com
It does what it says on the label – gives you the convenience of a one-stop source for horse racing tip sheets. You can buy these for a selection of tracks. There is a page of links to practically every racetrack in North America.
e-mail: Info@tipshop.com

Premier-info

www.premier-info.com
They claim to be the Europe's leading racing advisory and information service on UK racing. The information package includes tips, racing links, news and betting. Ashley Carr, the leading light of the site, promises to provide a most informative online resource and give users the ability to beat the bookmakers and profit from betting.
e-mail: via online form

Race Base

www.racebase.co.nz
Complete statistical analysis of New Zealand horse racing. For $60 you can get computer software containing NZ race results since 1992, histories of over 20,000 horses, all NZ sires and dams for the past 4 years. The program also includes the complete histories of all their progeny, horse ratings, jockey career histories, time ratings and barrier draw statistics. They promise a one-month data update. Cheap at the price if you need it.
e-mail: racebase-subscribe@egroups.com

Race-hourses.com

www.race-horses.com
Racing clubs, trainers, horses for sale and links to other horseracing information and betting sites. To search, click on the topics.
e-mail: not available

Racenews

www.racenews.co.uk

Free news service provided twice daily on all aspects of British and International thoroughbred horse racing. The Value Betting Column has a comprehensive guide to the biggest betting. Online links take you touring around all the UK racecourses and international racing events.

e-mail: racenews@compuserve.com

Racing Channel On Line

www.racingchannel.com

Real-time racing information under 5 headings – thoroughbred tracks, harness tracks, greyhound tracks, all tracks and frames version. Daily entries, odds, results and other horse racing-related subjects in the USA are faithfully included on this site.

e-mail: Webmaster@racingchannel.com

Racing Legends Commemorative

www.racinglegends.com

One of the most exciting collections of horse racing memorabilia in the world. You can browse fascinating artefacts, purchase individually autographed items and gifts and learn about the sport of kings at your leisure. Links to other horse related sites take you to the jockey club, museum, race tracks and stables.

e-mail: Rlsales@racinglegends.com

Racing Pages

www.racingpages.com.au

They tell you almost everything you need to know about racing. There are links to UK racecourses, tips for choosing horses and jockeys, links to online betting sites and an online bookstore for horse racing publications. And it's all as easy as it sounds, a few clicks on the keyboard get you right where the action is.

e-mail: talktous@racylacy.com

Racing Pages

www.racingpages.com.au

Complete guide to Australian horse racing and thoroughbred studs. Sydney Selections, blood stock agents, live broadcasts, fields and riders add to general news items and photo pages. All information is also in Japanese.

e-mail: via online form

Racing –systems.co.uk

www.racing-systems.co.uk

Who are the true horse racing professionals? Are they all con men? How do I find out which services are genuine? Who provides the best services? What are the techniques of the professional gambler? How do I place my bets on horse racing? If you want the answers to any of these questions, visit this site. This online magazine will not only answer them but also provide a comprehensive racing system for the UK.

e-mail: Subscribe@racing-systems.co.uk

Racing-Chronicle

www.racing-chronicle.co.uk

All the excitement of races online on this best of UK horse racing sites. Click on the pictures on the home page and you can browse the hall of fame, race morning images and the latest racing clips. There is a very good link page for access to UK and international racecourses and horse racing web sites. If your modem is slow, update it to thoroughly enjoy this site.

e-mail: editor@racing-chronicle.co.uk

Richard P. Hazelton Inc

www.richardhazelton.com
Richard P. Hazelton is one of few trainers
who have saddled over 400 winners.
On this site, you will find all the records
of winning races and training information.
For local and National Thoroughbred
News, go to the Chicago Thoroughbred
Survey page. If you would like your
horse considered by the experienced
trainer, just give him a call or email him.
e-mail: Stock2no@ix.netcom.com

Saddleright.com

www.saddleright.com/links2.html
This is a directory of horse racing
associations and racetracks in the USA.
It is part of a shopping site offering
orthopaedic competition saddle pads.
You will find a good collection of links
to take you to horse competition sites
all over the USA. This is a one-stop shop
for anyone interested in US horseracing.
e-mail: saddle@webcom.com

SB0765

**www.senate.state.mo.us/98bills/bills/
SB765.htm**
Useful site for those interested in
pari-mutuel betting. Online you will
find the full text and a summary of
current Missouri State Bill SB765.
This bill authorises the regulation of
off-track pari-mutuel wagering in the
State. The debates in the Legislature
and a list of other 1998 bills of the
State are on the home page.
e-mail: senadmin@services.state.mo.us

Sports-Day.com

**www.sports-days.com/members/
index.html**
Leading UK Internet racehorse owners

club. Race reviews, free tips, competitions
and horses to follow are set out on the
home page. The Shadowfax stable page
brings you news, stories and articles on
jockeys and trainers.
e-mail: info@sports-days.com

The British Horse Racing Board

www.bhb.co.uk
Governing Authority for horseracing in
Great Britain. This official site has a
trainers' directory, racecourses and
racing calendars for the whole of the
UK. The latest news includes articles
on policy matters and the site as a
whole gives a complete picture of
British horseracing in the 20th Century.
e-mail: info@bhb.co.uk

The History of Horse Racing

www.mrmike.com/explore/hrhist.htm
Competitive racing of horses is one of
man's most ancient sports. You can
discover the history of this sport in less
than an hour. The site gives a brief
summary of thoroughbred racing,

breeding, betting, handicapping, harness Racing, the steeplechase and more. All the content is in plain text; a few pictures would upgrade this site from good to very good.
e-mail: not available

The Hong Kong Jockey Club

www.hkjockeyclub.com/hkjc/english/
Harking back to the days of Empire horseracing stands as a solid and profitable institution in Hong Kong. The two racecourses - one in Shatin on the Kowloon Peninsula the other in Happy Valley on Hong Kong Island – run weekend meetings from October to June each year. The web pages detail all race days, international competitions and online betting services. You can peek into the Hong Kong Racing Museum online.
e-mail: bs_hotline02@hkjc.org.hk

The Jockey Club

Home.jockeyclub.com
Get to know what you want to know about thoroughbreds in the USA - physical description, industry and breeding statistics, registration, fee schedule, rules and requirements. There is an online name book with recently released names and the FAQ may just answer the question that has been bugging you for days.
e-mail: via online form

The National Horse Racing Museum

www.nhrm.co.uk
The history of racing from its royal origins to the present day is beautifully put on display. The Museum is peopled by legends of the past and modern heroes like Lester Piggott and Frankie

Dettori and pride of place is no less accorded to the greatest horses that ran on the flat and jumped the fences. A site worth visiting when the racing season is over or between meetings.
e-mail: not available

The Racecourse Association

www.comeracing.co.uk
59 racecourses in Britain are members of this association. The web site has a directory to all 59, a guide to major races and reviews to each month's events. Another guide deals with special races and yet another helps beginners find their way around the sport. In fact you are likely to find anything you want to know about British racing.
e-mail: info@rcarcl.co.uk

The Racing Pages

www.theracingpages.freeserve.co.uk
The web site has pages of UK horse racing and especially the National Hunt. You will find the Welsh National, Grand National, news about racing horses and racing links online. Racing news brings you up to date with the latest events on the turf.
e-mail: davenurse@bigfoot.com

The Track Traveller

www.tracktraveler.com
The site does not have much to offer in itself but there are some very good horse racing sites such as Philadelphia Park racetrack and Wang's Thoroughbred Horse Racing, well worth a visit.
e-mail: InfoReqyest@tracktraveler.com

thehorsesmouth.co.uk

www.thehorsesmouth.co.uk
The ultimate online horseracing experience. The site covers all the important races in the UK, gives advice online and reports chat from trainers about their runners up and down the country with a liberal selection of betting tips. Even if you know nothing about horseracing you will be a lot wiser after visiting this site.
e-mail: feedback@thehorsesmouth.co.uk

Thoroughbred Champions

www.thoroughbredchampions.com
A gallery of greats, a research library and a racing round table make this an interesting US site not least because of the truly beautiful photographs.
e-mail: Editor@thoroughbred. champions.com

Thoroughbred Horse Racing

Wang.pimpin.net/horse.html
Thoroughbred racing in the USA with a flourish. If you do not find what you are looking for try the many links, enough to satisfy any handicapper.
e-mail: via online form

Vinery Kentucky

www.vinerykentucky.com
Premier thoroughbred breeding location in Australia with one of the world's finest rosters of stallions. News on champions, promotions and current stocks is well set out. If you happen to be going their way contact them by e-mail and they will be delighted to receive you.
e-mail: info@vinery.net

Winner Online

www.winneronline.com/horses/ horses.htm
This great web site brings you links to all the best horseracing resources on the Net in a gigantic database!
In addition it carries daily news and information about races and a good selection of audio-visual broadcasts from major US racetracks. If you know a site that should be added to these pages, get in touch.
e-mail: chuck@winneronline.com

www.Ausracing.net.au

www.ausracing.net.au/frontpag.htm
Horse racing and breeding around the world. Articles, news and a great deal of information world wide can be sourced online.
e-mail: jsingh@ausracing.net.au

Courses, Races and Clubs

Aintree

www.aintree.co.uk
The home of the annual Grand National, probably the most spectacular race in the calendar. The web site has excellent photographs with as much glamour as the event and a good deal of information about the competition and all the latest results.
e-mail: aintree@rht.net

Aqueduct

www.nyra.com/aqueduct/index2.html
e-mail: not available

Assiniboia Downs Racetrack

www.assiniboiadowns.com
e-mail: info@assiniboiadowns.com

Balmoral Park

www.balmoralpark.com
e-mail: info@balmoralpark.com

Bangordee Racecourse

www.bangordee.co.uk
Bangor-on-Dee in glorious countryside beside the River Dee in Wrexham, hosts National Hunt racing throughout the year. This perfect country course and its friendly atmosphere teem with all the excitement of the turf. Newcomers to the racetrack will find this site particularly attractive. There are advance booking services online.
e-mail: racing@bangordee. sagehost.co.uk

Bay Meadows Racecourse

www.baymeadows.com
e-mail: help@baymeadows.com

Belmont

www.nyra.com/belmont/index2.html
e-mail: via online form

Brighton Racecourse

www.brighton-racecourse.co.uk
They race from April to October. The online information centre gives you all the news, reports on race meetings, shows off the course facilities and services and has guides to the racecourse and its history that make for enjoyable reading. You can book tickets online.
e-mail: info@brighton-racecourse.co.uk

Carlisle Racecourse

www.carlisle-races.co.uk
Situated at Blackwell on the outskirts of the historic border city of Carlisle, this racecourse hosts quality racing every month of the year staging eleven national hunt meetings from September to April and nine flat meetings between April and August. On its site, you will find all the information. Online booking is available.
e-mail: info@carlisle-races.co.uk

Caymanas Track Limited

www.caymanastrack.com
They promote horse racing in Caymanas Park in Jamaica. Race meetings are held on Saturdays, most Wednesdays and all public holidays except Christmas Day and Good Friday. The web site has information on the top horses, jockeys and trainers, a few racing features and lots of statistics.
e-mail: racing@cwjamaica.com

Cheltenham

www.cheltenham.co.uk
This is the home of National Hunt
Racing in the UK. The web site has the
calendar of meetings, all the latest
news and views and a Hall of Fame to
enshrine past glories. There are
telephone contacts to help you book
accommodation and tickets.
e-mail: cheltenham@rht.net

Chepstow Racecourse

www.chepstow-racecourse.co.uk
Premier racecourse and home of the
famous Welsh National. Set in the
grounds of historic Piercefield Park, the
club is surrounded by outstanding
natural beauty between the Severn and
Wye rivers. The racing page has the
schedule of flat and jump races from
March to December.
e-mail: enquiries@chepstow-
racecourse.co.uk

Chester Racing Company

www.chester-races.co.uk
The racecourse hosts the Chester Cup
every year. The web site blends the
excitement of the track with ancient
Roman history. The city was the site
of a major Roman camp in the first
century. This enjoyable site does not
restrict itself to the flat races; there is a
lot more you may find interesting.
An online booking service helps you
with arrangements.
e-mail: not available

Churchill Downs

www.kentuckyderby.com
e-mail: not available

Dairyland Greyhound Park

www.dairylandgreyhoundpark.com
e-mail: dgpsimul@execpc.com

Del Mar Thoroughbred Club

www.dmtc.com
e-mail: marys@dmtc.com

Doncaster Racecourse

www.britishracing.com
Doncaster is where tradition meets
excellence. In September it hosts
the world's oldest and fifth and final
Classic of the British flat-racing season.
Other well-known events include the
4-day St Leger Festival and the winter
season features the Great Yorkshire
Steeplechase in January.
Transportation and hospitality
arrangements are nicely set out.
e-mail: info@british-racing.com

Down Royal Racecourse

www.downroyal.com
Home of Ulster Harp Derby. The web

site features the racing festivals, scrolls all the results, parcels out the news on and off-course and outlines the history of this well-known Irish racetrack. There is a ticket-booking service online.
e-mail: info@downroyal.com

Finger Lakes Race Track Home Page
www.fingerlakesracetrack.com
e-mail: kolomic@prodigy.net

Florida Turf
floridaturf.com
e-mail: inquire@floridaturf.com

Fontwell Park Steeplechase
www.fontwellpark.co.uk
Racing season in Fontwell Park is short, from August to December each year. Conveniently situated on the A27, you get clear information on how to get there, ticket prices, hospitality and special events.
e-mail: brooke@fontwellpark.co.uk

Go Racing In Yorkshire
www.goracing.co.uk
Consortium of nine racecourses, which together provide some of the best race meetings in the UK – high quality racing throughout the year, delightful surroundings with facilities and events to cater for all ages. The site has an events bulletin and sells season tickets online. The press column tells you a lot about the racecourses.
e-mail: enquiries@redcarracing.co.uk

Gulfstream Park
www.gulfstreampark.com
e-mail: vdoherty@Gulfstreampark.com

Hawthorne Race Course
www.hawthorneracecourse.com
e-mail: davezenner@worldnet.att.net

Haydock Park Racecourse
www.haydock-park.com
This racecourse, nicely within a rural setting but convenient for the major cities of the North West like Manchester and Liverpool, as well as the Midlands. With its user-friendly page design, you can quickly find information on race days, hospitality, bookings, weather and upcoming events.
e-mail: info@haydock-park.com

Hollywood Park
www.hollywoodpark.com
e-mail: via online form

Huntingdon Racecourse
www.huntingdonracing.co.uk
Easily accessible from the north, south, east and west via road and rail links, Huntingdon Racecourse sits in the Cambridgeshire countryside just outside the town. Competitive racing is offered throughout the year.
e-mail: huntingdon@rht.net

Kelso Races
www.kelso-races.co.uk
Situated in the Scottish Borders, Kelso is set on the confluence of the rivers Teviot and Tweed. As the home of Scottish Borders horse racing, Klso hosts various races throughout the year. On the web site, you will find the information on events and hospitality, a news page and online ticket sales and betting service. You can pay by cheque or credit card.
e-mail: kelso@cqm.co.uk

Kempton Park

www.kempton.co.uk
London's own racecourse situated in beautiful Kempton Park. The whole area is landscaped with a new grandstand, which includes the Premier and Paddock enclosures and the Jubilee Club. Its outstanding facilities for race goers make it equal to any racecourse in the country. The news section has all the latest on race fixtures and results. As a member you can enjoy the glamour and glitter of the popular race evenings during the summer including the regular Gala Night and Irish Night.
e-mail: kempton@rht.net

Lingfield

www.arena-online.com/lingfieldpark
Here you have racing all year around. It is located near East Grinstead on the borders of Kent, Surrey and Sussex and is only 20 minutes from Gatwick Airport. London is a one-hour drive away or just 50 minutes train journey from Victoria. Go to its fixtures page for race meetings from January to December.
e-mail: info@lingfieldpark.co.uk

Lone Star Park at Grand Prairie

www.lonestarpark.com
e-mail: via online form

Ludlow

www.ludlow-racecourse.co.uk
The Racecourse is situated one and a half miles North of Ludlow, and half a mile East of the A49. With horserace meetings all year around and one of friendliest club in the UK. Races, admission prices and transportation are fully detailed. If you are interested

in the history of Ludlow Castle, check out this section online.
e-mail: br-davies@lineone.net

Market Rasen Racecourse

www.marketrasenraces.co.uk
Located in a beautiful rural setting in the heart of the Lincolnshire countryside the racecourse offers good competitive racing virtually every month of the year. More than half the meetings are at weekends. Renowned for its friendly atmosphere, it caters to all sections of the population.
e-mail: marketrasen@rhtnet

Mussellburgh

www.musselburgh-racecourse.co.uk
This Scottish racecourse, originally known as the Edinburgh Races, has hosted horseracing since 1816. There are 22 race days in the year, including Flat Racing and National Hunt meetings. You can make reservations online.
e-mail: info@musselburgh-racecourse.co.uk

Newbury Racecourse

www.newbury-racecourse.co.uk
This beautifully designed web site gives you a friendly information pack including current racing events, stable yard, leisure lounge, library and an online box office. It hosts races all year round.
e-mail: info@newbury-racecourse.co.uk

Newmarket Racecourses

www.newmarketracecourses.co.uk
Newmarket, North east of London, runs races of the highest order, including two of the five UK Classics,

the 1000 and 2000 Guineas in May and one of the richest race days, Champions' Day in October. June, July and August have the best events. Check out the race bulletin and the many special offers for online booking.
e-mail: not available

Newton Abbot Racecourse

www.naracecourse.co.uk
Newton Abbot in the heart of South West England with excellent communication links is home to horse and greyhound racing. The 21 days of competitive jump racing pays out huge prize money. The Sunday meetings have been a family favourite since the 1950s.
e-mail: enquiries@naracecourse.co.uk

Nottingham Racecourse

www.nottinghamracecourse.co.uk
With over 100 years of history, this racecourse offers all the enjoyment of 20 days at the races from March through to October. The web site shows you the full range of facilities available at the course, the Centenary Stand and the Grandstand, the bars and restaurants.
e-mail: nottingham@rht.net

Ocean Downs

www.oceandowns.com
e-mail: info@oceandowns.com

Plumpton

www.plumptonracecourse.co.uk
Hosting horse racing for over 200 years, this racecourse nestles below the South Downs close to the old Sussex town of Lewes. Close to the rails, this modern stand now offers the oldest steeplechasing course in Sussex.

On its web page, you will find information of races, hospitality and latest news. A great day out from London or Brighton.
e-mail: plumptonracecourse@ dial.pipex.com

Pontefract

www.pontefract-races.co.uk
Pontefract is one of the best appointed courses of its kind in the Country for an exciting racing experience. Information includes yearly fixtures and transportation directions.
e-mail: pontefract-races@ic24.net

Prescott Downs Race Track!

www.amdest.com/az/Prescott/pd/ prescottdowns.html
e-mail: not available

Remington Park

www.remingtonpark.com
e-mail: rp-mis@remingtonpark.com

Royal Windsor Racecourse

www.windsorracing.co.uk
Picturesque racecourse on the banks of the Thames with races from March to November, mostly in the evening. Admission is free to under 17s and the wheelchair-bound. Aside from the races you get the low-down on tourist attractions in Windsor.
e-mail: office@windsorracing.co.uk

Salisbury Racecourse

www.salisburyracecourse.co.uk
Salisbury is the home of the Bibury Club, the oldest racing club in England. Racing started there in the sixteenth century and today it hosts a number of valuable races throughout the season.

Forthcoming events and other entertainments are listed.
e-mail: biburyclub@ salisburyracecourse.fsnet.co.uk

Sandown

www.sandown.co.uk
Compared with some old British racecourses, this eight year old race course has won itself a lot of praise for high class facilities and services. With racing staged all year round, you can enjoy both the Flat and over. You get a guide to meetings, facilities, entertainment and transportation.
e-mail: adam@southwellracecourse.co.uk

Santa Anita Park

www.santaanita.com
e-mail: comments@santaanita.com

Southwell

www.southwell-racecourse.co.uk
All-weather racecourse with long sweeping bends that make it a match for any artificial track in the world. A comprehensive introduction gives all the details - race meetings, in-house facilities, entertainment and transportation.
e-mail: claudia@lingfieldpark.co.uk

Stratford Racecourse

www.stratfordracecourse.net
Since 1775, Stratford Racecourse has been host to steeple-chasing events. Today it runs fourteen meetings a year, mostly in summer. It is one of Britain's best smaller courses. Booking in advance entitles you to worthwhile concessions.
e-mail: info@stratfordracecourse.net

Taunton

www.tauntonracecourse.co.uk
Taunton Racecourse is the youngest Racecourse in Britain and one of the most beautifully located courses in the country. On its web page, you will find a race bulletin, entertainment, transportation and a course map. Whether you enjoy a day at the races or wish to use the racecourse for that special occasion, you are guaranteed a complete service. The FAQ should answer all your enquiries.
e-mail: info@tauntonracecourse.co.uk

The Hamilton Park Racecourse

www.hamilton-park.co.uk
10 miles south of Glasgow and a horseracing history that goes back to the 16th century. The racing schedule mixes day, night and weekend meetings from April to September. The site has information on race days, ticket booking, accommodation and catering.
e-mail: hamilton@cqm.co.uk

The Perth Hunt

www.perth-races.co.uk
Scone Palace Park, Perth, Scotland, considered the best small racecourse in the UK, run race meetings from April to September. The web pages describe their facilities, exhibitions and races and provide a course map. You can buy tickets online. This must be a grand way to spend the day outdoors.
e-mail: Sam@perth-races.co.uk

Towcester

www.towcester-racecourse.co.uk
Towcester Racecourse is set in the beautiful parkland estate of Easton Neston, the family home of Lord Hesketh. It is one of the most scenic racecourses

in Britain. It hosts meetings from October to May each year. Information on the site is sparse so a brochure via the online form.
e-mail: info@towcester-racecourse.co.uk

Track Expert Horse Racing Information

www.trackexpert.com/contact_us.html
e-mail: info@trackexpert.com

Warwick Racecourse

www.warwickracecourse.co.uk
The racecourse offers the thrills of flat racing from April to September and the tumbles of the National Hunt from November to May. The National Hunt programme includes the Tote Warwick National in January and the Michael Page International Kingmaker Novices Chase. The web site updates information bringing the latest news online.
e-mail: warwick@rht.net

Will Rogers Downs

www.willrogersdowns.com/ homefrmst.htm
e-mail: menterline@willrogersdowns.com

Wincanton Racecourse

www.wincantonracecourse.co.uk
In the heart of the Somerset countryside the course presents an excellent programme of National Hunt racing from October through to May. Among the best known horses that have raced here are Double Thriller, Teeton Mill and Grey Shot.
e-mail: wincanton@rht.net

Windsor Raceway

www.windsorraceway.com
e-mail: youbet@wincom.net

York

www.yorkracecourse.co.uk
Here you find one of Britain's most exciting horse racing courses opened in recent years, offering meetings from May to October each year. The web pages are well supplied with pertinent information.
e-mail: info@yorkracecourse.co.uk

Ice Hockey

General Sites

A to Z Encyclopaedia of Ice Hockey

www.azhockey.com
e-mail: not available

All Hockey Links

www.hockeylinks.com
e-mail: not available

Canadian Hockey Association

www.canadianhockey.ca
e-mail: not available

Faceoff.com

www.faceoff.com
e-mail: not available

Hockey Injuries

www.hockeyinjuries.com
e-mail: not available

Hockey Over Time

www.lcshockey.com/history
e-mail: not available

Hockey Phreak

www.hockeyphreak.com
e-mail: not available

HockeyChat

www.4-lane.com/sportschat/newsc/
hk_index.html
e-mail: not available

Ice Hockey World Championships

www.ihwc.net
e-mail: not available

International Ice Hockey Federation

www.iihf.com
e-mail: not available

Joy of Hockey

joyofhockey.com
e-mail: not available

NHL.com

www.nhl.com
e-mail: not available

Safehockey.com

www.safehockey.com
e-mail: not available

TheHockey.Net

www.thehockey.net
e-mail: not available

USA Hockey, Inc

www.usahockey.com
e-mail: not available

Teams

ANAHEIM MIGHTY DUCKS

Anaheim Mighty Ducks

www.mightyducks.com
A Flash introduction is followed by club and team news, online chat, message boards and a mailing list you can join. Match schedules and statistics keep you in touch. Desktop pictures for Windows or Mac computers are freely downloadable.
e-mail: not available

Anaheim Mighty Ducks - Mighty Ducks

www.geocities.com/Colosseum/Field/6675
e-mail: not available

Anaheim Mighty Ducks - Mighty Ducks Alternative Website

www.duckpuck.com
e-mail: not available

ATLANTA

Atlanta Thrashers

www.atlantathrashers.com
The Live Game Audio service is where you listen to the Atlanta Thrashers in action. Audio comes in Real G2 Audio and Windows Media Player while the Thrashers Tribute Video is in MOV format. Statistics and club news blend in with a marvellous photo archive.
e-mail: not available

Atlanta Thrashers - Unofficial Atlanta Thrashers

www.atlantahockey.freeservers.com
e-mail: not available

BOSTON BRUINS

Boston Bruins

www.bostonbruins.com
Great collection of multimedia files you can download - all the action from the regular season and video highlight clips from the last four seasons. The Fans Centre has downloadable club Windows wallpaper for your desktop and a selection of Bruins postcards to send to friends online.
e-mail: not available

Boston Bruins - Unofficial Marty McSorley Homepage

www.execulink.com/~karent/marty.htm
e-mail: not available

BUFFALO SABRES

Buffalo Sabres

www.sabres.com
Aside from news and player profiles with mug shots, fans can sign up for an e-mail address customised with the club name. The club shop has a catalogue of all its stock items and you can purchase by telephone, mail or fax.
e-mail: via online form

Buffalo Sabres - Sabres Rule

www.sabresrule.com
e-mail: not available

Buffalo Sabres - Sabres Source

www.angelfire.com/ny3/BuffaloSabres2
e-mail: not available

CALGARY FLAMES - FLAMES NET

Calgary Flames

www.calgaryflames.com
An animated Flash introduction page leads on to the latest news, fixtures and results. They tell you about their community work and guide you to their Fan Attic Store. When you register for an e-mail account you get a customised e-mail address @Flamesfanmail.com.
e-mail: not available

Calgary Flames - Flames Net

www.geocities.com/Colosseum/Loge/6055
e-mail: not available

Calgary Flames - Hnat's Page

www.geocities.com/Colosseum/Track/2499
e-mail: not available

CAROLINA HURRICANES

Carolina Hurricanes

www.caneshockey.com
Designed with ShockWave Flash and sound effects the web site keeps you up to date with team progress. Tickets can be purchased online through Ticketmaster and the catalogue tells you what is available in the shop.
e-mail: not available

Carolina Hurricanes - Hurricane Warning

home.beseen.com/sports/drewpiece
e-mail: not available

CHICAGO BLACK HAWKS

Chicago Black Hawks

www.chiblackhawks.com
Live commentary of their games, via Broadcast.com, in RealAudio format. Presently they are adding a camera so you can also watch games in action. They proudly describe their activities in youth hockey, the community and charity work.
e-mail: via online form

Chicago Black Hawks – Chicagofighters

www.chicagofighters.com
e-mail: not available

Chicago Black Hawks - Free The Hawks

www.freethehawks.com
e-mail: not available

COLORADO AVALANCHE

Colorado Avalanche

www.coloradoavalanche.com
KKFN AM-950 is the Fan-Flagship Station of the Colorado Avalanche team and runs commentaries on all their games. Match reports and player statistics lead on to the club program of education, sports and health initiatives.
e-mail: via online form

Colorado Avalanche – Coloradohockey

www.coloradohockey.com
e-mail: not available

Colorado Avalanche - Danger Avalanche Warning

avalanche.rivals.com
e-mail: not available

DALLAS STARS

Dallas Stars

www.dallasstarshockey.com
StarsNet updates you on players and each game has live commentary. The Fan Zone informs you of events and hockey opportunities at the Star Center. If you have QuickTime you can see the Stanley Cup in Virtual Reality. There's a video section and e-postcards come free online.
e-mail: via online form

Dallas Stars - Dallas Stars Photo Gallery

www.thedallasstars.com
e-mail: not available

Dallas Stars – Starsrule

www.starsrule.com
e-mail: not available

DETROIT RED WINGS

Detroit Red Wings

www.detroitredwings.com
A great site for fans with special features like Heart of Hockeytown, the pro-active outreach community programme and the Wish Club that raises money for charity. Keeping up to date with club news, stats, ticket status and club publications is made easy for you. The photo gallery shows players on and off the field and the Wings Chat room is constantly talking. You need Flash 4 and Acrobat Reader to view this site.
e-mail: not available

Detroit Red Wings - Archies Red Wings Page

www.geocities.com/Colosseum/Field/4359
e-mail: not available

Detroit Red Wings - Red Wing Zone

www.css.tayloru.edu/~bmahan/rwz
e-mail: not available

EDMONTON OILERS

Edmonton Oilers

www.edmontonoilers.com
It's all on board and you don't have to look very far. The team, coaches, management, news, stats and Fast Facts, the club store, schedules and ticket sales are easily accessed. Club history and traditions are a pretty good read and you can join the lively discussions in the Fans Forum. Make sure you have Realplayer and WinZip software for the video and audio footage.
e-mail: not available

Edmonton Oilers – Pipeline

www.geocities.com/no1oilerfan/oilers1.html
e-mail: not available

Edmonton Oilers - The Oil Rox

come.to/theoilrox
e-mail: not available

FLORIDA PANTHERS

Florida Panthers

www.flpanthers.com
Official site with all the regular features and a link to ticketmaster.com to purchase match tickets online.
e-mail: not available

Florida Panthers - Home Ice

www.homeice.net
e-mail: not available

Florida Panthers - Inside Edge

www.binzinc.com/panthers
e-mail: not available

LOS ANGELES KINGS

Los Angeles Kings

www.lakings.com
Top Stories make this a very newsy official web site. Keep up to scratch with the team, fixtures, local hockey and the community and ask as many questions as you want in the Fans Forum. Download a club screen saver for free.
e-mail: didyouknow@lakings.com

Los Angeles Kings - LA Kings

www.la-kings.com
e-mail: not available

Los Angeles Kings - LA Kings

www.kingshockey.com
e-mail: not available

MINNESOTA WILD

Minnesota Wild

www.wild.com
Between Cool News, team information and a section called Know It you should get a good handle on national and local hockey leagues. The ticket information centre has a map of the arena and the shop displays team shirts for sale.
e-mail: not available

MONTREAL CANADIENS

Montreal Canadiens

www.canadiens.com
They tell you how to listen to their matches via Internet Radio for which you'll need Windows Media Player or RealPlayer, but you can follow the action of all their games from your desktop by downloading the software. Visit their virtual dressing room if you have QuickTime. Text is in English and French.
e-mail: via online form

Montreal Canadiens - Hab Fans

www.habfans.com
e-mail: not available

Montreal Canadiens – MyHabs

www.myhabs.com
e-mail: not available

NASHVILLE PREDATORS

Nashville Predators

www.nashvillepredators.com
Adults and youngsters have it made on this great web site. The Kids' section is loaded with games and other diversions and the adults, including hardened fans, get all the info they need and the convenience of a shop. Send e-mail, leave your messages and read what others have said in Feedback.
e-mail: predators@nashvillearena.com

Nashville Predators - Unofficial site

www.icewind.net/hockey
e-mail: not available

NEW JERSEY DEVILS

New Jersey Devils

www.newjerseydevils.com
The QuickTime video highlights and
RealAudio interviews are first rate.
They also dish up a little club history,
player profiles, press releases and
statistics and tell you how to buy
tickets and merchandise.
e-mail: not available

New Jersey Devils - Devils Centre

www.jmiz5.hypermart.net
e-mail: not available

New Jersey Devils - NJ Devils

www.allsports.com/nhl/devils
e-mail: not available

NEW YORK ISLANDERS

New York Islanders

www.newyorkislanders.com
You get club history, player profiles
with snapshots, forthcoming fixtures,
reviews of seasons past and a good
selection of audio-video clips in
QuickTime, RealAudio and Windows
MediaPlayer formats.
e-mail: not available

New York Islanders - NY Islanders Online

www.detrinet.com/islanders
e-mail: not available

NEW YORK RANGERS

New York Rangers

www.newyorkrangers.com
Use the search facility to take you
directly to multimedia clips of players
in action in RealAudio and QuickTime
formats. The interaction bit comes in
the Player Q & A section and the
Bulletin Board. Club screensavers and
personalised postcards come free.
e-mail: via online form

New York Rangers - Andrew and Ben's page

www.magiccarpet.com/~afeldman/ranger
e-mail: not available

New York Rangers - New York Rangers Café

www.newyorkrangerscafe.com
e-mail: not available

New York Rangers - New York Rangers Fan Club

www.nyrfanclub.com
e-mail: not available

OTTAWA SENATORS

Ottawa Senators

www.ottawasenators.com
Up-to-date information on the team
and its progress, merchandise displayed
in the club shop and a guest book to leave
comments, good, bad or indifferent.
e-mail: via online form

Ottawa Senators
www.ottawahockey.com
e-mail: not available

Ottawa Senators - Lavinia's page
www.relativedata.com/sens
e-mail: not available

PHILADELPHIA FLYERS
Philadelphia Flyers
www.philadelphiaflyers.com
Audio and video clips online, links to match commentaries, a chat room to interact with other fans and a long club history just about wrap up this official site.
e-mail: not available

Philadelphia Flyers – FlyersZone
www.flyerszone.com
e-mail: not available

Philadelphia Flyers - Mark's Tribute
www.interlog.com/~1wiseguy
e-mail: not available

PHILADELPHIA FLYERS
Phoenix Coyotes
www.nhlcoyotes.com
This official club site is short of nothing; news, stats, schedules, ticket information, a merchandise catalogue, kids' corner, a bit of history and records of the club fill the pages. Video and audio clips need QuickTime and RealAudio software and if you're looking for interaction go straight to the Fans Forum.
e-mail: brian.wilkinson@ phoenixcoyotes.com

PHOENIX COYOTES – COYOTE
Phoenix Coyotes – Coyote
www.nt.net/~jubyss
e-mail: not available

Phoenix Coyotes – Coyotes
www.azcentral.com/sports/coyotes/coyoteindex.shtml
e-mail: not available

PITTSBURGH PENGUINS
Pittsburgh Penguins
www.pittsburghpenguins.com
If you have the Flash plug-in installed you can view the splash page introduction. The multimedia section has a great collection of video clips and the site gives you ticket prices, news, stats, fixtures and results. The very popular Penguins Message Board gets a lot of traffic.
e-mail: not available

Pittsburgh Penguins - Let's Go Pens
www.letsgopens.com
e-mail: not available

Pittsburgh Penguins - Penguin Fan
www.fancentral.net/pfc
e-mail: not available

SAN JOSE SHARKS
San Jose Sharks
www.sj-sharks.com
Packed with info about the team, the community and the game. Fans have a special one-to-one service with a dozen changing interactive elements; the chat room and e-mail facilities put you in direct touch with players and fellow

fans. Game coverage on TV and Radio is listed and the shop is stocked with club merchandise. The kids' section is a lot of fun at any age.
e-mail: not available

San Jose Sharks - Chumming For Sharks

www.tealtown.com
e-mail: not available

San Jose Sharks - Sharkspage.com

www.sharkspage.com
e-mail: not available

ST LOUIS BLUES

St Louis Blues

www.stlouisblues.com
All the usual club news, team stories, schedules, ticket details, stats and club history and a live scoreboard bring you up to speed on this official web site. The Fans Stuff section takes you on a virtual tour of the locker room and regularly polls fans for opinions. The chat room and kid's section complete the site.
e-mail: webmaster@stlblues.com

St Louis Blues - Blues Net

www.bluesnet.brick.net
e-mail: not available

St Louis Blues - St. Louis Blues Bluenote Bandwagon

www.cchat.com/grayj/stlouis.html
e-mail: not available

TAMPA BAY LIGHTNING

Tampa Bay Lightning

www.tampabaylightning.com
Great visual and lightning sound effects

greet you as you enter this official web site. News, player and coach information, a brief club history, merchandise and ticket details are easy to access. Live radio broadcasts and video highlights require RealAudio and Windows Media Player. Don't be shy, e-mail any player or say what you like in the feedback section.
email: not available

Tampa Bay Lightning - Lightning Strikes

www.tblightning.com
e-mail: not available

Tampa Bay Lightning - Tampa Bay Lightning Club House

www.lightningclubhouse.com
e-mail: not available

THE COLUMBUS BLUE JACKETS

The Columbus Blue Jackets

www.columbusbluejackets.com
A good site with no unusual features. The latest club news and results, ticket information, a guide to where you can buy club merchandise, a chat room and message board, a bit of club history and player profiles sum it up.
e-mail: via online form

The Columbus Blue Jackets - Blue Jackets

www.greenapple.com/~tosgood/jackets/index.html
e-mail: not available

The Columbus Blue Jackets – BlueJacketsFans

www.bluejacketsfans.com
e-mail: not available

THE WASHINGTON CAPITALS

The Washington Capitals

www.washingtoncaps.com
Videos of match highlights can be downloaded in RealPlayer and Windows Media Player formats on this official site which also runs all the latest club news. The last season is reviewed with great soul searching and you can have your say on the message board and in the chat room.
e-mail: customerservice@washcaps.com

The Washington Capitals - Capital Offence

www.geocities.com/Colosseum/Midfield/4190
e-mail: not available

The Washington Capitals - Chris' Capitals Page

www.polsci.wvu.edu/grad/CCampbell/caps.html
e-mail: not available

TORONTO MAPLE LEAFS

Toronto Maple Leafs

www.torontomapleleafs.com
Club history, profiles of some players, fixtures, results and stats with a multimedia section screening QuickTime action videos online. You can download Windows club wallpaper and a screensaver for free.
e-mail: not available

Toronto Maple Leafs - Fifty Mission Cap

www.interlog.com/~robdm/fifty.html
e-mail: not available

Toronto Maple Leafs - Graham's Leaf Page

www.drpeace.com/leafs/leafs.html
e-mail: not available

Toronto Maple Leafs - Leafs Report

www.iaw.on.ca/~maven
e-mail: not available

VANCOUVER CANUCKS

Vancouver Canucks

www.orcabay.com/canucks
Everything you want to know is conveniently online - news, team updates, schedules, statistics, ticket information and results. The general manager Brian Burke will promptly answer any questions you pose on the site. Audio and video clips and live commentary require QuickTime and RealAudio. You can enrol for the free newsletter and send e-mail online.
e-mail: comments@orcabay.com

Vancouver Canucks - Canucks Blue Line

www.geocities.com/Colosseum/Stadium/4631/index.html
e-mail: not available

Vancouver Canucks - CanucksCentral.com

www.canuckscentral.com
e-mail: not available

Motor Racing

The Tournaments

Active World Wide Sports - United States Formula

www.usf3.net

Official site of the US championship. You can check the racing schedule, teams and latest news and preview the new cars for the current season. The teams and manufacturers are listed with contact details including e-mail addresses. If you want to trade in your hatchback, there are pages of used F3 cars and engines for sale.

e-mail: via online form

Alfred Blackmore Historic Racing Saloon Championship

www.historicsaloons.fsnet.co.uk

All details of this racing championship come online – entry requirements, where they race and how the season is progressing. The cars have historical relevance and a photo gallery shows you the entrants with some action shots from the season. For practical help look at the Service pages for advice and links to companies that stock spare parts and rebuild classic cars.

e-mail: Adrian@historicsaloons.fsnet.co.uk

American Motor Racing Association

www.amramodified.com/index.htm

This governing body sanctions auto racing throughout North America and the site provides easy access to all associated rules and regulations, car specifications and how to join, with lots of good photos. Current news from the racing season accompanies results from the last two seasons, archived for comparison. You can also check out track details, drivers and information on sponsors.

e-mail: wehpah@ecr.net

Arrows F1 team

www.arrows.com

Fans of the Arrows racing team can follow the dash and daring of the boys at the

wheel, their test results, driver interviews and check progress within Formula 3000. A preview of the next Formula 1 race of the season comes online with a track guide. A press area, jobs page, an online set up for regular updates sent as text messages to your mobile phone and archives of all articles complete the site.
e-mail: not available

Asia Motor Sports

www.asiamotorsports.com
You can read up on motor sport news from around the globe, check the online calendar and browse through a series of pages on motor racing organisations and circuits world wide. Regular columns discuss major sporting issues and you are invited to vote yea or nay. This site is WAP enabled and updated daily.
e-mail: not available

Australian Motorsport Internet Bulletin

www.ecn.net.au/~amib/frames.htm
This site does exactly what it says on the label – it is a bulletin board for motor racing around the globe. Ten major championships including Formula 1, British Touring Cars and World Rallying have their own pages with lists of results and driver-team championship points to date. There are not one, not two, but fourteen galleries of current racing photos to browse through and a links page with a line-up of first-rate racing web sites.
e-mail: not available

Autosport Online

www.autosport.com
On this large site you can browse

through pages dedicated to all major forms of motor racing around the world. Each competition has its own news page, a calendar of events for coming months, championship tables, driver and circuit profiles. To listen to post race reports, check out the radio page for live broadcasts over the Internet. This feature requires RealPlayer G2 software. You can subscribe to receive e-mail news.
e-mail: via online form

Brands Hatch Leisure Group

www.brands-hatch.co.uk
The site covers four circuits in Britain with pages about each and its events. Special facilities are offered, such as driving high performance sports cars round the circuits. The database can be searched for events by month and circuit. Read about the Brands Hatch Club and join with the details provided.
e-mail: pressoffice@bhlg. brands-hatch.co.uk

British Automobile Racing Club

www.barc.net
They run several championships around the UK, all listed on the site. You'll find details accompanying each competition and information on the club, how to join and a list of driving schools. A picture gallery and links to other sites can be accessed from the home page.
e-mail: not available

British Touring Car Championship

www.btcc.co.uk
Official and full news service for the UK championship. Results and tables are laid out so that you can compare them

with the previous year's and read up on the teams and drivers. The TV listings cover the whole season of BBC Grandstand programs. There are notes on the history of the championship, a whole catalogue of photos and you get timings live online during racing events.
e-mail: btcc@mpafingal.co.uk

Brookspeed

www.brookspeed.com
Follow the fortunes of the team and its build up at each year's 24-hour Le Mans race. The full story is published along with details of the cars and their drivers. Race dates are featured, with sponsors and car conversions. You can check their merchandise online and e-mail your order.
e-mail: via online form

Canadian Motorcycle Drag Racing Association

www.cmdra.com
Follow the racing, view schedules and read event reports. There are pictures, details of sponsors and rider profiles. Items for sale come with brief descriptions, a link to a photo and an e-mail address. Useful links and a new forum for debate complete the site.
e-mail: cmdra@mortimer.com

CART

www.cart.com
Keep your finger on the pulse of this global sport with race reports, forthcoming schedules and profiles of all the teams and drivers. Check TV and radio listings world wide by selecting the region and clicking. There are special news reports about everything associated with the sport,

games for amusement, a community area with fan messages to drivers and teams and an online shopping area where you can buy merchandise over a secure server using a virtual basket system.
e-mail: feedback@cart.com

Castrol Honda World Superbike Team

www.castrol-honda.com
Official site of the racing team with results following as the races happen. The championship calendar, standing and track information appear on the Supersport page. Each rider has a designated area of the site for a biography, career history and a Q & A page. Team merchandise is for sale online using a secure server and virtual shopping basket system. Click on the Team Gear link to open a new window; all items are listed in the drop down menu.
e-mail: not available

Classic Formula Ford

www.classicformulaford.com
Exclusive to this racing formula and within the UK only, info is updated continuously through the season with a full results and reports service. Championship positions can be read against driver profiles and compared with archives of last season's results. You get information about the club shop and goods can be ordered by telephone.
e-mail: Shineracing@tesco.net

Clipsal 500 – Adelaide

www.clipsal500.com.au
If you are into V8 Supercars then check out this site from down under, covering

the Shell series of endurance races. You get the program for the whole weekend, ticket prices and a link to an online booking company, a race route map and an archive of previous results. The link to the Adelaide Tourist Board web site helps you with accommodation.
e-mail: via online form

Daytona International Speedway

www.daytonaspeedway.com
The history and details of current events at this world famous circuit, with racing news, schedules, archives and track specifications. You can buy tickets online over a secure server and get the low down on the Dayton Club and its corporate entertainment service. If you'd like to get your hands on the merchandise then check out the souvenirs page with items available online.
e-mail: not available

F1 Now

www.f1-now.co.uk
As well as access to the latest stories from the world of F1 racing, this site has a host of other features. Weather forecasts for the next race, predictions of how the results might look after the impending race and the whole season of races. There are weekly polls and surveys and you can register on the mailing list to receive constant updates. There is a link on the home page for the F1 shop which sells only computer hardware and software, not F1 merchandise as you might expect.
e-mail: via online form

Fantasy Racing

www.fantasyracing.co.uk
If you love the sport, here is a site with

more than a hundred great racing games to play online. They are divided into groups representing all the motor racing championships. Most are organised and maintained here, but a few are through links to other sites.
e-mail: not available

Federation Internationale de l'Automobile

www.fia.com
There are two main sections, only one of which concerns motor racing fans - the sports bit. The Federation is the main governing body for motor sports so you are bound to discover everything you need to know about racing cars from Formula One to your local kart race. There is a whole starting line of links to other sites for press releases, competition regulations and a lot else. Use the drop down menu at the top of the screen to navigate around the site quickly. Text is in English and French.
e-mail: www.fia.comnot available

Ford Racing

www.fordracing.net
All about Ford's global racing in the British Touring Car and World Rally championships. You get the latest results, team news, the racing diary, team and driver profiles. There is a section of downloadable photos and video footage and you can purchase merchandise. The online shop uses a virtual shopping basket and a secure server to protect your credit card details. Text is in English and Spanish.
e-mail: via online form

Formula 1 Online

www.f1-online.com

One of many Formula 1 sites. This one covers all current information, the racing calendar, archives of previous years' results and an impressive album of photographs. Articles about teams and drivers, a look ahead to the next race, chat forum, opinion poll, championship tables and statistics take up a lot more pages, followed by live updates on race days. Links take you to lots of other racing sites, not all F1. Text is in English, French and German.

e-mail: team@f1-live.com

Formula 3 Association - Great Britain

www.fota.co.uk

You'll find information about the British Championship only, although all competing teams from around the world get a mention. An online guide and history page explaining the sport and its status will bring those unfamiliar with F3 up to speed. The annual calendar and a photo gallery from previous events take you up to the Fun page for screen savers and games and some streamed video footage.

e-mail: info@fota.co.uk

Formula One Supporters Association

www.fosa.org

Answer three short questions on the right of the home page and you become a member of this international supporters' site for free. Then you can follow the racing season in full, enjoy the fun pages, keep up with F1 news, statistics, live relays and a chat forum, F1 games and cartoons, a guest book

and buy goods at the FOSA shopping mall. Not bad for just three quick answers. Text is in English, German, French, Italian, Spanish and Portuguese.

e-mail: fosa@fosa.org

Formula1.com

www.formula1.com

This unofficial Formula 1 site covers all aspects of the championships. Pages bulge with current news stories about teams and circuits and an online store sells tournament tickets and arranges hospitality wherever races are staged. Times and results are updated live during races and a dedicated audio-visual page lets you download interviews and clips from major events. Text is in English and Portuguese.

e-mail: via online form

Grand American Road Racing

www.grandamerican.com

Official site of the motor sports association with lots of information on professional road racing. The events calendar and overall ranking are on separate pages. You can download the rules and regulations that apply to each racing class in PDF format and also check out prizes that can be won in the competitions. The home page has a list of TV coverage for each event.

e-mail: not available

Grand Prix Tours

www.gptours.com

They organise special tours to the major racing events around the world - the full F1 season, NASCAR, CART and vintage racing. You'll find all the packages available to fans and what you have to pay, and if you join the mailing list you'll get to know all the deals going. The Downloads page has files with race and tour information and instructions on how to book in PDF and Word '97 format.

e-mail: reservations@gptours.com

Hawaii Motorsports Centre

www.hawaiiracewaypark.com
Details of all motor sport in Hawaii, not just for professionals either; anyone who wants to test his or her racing skills at the circuit can apply. Schedules, photos and track information are all published along with a guide to facilities at this racetrack. Related legislation from the State government is included for the benefit of potential participants. A separate page shows the location of the raceway and directions on how to get there.

e-mail: info@hawaiiracewaypark.com

Honda Racing

www.hondaracing.com
Everything you ever wanted to know about Honda's racing activities is on this site. Each page uses drop down menus to quickly navigate through the huge fund of information including racing schedules, track information, driver details and press releases. You can check out particular tracks and download RealAudio clips of interviews from previous races. The shopping page has a catalogue of all available Honda goods.

e-mail: not available

Indy 500

www.indy500.com
Official site for the Indy 500, with the latest news articles and two search

engines - one for general search of the whole site and the other for a special track search. Other information pages include the racing schedule, stats and ticket status. A neat extra feature is the See/Hear page where you can watch Real Video clips of a lap of the circuit and listen to audio clips from exciting racing moments.

e-mail: imspr@brickyard.com

Indy Racing Online

www.indyracingleague.com
Internet equivalent to a one-stop shop for Indy Car racing news with full coverage of all aspects of the US sport, news and reviews, reports and schedules, statistics, driver profiles and team stories. Each race is expertly written up and what's more you can watch streamed video sequences of races. Sign up for an e-mail newsletter and bone up on the rules and regulations of Indy racing. Then, if you like, visit the online store to buy racing items.

e-mail: via online form

International Hot Rod Association Drag Racing

www.ihra.com
A huge amount of information about drag racing in North America. Pages cover the association, news, drivers, tracks, rules and regulations and the sponsors. You can check the online schedules, stats and TV listings for each event. There are loads of pictures, a chat room and message board in the Community area of the site.

e-mail: comments@ihra.com

International Motor Sports Hall of Fame

www.motorsportshalloffame.com/default.htm

You can see what's on show in this US museum. When you enter the Hall of Fame itself you'll find an index of all drivers honoured by the museum, loads of photos and articles about the cars and stars of the sport. They publish a newsletter which you can subscribe to online and a search engine helps find items quickly. Use e-mail to find out how to get there.
e-mail: via online form

ITV Formula 1

www.itv-f1.com

TV run this site and profile the commentary team who present the races. They give a full TV schedule for all F1 events including qualifying, stack up news articles, race reports and photos and profile the drivers, teams and circuits. You can sign up for their newsletter, enter competitions online and wise up on how to purchase tickets for races anywhere in the world. The shopping link takes you to a separate web site called Grand Prix Legends which has an online shopping mall.
e-mail: not available

Jaguar Racing

www.jaguar-racing.com

The team's official Formula 1 site, which requires Flash 4 to enjoy the animations. You can read team news, what they're doing and where they're going, revel in the photos of cars standing still and in action in the last race; join the virtual club by registering online and receive a newsletter in exchange for your e-mail address. Merchandise is sold online through a secure server and text is in English and German.
e-mail: not available

Jordan

www.fijordan.com

Grand Prix site housing all the current news of the team. A racing calendar, championship tables and a gallery of the season's action shots fill more pages. For avid team fans there are details on the Club Jordan page on how to join and a link to the online registration form. To cover yourself with team colours, shop online.
e-mail: via online form

Karnac Motor Sports Community

www.karnac.com

US site for news and information about all types of racing in the States with a section on motor racing around the world. You can check out the latest

Nascar news, read up on competitors or shop for a roll cage online. A drop down menu of forums is at the bottom of the home page; if you are a young racer trying to get started or make a name for yourself the site will help with advice and sponsorship.

e-mail: info@karnac.com

Minardi Team F1

www.minardi.it
Another team site for fans to keep up to date with racing news and browse through the huge number of photographs. Text is in English and Italian.

e-mail: not available

NASCAR Online

www.nascar.com
An official web site for NASCAR racing in America. All three series have pages with results, competitor standing, schedules, team and current race information. There are programmed live chats with drivers, the NASCAR poll where you are invited to vote and a camera which constantly updates images from one of the garages at the Lowe's motor speedway. This very packed site has an online store, track databases and a whole section stuffed with racing news that keeps you up to date.

e-mail: not available

New Zealand Touring Car Championship

www.nztouringcars.co.nz
The latest motor racing news from Touring Car championships in New Zealand. Every detail from race dates through qualifying times to up-to-the-minute results on the day is published on this site. You can check the weather at the racetrack, updated daily, and watch video footage of racing around a lap. A useful feature is the Bookstore page that lists a library of titles on all aspects of the sport with a direct link to Amazon.com.

e-mail: editor@nztouringcars.co.nz

Northern Ireland Rally Network

www.nirallynetwork.co.uk
On this small site you follow rally events and get the latest news. The home page lists all the news in an archive and you are invited to submit your own if you have some. Three other areas give race results for the previous month, championship standing and a motor sport links page. Track marshals' jobs are also advertised on the same page.

e-mail: mail@nirallynetwork.co.uk

PACE Supercross

www.pacesupercross.com
All-in-one site for this class of motor racing, with the home page crammed with racing news. The ticket section gives you seating plans and prices for all races; results and press releases are continuously updated and you can download stacks of pictures and video clips. Both riders and tracks are profiled online, and don't overlook the very good interviews. There is a store connected to the Yahoo.com site with a secure server for purchasing online.

e-mail: webmaster@pacesupercross.com

Pacenotes

www.pacenotes.co.uk
Big rally fans will enjoy this site as it has updates on all major events around the world. The three news areas cover

general news, the British Rally Championship and the World Rally Championship. Then you get driver profiles and a page of classified adverts. If you have an interesting article you think other readers might enjoy, submit it online. An online store for rally related items is just around the corner.
e-mail: via online form

Phoenix International Raceway

www.phoenixintlraceway.com
A major US raceway web site well worth a visit. The history of the circuit, track statistics and racing schedules are well laid out. You can purchase tickets online to any event by completing an order form but first check out ticket types and prices. A web page shows their special fan suite which provides the best seats in the house with details on how to book.
e-mail: not available

Pontiac Racing

www.pontiacracing.com
Follow the fortunes of this racing team and its drivers in the NASCAR and NHRA championships held in the USA. Each has its own page with news, race results, profiles and an over-all season schedule. The home page links up with their online store and official fan club. Use the form to sign up for membership. The Racing News page has a complete list of all racing articles by headline and competition.
e-mail: not available

Promotorsport

www.promotorsport.co.uk
The Scottish touring car team makes its debut this year in the British Touring Car Championship. As there isn't much history to record, you will have to do with results and reports for the current season. Just the same, the full team and driver profiles are published. There is a full racing calendar and several photos to browse through and you can join the team fan club online for an annual subscription.
e-mail: info@promotorsport.co.uk

Prost Grand Prix Formula 1

www.prostgp.com
The front page will ask you to choose English or French, and you'll need Flash 4 for all the great animations. Then you can read up on team news, keep track of the racing live with continuous updates online and check all the championship tables for the current season. The entertainment area lets you send web cards of team photos to your mates and view multimedia presentations. The link at the bottom of the home page takes you to the Prost Team club.
e-mail: via online form

Racin.net

www.racin.net
Follow the Winston cup series of NASCAR racing in the USA on this site. Full race results from qualifying to overall standing within each championship are displayed with all the latest news articles summarised on the home page. There are links to weather information at each race circuit and to other racing sites. You can have all NASCAR results e-mailed to you by registering online.
e-mail: about@racin.net

Rally Sport

www.rallysport.com

All about the World Rally Championship, where you can keep in touch with developments in the sport. The full racing calendar and results are ready to browse, with last year's results displayed for comparison. There is a separate page for UK rally news updates and all articles can be e-mailed to your phone, as the site is WAP enabled. An online store is under construction for rally merchandise; for now you can buy videos using a virtual shopping basket and secure server system.

e-mail: via online form

Rally UK

www.rallyuk.8m.com

This site, dedicated to the art of rallying, certainly lives up to its name. There are pages for news, events, photographs, driver profiles and racing calendars. Then, moving on from the competition, there are pages for car specifications, rally schools, a classified ads page where you can check out cars for sale and a link to a chat forum.

e-mail: rallyuk@netcomuk.co.uk

Red Bull Yamaha Motorcycle Grand Prix Team

www.redbull-yamaha.com

Although this site does not get the prize for good looks, it still provides a good way of keeping up-to-date with this racing team. There are pages for team news, team structure and individual drivers with brilliant photos from each event in the news section, with yet more for all things technical.

e-mail: Peterclifford@ redbull-yamaha.com

Roberts Group - 500 cc Grand Prix Motorcycle Racing

www.robertsgroup.com

News, race results and lots of pictures of this racing team. Although their main interest is in 500 cc racing you'll find quite a bit about their Asian 250 cc group and their riding school in Spain. There is plenty of tech-talk on the bikes they build and pages for teams, drivers and staff. You can buy team merchandise online through a secure server and all products are displayed with pictures and prices in US$.

e-mail: via online form

Sauber Petronas

www.sauber.ch

The two sets of menus on the home page and those at the top of the screen are not the most intuitive to use. Place your mouse over one topic and wait for the yellow four-square and text to appear. Click on the square that has the information you want and the text turns yellow as well. You get all current team information, a boutique to buy goods over a secure connection and an entertainment area with screen savers and greeting cards.

e-mail: via online form

Scottish Rally Championship

www.scottishrallychampionship.co.uk

The championship is fully detailed on this site. You can check rules of entry, vehicle classes and awards made, browse through location maps and route notes. There are pages for the latest press releases, current points table and registration for rallying. If you prefer to talk your way round these courses, go to the special page devoted

to co-driving for details of the Colleen McRae rally scholarships. You can also check out various car clubs in Scotland and a page of rally cars for sale.
e-mail: not available

Seventh Gear

www.seventhgear.com
Mainly cart racing in the USA with a few articles from other racing events. The home page has links to all current news articles. Other pages divide into sections on drivers and teams, schedules and tracks. Feature articles give the low-down on sports personalities and a forum lets you air your views. The online store has a list of racing books, briefly reviewed, and clicking on any will take you direct to the Amazon.com web site.
e-mail: webmaster@seventhgear.com

Shell Championship Series V8 Supercars

www.shellseries.com.au
Official site of the annual Australian championship. You can check out all the teams and drivers, browse race results and reports and read the history of the event. There are photos from the current year's racing and animated screen savers to download. The site gives links to other V8 and Shell affiliated web sites. If you get a buzz predicting winners then try the Tipping Competition page and hopefully race away with the prize given at each round of the championship.
e-mail: not available

Shell-Ferrari

www.shell-ferrari.com
The team and main contributor collaborate to bring you this site that has all the F1 and Ferrari team news, updated weekly, before and after each race. Read the driver interviews, test yourself with the team quiz or enter their chat forum. In the bottom left corner of the home page you'll find their current poll for your vote. One page has a whole chain of good links to other F1 teams and Ferrari fan sites world wide.
e-mail: not available

Sidecar World Cup

www.sidecar.org
A very particular racing championship with a lot of information about each event in the season. Teams are listed with photos and other pages are taken up with a racing calendar, news stories and overall team standing. There are links to other motorcycle racing and track sites and a separate gallery of great action shots. One page deals with techie stuff, rules and regulations.
e-mail: info@sidecar.org

Silverstone

www.silverstone-circuit.co.uk
The most famous racing circuit in Britain. Online you get a well-documented tour of the circuit and its facilities with an outstanding photo gallery and a lap of the track with F1 driver Eddie Irvine. You can order an event calendar and tickets online using their secure connection credit card system. There are details of how to book online to drive on the circuit with tutored sessions in high performance cars.
e-mail: info@silverstone-circuit.co.uk

South African Motorsport Paddock

www.msport.co.za/index.html

Although the focus of this site is motor racing news from South Africa, it does include international racing reports. It publishes a track guide, team guide and calendar of racing events and you can subscribe to a newsletter. If you missed a particular event and would like to catch up, the news archive will help you.

e-mail: pitcrew@msport.co.za

Spirit of America

www.spiritofamerica.com

Team with an unusual motor racing dream - to beat the British held land speed record. The site explains how they intend to do it. There are details of the cars they build and a profile of the driver; the history of this record is told and technical details explained. Team merchandise can be ordered online with shipping costs listed at the bottom of the order form. Check out the photo gallery for some superb action shots of these extreme vehicles.

e-mail: via online form

Supercross

www.supercross.com

You can follow Supercross competition in both racing and freestyle forms. There are articles on the AMA trucks events, TV listings for the USA and a newsletter you can subscribe to for a results service. All racing results are illustrated with photos and interviews. The home page has an excellent links section that uses multiple drop down menus from which you can get to any motor racing web site in the world.

e-mail: race@supercross.com

Ten Tenths Motorsport

www.ten-tenths.com

A massive site where you can read about all forms of motor racing around the world. Aside from current racing news it has track guides, an events diary, a polling booth and several chat forums. There are pages of classified adverts, a store for all kinds of merchandise and TV schedules for live racing coverage. The site has a battery of links and you can subscribe to the weekly e-newsletter. There's also fun stuff like racing cartoons and competitions to enter.

e-mail: via online form

The Australian Motor Sports Report Online

www.ozmotorsport.com

Australian motor racing news, views and interviews from all types of motor racing, updated weekly. Most of the information comes in streamed format with audio and video enhancement, so you'll need RealPlayer G2. There are scheduled chats and a picture gallery to browse through.

e-mail: motorsport@speedlink.com.au

The Drivers Room

www.driversroom.com

Drag racing in the US attracts fans from all over the world. The site has pages for well known drivers and teams, lots of action shots and links to racetracks, related companies and a gift shop for drag racing merchandise. The racing calendar for two major championships is posted online and a guide to live action on US TV.

e-mail: info@driversroom.com

The F1 Rumors Site

www.f1rumors.net

Remember you heard it here first seems to be the motto of this site. They try to get in with the latest F1 stories ahead of the pack so their stories are published online as rumours. At the same time they provide a complete news service which can be e-mailed to you if you join their mailing list. Pictures and cartoons, statistics and a fantasy F1 game are some of the other features. There are live updates from the races and a chat forum.

e-mail: f1rumours@f1rumors.net

The Formula 1 Fan Club

www.f1fanclub.co.uk

This is the site for any discerning F1 fan to bookmark if he wants to remain in touch with day-by-day developments in the sport. Membership is free and only requires completion of the simple form online. Apart from news updates and a news archive you can also purchase merchandise, books, videos and clothing. There is an F1 database online and a page of monthly competitions.

e-mail: feedback@f1fanclub.co.uk

The North American Motor Sports Pages

www.na-motorsports.com

Unofficial web site for racing enthusiasts. It runs its own information service and carries links and contact details to many major motor racing bodies in North America. The search engine will take you by the express route through a track database and online magazine. Race results and reports appear weekly; there is a chat room to exchange ideas and a gallery of racing photographs.

A motor sports classified advertising page will soon be added.

e-mail: rwelty@wizvax.net

The Official McLaren Online Magazine

www.mclaren.co.uk

On this large team site you can browse through the team's race listings and results and enter the World of McLaren. The online shopping mall has an attractive range of goods to pick up and drop into a virtual shopping basket then pay for via the secure link. Register as a member to take advantage of special offers and discounts and get access to chat forums.

e-mail: not available

The UK Motorsport Index

www.ukmotorsport.com/racmsa

A partnership between the Motorsport Index and one of the governing bodies, the Motorsports Association of the UK. The site is very large and contains just about everything you could possibly want to know about the sport within the UK. Pages include events and championship details, jobs, contacts for young drivers, press releases and a link to the owners' club. Special pages are devoted to disabled driver training and women driver publications by the MSA. Use the drop down menu to search by race category or the search engine for more general information.

e-mail: msa_mail@compuserve.com

The Welsh Racing Drivers Association

www.wrda.co.uk

Whether a competitor or fan of Welsh motor racing you'll find something of

interest on this site. Details of the
association, how to join, news, articles
and a racing calendar for the current
season come online. Test yourself with
the quiz and use the links to the classified
adverts of cars and parts. News archives
go back to the beginning of the 1998
season.
e-mail: wrda@iclwebkit.co.uk

TOCA Australia

www.toca.com.au
Keep track of the Super Touring Car
racing news from down under. The full
season of events is listed with news
reports as they occur, championship
tables and guides to teams, drivers and
circuits. All the technical data and
regulations of the sport get full coverage
together with details of sponsorship.
TV racing programs are listed for the
week and as an extra the site reports
the latest events in the British Touring
Car Championship.
e-mail: koreilly@bigpond.net.au

Toyota Motorsport

www.tte.de
Toyota tell you about themselves, their
efforts in world rally racing and the Le
Mans 24-hour endurance race. Both
these competitions have their own web
pages packed with pictures, articles and
information on the team and drivers.
Toyota merchandise can be seen online
but purchasing is limited to a few
countries.
e-mail: not available

UK Karting

www2.karting.co.uk
Extensive guide to Karting in the UK.
The ten main pages contain a lot of

information about how to get into the
sport, what's going on, photographs
and classified adverts. If you are a little
daunted by everything there is to read,
try the quick guide link located at the
top of the home page under the main
page choices. The home page has a
list of all the latest articles.
e-mail: mail@karting.co.uk

US Rally

www.usrally.com
Best described as an online database
of motor racing around the world, it
has several categories, each with a
search engine for easy browsing and
links to add other pages. The categories
are events, clubs, teams, stories and
FAQ section. A page is set aside for
motor racing links.
e-mail: via online form

Watkins Glen Motor Racing
Research Library

www.racingarchives.org
Large racing archive online and
research service by e-mail. You may
have to pay for detailed research and
photocopying of material. The database
is still under construction; meantime a
list of useful books and a bookshop link
come on the reference page. Posters
and postcards from memorable racing
moments can be ordered online for a
small donation. Prices are in US$. The
full library list is on a separate page.
e-mail: research@racingaarchives.org

Williams F1

www.williamsf1.co.uk
One of the most famous racing teams
around with a web site that covers not
only their activities but their story, other

ventures and partners in this high tech
sport. Current news features the team
as a whole and drivers individually with
an eye on the next race; discussions of
the previous years' results come from
the online archive. You can also
download high-res pictures and a
screen saver.
e-mail: via online form

World Superbike Championship

www.superbike.it
The home page offers access to some
of the features and the choice of two
versions of the site. One is fully
animated and enhanced and requires a
recent browser, the other is text-based.
Both these sites give you racing news,
profiles of riders and teams, sponsorship
information and a racing calendar.
Check out the web cam page which has
continuous live images from the Ducati
garages on race days.
e-mail: via online form

The Drivers

Andretti Web Site

www.andretti.com
There are three Andrettis who race
today and their site covers all of them.
Details of their lives blend with their
aspirations and personalities. Current
racing results come online; you can
check out the fan club and merchandise
on sale. There is also a classified
adverts page and a business page that
deals with Andretti family projects.
e-mail: staff@andretti.com

Andy Priaulx - F3 Driver

www.andypriaulx.com
This up and coming driver's site charts
his rise through the sport and has
results of his current racing season.
Both his overall championship standing
and personal results are published with
his racing schedule. You can browse
through photos and press releases,
learn about his sponsors and soon you
can buy personal merchandise online.
Register for future e-mail updates on
the home page.
e-mail: priaulx@btinternet.com

Carl Fogarty

www.carlfogarty.org.uk
Take part in a fantasy superbike game
online or enter the Fogarty chat forum.
The motorcycle champion's career
history and results of the last two and
current seasons are shown with pictures,
a signed print you can purchase and a
guest book to sign. World superbike
stats and information on other riders
are published.
e-mail: not available

Exclusively Eddie Irvine

www.exclusively-irvine.com
The site, as the title says, is all his. To get the best of it you need to join online using a credit card through a secure server. There are benefits to be had like an embroidered shirt and a chance to meet the man himself. If you don't want to become a member you can still read his biography and see him in action.
e-mail: via online form

Heinz Harald Frentzen Online

www.frentzen.de
The site blends both current F1 Grand Prix racing news with a good write-up about the driver and his rise within this high-tech sport. Results are posted on the stats page together with all championship standings. Chat rooms and the Frentzen Club have open and members only areas. You'll need Flash 4 to appreciate all the animations.
e-mail: mail@frentzen.de

Jacques Villeneuve

www.jacques.villeneuve.com
This is the life of the Formula 1 driver blended with news about him and profiles of the cars he drives, the team he works with and the previous and current racing seasons. There is a gallery of photos and another of cartoons, a guest book to sign with a link to a special Villeneuve chat room. The site is seen best with Flash 4 software.
e-mail: not available

Jarno Trulli

www.jarnotrulli.com
This is definitely the official site of the Formula 1 driver. There is an excellent animated Flash 4 version and a simpler text based site. Once inside you get biography, career history, a gallery of photos and the latest news. One page offers downloads of screen savers and other images, another page has links to other racing sites. The online store area is currently under construction.
e-mail: not available

Jason Plato online

www.jasonplato.com
Touring car race driver who competes in the UK. You can read Jason's profile and racing diary, reports and opinions on races and car developments and join Club Plato. The fan club requires an annual subscription; you can apply for membership online via a secure server and subscribe to a Plato newsletter.
e-mail: not available

Jenson Button

www.racecar.co.uk
Great site for the F1 enthusiast because aside from a profile of the driver, you get a guide to the racing scene. Every race is covered - where it's held, relative statistics and comparisons with previous seasons. There are online chat rooms, a multimedia page with downloadable images, video clips and an F1 game to play online. Joining the fan club is fully detailed and an online application form accelerates the process. A shop will be added to the site soon but for the moment you can buy goodies from his team web site.
e-mail: judem.jensonracing@
btinternet.com

Johnny Herbert

www.johnnyherbert.co.uk
A much more extensive web site compared with most other driver sites. This patriotic British driver posts up-to-date racing news with pictures, articles and interviews. There are chat rooms, discussion forums, message boards and a visitors' book. You can join the fan club online and buy Herbert goods at the store using a secure server.
e-mail: dc@johnnyherbert.co.uk

Pedro Diniz

www.pedrodiniz.com
Formula 1 driver and his official fan club site. Each racing weekend, news is updated under qualifying and racing headings in addition to reports for the whole season. The story of his career so far with a clutch of pictures takes you up to the fan club pages. The fan club discusses the events it organises and offers some of its members an opportunity to meet the man himself. Text is in English and Portuguese.
e-mail: fansclub@pedrodiniz.com

The Boss

www.the-boss.nl
Private fan site for F1 and in particular, Dutch drivers who compete in the sport. They are sketched in profile with news updates from each racing event. There are galleries of photos with action shots and massive crashes, cartoons and videos plus a list of other Formula 1 racing links. The site is in English and Dutch.
e-mail: info@the-boss.nl

The Earnhardt Connection

www.daleearnhardt.net
Every NASCAR fan has heard of Dale Earnhardt; this is his site. His career, history, family and sponsors are fully covered and racing news is continuously updated. A fan centre and merchandise page will soon join the chat room and message board. There are links to other racing sites, some details of his business interests and a newsletter.
e-mail: mail@daleearnhardt.net

The Johnny Benson Fan Club

www.johnnybenson-fanclub.com
Two-in-one web site - the official one and the fan club site run by his sister. You can join the fan club online by printing out a page from the site and sending it to the club office. His crew, racing schedule and press releases are all published online and you can check out the message board, sign the guest book and enter a special chat room. Merchandise can be viewed and to buy, either e-mail or fax your order to the fan club office.
e-mail: jbfc@iserv.net

The Official Jacques Villeneuve Fan Club

www.jvfan.villeneuve.com
This is the other Villeneuve site where you get details on how to join the fan club and what you will receive as a member. Complete the form provided, print and send it off to the fan club. Prices are in Swiss Francs but the online currency converter will help. Text is in English and French.
e-mail: not available

The Official Jeff Gordon Web site

www.jeffgordon.com
Click Jeff Gordon's picture and he
welcomes you to his site. You get
general news about NASCAR and more
specific news about the man himself.
You can become a member of the fan
club, keep up to date with NASCAR
tournaments, read about Jeff's racing
history and flick through his photo
album. There are weekly audio
downloads of post race interviews
and a large shopping section where
you can buy all kinds of merchandise
from videos to a special edition of
Monopoly.
e-mail: not available

The Tifosi Club

www.tifosi-club.com
Ferrari Formula 1 team and drivers
Michael Schumacher and Rubens
Barrichello. This is not an official site,
yet it is updated regularly with all the
latest news and results posted with
articles about the drivers. There are chat
forums to take part in, a technology page
that explains the latest advancements in
the sport and a multimedia page where
you can download screen savers and
video clips. Text is in English, Spanish,
Italian and French.
e-mail: via online form

Tony Stewart

www.tonystewart.com
The official web site of the driver and
his fan club. His racing schedule and
results come with news stories from
each race and an archive. There are
multimedia downloads - audio and
video clips. The easiest way to navigate
is to use the menu on the left which
scrolls out into the screen if you put
the mouse over it. The fan club page
tells you how to join and a link takes
you to their online store for merchandise.
e-mail: not available

Olympics

Ancient and Modern Olympic Sports

olympics.tufts.edu

Using the information from the Perseus Project, Tufts University has come up with a site where you can compare ancient and modern Olympic Games. Follow a tour of the site of Olympia as it is today and the Games themselves; discover the Olympic spirit and read about the athletes who were famous millennia ago, all on this site.
e-mail: webmaster@perseus.tufts.edu

Australian Sports Commission

www.ausport.gov.aul

There are special pages on this official site that take you to Sydney 2000, an introduction to the Olympic Family, news of future Olympic Games and bid cities and links to Olympic-related sites, making this an excellent place to get an overview of the greatest international tournament. The Australian side of the picture comes in the form of records of their Games medallists from 1896 to the present and profiles of current and former athletes.
e-mail: not available

Australian Sports Commission

www.ausport.gov.au

Information on organisational involvement in sport at a national, State and local level, with details of the Australian Sports Commission, the Australian Institute of Sport, national sporting directories and most importantly, the Sydney 2000 Olympics.
e-mail: webmaster@ausport.gov.au

Beijing Olympic Committee

www.beijing-olympic.org.cn

The Beijing Olympic Committee's bid for the 2008 Olympic Games is fronted by this web site. Olympic history, Chinese culture, Olympic sports and International Committees take up several pages. If you are interested in Chinese culture and how China views the Olympic Games, you'll find lots to read on the site. Text is in English and Chinese.
e-mail: 2008@beijing-olympic.org.cn

Big West – Olympic Sports

www.bigwest.org/sports/olympic
Influential sports conference held in
the USA. The official site has pages
specially featuring women's gymnastics,
men's and women's golf, tennis, track
and field events at Olympic level.
e-mail: mvillamor@bigwest.org

Big12sports.com

www.big12sports.com/teams/oly
Online coverage of news, results and
several Olympic events with championship
records and quick facts on national teams.
e-mail: via online form

Bulgarian Olympic Committee

www.infotel.bg/bocbg
e-mail: bocbg@main.infotel.bg

Chinese Olympic Team

www.chinaolympics.com
e-mail: via online form

Croatian Olympic Committee

www.tel.hr/hoo
e-mail: adresu hoo@hoo.tel.hr

Denmark Olympic Team

www.dif.dk
e-mail: not available

Estonia Olympic Committee

www.online.ee/~eok/committee.html
e-mail: eok@online.ee

Federations For Olympic Sports

www.roc.ru/eng/federat_e.htm
e-mail: roc@orc.ru

General Secretariat for Sports

www.sport.gov.gr
Sports news online covers forthcoming
Olympic games in 2000, 2002 and 2004.
The Olympic Youth Festival, links to
international and national Olympic
Committees, event calendars and
sports conferences complete the site.
e-mail: not available

Georgian Olympic Team

www.sanet.ge/atlanta96/index.html
e-mail: not available

German Sport and Olympic Museum

www.sportmuseum-koeln.de/
sportmuseum/eng/home.htm
German sport, development, national
involvement in the Olympic Games,
their achievements, teams and
structure. To search, click on the
images on the home page. Text is
in English and German.
e-mail: sportmuseum@
sportmuseum-koeln.de

Guam National Olympic

www.gnoc.com
e-mail: gnoc@ite.net

Ingrid O'Neil Sport and Memorabilia

www.ioneil.com
Leading source for Olympic memorabilia
through auctions across the world.
Goods for sale include participants'
and winners' medals, torches, badges,
pins, official reports, programs, tickets,
posters, diplomas and souvenirs.
e-mail: info@ioneil.com

International Olympic Committee

www.olympic.org
A very easy official site to navigate,
information is plentiful about members

and activities. The home page has links to National Olympics Committees, International Sports Federations, Olympics Television Archives and a Museum. Text is in English and French.
e-mail: not available

International Sailing Federation

www.sailing.org
The governing body of the Olympic sailing competition. Pages cover Federation activities, sailing updates, the latest news and Olympic issues, ranking, elections, committee nomination and a host of sailing topics.
e-mail: sail@isaf.co.uk

Japanese Olympic Committee

www.joc.or.jp/eng
e-mail: not available

Kenya Olympic Team

www.africaonline.co.ke/AfricaOnline/olympics.html
e-mail: not available

Korea Olympic Committee and Korea Sports

www.sports.or.kr/english/enew.html
e-mail: not available

Macedonian Olympic Committee

www.mok.org.mk
e-mail: not available

Malta Olympic Committee

www.digigate.net/moc
e-mail: nocmalta@waldonet.net.mt

New Zealand Olympic Committee

www.olympic.org.nz
e-mail: office@olympic.org.nz

Olympic Games

www.nbcolympics.com
Well designed site with loads of interactive stuff on all forms of sport. Scroll through the pages for special columns on the Olympics, the athletes and future events in Sydney 2000 and Athens 2004.
e-mail: nbc-feedback@nbcolympics.com

Olympic Regional Development Authority

www.orda.org
e-mail: info@orda.org

Olympic Tour

olympic.tour.d9.com
If you're not a lucky ticket holder to what is likely to be a truly great sports pageant in Sydney, take advantage of an organised tour by visiting the site and experience the history of the Olympics online.
e-mail: via online form

OVC

www.ovcsports.com/oly/oly
e-mail: information@ovc.org

Salt Lake 2002

www.slc2002.org
Salt Lake City will host the Winter Olympic Games in 2002. The official site gives

year-round training and competition for more than one million athletes in 150 countries. They tell you what they do and where they are and offer an online shop.
e-mail: not available

Special Olympics Connecticut

www.soct.org
Each year these special Olympics host more than 50 tournaments and competitions in 21 different fields of sport for mentally retarded children and adults. This United States program offers year-round training and athletic competition. The home page introduces you to the Special Olympics and the 2001 World Winter Games.
e-mail: maryc@soct.org

Special Olympics Pennsylvania

www.paso.org
A new page in sports history where several summer competitions for mentally retarded and disabled athletes are hosted. The organisers give year-round training for Olympic-style sport. The pages tell you a lot about these special Olympics and the training program.
e-mail: esmith@paso.org

Sports Stars USA

sportsstarsusa.com/Olympians
Directory of US sports stars, their memorable performances and mug shots, all searchable by name or sport. Olympic gold medallists are also listed.
e-mail: bill@sportsstarsusa.com

you the full program, venues, how to get tickets, whom to contact and anything else you need to know to get you there. If you wish to volunteer your services, you can do so online and while you're at it check out the shopping directory.
e-mail: via online form

SEC

www.secsports.com/teams/oly
Sport across the United States, Olympic Sports and great links to national and international Olympic organisations, federations and committees. If you want to check out the latest schedules for the Olympic Games, go and see its Olympic Sports pages.
e-mail: not available

SOSFO

www.sosfo.or.kr
e-mail: not available

Special Olympics

www.specialolympics.org
Global online headquarters of the world wide Special Olympics Movement for

sportsjones

www.sportsjones.com/sports/olympics.htm
Daily online sports magazine with a

lively section on the Olympics. Fascinating articles cover all forms of sport - baseball, boxing, fitness, wrestling, basketball and then you get great stories about athletes, reviews and re-runs of previous competitions.
e-mail: sjeditor@sportsjones.com

Sportsline.com

www.sportsline.com/u/olympics
Another site on which to follow the summer Olympic Games in Sydney, Australia. All the teams, events and competitions are detailed online.
e-mail: not available

Sydney Athletics Web

www.oztrack.com
e-mail: sydneyathletics@oztrack.com

The Ancient Olympic Games Virtual Museum

devlab.dartmouth.edu/Olympic
Virtual museum that goes into the

Olympic sports battles of the ancients. To search, click on the online map for an exhibition that presents history, contests, anecdotes and stories of the competitors in a marvellous parade. There are links to related sites.
e-mail: via online form

The British Olympic Association

www.olympics.org.uk
They select and manage the British Olympic Games team. You'll find information dealing with specific sport and a record of medal winners. The Medal Zone runs a monthly competition and Hot Issues gives you access to the latest news and recent press releases.
e-mail: talkolympic@boa.org.uk

The Cyprus Olympic Committee

www.olympic.org.cy
e-mail: not available

The First Olympia Games, Athens 1896

orama.com/athens1896
For a vivid description of the first meeting of the great event in 1896, visit this site. Then you can follow up on more modern Olympic Games including the last great event in Atlanta, USA.
e-mail: orama@orama.com

The Lithuanian National Olympic Committee

www.ltok.lt/indexeng.html
e-mail: komitetas@ltok.lt

The Olympic Century

www.olympiccentury.com
A definitive reference on the modern Olympics movement in 24 volumes, with a series index, core curriculum

guides and lesson plans. The series is introduced, customer services explained and links take you to international and national Olympic committees. For the serious Olympic student.
e-mail: via online form

The Olympics and Sports Study Centre

www.blues.uab.es/olympic.studies/activities.html
The centre located in Symposia, Spain collaborates with the Olympic Museum in Lausanne in hosting studies, seminars and research projects all over the world. Topics include Olympic villages, ceremonies and games. This site gives a greater in-depth coverage of Olympic activities for the serious researcher.
e-mail: Berta.Cerezuela@uab.es

The Sacramento Sports Commission

www.sacsports.com
e-mail: bburns@sacsports.com

The Virtual Resource Centre for Sport Information

www.sportquest.com/wintolym.shtml
This sports information centre has a resource you can search by sport or topic. The Winter Olympic Sports section covers eleven separate activities. It makes up a very useful site for research or just plain entertainment.
e-mail: moreinfo@sirc.ca

United States Olympic Committee

www.usoc.org
The US Olympics team is generally one of the largest and runs off with the top honours. These pages tell you about

the team and how it is organised; you get a look at athletes in training and a count of US medals. An online shop is at your service.
e-mail: via online form

USA Shooting

www.usashooting.com
Home of the national governing body of the Olympics shooting competition with a countdown to the 2000 Games. The US team tells you how it has done in national competitions and the previous Olympic Games. US team selection procedures are explained online.
e-mail: Admin.Info@usashooting.org

Volleyball In The Olympics

www.volleyball.org/olympics/index.html
The past, present and future of Olympic, indoor and beach volleyball are nicely detailed on this site. In addition you get an overview of the original and modern Olympic Games with links to International and National Olympic Committees.
e-mail: via online form

Winter and Summer Olympic Sports

www.walkercenter.com/walkercenterihpc/summersports.html
More or less an encyclopaedia of Olympic sports. Summer and winter games are broken down into individual events and each is dealt with in great detail. If you have further questions, consult the Q & A section. There are links to forthcoming Games including Sydney 2000, Salt Lake 2002 and Athens 2004.
e-mail: staff@walkercenter.com

Wotz On

www.wotzon.com.au
A special visual tour of the Sydney
Olympic Games. By following the tour
you'll find interactive stadium floor
plans, a calendar of events and many
useful links to local facilities, media
and public transport in Sydney.
e-mail: not available

www.theACC.com – Olympic Sports

theacc.fansonly.com/olympic/
acc-olympic.html
Mainly introductions and reviews of all
manner of Olympics events including
field hockey, tennis, soccer, golf,
volleyball and wrestling. There are
features on baseball, football and
basketball across the USA.
e-mail: via online form

Rugby

General Rugby Sites

About: Rugby

rugby.about.com/sports/rugby/
Rugby section of the popular
About.Com guides to the web.
Stuart Duncan a freelance writer and
long-time rugby enthusiast wrote the
words. An army of links, assembled
into categories, takes you to sites that
would rivet any rugby fan. A newsletter,
chat facility and message board give
you an opportunity to interact.
e-mail: rugby.guide@about.com

European Rugby

www.officialeuropeanrugby.com
Informative official web site, though a
little restrained. As the showcase of
the European and Six Nations Rugby
the site brings you up to speed on the
Heineken Cup, the European Shield
and the Lloyds-TSB Six Nations
Championship. The summer tours of
the Home Unions are added on to do
justice to regional events. In any case
you can sign on to receive the
newsletter regularly by e-mail.
e-mail: not available

NRL What A Game

www.nrl.com.au
Australia's National Rugby League
site does it all online. Teams and
players with their profiles, match
results, league tables and a thumbnail
sketch of every club. Screensaver and
wallpaper will download directly on to
your computer. A photo gallery of
match highlights from umpteen games,
sound gallery of interviews and match
previews, which can be found on the
sight and sound page, require MP3
player. So what's left to do?
e-mail: not available

Planet Rugby

www.planet-rugby.com

Highly respected resource and one of the best, if not the very best rugby site on the web. Everything you can possibly want to know about international rugby, players, fixtures results, statistics, online rugby trivia quiz and message boards, an e-mail newsletter service. Club level rugby is also featured with latest news and photos. You can't ask for more without being greedy.

e-mail: via online form

Rugby League - The Greatest Game on the Web

www.rlsa.org.uk

This is it – the official web site of the UK Rugby League Supporters Association. It's all here, what they do, what they want to do, how to get in touch and how to join up. And then some more - the online edition of The Greatest Game Rugby League fanzine and The Virtual Terrace message board for all fans.

e-mail: info@rlsa.org.uk

Rugby365

www.rugby365.com

As the Rugby section of the popular 365 series of web sites this portal covers the game globally and with style. Tournaments, internationals, national club competitions at every level and pretty much everything else in English, French, Spanish, and Afrikaans.

e-mail: via online form

Scrum.Com

www.scrum.com

The rugby wing of the Sportal Network covering Rugby Union tournaments,

internationals, national leagues world wide, women's and student rugby. Weekly columnists include BBC's sports broadcasters John Inverdale and the respected rugby player Lawrence Dallaglio. Sportswear and accessories can be purchased in the Shopping Mall. As a bonus you can post your messages on the highly popular bulletin board. Keep this site in view.

e-mail: via online form

USRL.com

www.usrl.com

The United States Rugby League fills its web site with league news, tables, fixtures, player lists and contact details for each of their affiliated teams. Each week the best players are scored on the Total Gym from which the Player of the Year is chosen. You can track progress online.

e-mail: sgormley@usrl.com

Tournaments

These official tournament sites give close coverage of competitions under their control. The tournaments themselves are also featured on the National Federation and Union sites listed in this directory.

Epson Cup Pacific Rim

www.irfb.com/epsoncup
e-mail: not available

Official World Sevens Site

www.irbsevens.org
e-mail: not available

The rest of this chapter is divided into two main sections - Rugby League and Rugby Union.

Rugby League

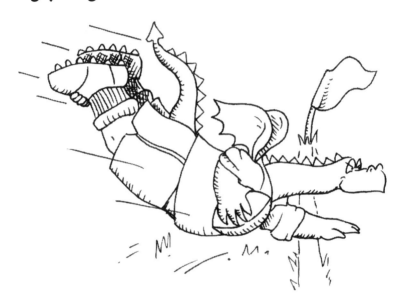

AUSTRALIA

AUCKLAND WARRIORS

Auckland Warriors Official Website

www.warriors.co.nz
Full-blooded official web site covering all aspects of the club and team. The chat room has a special feature for fans to talk live together during and after games or with players at special chat events which are fully transcribed so you miss nothing but the drama if you miss the session. The online store sells kit, memorabilia and season tickets.
e-mail: via online form

Auckland Warriors - Auckland Warriors

www.geocities.com/Colosseum/Field/2382/
e-mail: not available

Auckland Warriors - Home Away From Home

homepages.ihug.co.nz/~field_7/
e-mail: not available

BRISBANE BRONCOS

Brisbane Broncos

www.broncos.com.au
The official site of the Brisbane Broncos with a club history, player profiles and photographs, and a message board and chat facility. Online shopping for club merchandise can be done in the Raiders accessories store. Some sections require Flash plug-in.
e-mail: not available

Brisbane Broncos - Kelly's Broncos Page

www.geocities.com/Eureka/Plaza/6642/
e-mail: not available

Brisbane Broncos - Let's Go Broncos

members.xoom.com/broncoland/
e-mail: not available

Brisbane Broncos - Unofficial Home of the Brisbane Broncos

www.bronconet.com
e-mail: not available

CANBERRA RAIDERS

Canberra Raiders

www.raiders.com.au
Some sections of this official site require the Flash plug-in. Reporting of matches and club news, player profiles with photographs and an album of pictures from key moments in the club's history make entertaining reading. All the fan and shopping facilities are geared to making this a friendly site.
e-mail: not available

Canberra Raiders - Canberra Raiders Army

www.geocities.com/Colosseum/Arena/9776/
e-mail: not available

Canberra Raiders - Canberra Raiders E Group

www.egroups.com/group/raiders82
e-mail: not available

Canberra Raiders - Mals Green Machine

greenmachine.8m.com
e-mail: not available

Canberra Raiders - Season '82

raiders.rleague.com
e-mail: not available

CANTERBURY BULLDOGS

Canterbury Bulldogs

www.bulldogs.com.au
They tell you their story back to the 1930s. The Howling Wall is where you post your messages, the Injured Dog tells you who is in the treatment room and why; elsewhere you get news and stats. The online store has a few unusual items on offer.
e-mail: debs@zeta.org.au

Canterbury Bulldogs - Canterbury Bulldogs eGroup

www.egroups.com/group/canterbury
e-mail: not available

Canterbury Bulldogs - Canterbury Bulldogs Supporters Site

www.rleague.com/bulldogs/
e-mail: not available

CRONULLA SHARKS

Cronulla Sharks

www.sharks.com.au
There are loads of freebies on this official site. In addition to screensavers, wallpaper, video and audio downloads, you can do the same with a Browser Skin to customise your own. The Shark Theatre has loads of MPEG video games that can be played online or downloaded. Aside from this you get a club history and team photos that go back to 1967.
e-mail: sharks@sharks.com.au

Cronulla Sharks - Coonsta's Sharks Site

www.geocities.com/SunsetStrip/Garage/3315/
e-mail: not available

Cronulla Sharks - Srini's Shark Page
www.geocities.com/sharks2000_au/
e-mail: not available

DRAGONS ST GEORGE ILLAWARRA

Dragons St George Illawarra
www.dragons.com.au
As official home of this League Club, the site has the latest club and team news, results and tables. The online club store is well-stocked with team kit and memorabilia. Player profiles blend in with a lively photo gallery.
e-mail: via online form

Dragons St George Illawarra - Saints On TV
www.showroom.com.au/dragons/
e-mail: not available

Dragons St George Illawarra - The Unofficial St George-Illawarra Dragons Website
www.ozemail.com.au/~dsmart/saints/
e-mail: not available

MELBOURNE STORMS

Melbourne Storms
www.melbournestorm.com.au
Another site loaded with freebies - wallpaper and screensavers from the Kids Zone, a quiz to test your knowledge of the team and if you have Flash plug-in you can play the Melbourne Storm Memory Game. The serious part of this official web site gives all the stats, fixtures and an online shop.
e-mail: via online form

Melbourne Storms - Dust Storm
www.zeustech.com.au/storm/
e-mail: not available

Melbourne Storms - Melbourne Storm Supporters Club
members.xoom.com/stormfans/
e-mail: stormfans@hotmail.com

NEWCASTLE KNIGHTS

Newcastle Knights
knights.hunterlink.net.au
The newsroom has an almost endless list of items dating back some six months. You can e-mail any player by filling out the online form, meet players and cheerleaders, listen to the club theme song and purchase merchandise in the club shop.
e-mail: knights@newcastleknights.com.au

Newcastle Knights - Newcastle Knights Photo Archive
www.geocities.com/marathonstadium/
e-mail: not available

Newcastle Knights - Newcastle Knights Results and Statistics
www.users.bigpond.com/apfrith/default.htm
e-mail: not available

North Queensland Cowboys
www.cowboys.com.au
Breaking news and sponsorship opportunities are just two aspects of what you get on this packed site. Ticket prices and status can be checked online and if you become a Net Member you can access the more hallowed parts of the site for free.
e-mail: cowboys@cowboys.com.au

NORTHERN EAGLES 2000

Northern Eagles 2000

www.northerneagles.com.au
They promise to add free audio and video clips to their other downloadable goodies. Judging by the amount of traffic, the chat room and bulletin board must be very popular. The club has a Junior Development Program and Junior Rugby League.
e-mail: info@northerneagles.com.au

Northern Eagles - Another Unofficial Northern Eagles Website

www.markie.com.au/eagles/main.htm
e-mail: not available

Northern Eagles - Northern Eagles

www.zipworld.com.au/~gfiveash/
e-mail: not available

PARRAMATTA EELS

Parramatta Eels

www.parraeels.com.au
The Eels go out and about in a community program, which in part gives people a chance to meet the players. The web site not only tells you all about the club but offers very useful coaching tips and free downloads of screensavers and wallpaper. The online shop sells children's wear and supporters' gear.
e-mail: via online form

Parramatta Eels - The Greatest Club

www.geocities.com/Colosseum/Rink/9229/clubs/parra/index.htm
e-mail: conder@globe.net.nz

Parramatta Eels - The Unofficial Parramatta Eels Web Page

www.blueandgoldarmy.com
e-mail: deano@blueandgoldarmy.com

PENRITH PANTHERS

Penrith Panthers

www.panthers.com.au
If you have RealPlayer you can pick up the team song. The site has a lot to say about club players with biogs of Immortals from the past, a photo gallery and profiles of current players. You can also e-mail the players.
e-mail: not available

Penrith Panthers -Panthers Den

www.panthersden.cjb.net
e-mail: cthomas@start.com.au

Penrith Panthers -Scarters Army

www.scarters.cjb.net
e-mail: not available

THE SYDNEY ROOSTERS

The Sydney Roosters

www.sydneyroosters.com.au
e-mail: not available

The Sydney Roosters - Rooster Net

www.dovenetq.net.au/~pcallen/index/index.htm
e-mail: not available

The Sydney Roosters - The Rooster Pen

www.insidetheweb.com/mbs.cgi/mb910263
e-mail: not available

The Sydney Roosters - Unofficial Site

www.ozemail.com.au/~ovelar/
roosters.html
e-mail: not available

WESTS TIGERS

Wests Tigers

www.weststigers.com.au
Supporters are very much in mind on
this official site. A chat room to talk
with other fans or players at appointed
times, a notice board and a membership
application form. The club does a lot
of work in the local community and
players go out to meet the people.
There is of course a picture gallery,
match results and reports and player
profiles.
e-mail: via online form

Wests Tigers - The Wests Tigers Den

www.geocities.com/Colosseum/
Sideline/7915/
e-mail: not available

Wests Tigers - Wests Tigers On The Web

rleague.com/weststigers/
e-mail: not available

ENGLAND

Aye of the Tigers

www.ayeofthetigers.fsnet.co.uk
e-mail:
contribute@ayeofthetigers.fsnet.co.uk

Barrow Border Raiders

www.raiders.org.uk
Because of its unusual design the
Raiders web site appears to have little
content. But double click on the page

and a pop up menu appears. This
enables you to navigate around the
site, which has a guide to club history,
the latest news, results and a message
board for fans to chat. Guest writer
Alan Tucker comments on current club
business.
e-mail: not available

Bradford Bulls

www.bradfordbulls.co.uk
Articles by regular columnist James
Lowe, a free newsletter and sign up
details for the Bulls Summer Camp
form the mainstay of this official web
site. You get some more about the
team and its progress, then the rest is
for fans. E-mail addresses of other
fans looking for pen pals, a message
board, guest book, and chat room give
you lots of opportunity to interact.
e-mail: info@bradfordbulls.co.uk

Breathing Fire

www.doncasterdragons.org.uk
This is the official Doncaster Dragons
web site bringing you the latest club
news, match results, reports and
previews of forthcoming fixtures.
There is a little about club merchandise

and a Terrace Talk page where fans get to voice their opinions. The site has been optimised for Internet Explorer version 5.
e-mail: robclayton@cableinet.co.uk

Castleford Tigers Unofficial Rugby League Club Website

www.rangey.demon.co.uk/tigers.htm
Fan site with stats, fixtures, results, match reports, player biographies and a packed photo gallery. The Who Are Yer page encourages you to reveal a bit about yourself on the site. You can download Tigers wallpaper and screensavers for your PC and music in RealPlayer, MP3, and MIDI formats. Here's a chance to send a Castleford Tigers postcard - simply select a photo and music from those available and fill the online form.
e-mail: mraynor@rangey.demon.co.uk

Dewsbury Rams

www.dewsburyrams.com
Fixtures, results, match reports and all the latest team news are followed by a mailing list you can join if you want to receive club news by e-mail. You can leave comments and questions for other fans on the message board. Each week The Boot Room focuses on a different match from Rams history.
e-mail: dewsburyrams@bigfoot.com

Featherstone Rovers Club

www.btinternet.com/%7Erovers/fev.html
The club was formed in 1902. The official web site gives its history, photographs, a list of honours won and a focus on the great matches. The club shop catalogue tells you what you can

buy and a guest book asks for your comments about the site.
e-mail: rovers@btinternet.com

Halifax Blue Sox

www.bluesox.co.uk/index.htm
Official site with club news and information. To sponsor the team, check out the packages detailed online and take your pick. The online shop sells videos and replica kits. You can get yourself a Blue Sox Visa Card.
e-mail: murgatroyd@breathe.co.uk

Hull FC

www.hullfc.com
Previously known as the Hull Sharks this official site features a club history, illustrated tour of the grounds and a soon-to-open online club shop. Send a personal message to your favourite Hull FC player, write in the guest book, use the chat room or message board and get yourself on the mailing list. You can download a Hull FC Space Invaders Screensaver and Game.
e-mail: chris@hullfc.com

Hull FC Unofficial

www.hull-fc.co.uk
e-mail: shaun@hull-fc.co.uk

Leeds Rhinos

www.leedsrugby.com/rhinos/frames.htm
Packed with content to satisfy any fan, the official club site has all match details, selections from the tournament programme and you get a chance to have your say. Download the Rhinos wallpaper for your desktop while you check out the history of the club. The online shop sells replica kit, accessories and season tickets and you can keep in

touch by subscribing to the Official E-mail News Service.
e-mail: corporate@leedsrugby.com

Leeds Rhinos Unofficial

www.cowardathome.demon.co.uk
Can you pick a team of Rhinos greats from the 1990s? If you want to give it a try, send off to this site and see it online alongside a growing number of teams selected by fellow fans. The site brings you thoughts on the club, fixtures, results, league tables and match reports.
e-mail: paul@cowardathome. demon.co.uk

London Broncos

www.londonbroncos.co.uk
Keep up to date with team progress, match previews, reports and events at the club. Coach's Corner gives an insight into the coaching staff and their aspirations. If you are a junior find out how to join that part of the club reserved for your age group. Tickets, replica kit and a range of other items can be purchased online in the club shop.
e-mail: via online form

Nick's Riverside

www.angelfire.com/nd/rleague/
e-mail: ndraper@mailexcite.com

P & B Online

www.unofficialwolves.freeserve.co.uk
The Wolves fan site has a petition asking fans to support the move to a new stadium by signing online. If you want a print version of the Primrose and Blue fanzine and an archive of past articles check out the request details. Matches, news and comments conclude the web business.
e-mail: nathanashurst@yahoo.com

Ram It Home

freespace.virgin.net/cris.tout/rams/ index.htm
Ram It Home is a very impressive fansite devoted to the Dewsbury Rams.
e-mail: cris.tout@virgin.net

Rugby Leaguer

www.rugbyleaguer.co.uk
Online companion to the Wigan-based Rugby Leaguer magazine. The coverage is simply enormous - news from the UK and the world, fixtures, results, statistics and tables; regular columnists write from their intimate knowledge of the sport. If you want to subscribe to the magazine, fill out the online form. And what would such a site be without a message board?
e-mail: rugby.leaguer@rim.co.uk

Saints

saints.merseyworld.com
Match reports, fixtures and results of all the competitive games played by the club and a bundle of images of the team in action. Each week Apollo Perelini will answer five questions e-mailed by fans. You can exchange views with other fans via the message board and chat room or join the mailing list.
e-mail: not available

Salford City Reds

www.reds.co.uk
Rare example of an official club site that uses Macromedia Flash. Appearance and presentation are that much more visually appealing. The use of sound lets you select from four backing tracks from classical to disco so you read to the sound of music.

You get all the statistics and club news, a chat room and online shop.
e-mail: via online form

The Giants

www.giantsonline.co.uk
As an official web site it is well stocked with club details and their record. Hot Gossip gives an insider view of goings, on and off the pitch. Illustrated player profiles, match fixtures, results and reports take up the remaining pages.
e-mail: enquiries@giantsonline.co.uk

The Saints Heritage Society

www.saints.org.uk
Community run web site with an emphasis on the history of the club from the fans' point of view, nicely illustrated with photographs and quotes. Screensavers and wallpaper can be downloaded as well as video clips of players in action. These require Windows Media Player.
e-mail: paul@saints.org.uk

The Saints Online

www.supersaints.freeservers.com/ index.htm
If you have Shockwave plug-in you can watch a slide show of the team in action in the 1999 Grand Final. A few clicks on the map will help you locate the club. The player profiles and photos from the past few seasons are particularly good. The latest news, fixtures and results finish off this unofficial site.
e-mail: supersaints@cableinet.co.uk

The Tigers Den

www.hagis.freeserve.co.uk/theden.htm
e-mail: not available

The Voice of the Crowd

www.unofficial-bluesox.co.uk
There is an impressive collection of material on this fan site. Player profiles, statistics, an illustrated club history and directions to the grounds. Fans can converse using the chat room, message boards and the guest book. Have a laugh if you are privy to the partisan jokes.
e-mail: andi@unofficial-bluesox.co.uk

The Wildcats Lair

www.trinitywildcats.co.uk
To make your PC completely Wildcat friendly download the screensavers and wallpaper images supplied free of charge. The official web site of Wakefield Trinity Rugby Club has all the latest news, match facts and figures, a message board and chat room. You can try your luck at the Tipping Competitions where you predict match winners to win points.
e-mail: info@trinitywildcats.co.uk

Tiger Town

members.xoom.com/_XMCM/ tigertownweb/index.htm
Unofficial fan site by Stuart Main devoted to the Castleford Tigers which has plenty of stats and information. Regularly updated news about the club and results reports and tables. Have your say on the TigertownWeb Interactive Message Board.
e-mail: tigertown_web@hotmail.com

Tigers TeamTalk

www.tigers.teamtalk.com
Club news, forthcoming fixtures and details of Sky TV televised matches take up a few pages of the official Castleford Tigers web site. There are photographs

of team successes in the Challenge Cup, Regal Trophy, Yorkshire Cup, Yorkshire League, and the BBC 2 Floodlit Trophy and illustrated player profiles. They will shortly move to a new site at http://www.castigers.com/.
e-mail: not available

Unofficial Wakefield Trinity Wildcats

www.adaley.freeserve.co.uk/index.html
Fansite for Wakefield Trinity Wildcats. Meet The Team has player biographies with photographs, full fixtures and results; league tables can be downloaded in Microsoft Word format. There are stats for the top 5 players of 1999 in categories such as Metres Made and Clean Breaks, an archive of past players, league tables and a popular message board.
e-mail: not available

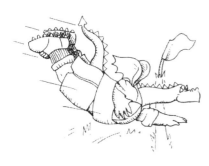

Wigan Warriors

www.wigan-warriors.co.uk
Official Wigan Warriors presence on the Internet with all the news, player details, club and team information, supporters' letters, results and match coverage. You can post your views and read the opinions of other fans on message board.
e-mail: via online form

Wigan-Warriors.com

www.wigan-warriors.com
This unofficial fan site claims to be the most comprehensive resource online for Wigan Warriors Rugby League. Loads of stats, records and news come with an audio-video section showing players in action. You get to interact with other fans on the message board and take part in a poll to rate favourite players and select the best team.
e-mail: not available

Wolf Web

www.wwrlfc.co.uk
Wolf Web is the excellent official web site of the Warrington Wolves with an illustrated history of the club from 1879 to the present day. A downloadable section has desktop wallpaper and games. There are details on how to join the Pack, a photo gallery, player profiles, a busy and popular fans forum and club shop. The audio/video content requires RealPlayer.
e-mail: not available

World of Rugby League

www.rleague.com
Probably the largest and best site for global Rugby League. Australian and UK league news, stats, tables, teams, fixtures, national games coverage, stories and articles, history, trivia and then wallpaper to change the face of your computer. To keep in touch, get the e-mail newsletter. The fan forum and chat room want to hear from you. Definitely a site not to be missed and certainly one to bookmark.
e-mail: matthew@rleague.com

Rugby Union

ENGLAND

Bath

www.bathrugby.co.uk
Internet home of Bath Rugby with selected items from match programs once the game commences. Player profiles of all the team come with statistics and photographs. The online store will sell you most of the goods found in their official store.
e-mail: hmercer@bathrugby.co.uk

Bedford Rugby Club

www.bedfordrugby.co.uk
They tell you what the papers say about them and give you all the stats and coverage for the first team and the Junior Blues of all ages. Browsing in the club shop for sportswear is bound to come up with something you want and to make it easy you can order online.
e-mail: info@bedfordrugby.co.uk

Bristol Rugby Club

www.bristolrugby.co.uk
News and results spiced with a photo gallery of players in action and a plan to put on live broadcasts of all matches. Club history, statistics, player biographies and coaching staff back up the club shop and online ticket office, which have secure online payment. The message board encourages you to interact with fellow fans.
e-mail: lynn.coles@bristolrugby.co.uk

Coventry

www.coventry.co.uk
Official site for Coventry Rugby Club. This site is currently Under Extensive Re-Construction. No content at present.
e-mail: not available

Gloucester Rugby Football Club

www.kingsholm-chronicle.org.uk
If you have a passion for statistics or just want a past result, you will find them online going all the way back to 1873. The club shop sells you fan kit while video and audio clips, screensavers and animations come free if you have Shockwave plug-in, RealPlayer and speakers.
e-mail: gloucester_rugby@hotmail.com

Harlequins

www.quins.co.uk
Fixtures, results and match reports support a large squad of illustrated player profiles. The online shop, powered by Kitbag.com offers a range of Harlequins official leisurewear to buy online including jerseys, fleeces and caps; kit out your baby, if you have one, in team colours with the Harlequins Romper suit.
e-mail: not available

Henley

www.henleyrugbyclub.org.uk
All levels of the club's teams - juniors and seniors, men and women – are given the full treatment including a detailed report on the International Henley Sevens. There is a great selection of goodies in the club shop.
e-mail: scoop.hrfc@virgin.net

Leeds Tykes

www.leedsrugby.com/tykes/frames.htm
Just so you don't forget them, as if any fan could, they give you Tykes Wallpaper to download onto your desktop. The official site has all the club news and match details. The current squad is discussed together with lively player profiles. You can buy your club kit and tickets online and enter future events and functions into your diary.
e-mail: corporate@leedsrugby.com

Leicester Tigers

www.tigers.co.uk
Re-live past matches in the photo gallery and savour those delicious moments of glory in the Days Gone By section. The official web site tells you about fixtures for the first team, the under-21s and the youth with all the results and tables. You can buy replica kit and sportswear online and fans can talk themselves hoarse in the busy Tigers Forum. A really good site
e-mail: tigers@tigers.co.uk

London Irish

www.london-irish-rugby.com
Aside from all the information you would expect about the club, there are details of the London Irish Rugby Rewards Cashback scheme. Loads of press releases and a picture gallery of players in action follow match reports.
e-mail: londonirishrfc@aol.com

London Welsh RFC

www.london-welsh.co.uk
Fans will enjoy following the progress of their team on this official site. Matches, stats and a potted club history take you up to a membership application form which you can send online for a quick answer. The club shop also operates on the same basis. All players have their careers and mugshots recorded online.
e-mail: commercial@london-welsh.co.uk

Manchester Rugby Club

www.manchester-rugby.co.uk
Fixtures, match results, league record
and directions to the grounds in case
you've forgotten. A history of the club
starts from the earliest years to the
present brought to life with pictures
and profiles of key players.
e-mail: rugby@manchester-rugby.co.uk

Moseley

www.moseleyrugby.co.uk
Find out online how you can sponsor
players and their cars or the match ball.
Fans can discuss club progress by
posting questions and comments, kind
or cutting, on the board. Match results,
player profiles and a club shop
complete the site.
e-mail: alan.escott@virgin.net

Newcastle Falcons

**www.newcastle-falcons.co.uk/
default.htm**
Read the latest club news, full match
reports, player profiles and of course all
the gossip. The catalogue lists the goods
you can buy from the club shop and if
you are planning to be at a game,
check out ticket prices and the map for
how to get there.
e-mail: not available

Northampton Saints

www.northamptonsaints.co.uk
There is no shortage of news and results
on this official club web site. Clothes,
videos, books, teddy bears and tankards
can be bought online in the club shop.
Post messages on the club message
board and if you want to contact a player
check out his e-mail address online.
e-mail: clubinfo@northamptonsaints.co.uk

Rotherham RUFC

www.rrufc.co.uk
It's all online – fixtures, match reports,
a brief club history, location map, the
latest news of events and new signings
and a full league table. Click on the
face of a player in the team photo and
his profile and mugshot appear. Post
your comments in the supporters'
forum.
e-mail: not available

Rugby Lions

www.rugbylions.co.uk
Everyone knows that when William
Webb Ellis, a Rugby schoolboy, picked
up the ball and ran with it whilst playing
football, he gave birth to the sport that
is played internationally to millions of
spectators. This is the official web site
of the only team from the birthplace of
the great game. Their home ground is
named after Ellis and the web site tells
you about the club and the team.
e-mail: info@rugbylions.co.uk

Sale Sharks

www.mansalerugby.com

Along with fixtures, results and match reports come player details and photographs. Shop for club merchandise in the online store and post your comments everywhere you can.
e-mail: not available

The Saracens Rugby Club Online

www.saracens.com

On this very interactive site you can send a friend or rival fan a Saracens postcard of your choice that they can pick up by visiting this official web site. Put yourself or a fellow fan forward for Fan of the Month by filling out an online form. Use the message boards and chat room to say your piece and check out player fitness in the Who's in the Physio Room section.
e-mail: comments@saracens.net

W 4+ +

subnet.virtual-pc.com/~be498476/

Strange name but not so strange a fan site, dedicated to the London Wasps. Gossip, views and news come on The Wasp Telegraf. The Wasp-to-Wasp bulletin board buzzes with comments.
e-mail: Dominic.Benson@brunel.ac.uk

Wakefield RFC Supporters Club

www.rugbysupporters.co.uk

Though supporters constructed this site, it officially represents the Yorkshire club. Match reports appear on the same day with results and statistics. A mailing list, guest book, message board and polls give you lots of opportunities to interact with your fellows.
e-mail: tackler7@yahoo.com

Wasps on the Web

www.wasps.co.uk

Keep up to date on the London club's official web site. Match results, fixtures and reports come to you with live audio clips if you have RealPlayer. You can buy club replica kit, fleece jackets and leisurewear online.
e-mail: wasps@loftusroadplc.co.uk

West Hartlepool Rugby Club

www.west-rugby.org.uk

Player profiles tell you who they are and Terrace Talk tells you where to chat about them with other fans. Read about the fixtures, results and match reports then find out how to sponsor the team and hire club facilities for your celebrations.
e-mail: not available

Worcester Rugby Football Club

www.wrfc.co.uk

They've done a great job of the club's official web site. You can bone up on club history, check out the ladies, senior and junior teams, keep up with regularly updated news and fixture list and shop online. If you want to host a party, check out the Sixways Conference Centre.
e-mail: via online form

All sites below are the official pages of lower ranked English Rugby Union clubs. Generally, you'll find information on fixtures and match results, a little about the club, its history and contact details for those wanting to become involved.

Andover Rugby Club

www.theknife.freeserve.co.uk
e-mail: not available

Army Rugby Union

www.armyrugbyunion.clara.net
e-mail: not available

Barbarians

www.barbarianfc.co.uk
e-mail: not available

Basingstoke Rugby Club

www.basingstoke.net/brfc.htm
e-mail: not available

Beckenham Rugby Football Club

www.guruconsultancy.com/rugby/index.htm
e-mail: not available

Blackheath Rugby Club

www.blackheathrugby.co.uk
e-mail: not available

Bolton Rugby Club

www.boltonrugby.co.uk
e-mail: not available

Bournemouth RFC

www.bournemouthrfc.org.uk
e-mail: not available

Bracknell Rugby Football Club

www.bracknellrugbyclub.com
e-mail: not available

Brighton Football Club (RFU)

www.brightonrugby.freeuk.com
e-mail: not available

Cambridge RUFC

www.crufc.co.uk
e-mail: not available

Chelmsford Rugby Club

www.terminator.co.uk/chelmsford
e-mail: not available

Chester RUFC

www.chester-rufc.com
e-mail: not available

Colchester RFC

www.colchester-rugby.freeserve.co.uk
e-mail: not available

Consett Rugby Football Club

www.derwentside.org.uk/community/demi/
e-mail: not available

Doncaster Rugby Football Club

www.drfc.co.uk
e-mail: not available

Dorking RFC

www.dorkingrugbyclub.co.uk
e-mail: not available

Eccles RFC

www.ecclesrfc.org.uk
e-mail: not available

Erith RFC

www.erithrfc.co.uk
e-mail: not available

Esher RFC

www.esherrfc.org.uk
e-mail: not available

Guernsey Rugby

www.guernseyrugby.swinternet.co.uk
e-mail: not available

Harlow Rugby Club

www.ramlogic.demon.co.uk/harlowrf.html
e-mail: not available

Horsham RUFC

come.to/HorshamRUFC
e-mail: not available

Hove RFC

www.hoverfc.com
e-mail: not available

Hull RUFC

www.come.to/hull.hornets
e-mail: not available

Huntingdon RUFC

members.aol.com/hrufc/
e-mail: not available

Jersey RFC

jrfc.jumpsports.com
e-mail: not available

Kendal RUFC

welcome.to/kendalrufc
e-mail: not available

Lowestoft

www.lowestoftandyarmouthrfc.co.uk
e-mail: not available

Maidenhead Rugby Club

www.maidenheadrfc.com
e-mail: not available

Maidstone Rugby Club

www.maidstonerugby.org.uk
e-mail: not available

Malvern College Rugby Club

www.malcol.org/web/Sports/Rugby/
home.html
e-mail: not available

Malvern RFC

www.geocities.com/rugbypost/
e-mail: not available

Marlow RFC

www.marlowrfc.com
e-mail: not available

Mellish RFC

www.juniormellish.fsnet.co.uk
e-mail: not available

Melton Mowbray RFC

www.mmrfc.freeserve.co.uk
e-mail: not available

Moore RUFC

www.moorerufc.co.uk
e-mail: not available

Newcastle (Staffs) Rugby Club

www.newcastlestaffsrufc.co.uk
e-mail: not available

Old Actonians

www.oldactoniansrfc.co.uk
e-mail: not available

Old Bedians RFC

www.oldbedians.freeserve.co.uk
e-mail: not available

Old Brentwoods Rugby Football Club

www.obrfc.org
e-mail: not available

Old Brodleians
www.johnkett.force9.co.uk/
oldbrodleians.htm
e-mail: not available

Old Edwardians RFC
www.oldedwardians.freeservers.com
e-mail: not available

Old Elthamians
www.old-elthamians-rfc.org.uk
e-mail: not available

Old Emanuel Rugby Football Club
www.old.emanuel.net
e-mail: not available

Old Northamptonians
www.oldnorthamptonians-rfc.co.uk
e-mail: not available

Old Reigatian Rugby Club
www.oldreigatianrufc.co.uk
e-mail: not available

Pennanians Rugby Union Football Club
www.PennsRUFC.org.uk
e-mail: not available

Penzance & Newlyn RFC
www.pirates-rfc.co.uk
e-mail: not available

Phoenix Rugby Union Football Club
members.aol.com/phoenixrfc
e-mail: not available

Plymouth Albion RFC
www.members.tripod.com/
beaconpark/index.htm
e-mail: not available

Port Sunlight Rugby Football Club
portsunlightrfc.merseyside.org
e-mail: not available

Richmond RFC
www.geocities.com/richmondvikings
e-mail: not available

Ripley Rhinos
www.dtrubee.dircon.co.uk/index.htm
e-mail: not available

Rotherham RUFC
www.rotherhamrugby.co.uk
e-mail: not available

Royal Navy Rugby Union
www.navyrugbyunion.co.uk
e-mail: not available

Runcorn RUFC
www.runcornrufc.f9.co.uk
e-mail: not available

Rushden & Higham Rugby Club
www.rhrufc.co.uk/rugby
e-mail: not available

Salians Rugby Club

www.saliansrufc.org.uk
e-mail: not available

Sandbach RUFC

www.sandbachrufc.co.uk
e-mail: not available

Scarborough Rugby Club

www.srufc.co.uk
e-mail: not available

Sedgley Park RUFC

www.sprufc.com
e-mail: not available

Sevenoaks Rugby Club

www.sevenoaks-rugby.org.uk
e-mail: not available

Sheffield Tigers RUFC

www.sheffieldtigers.co.uk
e-mail: not available

Stockport Rugby

www.stockportrugby.co.uk
e-mail: not available

Stoke on Trent RUFC

www.stokerugbyclub.co.uk
e-mail: not available

Stourbridge Rugby Football Club

www.stourbridge-rfc.co.uk
e-mail: not available

Suffolk Rugby Union

www.suffolk-ru.fsnet.co.uk
e-mail: not available

Tunbridge Wells RFC

www.pembury.freeserve.co.uk/twrfc.htm
e-mail: not available

Twickenham RFC

www.twickenhamrugby.com
e-mail: not available

Tyldesley RUFC

www.tyldesleyru.net
e-mail: not available

Warwickshire Colts RFU

www.warwickshirecolts.fsnet.co.uk
e-mail: not available

Warwickshire rugby

www.warwickshire-rfu.co.uk
e-mail: not available

Wellingborough RFC

websites.ntl.com./~c.ashby
e-mail: not available

Wellington Rugby Football Club

www.wellingtonrfc.co.uk
e-mail: not available

Westbury-on-Severn Rugby Club

www.xtravision.com/wosrfc
e-mail: not available

Wharfedale RUFC

www.wharfedalerugby.co.uk
e-mail: not available

Woking RFC

www.WokingRugby.com
e-mail: not available

Wyvern RFC

www.wyvernrfc.co.uk/home.htm
e-mail: not available

All Blacks-The Official NZ Site

www.nzrugby.com
e-mail: not available

INTERNATIONAL

The following addresses are the official sites of National Rugby Unions and Federations; all are in English or have an English translation. Taken individually, they are excellent starting points for basic information about the sport in a particular nation; combined they bring together the whole world of rugby. Each site has something to say about the national team, local leagues and competitions; it also describes the activities and members of the organisation and gives contact details.

Australian Rugby Union
www.rugby.com.au
e-mail: not available

Austrian Rugby Union
www.rugby-austria.com
e-mail: cjones@osce.org

Canadian Rugby
www.rugbycanada.ca
e-mail: RugbyCanada@rugbycanada.ca

England Rugby Football Union
www.rfu.com
e-mail: steveelliott@rfu.com

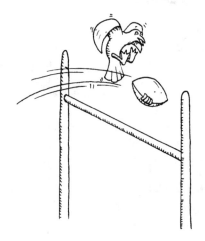

French Rugby Union
www.ffr.fr
e-mail: via online form

Hong Kong Rugby Union
www.hkrfu.com
e-mail: hkrfu@pacific.net.hk

Irish Rugby Union
www.irfu.ie
e-mail: not available

Japanese Rugby Site
www.rugby-japan.or.jp
e-mail: jrfu@rugby-japan.or.jp

Manu Samoa
www.manusamoa.com.ws
e-mail: not available

New Zealand Rugby Union
www.nzrugby.co.nz
e-mail: info@nzrugby.co.nz

Scottish Rugby Union
www.sru.org.uk
e-mail: feedback@sru.org.uk

South African Rugby Union
www.sarfu.org.za
e-mail: sarfu@icon.co.za

Trinidad and Tobago
www.ttrfu.com
e-mail: contact@ttrfu.com

USA Rugby Union
www.usarugby.org
e-mail: info@usarugby.org

Welsh Rugby Union
www.wru.co.uk
e-mail: not available

IRELAND

Ballymena
www.ballymena.rfc.mcmail.com
A photo gallery of smiling Irish eyes
and links to player profiles. Fixtures,
results and tables for the club's seven
teams can be viewed online with a
review of the last season. They run
a well-stocked online shop.
e-mail: ballymenarfc@mcmail.com

Bective Rangers
www.bectiverangersfc.com
e-mail: not available

Belfast Harlequins
www.belfastharlequins.com
e-mail: not available

Buccaneers
www.buccaneersrfc.com
A Who's Who of the club executive comes
with contact details to give you easy
access to the guiding spirits. Match
results, fixtures, reports and player
profiles take up several web pages.
The Pirate Club is linked to the shop
and you can chat online or draw swords
with other fans in the Cutlass Bar.
e-mail: info@buccaneersrfc.com

Cork Constitution
www.corkcon.ie
Home of the All Ireland League

Champions 1990-91 and 1998-99.
A thoroughly good and well-illustrated
history of the club from its origins in
the late 19th century to the present day
backs up the latest news, fixtures,
league tables, squad details and
instructions on how to get to the
ground.
e-mail: not available

Dundalk RFC
www.dundalkrfc.com
e-mail: not available

Dungannon
www.dungannon-rugby.co.uk
e-mail: not available

Enniscorthy RFC
www.geocities.com/enniscorthyrfc
e-mail: not available

Garryowen
www.garryowen-rugby.com
One of Ireland's oldest rugby clubs
publishes its fixture list, match results
and reports, news and press releases
on this site. A potted history tells
something about the club enlivened by
profiles of past and current players.
e-mail: via online form

Malahide RFC
www.malahide.ie
e-mail: not available

Old Crescent RFC
members.tripod.com/oldcrescent
e-mail: not available

Old Wesley RFC
www.oldwesley.ie
e-mail: not available

Shannon

www.shannonrfc.com
You can download the team songs -
Shannon, You Are Our Pride and The
Isle, purchase at the club shop from
an illustrated guide and walk down
Memory Lane looking back at grand
moments in club history. You return
to the present with fixtures and results,
player profiles and honours won.
e-mail: not available

St. Mary's College

www.stmarysrfc.com
Get yourself an e-mail address that
puts you firmly in with the club. An
album of photographs helps you re-live
recent matches while match fixtures,
team news and player profiles bring
you up to date.
e-mail: info@stmarysrfc.com

Terenure College

www.iol.ie/~tcrfc
To join the club, use the membership
application form online. The rest of
the site gives you team news and
match fixtures, league tables club
news and a bit of history.
e-mail: tcrfc@iol.ie

Trinity College

www2.tcd.ie/Clubs/Rugby/index.html
e-mail: not available

Young Munster

www.angelfire.com/on/youngmunster
e-mail: kenneth_real@dell.com

SCOTLAND

Annan RFC

**www.geocities.com/Colosseum/1920/
index.html**
Though this is an unofficial web site it
lays claim to being the first Scottish
Rugby club on the Net. Fixtures and
match reports blend in with club news
and details of the Ladies XI and how to
join them. The chat facility and photo
gallery finish off this interesting site.
e-mail: annanRFC@hotmail.com

Edinburgh Reivers

www.edinburghreivers.com
Full multimedia presentation using
QuickTime, RealPlayer and ShockWave
Flash. There is another version of the
site if you do not have the plug-ins.
They bring you up to speed in great
style with the latest news, team stories
and player profiles. The chat facility is
always busy and screensavers can be
downloaded for free.
e-mail: via online form

Glasgow Hawks

www.glasgowhawks.com
Basic site but with enough to keep you
in the picture. Fixtures and results, player
profiles, club news and membership
details are easily accessible. The club
shop has a few items for sale.
e-mail: ken@glasgowhawks.com

Hawick Rugby Football Club

hawickrfc.co.uk
Regular official site with all the info on
what's happening at Mansfield Park.
Club history, fixtures, results, match
reports and player profiles are all in
place. All the goods available from the

club shop are listed.
e-mail: via online form

Langholm RFC

homepages.enterprise.net/iainlogan/lrfc/index.html
Founded in 1871, Langholm is the oldest rugby club in the Borders. Their web site gives you all the fixtures and results, current news and a look over the shoulder at the last season.
e-mail: iainlogan@enterprise.net

Livingston RFC

www.sniffout.net/HOME/CWILSON
Basic site with a little of everything - club details and history, fixtures and results, news and views. There are also league tables for the first and second teams.
e-mail: lrfc@sniffout.com

Melrose Rugby Football Club

www.melrose.bordernet.co.uk/traders/rfc/
The club that founded Seven-a-Side Rugby tells you all about the game in the Club History section. Results of this particular competition come online. You can follow their progress in the more mainstream Premiership League Division One. The online shop has a catalogue.
e-mail: mrfc@melrose.bordernet.co.uk

Murrayfield Wanderers

www.geocities.com/colosseum/stadium/5960
Founded in 1868 as the Edinburgh Wanderers FC, Murrayfield Wanderers are thus among the oldest rugby clubs in Scotland. Aside from all the usual news and reports, the site covers the club's Mini-Midi Rugby, has sections

for Ladies and Men and a list of club officials.
e-mail: mwfc@edin13.freeserve.co.uk

The Reds

www.scottishrugby.com/thereds/
The Glasgow Caledonians are one of only two fully professional teams in Scotland. Their web site goes some way to tell you who they are, what they've done and where they're going. Get in with the gossip, try your hand at the competitions and enjoy the exclusive interviews.
e-mail: not available

Watsonian Football Club

www.watsoniansrugby.com
A site without frills – a brief club history, contacts and details of fixtures and how you can sponsor the club.
e-mail: mike@geoghegans.co.uk

The clubs listed below include just about every notable Scottish rugby team outside the Premier League. In general, the web sites tell you about the club, chart the team's progress through the season and keep you up to date with all their fixtures, match reports, statistics in fine detail, player profiles and club news.

Aberdeen University RFC

www.abdn.ac.uk/~aus030/rugby.htm
e-mail: not available

Aberdeen Wanderers RFC

members.tripod.com/aberdeenwanderers/home.htm
e-mail: not available

Aberdeenshire RFC

members.tripod.co.uk/
aberdeenshirerfc/index.htm
e-mail: not available

Aboyne RFC

www.royal-deeside.org.uk/arfc.htm
e-mail: not available

Allan Glens RFC

www.allan-glens.org.uk
e-mail: not available

Ayr RFC

dspace.dial.pipex.com/paul.lang/
ayrrfc/index.htm
e-mail: not available

Banff RFC

www.robbins-associates.co.uk/banffrc
e-mail: not available

Bannockburn RFC

www.stir.ac.uk/dsdc/brfc.html
e-mail: not available

Birkmyre Rugby Club

www.colloquium.co.uk/birkmyre
e-mail: not available

Bishopton RFC

members.tripod.com/~neridum/
rugby.html
e-mail: not available

Boroughmuir RFC

www.boroughmuirrfc.co.uk
e-mail: not available

Cambuslang RFC

www.crfc.freeserve.co.uk
e-mail: not available

Corstorphine RFC

www.corstorphine-rfc.co.uk
e-mail: not available

Dalkieth RFC

www.geocities.com/colosseum/
Track/9613/
e-mail: not available

Earlston RFC

www.earlstonrfc.org.uk
e-mail: not available

Edinburgh North

hometown.aol.com/garft/enrfc.html
e-mail: not available

Ellon RFC

www.erfc.fsnet.co.uk
e-mail: not available

Forrester RFC

www.forresterrfc.freeserve.co.uk
e-mail: not available

Glasgow Academicals RFC

come.to/glasgowaccies
e-mail: not available

Greenock Wanderers

www.geocities.com/gwrfc/
e-mail: not available

Hawick RFC

hawickrfc.co.uk
e-mail: not available

Isle of Arran RFC

www.geocities.com/arranrfc/
e-mail: not available

Leith Rugby Club

members.aol.com/larfc/
e-mail: not available

Linwood RFC

www.members.tripod.com/linwoodrc/
e-mail: not available

Lismore RFC

www.lismorerfc.co.uk
e-mail: not available

Lossiemouth RUFC

www.lossiemouth-rufc.co.uk
e-mail: not available

Moray House Rugby Club

www.ed.ac.uk/~ebot09/house.htm
e-mail: not available

Musselburgh RFC

www.mrfc.co.uk
e-mail: not available

Orkney RFC

www.orkneyrfc.co.uk
e-mail: not available

Paisley RFC

members.tripod.com/~Paisley_RFC/
e-mail: not available

Paisley RFC (Mini/Midi Club)

members.tripod.co.uk/lewisjs99
e-mail: not available

Peterhead RFC

www.hood-99.freeserve.co.uk/
rugby.htm
e-mail: not available

Strathmore RFC

www.strathierfc.fsnet.co.uk
e-mail: not available

Striling University RFC

www.surfc.co.uk
e-mail: not available

Uddingston Minis

www.uddingstonrfc.co.uk
e-mail: not available

Waid Academy FP RFC

users.tinyonline.co.uk/waidfp/
e-mail: not available

WALES

Aberavon Wizards R.F.C.

www.aberavonwizards.co.uk
One of the top Welsh rugby clubs since
its foundation in 1876. The site keeps
information about the club up to date.
Fixtures and results, squad details with
photographs, an impressive and well-
illustrated club history section and a
Brief History written by Tony Poole of the
Evening Post are altogether very readable.
e-mail: gareth.gange@
aberavonwizards.co.uk

Abertillery RFC

www.abertillery-rfc.co.uk
Fixtures, match reports, league tables,

a message board for fans to interact and a club shop are all in place. To apply for membership, print out the online form and send it to the club.
e-mail: tyleri@abertillery-rfc.co.uk

Blackwood RFC

freespace.virgin.net/martyn.rees/ bwrfc.html
The home page has trailers for match reports of recent encounters. Fixtures and stats, a club Who's Who and player profiles with mug shots tell you what you need to know.
e-mail: martyn.rees@virgin.net

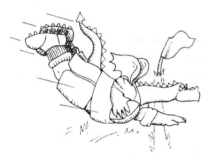

Bridgend RFC

www.bridgendrfc.co.uk
e-mail: not available

Bridgend RFC - Bridgend RFC Unofficial

www.bridgend-pages.com/brfc/ index.htm
e-mail: not available

Caerphilly RFC

www.caerphillyrfc.co.uk
A Brief History of the Club from 1887 to 1998 takes centre stage. They give you the latest news and tell you all the ways

you can sponsor the team. The squad gets the full treatment with photographs and profiles together with all their fixtures, results and tables.
e-mail: clubhouse@caerphillyrfc.co.uk

Cardiff Rugby

www.cardiffrfc.com
Fixtures, match results and reports, player pictures, biographies and interviews, squad details, stadium location and a shop on the way. You can get your tickets online using Ticketing Solutions paying by credit card on a secure server.
e-mail: not available

Cardiff Rugby - Blue & Black

www.cardiffrfcfans.freeserve.co.uk
e-mail: not available

Cardiff Rugby - Match reports for Cardiff RFC

www.homeusers.prestel.co.uk/gigg/
e-mail: not available

Cardiff Rugby - Unofficial Cardiff RFC Website

members.netscapeonline.co.uk/ garethwilliams42/
e-mail: not available

Ebbw Vale Rugby Football Club

www.ebbwvalerfc.co.uk
The site has been designed from a fan's eye view of the club. Remember That Game records memorable encounters with match program scans and witty banter. Results, news and a chat room give fans more to get their teeth into.
e-mail: ebbwrfc@baynet.co.uk

Ebbw Vale Rugby Football Club - Ebbw Vale R.F.C

www.spaceports.com/~ebbwrfc/
ebbwvalerfc.htm
e-mail: not available

Ebbw Vale Rugby Football Club - Ebbw Vale RFC Supporters Arena

www.insidetheweb.com/mbs.cgi/
mb240128
e-mail: not available

Llandovery RFC

www.geocities.com/Colosseum/
Pressbox/3531/index.html
Llandovery was a founder member of the WRU in 1881. The club's progress from the 19th century to the present is nicely set out and makes interesting reading. Fixtures, results and illustrated reports, a gallery of club merchandise and the latest news finish off the site.
e-mail: bweaver@acitt.org.uk

Llanelli RFC

www.scarlets.co.uk
They tell you how they got started, where they are and how to get to them. Then you get the latest news, results and fixtures, match reports, illustrated player profiles with autographs, stats from recent seasons and a message board.
e-mail: not available

Llanelli RFC - Llanelli (Unofficial)

www.expage.com/unofficialscarlets
e-mail: not available

Neath R.F.C.

www.k-c.co.uk/neathrfc
The Welsh All Blacks keep an archive with stories from 1998 to date and follow this with the current season's fixtures. Players are profiled with their pin-ups and statistics and the club shop has a lot on offer.
e-mail: admin@neathrfc.co.uk

Newbridge RFC

www.btinternet.com/~brookskwj
Much the usual information for a rugby site with fixtures and results, photos and news of the clubhouse and player profiles.
e-mail: brookskwj@hotmail.com

Newport Rugby Football Club

www.newport-rfc.co.uk
Press releases, club vacancies, fixtures and a run down of the players. Find out how to enrol in the Newport Rugby Academy Of Excellence and enjoy a page devoted to the Supporters Club. A catalogue tells you what you can buy from the club shop.
e-mail: via online form

Pontypool R.F.C

www.pontypoolrfc.co.uk
First you get a Shockwave Flash introduction to the site then everything follows - names and photographs of club officials, coaches and players, some of whom are profiled. Club history, fixtures, results and match reports take up the rest of the site.
e-mail: not available

Pontypridd RFC Official

www.pontypriddrfc.co.uk
Simple web site showing where they are on the map and how to get there, contact details and a listing of honours won.
e-mail: not available

Pontypridd RFC Official - Pontypridd RFC

www.ponty.net
e-mail: not available

Pontypridd RFC Official - Pontypridd Rugby Club

freespace.virginnet.co.uk/tembo.kubwa /frames.html
e-mail: not available

Rumney RFC

www.rumneyrfc.co.uk
Small official site with squad photographs of the first and youth teams, current fixtures and a look back over the shoulder to the last season. You can sign on for the e-mail newsletter online.
e-mail: rumneyrfc@madasafish.com

Swansea Rugby Club

www.swansearfc.co.uk
Pen Pics is where you look for profiles of all the players, their mug shots and e-mail addresses for contact. All the news and views, match fixtures and reports get the usual treatment. The club shop stocks desirable fan items and you can chalk up your comments on the message board.
e-mail: whites@swansearfc.co.uk

Swansea Rugby Club - Swansea R.F.C. (Unofficial)

come.to/swansearfc
e-mail: not available

All sites below are the official pages of lower ranked Welsh Rugby Union clubs. Generally, you'll find information on fixtures and match results, a little about the club, its history and contact details for those wanting to become involved.

Abercwmboi Rugby Club

freespace.virginnet.co.uk/geena.davis69 /index.html
e-mail: not available

Cardiff Saracens RFC

freespace.virgin.net/ray.diment/
e-mail: not available

Coventry Welsh RFC

ourworld.compuserve.com/ homepages/ianthatcher/
e-mail: not available

Crickhowell RFC

dialspace.dial.pipex.com/town/drive/ xyh12/
e-mail: not available

Haverfordwest Rugby Football Club

www.hrfc.co.uk
e-mail: not available

Llandudno Rugby Club

www.llandudno-rugby.co.uk
e-mail: not available

Llandudno Rugby Club

members.xoom.com/jjgreen/rugby clubsite/index.htm
e-mail: not available

Mumbles Rugby Football Club

website.lineone.net/~mumblesrfc
e-mail: not available

Nant Conwy Rugby Club
freespace.virgin.net/llifon.llifon/
e-mail: not available

Pentyrch RFC
www.uwcm.ac.uk/uwcm/hg/mills/
rugby/
e-mail: not available

Pontyclun RFC
www.pontyclunrfc.freeserve.co.uk
e-mail: not available

Tonyrefail RFC
www.tonrfc.freeserve.co.uk
e-mail: not available

Tywyn Rugby Club
www.tywynrugby.freeserve.co.uk
e-mail: not available

UMIST RFC
info.mcc.ac.uk/UMIST_Sport/rugu.html
e-mail: not available

Waunarlwydd RFC
www.waunarlwyddrfc.org.uk
e-mail: not available

Waunarlwydd RFC
websites.ntl.com/~paul.Phillips
e-mail: not available

Welshpool Rugby Club
www.geocities.com/Colosseum/Loge/
1736/index.html
e-mail: not available

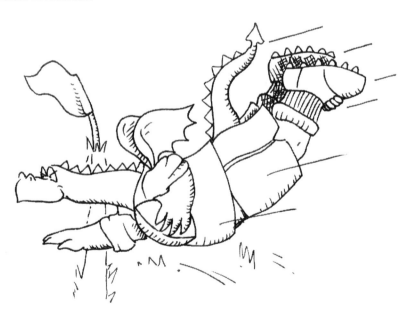

Show Jumping

Ability.org - Riding Show Jumping

www.ability.org.uk/riding_show_ jumping.html

A directory of show jumping sites around the world. When you click on a hyperlink you enter an official site like the British Show Jumping Association, Hampton Classic Horse Show in the USA, Scottish Show Jumping, Australian Show Jumping and so on.
e-mail: ability@ability.org.uk

American Miniature Horse Association

www.minihorses.com

A complete run down on all diminutive horse activities and techniques including single pleasure driving, harness viceroy driving, roadster driving and articles on driving, jumping and other forms.
e-mail: amha@flash.net

BCM

www.bcm.nl

Today the FEI - BCM World Show Jumping and the World Breeding Rankings are generally accepted as an essential part of the sport. Both riders and enthusiasts value ranking as the standard for comparing the strength of competitors and horses. You'll find top level show jumping, dressage, horse trials and driving blended with news, features, reports and previews from around the world. There are several useful horse racing links.
e-mail: info@bcm.nl

British Show Jumping Association

www.bsja.co.uk

The governing body of the sport in Britain. An events calendar, horses, riders and general information take up a few pages. The organisation runs classes for all levels of ability and manages more than 2,770 shows each year providing in excess of 2,800 days of show jumping for members.
e-mail: bsja@bsja.co.uk

CSIO Lisbon 2000

www.csio-lisbon.com

You get news, a calendar of events and the low down on the hippodrome of the annual international show jumping held in Lisbon, with details of the full

program. There are links to other equestrian sites. Text is in English and Portuguese.
e-mail: Info@ciso-lisbon.com

Cyberhorse.net
www.cyberhorse.net.au
Australian site for everything equestrian with links to horse sales, a form guide, news and competition results, breeding, dressage and more with an international diary of events. This is a bumper site with interesting stories about races and riders.
e-mail: tve@cyberhorse.net.au

equestrian.co.uk
equest.remus.com
One of the best UK Internet sites on show jumping, endurance, eventing, driving trials, pony and riding clubs. The latest stories give up-to-date rider rankings, meeting results and news from national and international competitions.
e-mail: editor@equestrian.co.uk

Equestris
www.equestris.com
A page of links to all things equestrian, including horses for sale, muscle massage therapy, feed suppliers, insurance, show jumping pages, results, world breeding, ranking and the standing of competition leagues.
e-mail: morag@equestris.com

Equimall
www.equimall.com
The blurb says that this is the world's largest equine information and shopping site on the Internet. Aside from news, horse shows, classifieds and lots of

links, there are special features on world equestrian games. The online bookstore has a show jumping magazine with interesting stories.
e-mail: lance@equimall.com

Equine-Net
www.equine-net.com
Ireland's premier equestrian information service on the Internet covers national and international horse competitions and has links to the Show Jumping Association of Ireland, Irish Horse Board and other Irish horse racing sites. It also has links to sports news from the media.
e-mail: markcasey@tinet.ie

Falcon Grey
www.falcongrey.com
Promotion of international show jumping in every respect - training of juniors, amateurs and professional show jumpers seeking to improve their skills both at home and through competitions abroad. There is a calendar of events, horses for sale and links to industry sites.
e-mail: jayduke@falcongrey.com

Flanders Christmas Horse Show
www.jumping-mechelen.com
The Christmas horse show in Flanders, Belgium. Check the program and tickets pages for the next show. There are results, statistics and records of past shows and very readable stories.
e-mail: via online form

Horse Click
www.horseclick.com
Directory of world wide show jumping where you'll also find information

about horses, dressage, eventing, an equestrian calendar, breeding and even painting horses. There are links to museums and horse magazines. An online encyclopaedia of things horsey.
e-mail: via online form

Horse Web

www.horseweb.com
On this informative and well presented US site you'll find a calendar of events, saddle clubs, articles on legal issues, horse tips, trails and press releases.
e-mail: articles@horseweb.com

Kick On – Show Jumping

www.kickon.com/Show_Jumping
A whole lot about horses, racing, show jumping, breeding, dressage, driving, pony and horse welfare. Good links take you to other horse-related sites.
e-mail: via online form

Linda Allen's Jump Smart

www.jumpsmartonline.com
News and links on this site cover the show jumping scene in the USA and around the world. There are pages on training courses, major international events and links to horse-related authorities. Information is well organised even for the uninitiated.
e-mail: llallen@usa.net

Maryland Equine International

www.mdequineintl.com
Premier boarding and training facility for riders and horses from novice to advanced competitor in the disciplines of show jumping to Grand Prix level, dressage to Prix St. George and eventing to advanced level. You'll find details of amenities, instructors, clinics, horses

for sale and news items.
e-mail: info@MdEquineIntl.com

Olympia International Show Jumping

www.olympia-show-jumping.co.uk
As this grand event is held every four years, results and information date back to 1997. The Olympia Show Jumping site at *www.olympiashow jumping.com*, reopened in July 2000, has the calendar of events and other information for the next tournament.
e-mail: nicola.c@olympiashow jumping.com

Open Directory Project

dmoz.org/Sports/Equestrian/ Show_Jumping
A page of links to show jumping sites around the world. Although the collection is limited, those that are included are worth a visit.
e-mail: via online form

Power & Speed

www.polaris.net/~cmfrank/ powerspeed.html
Original National Grand Prix League annual yearbook for show jumping, distributed free of charge to spectators at events in the USA. The publication has feature stories, results and conference champions. The Horsemen's Directory, a virtual Who's Who of the show jumping fraternity, lists all the important events across the country.
e-mail: cmfrank@polaris.net

Redland Hunt Pony Club

www.rhpc.org
Equestrian educational organisation for youths between 6 and 21. Riding,

mounted sport, horse management, and equestrian knowledge form the backbone of the curriculum. They compete in regional and national events, games, dressage, show jumping, combined training, tetrathalon, polo and polocrosse.

e-mail: webspinners@rhpc.org

Show Jumping Association of Ireland

www.sjai.ie

The country's governing body, with membership rules, news on local and international competitions, horse sales and links to other sites. Tournament results are updated weekly.

e-mail: via online form

Show Jumping Hall of Fame

www.showjumpinghalloffame.com

The hall of fame and museum promote the sport and keep alive the legends of the men, women and horses who have made great contributions to the sport. The pages have an events calendar, news stories, results and US standing.

e-mail: info@showjumping halloffame.com.

The Equestrian Times

www.horsenews.com

International network bringing together equestrian news, competition results, live event reports, breaking news, rider ranking and an events calendar. To get to the real substance of the site you must be a member; to join, use the online form.

e-mail: eqtimes@ultranet.com

The Whole Horse Network

www.microsyne.com/wholehorse

The California equine online directory lists breed registers, training and tips, trial information, stallions, clubs, organisations and horse magazines.

e-mail: g2@sierratel.com

US Equestrian Team

www.uset.org

Everything about the US Team including history, disciplines, competitions, scoring and styles. Events and results are continuously updated.

e-mail: ballyo@uset.org

World Wide Warmbloods

www.wwwarmbloods.com

Links to horse breeders and trainers and sport horse information world wide. The News pages have the latest from other horse associations. A useful contact site for those in the business.

e-mail: riverhouse@wwwarm bloods.com

www.horsesport.org

www.horsesport.org

The online home of the Fédération Equestre International, the international governing body for equestrian sport recognised by the International Olympic Committee. They establish the rules and regulations for the conduct of international equestrian events in the jumping, dressage, eventing, driving, vaulting and endurance riding disciplines. This includes supervision and maintenance of the health and welfare of the horses and respect for the principles of horsemanship.

e-mail: info@horsesport.org

Snooker & Billiards

Australian Billiards & Snooker

www.billsnook.com.au
Everything about Australian snooker - events, ranking, results, forthcoming competitions, sponsorships and more. In addition there is an overview of international snooker competitions and web site links, some of which are worth visiting.
e-mail: not available

Austrian Snooker Homepage

www.snooker.co.at
Site for fans with all you would want to know about the Austrian snooker scene from general information to ranking, international snooker to English billiards, players to snooker clubs with very little left out between. Text is in English and German.
e-mail: e8926006@stud1.tuwien.ac.at

Billiards and Snooker

www.ausport.gov.au/bilsp.html
This site provides information rather than entertainment. The pages give all the dope on Australian billiards and snooker, links to a number of official bodies and a page of the rules of the sport.
e-mail: not available

Billiards, Pool and Snooker on the Internet

www.kellys.com/poollink.html
Essentially a page of links from Kelly's Bar to snooker related web sites which present you with loads of history, major international and regional competitions and player ranking without the bother of long searches.
e-mail: not available

Canadian Billiards and Snooker Association

www.cbsa.ca
The governing body for Cue Sports in Canada. This is an official site with everything laid out including tournaments, clubs, players, coaches, amateurs and more. The site would benefit from a few photographs.
e-mail: info@cbsa.ca

Cardiff University Snooker Club

www.cf.ac.uk/suon/au/snooker/
index.html
One of the most successful sports
clubs in the University and one of the
most successful University snooker
clubs in Britain. They are current
British Champions, the third time they
have achieved this distinction. There
are profiles of current and past players
and information about a whole lot else.
e-mail: robert@idwal.chem.cf.ac.uk

Cornwall Snooker Scene

hometown.aol.com/snookermag
Online snooker magazine with so
much information and so many good
articles, you can easily lose yourself
while browsing. One thing you can
watch repeatedly is John Higgins'
recent 147 at the Benson & Hedges
Irish Masters, shot by shot in pictures
and comments, as well as clippings of
other historical moments in British
tournaments.
e-mail: via online form

Deeside Snooker League

web6.pipemedia.net/dsl
Association of snooker teams centred
on Deeside in North Wales. The site is
devoted mainly to the league's fixtures
and results. It has a bulletin of local
and national competitions and useful
links to snooker products.
e-mail: rt.dsl@pipemedia.co.uk

Egypt Billiard, Snooker Federation

www.angelfire.com/md/kammah/egypt
web.html
The first Egyptian cueing web site.
From its homepage you get an
overview of the Federation, tournament

timetables, local player ranking,
snooker clubs and an assortment of
links. Hot news and access to shopping
complete the business matters of this
enjoyable site.
e-mail: catrig@access.com.eg

Embassy World Snooker

www.embassysnooker.com
Visit the site for all the news and
excitement of their world matches.
You get the official listings of player
ranking and statistics, major
tournaments, event reports, ticket
information and anything else you
want to know about this elegant sport.
e-mail: not available

Gibraltar Billiards and Snooker Association

www.gibnynex.gi/home/gbsa
Not the most exciting of web sites but
for a newcomer to the Internet it gives
quite a lot of information on snooker
in a country that would otherwise be
unavailable. All major tournament
particulars for current and forthcoming
events are listed.
e-mail: GBSA@gibnynex.gi

International Billiards & Snooker Federation

www.ibsf.org.uk
Controlling body for amateur billiards
and snooker world wide. There are
over fifty national and continental
associations affiliated to the Federation
and this gives you access to snooker
clubs in Asia, Europe and Africa.
e-mail: tonythomas@ibsf.org.uk

L1 sport

**www.lineone.net/clubs/sport/
snooker/snooker_front-d.html**
This is a general sports site with an
up-to-date section of snooker news
that always keeps you informed of
competitions and winners. It also
produces a bulletin of competition
timetables.
e-mail: support@lineone.net

London Snooker

www.snooker.force9.co.uk
Information on a number of London
snooker clubs including some of the
best deals on membership and table
rates. The news section keeps you
wise about the capital's snooker
stories and events.
e-mail: gavin@bissett.prestel.co.uk

Malaysian Snooker & Billiards Federation

**members.wbs.net/homepages/r/a/y/
raylim/msbf.html**
You get the whole lot on this site -
Malaysian player profiles, ranking, past
champions and tournament results.
Most importantly it has an up-to-date
calendar of Asian competitions; to keep
in touch you'll need to visit the site
from time to time.
e-mail: wychin@eastmail.com

Online Sports

**www.knowledgehound.com/topics/
pool.htm**
A list of sites giving free advice on how
to play snooker, pool and billiards
including the rules, tips on game
improvement and all the tricks you can
learn. The guides could prove a little
daunting to a complete layman but you

never know until you try. You'll find a
lot of information about other sport
and links to online shopping.
e-mail: not available

Picasso's Belgian Snooker

www.snooker.org
Belgian snooker site featuring all
current competitions and players'
performance in the previous season
with records and statistics. Unfortunately
you cannot get to know the players by
face or story as there are no photographs
or biographies online.
e-mail: Picasso@belbone.be

Professional Snooker Players

**www.geocities.com/Colosseum/Dome/
6685/Players/players.html**
If you want a quick round-up of all the
professional snooker players in Britain
in one go, this site has the complete
profile package, with a particularly
good album of photographs you can
download for your personal collection.
If you click on the last picture on the
site, you can download a video of the
reckless Welsh potter Mark Williams
going through his routine.
e-mail: not available

Republic of Ireland Billiards and Snooker

www.ribsa.f2s.com
The snooker scene in Ireland, with the
latest news and events calendar. You'll
find rankings, a hall of fame, a coaching
section to improve your skills and a
photo gallery.
e-mail: not available

Sin Wen Yean's Snooker Page

www.geocities.com/Colosseum/Dome/6685/index.html
Snooker fan's page offering advice and good tips to help develop your skills. There's a fine collection of video clips, including some of Stephen Hendry, Mark Williams and John Higgins from past competitions that you can download for free.
e-mail: snooker@gmx.de

Snooker at Queen's University

quis.qub.ac.uk/snooker/welcome.htm
A small snooker club located in Queen's University Belfast, with a site really worth visiting. Information on British and Irish Championship rules and results including professional and amateur competitions are regularly updated so you get the very latest.
e-mail: not available

Snooker Aus

www.snookeraus.com
The world's first web site devoted entirely to local billiards, snooker and pool clubs, or so they say. Australian local clubs are listed and results posted; news and event calendars, coaching tips, club and competition rules complete the site.
e-mail: via online form

Snooker Coaching Online

www.snookercoaching.com
Online snooker coaching for all ages from beginners through advanced players to professionals. You can improve your snooker techniques, make higher breaks and receive personal coaching without leaving the table. Check it out for yourself.
e-mail: via online form

Snooker Images

www.snookerimages.co.uk
Wonderful snooker information site with a world-class collection of photographs, daily results, news, player rankings and lots of what you want to know about the sport. There are several links to other snooker sites, all worth a visit.
e-mail: eric@snookerimages.co.uk

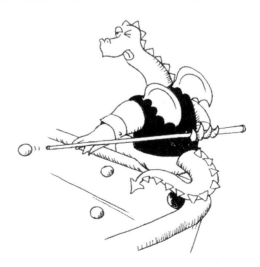

Snooker Loopy

www.snookerloopy.co.uk
Vote on who you think is the best player ever, or who makes the best cue. The site is being updated, so there should be more to follow.
e-mail: snooker.loopy@btinternet.com

Snooker Net

www.snookernet.com
UK site that informs and entertains with the elegance of the game itself. A spirited news service accompanies a huge amount of information with player profiles, match results and archives. You can search online for the nearest snooker club anywhere in the world by using the monumental club listing section. Snooker veteran Terry Griffiths gives online master classes and the site has a shop.
e-mail: info@snookernet.com

Snooker Ring

www.algonet.se/~bing/snooker.htm
If you want statistics about players' past performance, this is a good place to start, then check the links to other snooker sites.
e-mail: Bing@algonet.se

Snooker Training Center

www.robert-roos.com
Dutch snooker training centre out to promote the sport in the Netherlands. If you have leanings toward becoming a professional snooker player or just want to improve your game, contact them online for information.
e-mail: info@robert-roos.com

The Cookstown & District Snooker League

website.lineone.net/~cdsl
A league in Northern Ireland promoting snooker locally. Aside from contact information and league structure you get links to other snooker sites as well as sales of trophies and medals.
e-mail: not available

TSN Snooker

www.tsnsnooker.com
New site set up to provide full services to snooker fans. Online you'll find interactive gameplay, 24-hour tax free betting, a shopping mall, chat rooms, searchable archive material, audio commentary, competitions and tournaments. Most useful is the extensive list of biographies of the world's top players.
e-mail: sportsmasters@openkast.com

United States Snooker Association

www.snookerusa.com
The popularity of UK snooker spread out all over the USA. This is a small site but it brings with it all the news within the country, tournaments, a membership scheme for US players and a newsletter to keep you in touch.
e-mail: collins@interaccess.com

Virtual Snooker

www.interplay.com/games/snooker.html
This game of virtual snooker is so real you could believe your real world skills will improve. It has all the angles and all the shots of the real game. You can download a demo version and use the online technical support to help you.
e-mail: info@interplay.com

Welsh Snooker Web

www.abbey.animations.co.uk/snooker

Wales has shown its prowess at international sport on the snooker table as much as on the rugby pitch. Here you'll find profiles of all Welsh players, professional, amateur and world champions and major snooker centres in Wales. One very worthwhile feature is the section of WBSA news that covers just about everything on the Welsh side of the sport.

e-mail: not available

Wheels in Motion

www.wheelsinmotion.net

This new UK site come online last season, but if you are a pro or a would-be pro this is a must-visit site. There's advice on sponsorship, coaching and contact addresses to professional players. In addition you can catch up on player biographies, ranking and the results of six top players in the WIM table.

e-mail: via online form

World of Snooker

www.worldofsnooker.co.uk

All the current news and stories from the world of green baize, with the inside story on how the World Billiards and Snooker Association works and lists of current tournaments and competitions world wide. A good site that puts you in touch with the sport right from the outset.

e-mail: Webmaster@worldof snooker.co.uk

World Snooker Association

www.wpbsa.co.uk

International body governing and regulating professional and amateur snooker. As an official site it features the latest Embassy world ranking and tournament calendar and profiles players. Though still under construction the site is worth keeping in view as it will become a leading player in the Internet snooker frame.

e-mail: wsa@wpbsa.com

Yahoo Sport - Snooker

uk.sports.yahoo.com/snoo

All the sports news including snooker with up-to-date stories about players in ongoing competitions and links to other snooker sites.

e-mail: not available

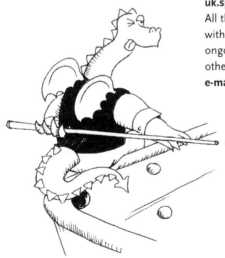

Soccer

Most teams have a great many fan sites, hate sites and unofficial sites constructed by devoted followers and others who have something to get off their chests. It is impossible to include the whole legion. That does not mean that the ones left out are dull and not worth a look in; on the contrary, some are very good, but there are just too many. If you check out some of these after visiting the official site, you could have a lot of fun just observing how fans and rivals see the same thing from different points of view.

ENGLAND

Premier League

CarlingNet - No Ordinary Web Site

www.fa-premier.com

A complete guide to all Premiership matches. Apart from information about all the clubs you'll find the latest results, club standing and future fixtures with news, rumours and gossip about transfers and player injuries. You can buy club gifts and match tickets online and have a go in the fan competitions.

e-mail: fast@fa-premier.com

Clubs

ARSENAL

Arsenal

www.arsenal.co.uk

Arsenal heaven. Following on from match results, statistics and fixtures the site goes on to report from the club's latest Premiership and Cup matches, show interviews with players and coaches, and give the latest news from Highbury. The match day live section puts you in mid-field with minute-by-minute reporting. Buy your match tickets online using their secure system. You can do the same at the

online shop where they sell club strip and collectibles. Let them know what you think in the chat room.
e-mail: cd@arsenalfc.net

Arsenal - Arsenal Mailinglist Homepage

www.satchmo.win-uk.net/arsehome
e-mail: maiser@itcarlow.ie

Arsenal - Arsenal: Probably the Best Club in the World

www.iol.ie/~killeen/arse.htm
e-mail: killeen@iol.ie

Arsenal - Arsenal Statto Shop

www.stattoshop.co.uk
e-mail: andy@stattoshop.co.uk

Arsenal - Arsenal World

www.arsenal-world.net
e-mail: chris@arsenal-world.com

Arsenal - Boring Boring Arsenal

www.boring-boring-arsenal.com
e-mail: via online form

Arsenal - Denis "The Menace" Nicholas Bergkamp

www.geocities.com/Heartland/Prairie/9935/bergkamp.html
e-mail: caglar@yifan.net

Arsenal - Up the Arse

www.upthearse.net
e-mail: via online form

ASTON VILLA FC

Aston Villa FC

www.astonvilla-fc.co.uk
Thoroughly good site with lots of information, up-to-the-minute results

and you can buy tickets to matches and make travel arrangements online. If you want to get something off your chest or celebrate with other fans, do it in the chat room. If you time it right you can talk to players and the coach online. The shopping department will sell you tickets, clothing, sports equipment and almost anything with the Villa crest on it and if you're sure of the odds, place your bets online. Information covers the latest results, tables, statistics, history, player and coach profiles and what the papers say about Villa matches. Fixtures are on the bulletin board.
email: via online form

Aston Villa FC - Aston Villa U.S. Supporters Page

www.transport.com/~seanc/
e-mail: usvillan@transport.com

Aston Villa FC - Aston Villa Worldwide Supporters Message Board

www.insidetheweb.com/messageboard/mbs.cgi/mb16593
e-mail: via online form

Aston Villa 6FC - Heroes & Villains Net

www.heroesandvillains.net
e-mail: mac@heroesandvillains.net

Aston Villa FC - The Villan's

www.villan.demon.co.uk
e-mail: Michael@villan.demon.co.uk

Aston Villa FC - Villa World

www.over.to/villa/
e-mail: villa@over.to

Aston Villa FC - Y2K Villa

champ.soccergaming.com/y2kvilla/
e-mail: y2kvilla@start.com.au

BRADFORD CITY AFC

Bradford City AFC

www.bradfordcityfc.co.uk
All the latest results, score tables and statistics are followed by players', supporters' and press comments and loads more about the team, reserves and the coach. The fixture list lets you to book tickets for home and away matches well in advance. The online shop sells club strip and memorabilia. If you want to share your views with other supporters use the message board.
e-mail: bradfordcityfc@compuserve.com

Bradford City AFC - Boy From Brazil

www.boyfrombrazil.co.uk
e-mail: not available

Bradford City AFC - Unofficial Bradford City Website

www.spufferoo.freeserve.co.uk
e-mail: salfordbantam@spufferoo.
freeserve.co.uk

CHARLTON ATHLETIC FC

Charlton Athletic FC

www.charlton-athletic.co.uk
Fixtures and reports, live broadcasts, league tables, score sheets, statistics, player profiles, a football academy and club information – all on the one site. You can buy season tickets, take part in competitions and prize draws and sign up for a football course online. All matches are covered by live audio broadcasts and there are video clips for entertainment. The archive holds match reports for the last four seasons, the online magazine links you to the supporters' club page and you can take a virtual tour around the stadium and look at the trophies.
e-mail: not available

Charlton Athletic FC – Addicks

www.addicks.org
e-mail: not available

Charlton Athletic FC - Charlton Net Addicks

charltonathletic.rivals.net
e-mail: trevor_f_@hotmail.com

Charlton Athletic FC - Forever Charlton

www.users.globalnet.co.uk/~davero/
cafcpage.htm
e-mail: infopilot@lieone.net

CHELSEA WEB SITE

Chelsea Web Site

www.chelseafc.co.uk
The essential site for all Chelsea fans. News and results are updated hourly and you can listen to live or recorded

audio feeds and watch videos. Go to the chat room, read all the previous mail then tell them how it really is. The megastore has match tickets, official Chelsea FC fan kit and other club gear. Through the ebookers.com link you get travel deals on the Internet. The miscellaneous page has Chelsea fan songs, facts about the team, forthcoming events and transfers, the history of the club, a trophy list and a great deal more.

e-mail: via online form

Chelsea Web Site - Chelsea Calling

chelseacalling.tripod.com/index.htm
e-mail: chelsea@zip.com.au

Chelsea Web Site - Chelsea FC Worship Page

www.geocities.com/Colosseum/Field/
5956/cfc/index.html
e-mail: mikec@zuken.co.uk

Chelsea Web Site - Chelsea Office

www.hello.to/chelsea.office
e-mail: asa_149@yahoo.com

Chelsea Web Site - Chelsea Shed Girl

uptheposh.prohosting.com/shedgirl
e-mail: shedgirl@chelseafc.net

Chelsea Web Site - Chelsea Supporters Registry

www.chelsea-fc.com/csr/
e-mail: not available

Chelsea Web Site - The History Of Chelsea Football Club

www.chelsea97.freeserve.co.uk/Chelsea/
frontpage.htm
e-mail: Paul@chelsea97.freeserve.co.uk

COVENTRY FOOTBALL CLUB

Coventry Football Club

www.ccfc.co.uk
Big on information, this site would be a whole lot bigger if it had more pictures, like some real action shots. Apart from up-to-the-minute results, club stats run all the way back to the beginning and the team, the coach and transfers get coverage. The online shop sells you tickets, club kit and souveniers. You can also pick up live radio broadcasts during matches.
e-mail: via online form

Coventry Football Club - Coventry City

www.geocities.com/CollegePark/Quad/
5699/indexcov.html
e-mail: rgau@fastnet.net.mt

Coventry Football Club - Hadji Interactive

hadji-interactive.com
e-mail: k.design@morocco.com

Coventry Football Club - Martin's Coventry City Page

members.xoom.com/mwildig/mwcov.htm
e-mail: not available

DERBY COUNTY FC

Derby County FC

www.dcfc.co.uk
You can see the complete history of the club, sing along, hang up pictures, read

press commentaries and check stats since the club was established. You'll find up-to-date news and rumours, the latest results, score-sheets and all the fixtures for the season. The multimedia side has a chat room and live radio and video feeds. You can buy tickets and club stuff in the shop.
e-mail: derby.county@dcfc.co.uk

Derby County FC - DCFC World
www.dcfcworld.com
e-mail: via online form

Derby County FC - Derby County on the Internet
www.therams.co.uk
e-mail: rams@derbytelegraph.co.uk

Derby County FC - From the eStand
www.derby.org/jeff/
e-mail: press.office@dcfc.co.uk

Derby County FC - Supporters on the Internet
easyweb.easynet.co.uk/~nickwheat/ramsnet.html
e-mail: wheaty@derby.org

EVERTON FOOTBALL CLUB

Everton Football Club
www.evertonfc.com
Aside from the history, you get club statistics, pictures from the past, a run down of the squad and the latest Premiership news with live updates and audio feeds. You can have a go at the manager in the chat room, buy match tickets, sort out away trips, order gear from the online store, place your bets or try your luck in the prize draws.
e-mail: feedback@everton-fc.net

Everton Football Club - Blue Horizons
www.blue-horizons.net
e-mail: stephen@bickerton.mersinet.co.uk

Everton Football Club - EFC – First Division Material
www.efc.cjb.net
e-mail: relegation.material2@virgin.net

Everton Football Club - Everton Online
www.everton-online.co.uk
e-mail: sdaleyeol@w3site-design.co.uk

Everton Football Club - Feeling(s) Blue
www4.ewebcity.com/feelingsblue
e-mail: rob@blandefc.freeserve.co.uk

Everton Football Club - The Blues
www.the-blues.com
e-mail: feedback@the-blues.com

Everton Football Club - The School of Science
www.zogmeister.com/sos/sos.html
e-mail: webmaster@zogmeister.com

LEEDS UNITED FC

Leeds United FC

www.lufc.co.uk

All the news and rumours from Ellan Road. The news section gives you up-to-date stories and the latest results with video feeds for last month's editions; information on transfers, injured players, matches and ticket availability. See who's in charge of what, read about the players and coach, see the history or follow the ups and downs of club fortunes, all in statistics and pictures.
e-mail: via online form

Leeds United FC - Everything Leeds

www.everythingleeds.co.uk
e-mail: CYMSteve@aol.com

Leeds United FC - HarryKewell.co.uk

www.harrykewell.co.uk
e-mail: webmaster@harrykewell.co.uk

Leeds United FC - Leeds United Fan Club

www.leeds-united-fan-club.co.uk
e-mail: Silverfox@ukgateway.not

Leeds United FC - Leeds United in Pictures

www.leedspics.freeserve.co.uk
e-mail: info@leedpics.freeserve.co.uk

Leeds United FC - Marching On Together

www.isfa.com/server/web/leeds/
e-mail: andy@marchingontogether.co.uk

Leeds United FC - Official Leeds United Songs Page

www.leedsunitedsongs.co.uk
e-mail: Mk@synchronisity.co.uk

LEICESTER CITY FC

Leicester City FC

www.lcfc.co.uk

The current story takes in today's players and manager, the latest rumours and transfers, Premiership tables, match results and fixtures. Club history includes stats, pictures and articles about past players. There's a huge multimedia and interactive section that puts you in the chat room with other fans and brings live audio and video feeds from matches. Use the online shop to buy match tickets and club gear.
e-mail: via online form

Leicester City FC – ForFoxSake

www.forfoxsake.com
e-mail: mail@forfoxsake.com

Leicester City FC - The Blarmy Online

www.feetup.demon.co.uk/lcfc/lcfc.html
e-mail: webmaster@feetup.demon.co.uk

Leicester City FC - The Unofficial Leicester Page

www.angelfire.com/ok/phillipspeople/leicester.html
e-mail: phillipspeople@angelfire.com

LIVERPOOL FC - THE KOPEND.COM

Liverpool FC

www.liverpoolfc.net
The latest news from Anfield with a good measure of press and players' comments. Club history is told in words and pictures with a lot of stuff on players and coaches. A news desk yanks you into the present with match results, tables, fixtures, facts and rumours about the club and team. If you have something bursting to get out that you need to share, do it in the chat room. The online shop is where you buy match tickets, club kit and other gear.
e-mail: webmaster@liverpoolfc.net

Liverpool FC - Arion's Liverpool FC Page

www.geocities.com/Colosseum/Field/6201
e-mail: ArionMemos@hotmail.com

Liverpool FC - LFC Online

www.lfconline.com
e-mail: mail@lfconline.com

Liverpool FC - Liverpool FC - Number 1!

www.lfc-1.co.uk
e-mail: via online form

Liverpool FC - Michael Owen Fan Club

www.geocities.com/Pipeline/Halfpipe/5588/index.html
e-mail: OwenFanClub@hotmail.com

Liverpool FC - The KopEnd.Com

www.thekopend.com
e-mail: hadi_dx@hotmail.com

MANCHESTER CITY FC

Manchester City FC

www.mcfc.co.uk
Check the current season's news, complete with results and player profiles. All the usual club information, history and management are well covered and there are even jobs on offer. The interactive part of the site runs a chat room to share with other fans, wallpaper to download and an online store to buy tickets and club gifts. You can order the Manchester City supporters' magazine online.
e-mail: via online form

Manchester City FC - King of the Kippax

www.kingkippax.fsnet.co.uk
e-mail: webmaster@kingkippax.fsnet.co.uk

Manchester City FC - Manchester City International Supporters

www.mancity.net
e-mail: lads@mancity.net

Manchester City FC - MCFC Supporters' Home Page

www.uit.no/mancity
e-mail: svenn@hanssen.priv.no

Manchester City FC - Virtual Manchester

www.manchester.com/nojava/sports/beautiful/cityhome.html
e-mail: not available

MANCHESTER UNITED

Manchester United

www.manutd.com

Undeniably the best online source of information past and present about the club, with fact and fiction, pictures and profiles from the earliest days to today. A huge news section delivers live coverage of matches and a lot more in print about the players and manager, United matches, Premiership tables and the best from English and world football. Fans get the lion's share of the fun; there's a chat room to vent your feelings, a newsletter and daily e-mail forum, competitions and prize draws. You can send questions to players and management and take a virtual tour of Old Trafford. The online megastore offers items in stock in the real world club shop.
e-mail: webmaster@office.manutd.com

Manchester United - 100% Red

www.geocities.com/Colosseum/Sideline/8492/
e-mail: via online form

Manchester United - A Theatre of Dreams

mufc.simplenet.com
e-mail: via online form

Manchester United - All Evils' Manchester United Website

www.geocities.com/Colosseum/Dome/3688/index.htm
e-mail: bryannks@yahoo.com

Manchester United - Better Dead Than Red

www.integrity.co.uk/football/better_red_than_dead/
e-mail: not available

Manchester United - David Beckham

www.geocities.com/Colosseum/Gym/4729/index.html
e-mail: DavidBeckham_MU7@hotmail.com

Manchester United - Everybody Hates Man U

wembley.fortunecity.com/1966/279/2.html
e-mail: not available

Manchester United - I Hate David Beckham

members.tripod.com/~gjohnk/beckham.html
e-mail: gjohnk@hotmail.com

Manchester United - Mad on Man Utd

www.callnetuk.com/home/cleverly/
e-mail: mad_on_man_u@fcmail.com

Manchester United - Manchester United Supporters Worldwide

musww.hypermart.net
e-mail: musww@yahoo.com

Manchester United - Manchester United Tribute Page

www.csn.ul.ie/~oasis/United/
e-mail: 9725431@student.ul.ie

Manchester United - MUFC United States Supporters Club

www.muscusa.com
e-mail: john@muscusa.com

Manchester United - Red Rants

www.redrants.co.uk
e-mail: webmaster@redrants.co.uk

Manchester United - Redcafe.net

www.redcafe.net/fans/forum/
e-mail: niall@scamall9.iol.ie

Manchester United - Stand Up if you hate Man U

users.d-n-a.net/dnetijcy/Scumchester.htm
e-mail: little.daffodil@dnet.co.uk

Manchester United - The Man Utd Haters Page

www.soft.net.uk/rik/hp.htm
e-mail: Rheath@rik.softnet.co.uk

Manchester United - Trafford Park - Who The F*!@ Are Man Utd?

www.angelfire.com/tx/thesaints/traf-fordpark.html
e-mail: thesaint@winningteam.com

MIDDLESBOROUGH FC

Middlesborough FC

www.mfc.co.uk
It's all here including an online shop, with the news from the club and the league, competitions and special travel offers for fans. The history and squad pages fill you in with facts, photos and press releases. Check out match results, browse through tables and score sheets, read match reports and introductions to fixtures. If you can't get to the match, watch it live online, but if you want tickets, use the online shop. There are multimedia freebies to download, job opportunities in the club, stuff for kids and information about the fan clubs.
e-mail: via online form

Middlesborough FC - Boro Index

www.boro69.freeserve.co.uk
e-mail: jon@boro69.freeserve.co.uk

Middlesborough FC - Boro Online

www.boro.co.uk
e-mail: not available

Middlesborough FC - Paul Gascoigne Photo Gallery

www.sr3.t.u-tokyo.ac.jp/~akishita/Gazza.html
e-mail: akishita@sr3.t.u-tokyo.ac.jp

Middlesborough FC - Riverside Reds

www.riversidereds.ac.psiweb.com
e-mail: ayresome@hotmail.com

NEWCASTLE UNITED FC

Newcastle United FC

www.nufc.co.uk
A must for any Magpie fan, with news, press releases, interviews with players and manager. You can sign up to join the supporters' club and try your luck in several competitions. There's a chat room to sound off with other fans and a complete club history with stats and pictures from the past. Check out the interviews with players and management or visit the online shop to buy tickets, arrange away travel and kit up with club gear.
e-mail: magpiesclub@nufc.co.uk

Newcastle United FC - Alan Shearer by Socceraction

www.socceraction.co.uk
e-mail:
david@marks999.freeserve.co.uk

Newcastle United FC - Magpie Web

www.magpieweb.co.uk
e-mail: not available

Newcastle United FC - Newcastle United Football Club Online

www.nufconline.co.uk
e-mail: steve@nufconline.co.uk

Newcastle United FC - Not Everything in Black & White Makes Sense

www.blackandwhite.fsnet.co.uk
e-mail: magpie@blackandwhite.fsnet.co.uk

Newcastle United FC - NUFC - The Truth

www.nufc-the-truth.com
e-mail: nufc.the.truth@cwcom.net

Newcastle United FC - The Magpies Zone 2000

www.geocities.com/Colosseum/Stadium/6778/index.html
e-mail: shearyadi@geocities.com

SOUTHAMPTON FC

Southampton FC

www.saintsfc.co.uk
Complete information site for all Saints' fans with multimedia freebies as a bonus. A complete club history, photo galleries, stories about players, match results, tables and news from Premiership football are updated daily. You can place bets, buy match tickets and away trip packages, supporters' kit and club stuff securely online. Check out the computer games, chat room and online magazine.
e-mail: via online form

Southampton FC - Rick Throbber's Bogus Saints FC Page

www.saintsnet.co.uk
e-mail: throbber@saintsnet.co.uk

Southampton FC - The Inside Loot @The Saints

members.tripod.com/~Colin1a/index3.html
2Colin1a@mailcity.com

SUNDERLAND FOOTBALL CLUB

Sunderland Football Club

www.sunderland-afc.com
A good site loaded with all the usual info and features – club history, photos, player profiles and all you want to know about past and forthcoming matches. The chat room will keep you busy for a while. You can buy match tickets and set yourself up for away matches with full travel packages.
e-mail: not available

Sunderland Football Club - Boldon Sunderland Supporters

www.arl-consultants.co.uk/bbranch/
e-mail: via online form

Sunderland Football Club - SAFC Magic

www.safc-magic.co.uk
e-mail: adam@safc-ftm.fsnet.co.uk

Sunderland Football Club - The Website of Light

www.websiteoflight.co.uk
e-mail: rob@ftm1973.freeserve.co.uk

TOTTENHAM HOTSPUR FC

Tottenham Hotspur FC

www.spurs.co.uk
Well presented site with all the style of a solidly good team. Match results and news are regularly updated so you are always up to speed. The online shop sells all the usual fan kit and you can get single and season tickets. Check out the interactive areas on the site.
e-mail: via online form

Tottenham Hotspur FC - Hotspur Hotspot

www.fotball.net/spurs/index.html
e-mail: thfc@fotball.net

Tottenham Hotspur FC - Spurs at The Legend

www.thelegend.co.uk
e-mail: hotspur@globalnet.co.uk

Tottenham Hotspur FC - Spurs Update

www.spurs-update.com
e-mail: webmaster@yidtalk.net

Tottenham Hotspur FC - The Hotspurs Hotsite

www.thehotspurshotsite.co.uk
e-mail: via online form

Tottenham Hotspur FC - What A Load Of Old Tottenham Hotspur FC

www.whataload.freeserve.co.uk
e-mail: webmaster@
whataload.freeserve.co.uk

WEST HAM UNITED FC

West Ham United FC

www.whufc.co.uk
Stats for all seasons and current fixtures are livened up with audio feeds of commentaries and interviews. Separate pages reveal all about the players and manager and tell you something about their careers with pics. To top up, they discuss the fan clubs, sell single and seasonal tickets in the online shop, provide live commentary on each match and give advice to youngsters who want to become footballers. The store will be happy to sell you supporters' kit, gifts, jewellery and tickets.
e-mail: via online form

West Ham United FC - C'mon You Irons!

**ourworld.compuserve.com/
homepages/jeff_parkins/**
e-mail: jeffparkins@yahoo.com

West Ham United FC - Hammer Time

www.hammertime.co.uk
e-mail: lee@theleezone.freeserve.co.uk

West Ham United FC - The Unofficial Irish West Ham Site

**www.angelfire.com/ri/richielyng/
westham.html**
e-mail: richielyng@hotmail.com

West Ham United FC - West Ham Independent Supporters Club

members.aol.com/whusc/
e-mail: drsandys@aol.com

West Ham United FC - West Ham Online

www.westhamonline.com
e-mail: alex@westhamonline.com

Other Divisions

Nationwide Football Site

www.football.nationwide.co.uk
Part of a larger web site maintained by
the Nationwide Building Society, one
of the sponsors of national football
including first, second and third division
teams. All league members are listed
with links to their official sites if they
have one, the latest results and standing.
The online shop sells football tickets
and you can bet on major sports events.
e-mail: via online form

Clubs

Barnsley FC

www.barnsleyfc.co.uk
You get up-to-date club news,
information about players, fixtures,
match results and tables from the
previous two seasons, player profiles,
a club history, statistics and weather
forecasts. The online shop will be
happy to fix your tickets and sell you
loads of club gift items. Have fun with
the games, download the wallpaper or

check out the chat room, competitions
and quizzes.
e-mail: via online form

Birmingham City FC

www.bcfc.com
All the latest news, fixtures, results,
player stories and profiles, a secure
online shop, box-office and a bundle of
multimedia features. You get to listen
not only to live audio broadcasts but also
to archived post-match commentaries.
The site advertises BCFC free Internet
access and offers an online betting
facility for football and other sport.
e-mail: via online form

Blackburn Rovers

www.rovers.co.uk
Up-to-date news, match results and
tables, the latest gossip and full match
reports. Apart from present day stuff
they include club history, players and
managers from the past with pics and
audio files. Fans can check ticket
availability in the box office or buy them
and a pile of other club goodies from
the online shop. Additional features
bring news from the supporters'
community, links to unofficial sites, live
audio match broadcasts and information
about the football academy.
e-mail: Guywignall@skynow.net

Bolton Wanderers FC

www.boltonwfc.co.uk
The latest news, results, club information, an online shop selling official
supporters' kit and gifts and an online
ticket box-office come as standard.
Aside from that you will find a
competition page and loads of goodies
for your PC including a Bolton game,

wallpaper, screensavers and a pile of video clips. Every match has a free live audio commentary and a chat room gives supporters a chance to sound off. **e-mail:** via online form

Crystal Palace

www.c-palace.org
There is no official page on this site as it does not speak for CPFC. But just the same you will find worthwhile information brought together and updated frequently. The author presents a history of the club with statistics, pictures and some videos of goal scoring. The latest results, tables and fixtures for the current season; player profiles and of course a good run down of the stadium take up a fair slice of the site. Tickets, multimedia bits to download onto your PC and advice for those who want to sign up with the football academy complete the picture.
e-mail: Postmaster@c-palace.demon.co.uk

Fulham Football Club

www.fulhamfc.co.uk
Apart from the latest news, club information and an online shop the site has several facilities for fans. You can subscribe to an official supporters' club, chat online with fellow members, check out facilities for the disabled and get to grips with the layout of the stadium. Then try to digest a huge amount of information about the club, its history, past and present players and sing along to club songs. Match commentaries come live and applicants for the junior academy can pick up some tips.
e-mail: paul@fulhamfc.net

Huddersfield Town Football Club

www.htafc.com
Regrettably the site is outdated and contains very little useful information, so use the Latest News link to a news page brought to you courtesy of a local paper where you'll find what you are looking for – all the latest match reports, player information and fixtures.
e-mail: ht.afc@Virgin.net

Mariners Net

www.gtfc.co.uk
Official web site of Grimsby Town FC, with match results, multimedia coverage including video feeds from matches with the all important goals, live audio commentaries and even wallpaper to decorate your desktop. The club history gives you a good look at player profiles. Use the online shop to buy match tickets and club gifts.
e-mail: Martin@isbl.demon.co.uk

Norwich City Football Club

www.canaries.co.uk
Club news, results, current tables are all updated regularly. The club writes its history in the hall of fame section,

profiles players and manager and provides information for juniors. Use the chat room to keep in touch with other fans.

e-mail: via online form

Nottingham Forest Online

www.nottinghamforest.co.uk
A must-see web site for club fans. Apart from a huge amount of information and the latest news, you can buy tickets, kits and gifts online, paying by credit card via a secure server. There is a newsroom and a chat room, NFFC screensavers for your computer and club news you can receive daily in your e-mail.

e-mail: webmaster@ nottinghamforest.co.uk

Portsmouth FC

www.pompeyfc.co.uk
A multimedia playground for all club supporters. Fans can shop online, listen to live radio broadcasts during club matches and blow off steam in the chat room. All the usual information about the club, players, latest match results, fixtures, tables and score sheets are in place.

e-mail: via online form

Preston North End FC

www.prestonnorthend.co.uk
The site combines the club's past and present and brings you all the news, match reports, press commentaries and the latest on players. In the merchandising section you can book your match tickets, kit up in fan gear and buy club memorabilia. Additional features are fun for kids, links to other PNE sites and wallpaper for your PC.

e-mail: enquiries@prestonnorthend.co.uk

Queens Park Rangers FC

www.qpr.co.uk
This is a supporters' web site with a difference - you can open a QPR savings account or apply for a QPR MasterCard. The news from Loftus Road is updated daily, and apart from being able to book and buy tickets, supporters' kits and club memorabilia can be bought online. Use the Internet chat room to get things off your chest, comment, discuss and criticise all you want.

e-mail: qpr@loftusroadplc.co.uk

Sheffield United Football Club

www.sufc.co.uk
Anything you want to know about the club, what's old, what's new, tables, statistics and whatever else. There is an online store to buy tickets, single or season, gear to kit yourself out, club souvenirs and whatnots. These make up the official club web site. A link takes you to an official supporters' site with details of fixtures for the current season and a ticket status report. The club offers conference and banqueting halls for rent.

e-mail: info@sufc.co.uk

Sheffield Wednesday

www.swfc.co.uk

Sheffield Wednesday FC has designed its site to please any true Owls' fan. News is updated as quick as a header and generally no more than a few minutes after the end of a match. Injuries, transfers and everything else about the club and players are recorded. Check out player profiles, club history and general gossip. The online shop sells tickets and club gifts; there is a chat room to share views with other fans and a collection of multimedia goodies to load into your computer.
e-mail: via online form

Stockport County FC

www.stockportmbc.gov.uk/scfc/

The web site is divided so that you get information neatly parcelled. Club history, players, manager and the football academy come in the general section. An online shop books tickets and sells you supporters' kit. Then there is something about the local community and the role of the club, with details of banqueting and conference facilities for rent. Additional attractions include RealAudio live match commentaries.
e-mail: info@iocounty.co.uk

The Gills On-Line

www.gillinghamfootballclub.com

Gillingham FC's site carries news, match results and league tables, profiles of the current squad, the manager and the stadium. You can check out ticket availability and make travel arrangements for away trips. There is a large information page on the supporters' community and the

latest travel news. Audio match commentaries and interviews with the team and manager complete the site.
e-mail: Information@gillingham footballclub.com

Tranmere Rovers

www.tranmererovers.co.uk

Apply for an official TRFC MasterCard, use the online betting service and check ticket availability for the forthcoming matches. News reports are always up-to-date and match results are posted immediately. The whole team gets star treatment and there is coverage of rival clubs the team faces in the First Division.
e-mail: via online form

Watford Football Club

www.watfordfc.com

Information galore on Watford FC and an online shop. Club history is fairly well covered with words and pictures and a bit of audio stuff; players are profiled with their manager and the whole coaching staff. You can subscribe to the supporters' club or sign up to a junior football school online. If you want to check the latest club results you can be sure the tables, score-sheets and latest news are up-to-the-minute. The online shop is always open for tickets, supporters' kit, club gifts and a whole lot more.
e-mail: via online form

West Bromwich Albion FC

www.wba.co.uk

The history of the club and stadium, statistics and pictures from the past make this an interesting site. More recent information brings the team and

management, match statistics, tables, results and news up to date. The online shop will sell you loyalty kit and other mementoes via a secure server.
e-mail: via online form

Wimbledon FC

www.wimbledon-fc.co.uk
The latest news, results, tables and score-sheets and the low down on the club. There are bits historical and bits not so historical about the Club. You can book and buy match tickets and arrange away trips, fit yourself out in the latest kit and buy gifts online.
If you can't make it to the stadium to support your team, then console yourself with the live online commentary right through the matches.
e-mail: via online form

Wolves FC

www.wolves.co.uk
Update what you already know with what the site has to offer and have a lot of fun doing it. News, along with results, current tables and fixtures is updated regularly, so you'll never miss a thing. There's a huge picture gallery with photos from the past and present and two online shops, one for general club goods selling supporters' kit and memorabilia and the other, a box office to buy your tickets and arrange away trips. You can even subscribe to a live match broadcast channel. Additional attractions are for junior supporters and future footballers and a club hall of fame.
e-mail: not available

SCOTLAND

The Scottish Football Association

www.scottishfa.co.uk
The Scottish Football Association's online home, with information on all member teams - the A-team, women's and junior teams. Coverage is fairly good with player and manager profiles, their pictures and careers. Reports from friendly and tournament matches, press commentaries and a comprehensive archive fill several more pages. There are links to other Scottish football sites and fan pages.
e-mail: info@scottishfa.co.uk

Scottish Premier League Official Web Site

www.scotprem.com
The Scottish Premier League sets out all the rules, and lists member clubs with links to their official sites, their players, up-to-date results and ranking. You get information on league TV broadcasts and programmes for the next few weeks. They've added computer games and wallpaper for your PC.
e-mail: via online form

Clubs

ABERDEEN FC

Aberdeen FC

www.afc.co.uk
Everything about the club brought together on one web site. Club news, match reports and results, league tables, interviews with players and press extracts – all updated daily. Add to this information on the club itself – history, ups and downs of

fortune, hall of fame, photos from the past and videos from the present, together with facts about the stadium, player and management profiles. There are pages for fans to share their views or blow their tops and more pages for members to enter competitions and talk to players. The online shop and box-office sell tickets, away trips and loads of club gifts. To complete the facilities, you can also bet online.
e-mail: feedback@afc.co.uk

Aberdeen FC - Aberdeen Football Club

www.pawprint.co.uk/afc/
e-mail: via online form

Aberdeen FC - Dons Division

www.geocities.com/dons_division
e-mail: ultramabel@hotmail.com

CELTIC FC

Celtic FC

www.celticfc.co.uk
You can follow the latest club news and results, enjoy the interactive features and shop online. Tables and score sheets are updated frequently; you get all the authorised interviews with players and management, videos and live match commentaries. Press stories, supporters' comments and daily match analyses fill out several more pages. There is a good deal on record about club history and supporters have their official club and fan web sites. The online shop will sell you fan kit and tickets and the online betting service guarantees security.
e-mail: Newsdesk@celticfc.co.uk

Celtic FC - Bhoyzone Celtic FC Fhansite

www.bhoyzone.com
e-mail: bhoyzone@bhoyzone.com

Celtic FC - Celtic Supporters' Club, Carfin

www.carfincsc.co.uk
e-mail: carfin@carfincsc.co.uk

Celtic FC - CelticFC.cjb.net

www.geocities.com/Colosseum/Dugout/7713/
e-mail: webmaster@celticfc.cjb.net

Celtic FC - Glasgow Celtic Football Club

www.geocities.com/Colosseum/8030/celtic.html
e-mail: petemac@vossnet.co.uk

Celtic FC - Montreal Glasgow Celtic Supporters Club

www.microimm.mcgill.ca/felix/mtlcelt.htm
e-mail: fjsieder@microimm.mcgill.ca

Celtic FC - The Bhoys Club

www.btinternet.com/~stevken/
e-mail: bhoysclub@btinternet.com

Celtic FC - The Big Green Book

www.donegalinternet.com/bgb/
e-mail: bgb@eircom.net

Celtic FC - The Celts Are Here

www.infj.ulst.ac.uk/~czwq22/celtic.html
e-mail: tp.mchugh@ulst.ac.uk

Celtic FC - The Official Singapore Celtic Supporters Club

www.9to5.com.sg/singtims/
e-mail: not available

DUNDEE FC

Dundee FC

www.dundeefc.co.uk
Loads of facts from club history, all the trophies won, profiles of past heroes, reminders of great games and a huge picture gallery. Present day players and management are highlighted in pictures with brief career summaries for all. The current season for senior and junior teams, news from league and cup performances, tables and score sheets are all well presented. Team sponsors and the stadium are mentioned and you get downloadable stuff to Dundeefy your computer. Tickets and kit can be bought online via a secure server.
e-mail: davidy@dundeefc.co.uk

Dundee FC - The Dee Online

www.ianrae.demon.co.uk/dfc/
dol_home.htm
e-mail: thedee@ianrae.demon.co.uk

DUNDEE UNITED

There's no official site for the club. Visit the unofficial web sites for information and fun.

Dundee United -Arab FC

dundeeunited.rivals.net
e-mail: arabjacques@yahoo.com

Dundee United -Arabland – A Dundee United Homepage

www.arabland.demon.co.uk
e-mail: mark@arabland.demon.co.uk

Dundee United -DundeeUtd.co.uk

www.dundeeutd.co.uk
e-mail: Dundeeutdcouk@hotmail.com

Dundee United -Proud to be an Arab

www.geocities.com/Colosseum/3504/
dufc.html
e-mail: arab_c_nesbit@geocities.com

Dundee United -Tangerine Dream

www.geocities.com/Colosseum/Park/
8250/united.htm
e-mail: s.m.maclean@sms.ed.ac.uk

Dundee United -Welcome to The Glory Years

www.gloryyears.com
e-mail: rob@gloryyears.co.uk

GLASGOW RANGERS FC

Glasgow Rangers FC

www.rangers.co.uk
Everything you want to know about the club with competitions, fan corners and an online shop. Club history is told, the stadium and players illuminated with pictures and interviews. You get the latest news and results at high speed plus live match commentaries, post-match interviews, newspaper reviews and rumours, tables and score sheets. Moreover, you can watch the

greatest goals in club history or check out past results. A newsletter and chat room, competitions and special offers are laid on for fans. You can book or buy match tickets, team strip and club gifts. Additional features include an interactive stadium tour and club contacts.
e-mail: via online form

Glasgow Rangers FC - Melbourne Glasgow Rangers Supporters Club

www.mgrsc.org.au
e-mail: newall@tig.com.au

Glasgow Rangers FC - Rangers Net

www.ibrox.dircon.co.uk
e-mail: ibrox@dircon.co.uk

Glasgow Rangers FC - The East Enclosure

www.ayeready.com
e-mail: via online form

Glasgow Rangers FC - The Nine in a Row Page of Rangers

www.gla.ac.uk/~ghg1a/Rangers.html
e-mail: g.galloway@compserv.gla.ac.uk

HEART OF MIDLOTHIAN FC

Heart of Midlothian FC

www.heartsfc.co.uk
Any fan will enjoy reading the history of the club and it comes in five languages. The latest news section has a summary of the most talked about rumours, club information and ticket status, updated daily. A club encyclopaedia keeps all the facts on the stadium, supporters' community, junior academy and club management. Match results, fixtures, tables, player profiles, coaches and interviews, a supporters' corner with competitions, chat forum and kids' stuff take up several pages. You can buy tickets, kit and gifts online. Additional attractions include a supporters' credit card offer, live match commentaries and audio and video sequences from previous seasons.
e-mail: scott@heartsfc.co.uk

Heart of Midlothian FC - and other Drunken Football Stories

www.fortunecity.co.uk/stadium/ soccer/14/main.htm
e-mail: jamtart18@hotmail.com

Heart of Midlothian FC - Heart of Midlothian Football Club News Page

www.geocities.com/Colosseum/Bench/ 4524/
e-mail: ken.adair@usa.net

Heart of Midlothian FC - London Hearts Supporters Club

www.btinternet.com/~london.jambos
e-mail: london.jambos@btinternet.com

Heart of Midlothian FC - Neil McCann - A Jambo Forever

www.angelfire.com/nm/neilmccann
e-mail: mccanns_page@hotmail.com

Heart of Midlothian FC - The Jambos Unofficial Page

www.geocities.com/k_scotland
e-mail: k.hunter@cableinet.co.uk

Hibernian FC

www.hibs.co.uk
The latest news, match results and club bulletins and an illustrated club history, video clips, audio interviews and other interactive features, including a secure online shop. There are player profiles for junior and senior teams and managers, leads to forthcoming matches, extracts from the press and interviews with team members. Tickets, supporters' kit and football items can be bought online. Take a virtual tour of the stadium, watch match videos and an interactive club history, listen to live match commentaries and browse through the hall of fame.
e-mail: club@hibernianfc.co.uk

Hibernian FC - Hibs.Net

hibernian.rivals.net
e-mail: Alex_Graham@bankofscotland.co.uk

Kilmarnock FC

www.kilmarnockfc.co.uk
An indispensable source of information for fans with the latest results, score sheets, tables, match commentaries and fixtures. As far as the club is concerned you get player profiles, the club history with lots of photographs, ticket prices and shop merchandise although no online service is yet available. The general club history includes archives with complete results and score sheets from three previous seasons and statistics from earlier years. Fans can subscribe to several supporters' clubs, chat rooms and message boards and take part in club prize draws.
e-mail: wcravens@kilmarnockfc.demon.co.uk

Kilmarnock FC - Canada/USA Supporters Club

www.geocities.com/Colosseum/Mound/8422/index.html
e-mail: Aulda@msn.com

Kilmarnock FC - Kilmarnock FC Fan Site

www.killiefc.com
e-mail: webmaster@killiefc.com

Kilmarnock FC - Stripes Forever

www.kilmarnockfc.freeserve.co.uk
e-mail: smillar@kilmarnockfc.freeserve.co.uk

Motherwell FC

www.motherwellfc.co.uk
All the latest about the club, the team and the supporters' community updated daily or e-mailed if you're on their mailing list. You get a brief club history and player profiles with pics. Although the site does not contain a merchandising page you can order the team kit. The latest results, fixtures, match commentaries and press releases are posted throughout

the season. There's a big archive of previous match commentaries, a letter board for fan mail and a page for young supporters. Additional attractions include an online quiz for youngsters to win free match tickets.
e-mail: alisdair.barron@ motherwellfc.co.uk

Motherwell FC - Fir Park Corner

www.jwok.demon.co.uk/well1.htm
e-mail: not available

Motherwell FC - Mighty Motherwell Web Ring

www.jwok.demon.co.uk/mweb.htm
e-mail: mightywell@jwok.demon.co.uk

Motherwell FC - Motherwell FC Exiles Club

www.geocities.com/Colosseum/ Pressbox/7389/
e-mail: andrew.b.m.paterson@ cableinet.co.uk

Motherwell FC - Virtual Fir Park

www.stewarts.freeserve.co.uk
e-mail: andrew@stewarts.freeserve.co.uk

St.Johnstone FC

www.stjohnstonefc.co.uk
The latest club news and results, chat rooms for fans and an online shop. You'll find brief information about the club, directors, home and away kits and in-depth profiles of players and management. There's a table with current results, a brief club history, chat about senior and junior fan clubs, a calendar of events and special competitions. An online shop lets you book and buy single and season tickets, club gear and souveniers. A fan forum stores letters from supporters about matches, players and the club.
e-mail: season@stjohnstonefc.co.uk

St.Johnstone FC - Blue Heaven

www.homeusers.prestel.co.uk/popr/ blueheaven/
e-mail: blueheaven@popr.prestel.co.uk

St.Johnstone FC - The Temple Of Saints

www.grange.demon.co.uk/saints/sjfc.htm
e-mail: via online form

INTERNATIONAL

Federation Internationale de Football Association

www.fifa2.com

The governing body of international football is the first place to look for results of international football matches. The site sets out the rules of international football, its own statutes and a calendar of all international tournaments. National football bodies, with guides to their international records are listed with

pictures and press releases. Additional features include present team ranking, a guide to TV broadcasts, future matches and official football publications.
e-mail: media@fifa.org

UEFA

www.uefa.com

A complete guide to all European football teams including A-teams, women's and junior teams and European national leagues with brief information on each club, its players and European record. All UEFA tournaments from European Club Cups to European Championships are covered. Also included are tournament rules, the history of European football and multimedia freebies for your computer.
e-mail: info@uefa.com

Clubs

Ajax

www.ajax.nl

Good source of information for any fan of the Amsterdam club. Up-to-date results and tables from most of the Dutch and European competitions with news about players, transfers and the club itself. You can visit club archives filled with results from their glorious past, pictures, videos and commentaries. The site has an online shop for tickets and club items. You can also talk to other supporters, subscribe to a fan club and take a virtual tour of the Amsterdam arena.
e-mail: info@ajax.nl

CBF Official Website

www.brasilfutebol.com/ select_language.sps

The official site of the Brazilian Football Association is in English, Portuguese and Spanish. Matches played by the national team are thoroughly analysed supported by pictures, statistics and press commentaries. Forthcoming matches and pre-match briefings cover all teams - senior, junior and women. There are player profiles and a rundown on management. Team history is told with pictures, video and audio feeds and matches played by the national team have continuous live commentaries.
e-mail: via online form

FC Barcelona

www.fcbarcelona.es

Several sports are covered, with football top of the list – latest rumours, transfer details, match results, tables and commentaries brought to you hot from the press. You can also listen to live broadcasts and watch match videos or browse through a huge picture gallery. Add to this player profiles, a stadium tour, links to supporters' pages, fan clubs and an online shop and you get a very good web site. Text is in English, Spanish and Catalan.

e-mail: via online form

FC Bayern München

www.bayernmuenchen.de

All the latest news and views from Munich in English and German, with results tables, post- match anaysis, an archive of past stories and a photo gallery. Get stuck into the newsletters and fan forum for opinions and chat. If you want to go yourself, they offer ticket sales online.

e-mail: not available

Fútbol en la Red

www.sportec.com/www/laliga_ing/ main.htm

An overview of Spanish football in Spanish and English. For both 1st and 2nd leagues you get the latest results, tables, statistics and cup finals. There is news about international tournaments wherever national teams and clubs are competing. Fans have a chat room and get briefings about foreign leagues.

e-mail: futbol@sportec.es

InterMilan

www.inter.it

You are offered the latest news from Internazionale Milan, forthcoming matches and interactive features. You get match results, tables, score sheets from current and previous seasons, a stadium tour and player profiles.

You can also watch videos, listen to live broadcasts, share your views with fellow supporters and take part in competitions and quizzes. The site has an online ticket office and club shop.

e-mail: via online form

Italian Soccer

www.italian-soccer.com

With text in English this Italian site provides the most up-to-date information about the national football scene – players, clubs and teams. You get information separately for Italian first, second and third leagues, Italian Cup and Super Cup, senior, junior and women national teams. There are archives of previous seasons to browse through and excellent links to Italian club and supporters' web sites, an online betting service and the latest rumours from the transfer market.

e-mail: alex@italian-soccer.com

Juventus FC

www.juventus.it

Indispensable guide to an outstanding club for supporters from anywhere in the world. Apart from the usual features – latest club news and rumours about players, results, tables and statistics - the site also has huge photo and video galleries. The online shop will sell you club gifts, match and season tickets. Fans can speak up in the chat room, leave messages on the board, join the forum and e-mail the players.

e-mail: via online form

Real Madrid CF

www.realmadrid.es

The site brings you not only the latest news and results, player stories and

club information, but also lots of features for fans including multimedia files, an online shop and more. You can subscribe to supporter clubs for access to chat rooms and message boards. Interactive freebies include computer wallpaper, a virtual tour of the stadium and trophies, as well as audio and video feeds from past matches.
e-mail: via online form

S.S. Lazio

www.sslazio.it
The most up-to-date news, the most thorough information and a lot of downloadable stuff. Online match reports follow fast on the heels of live broadcasts and video clips give you all the excitement of recent and past goals. Club history, profiles of players and management and stadium details keep you in touch. Fans can buy tickets and gifts online and bid at an auction of club memorabilia. Additional attractions include competitions, a Lazio credit card and links to the supporters' community.
e-mail: web.sslazio@sslazio.it

The Orange Team

www.orangeteam.com
This is an unofficial site for the Dutch international football team. You get the latest squad line-up, daily updated results, pictures, fixtures and match commentaries and a link to a football betting service. You can browse through historical results and thrill at their best goals. Fans have a chat room and notice board to share their views with other supporters.
e-mail: via online form

www.acmilan.com

www.acmilan.it
You get the latest results from club matches and tournaments, tables and fixture reports and you can listen to live match broadcasts. The club section has details about the stadium, club history, photo galleries and profiles of players and managers. Fans can take a stadium tour, seerecent and archived video clips, read the fan magazine and use the chat rooms and message boards.
e-mail: via online form

Sports Equipment

Sports Equipment

123-fun.com

www.123-fun.com

The sports department of the US online store 123. Products come under 15 sports categories. If you know exactly what you are looking for you can go directly to the section. They say you can get the latest equipment cheaper than in real world shops. Payment is guaranteed secure and they deliver anywhere in the world.

e-mail: Customerservice@vstore.com

4Check

www.fourcheck.demon.co.uk

The site is designed to sell equipment to online UK hockey enthusiasts. Their strip and gear come from top manufacturers. All products are described, displayed and priced. Order by e-mail.

e-mail: webmaster@fourcheck. demon.co.uk

Action Direct

www.action-direct.com

Gear for hunters, campers and the outdoor person. The online catalogue lists the full range with many items not available in stores and you can take advantage of special offers. You can order online, with most items being shipped within 48 hours.

e-mail: info@action-direct.com

Adventure DooDads

www.adv-doodads.com

Secure online shopping for outdoor gear and equipment. If you are looking for hiking, camping and climbing equipment, in fact anything for outdoor holidays, they seem to have it. Books, nature CDs and a range of travel accessories add to their inventory.

e-mail: Cust-serv@adv-doodads.com

Adventure Sports Online

www.adventuresports.com/new/ shopdir.htm
The products and shops section of this outdoor activity guide. All manner of great gear is available from a variety of suppliers, including winter sports, biking gear, climbing gear, tents, sleeping bags, backpacks, footwear and so on. You can also carry out an Outfitter Search or a Product Search by country or activity using the pull down menus.
e-mail: via online form

Aitken & Niven

www.aitken-niven.co.uk
Scottish online store, offering a large range of rugby equipment, clothes, protective wear and memorabilia. When you place your order, remember to include your delivery details; they ship anywhere in the world.
e-mail: aniven@dial.pipex.com

Alphamart.com

www.alphamart.com/prod/sports.shtml
This is the sports section of an online superstore with equipment for a whole range of sports. Most products are displayed and prices are below those of real world shops and they deliver anywhere in the world. You need to register online before you buy.
e-mail: sales@alphamart.com

Alternative Sporting Services

www.altservices.co.uk
Archery equipment for the enthusiast, laid out in a neat virtual shop. Online search is easy and every product is described and displayed. Use the secure form to pay by credit card, cheque or money transfer. All prices

are quoted in Sterling, Euros and US dollars. They ship world wide.
e-mail: sales@altservices.co.uk

Anaconda Sports

anacondasports.com
Online department of the New York store. Virtually everything for basketball, softball, soccer, American football and baseball. They also organise auctions of rare equipment and memorabilia. Major credit cards are accepted and international deliveries can be arranged but check the charges first.
e-mail: sales@anacondasports.com

Appalachian Mountain Supply

www.adventuresports.com/product/ams
Outdoor adventure gear with equipment of a type taken on several Himalayan expeditions. For a free catalogue, call or fill out the request form. You can transact online.
e-mail: amsupply@flash.net

Aqua Flite

aquaflite.com
Wetsuits and diving gear in a complete selection of standard sizes, which can be personalised to suit you. It will be difficult to find a bigger range of styles, colours and accessories and as if that's not enough, they will tailor suits to your dimensions and specifications. Most credit cards are accepted.
e-mail: not available

Aquatic Outfitters.com

www.aquatrec.com
Water sports equipment store offering a complete line of swimming, fitness and travel equipment and accessories. Search the catalogue for particular

equipment or click on a category for a wide selection. Credit card transactions are welcome.

e-mail: sales@aquaticoutfitters.com

Auto Steer

www.autosteer.com

UK manufacturer and retailer of yacht steering systems. Their products are fully detailed with good pictures, specifications and prices. They accept major credit cards but do not state whether they deliver abroad.

e-mail: info@autosteer.com

Avalon Guns

www.avalon-guns.com

One of UK's largest online gun, accessories, consumables, clothing and footwear retailers. The web site details their products, gives shooting sports news, lists training grounds and latest events. Order a hard catalogue or browse through their collection online. Their range is listed by product, described, depicted and priced. They accept major credit cards and deliver within the British Isles.

e-mail: info@avalon-guns.com

Backpackgear.com

www.backpackgear.com

Footwear is their speciality but they also run a backpackers' emporium with everything from tents to tea bags, all items illustrated and priced.

e-mail: backpack@backpackgear.com

Backpacking Gear Community

shop.affinia.com/travelexperiences/store

You can view the products by Merchant, Brand or Category, or use the search engine if you know what you want. The home page features a range of must-have products.

e-mail: not available

Baldas USA

www.adventuresports.com/product/baldas

High quality, high tech snowshoes in all sizes for men, women and children, designed for the worst snow and ice conditions. All models are made of space age materials and ordering from the drop down list cannot be easier.

e-mail: vanmgmt@aol.com

Bargain Travel Center

www.bargain-travel.com

Travel goods and accessories with immediate despatch to home or holiday destination. Browse through a great selection of luggage, books, converters, clocks, binoculars, videos and electronics. If you know what you want, type it in the search box and find it immediately.

e-mail: not available

Bass Pro Shops Outdoor World Online

www.basspro-shops.com/index.cfm

A full range of travel products from automotive accessories to fishing hooks. Select a main category and a list of all gear on offer is displayed. Shop by dropping your choices in the Cart.

e-mail: not available

Bavarian Village

www.skigolf.com

This consortium of shops sells ski and golf equipment and travel services. You can browse each separately. Equipment is also available for hire and you can buy discount lift tickets.

e-mail: not available

Berry Scuba

www.berryscuba.com

The ultimate diving outfitters from goggles to underwater cameras and everything between. The homepage lists their stores, training sessions, special offers and an informative online catalogue.

e-mail: orders@berryscuba.com

Body Active

www.bodyactive-superstore.co.uk

London fitness superstore with an online catalogue of fitness equipment, accessories and nutrition. All products are displayed with a number of technical details to help you decide. To buy online use the shopping basket system and secure credit card server to seal the deal.

e-mail: enquiries@bodyactive-superstore.co.uk

Boz's Rangs Pages

www.boomerangs.net

Boomerangs galore for beginners and enthusiasts. They show you how they are manufactured, teach you how to use them and give you an online catalogue of all the models you can imagine, which just keep coming back. You order by e-mail but first check costs as no prices are stated.

e-mail: Contact@boomerangs.net

Busy Body

www.busybody.com

US sports store network selling home gym equipment online. Steppers, free weights, treadmills, exercise bikes and a whole lot more are nicely displayed. Buying is completely secure but delivery is restricted to the USA.

e-mail: via online form

Carl Douglas Racing Shells

www.rowing-cdrs.demon.co.uk

UK manufacturer and retailer of rowing boat hulls and equipment. There is a lot of technical information online and a price list. They have dealers in the UK, Canada, the USA, Japan, Holland and Germany. You can order from their dealers or online.

e-mail: carldouglas@rowing-cdrs.demon.co.uk

Cencal

www.cencal.com

Travel accessories originally designed for the aviation industry, using materials many times stronger than normally available and durable enough for the top of Mount Everest. So if you plan on going there you know where to get your gear.

e-mail: cencal@c-zone.net

CMR International

www.btinternet.com/~cmr.international

UK shotgun retailer with a range of pistols, rifles and accessories, most of which are for collectors. You can browse through a catalogue preview showing sample products from all categories; order a catalogue by filling in your billing details, then place an order. Major cards are accepted and shipping is world wide.

e-mail: cmr.international@btinternet.com

Continental Sports Limited

www.contisports.co.uk

Gymnastics and trampolining equipment from the UK. They sell you the products and will also set out your gym hall if you like. The catalogue is well laid out with lots of technical detail and pictures.

To purchase complete the form, however credit card transactions are not available at the moment.
e-mail: sales@contisports.co.uk

Country Polo

www.countrypolo.com.au
Australian online sports store offering everything for polo enthusiasts except the horses. Each item has its own catalogue with pictures, details and prices. Order by e-mail.
e-mail: enquire@countrypolo.com.au

Cricket 1

www.cricket1.com
Cricket equipment for amateurs and professionals. To keep you in touch they present the latest cricket news, last results and some specials. Equipment is well displayed with lots of detail to help you choose. To purchase, register by completing the online form for your password.
e-mail: via online form

Cricket Direct

www.cricketdirect.co.uk
They sell cricket equipment of every

sort and claim to be the world's finest store of this type. Products are listed by category, player and manufacturer with prices lower than in retail shops; they provide a comparison. To order, print out, complete and mail the form provided for world wide shipment.
e-mail: sales@cricketdirect.co.uk

Cumberland Transit

www.ctransit.com
Practically everything you will need to travel confidently, as well as a good selection of sports equipment. Each product category features a number of brands, so click on the logo. There is a Warranty & Factory Repair link for some items.
e-mail: info@ctransit.com

Direct Martial Arts

www.neglobal.co.uk/dma
UK supplier of martial art accessories, training videos, uniforms, protective clothing and other equipment. They highlight their newest products and customers' opinions. Order by mail, e-mail, fax or phone; they accept various methods of payment.
e-mail: dmarts@talk21.com

Discount Divers Supply

www.discountdivers.com
The largest US supplier of new and used scuba diving equipment. Their catalogue is divided into categories and the latest offers are displayed on the home page. Check out the pictures and video clips, read diving tips and get on their mailing list if you wish. They ship world wide.
e-mail: via online form

Discount Luggage

www.luggageman.com
Major brand luggage at a discount.
The durability rating 1 to 10, taken from
warranty and damage records, gives
you an idea of what to expect from your
luggage. The Top 10 Sellers also gives
an indication of what to buy.
e-mail: smluggage@fix.net

Dragon Sports

www.dragonsports.co.uk
Online UK retailer with a good range
of equipment for darts, cricket, bowls,
badminton, football, golf, snooker,
squash and tennis. Type the keyword
in the search engine or look for what
you want by category or manufacturer.
Major credit cards are accepted and
your details are securely encrypted.
They deliver world wide.
e-mail: Info@dragonsports.co.uk

DSports.com

www.dsports.com
Online department of the sports store
network of the same name in the USA.
They sell equipment for more than fifty
sports disciplines at lower prices than
main street retailers. Type what you
want in the search engine or have fun
browsing through all the categories and
leading brands. Purchase after you
have registered; shipment is world wide.
e-mail: service@dsports.com

Eagle Creek

www.eaglecreek.com
Everything for the traveller to pack a
bag and go. Travel gear, backpacks,
wheelie bags, duffel bags, Pack It
systems and accessories. Each link has
a selection of products and a search
engine helps you find exactly what you
are looking for. You can purchase online.
e-mail: not available

Easy Golf

www.easygolf.co.uk
Online UK golf retailer offering the whole
bit, broken down into small categories
to simplify search. All their products
are detailed with pictures and prices.
You can shop as you browse putting
your purchases into the trolley. For
orders from outside the UK check
shipping charges before you order.
e-mail: Sales@easygolf.co.uk

Ellis Brigham

www.ellis-brigham.com
UK retailer offering a huge selection of
outdoor sports equipment online. The
products are neatly set out in a useful
network of categories and subcategories
for easy shopping. Each product is
described, ranged by size and displayed.
They ask you to register online on the
secure credit card form before you
purchase.
e-mail: via online form

Elverys

www.stauntonsintersport.com
Irish online sports retailer offering
equipment, clothing and memorabilia
for rugby and Gaelic football fans.
Each sport has its own catalogue.
Clicking on either gets you a list of
currently available products, all well
displayed and priced. Register online,
place your shopping in the basket and
your goods will be delivered free,
anywhere in the world.
e-mail: via online form

Eurogym Sport

www.eurogym.org
Swedish online retailer of amateur and professional gymnastics equipment. Accessories and equipment are divided into categories to suit all enthusiasts. Products are fully detailed with pictures and prices in Swedish Kroner. To order or get more information complete the enquiry form.
e-mail: info@eurogym.org

Europa Skilodge

www.europaskilodge.co.uk
UK online retailer of all types of ski equipment. Their products, which come from top ski manufacturers, are catalogued by type and displayed with a short description and price comparison between their own and high street retailers. They accept major credit cards and you can order by post, fax or telephone. They offer repair services.
e-mail: sales@europaskilodge.co.uk

Fionn Fitnesswear

www.fionn.net
UK supplier of swimwear, exercise wear and body armour for sportswomen. The range of designs and colours is spectacular. Each design is modelled and in a wide range of sizes. Currency and measurement converters simplify shopping, which is just a matter of dropping your items into a basket and checking out. Payment is by secure credit card form.
e-mail: fionn@easynet.co.uk

Fitness Wholesale Online

fitnesswholesale.com
Fitness equipment for professional and home gyms. Browse online or order from the offline catalogue; either way prices are lower than in non-virtual stores and delivery is to your door within the USA and Canada. Check out special offers and clearance items.
e-mail: fw@fitnesswholesale.com

Flymail

www.flymail.com
All the flies in the world for game fishing. There are so many categories and subcategories it is impossible to imagine you will not find exactly what you are looking for. They fly to anywhere in the world and your credit card details are kept secure.
e-mail: flymailuk@aol.com

Fogdog Sports

www.fogdog.com
Equipment for any sport from leading manufacturers. This is a regular US online store with much the same way of finding your way around the products. They accept major credit cards and deliver world wide.
e-mail: customer_service@fogdog.com

Footprint Designs

www.adventuresports.com/product/footprint
End-of-line and surplus stock items at discounts. Click on the picture for details and use the secure link for ordering online.
e-mail: not available

Footsloggers

www.footsloggers.com
Hiking, backpacking, climbing, camping and outdoor equipment and then some more. All major brands are available with online icon for current specials.

To get quotes, use the Request page.
e-mail: footsloggers@helicon.net

GearDirect.com

www.geardirect.com
Online US sports superstore with a
catalogue of more than 50,000 items
for individual, team, winter, extreme
and recreational sports. You will find
equipment by particular sport, best-sellers,
best value and current special offers.
Major credit cards are accepted and
shipping is world wide.
e-mail: info@geardirect.com

GearHead

www.gearhd.com
Equipment advice service aimed at the
beginner preparing for his first adventure
without much of a clue or no time to
shop around. You'll get a complete
gear list from which to make your
purchases, for which you pay the cost
plus a small service fee to Gearhead.
Major credit cards are accepted.
e-mail: Wct1359@aol.com

Gearoom.com

www.gearoom.com
Outdoor enthusiasts who love
equipment and have a mission to help
others to get a feel for gear. Reviews
are product-based and in-depth. The
Book Store page and Gear Auction
section are very useful.
e-mail: not available

Gefen Sports

**dialspace.dial.pipex.com/town/street/
xnf37**
Gear for racket sports from UK suppliers.
You can search by sport or manufacturer
and get prices online. Order by e-mail.

Delivery is standard within the EU; for
other countries arrangements must be
made.
e-mail: Sales@gefensports.com

Gemini Racquetball

www.geminisports.com
Online US racquetball store. Click on
a product image and you get lots of
information. They ship world wide.
e-mail: gemrac@usa.net

George Wood Mallets

www.woodmallets.com
Polo, croquet and cricket players get
catalogues for each sport with prices
and good pictures. Order by e-mail or
snailmail for shipment world wide.
There are links to international
governing bodies for all three sports.
e-mail: gwoodm@xtra.co.nz

Gerrys of Morecambe

gerrys-of-morecambe.co.uk
Reputed to be UK's leading supplier
of seawater angling equipment. You'll
find thousands of products from top
manufacturers divided by category, fully
detailed with prices and pictures.
Before you order, open an account to
make shopping easy; you just pick
items as you see them and add them to
your list. The credit card form is secure
and you can order from anywhere on
the globe.
e-mail: sales@gerrys-of-morecambe.
co.uk

Godfrey Rowsports

www.godfrey.co.uk
Rowing equipment and accessories
from UK manufacturer and retailer.
Each category of gear has a materials

specification and manufacturing details. Make your choice and add it to the trolley before placing your order.
e-mail: enquiries@godfrey.co.uk

Golf Aids

www.golfaids.co.uk
Accessories for advanced golfers. Products are neatly listed with each in turn described, displayed and priced. Additionally there are links to other Internet suppliers of golf equipment. Order by e-mail.
e-mail: via online form

Golf Warehouse

www.thegolfwarehouse.com
They say they are dedicated to providing the largest and broadest selection of golf products in the world. The online catalogue contains literally thousands of items covering every aspect of the sport, with items specifically for women, children and beginners. You can order by e-mail, phone or fax.
e-mail: customerservice@tgw.com

Gordon Griffiths Fishing Tackle

www.gordon-griffiths.co.uk
Fishing equipment suppliers to dealers and distributors world wide. With what they offer, fish don't have much of a chance. For more information, click on the product.
e-mail: fishingtackle@gordon_griffiths.co.uk

Gorp

www.gorp.com
Gear for hiking, camping, boating, fishing, winter sports, kids, gear repair and general travel. Each category has a product guide and tips on choosing the right gear. There is a boutique section, a women's corner, books and maps, video and CD pages and Gear Discussion to share tips on buying, using and swapping gear.
e-mail: sales@gorp.com

Great Outdoor Emporium Mall

www.tgoemall.com
This is probably the largest, most visited service for shoppers of outdoor recreation gear. There are more than 2000 departments and outdoor enthusiasts will find everything for all sports and outdoor activities.
e-mail: help@tgoemall.com

Grind

www.grind.co.uk
Two stores in Northern England, distributing skateboards, skates, BMX cycles and all the clothes and gear to go with them. The online catalogue gives you clear descriptions and pictures of the products. They accept major credit cards, cheques, postal orders and international money orders. You can order by e-mail.
e-mail: grind@grind.co.uk

Hammerbrush.com

www.hammerbrush.com
Canadian online sports store selling brushes for curling in two categories. Ordering is by secure online form and delivery is world wide.
e-mail: info@hammerbrush.com

Huntingtons on the Web

www.jcn.com/huntingtons
As luggage and leather goods merchants they go back several generations and they will personalise your purchases for

free. Click on the items on the home page for pictures and details of products. Order by fax or e-mail.
e-mail: hunthelp@huntweb.com

Jagged Edge Mountain Gear

www.jagged-edge.com
Clothing for winter camping and mountaineering. The online catalogue gives the full range. Navigate the store by clicking the category you want to browse; when you find something you want to buy, click the Add Item button beneath. To complete your order, click the Check Out button.
e-mail: jemg@jagged-edge.com

Just Balls!

www.justballs.com
They sell balls of every description, for sport and fitness, toys, collectible balls and ball accessories. Use the search engine or browse through the categories. Online you will find the latest products, ball game rules, discount offers and advice on ball care. Before purchasing get an account and pay by major credit card. Orders are delivered world wide from the USA.
e-mail: Customerservice@justballs.com

Kamae International

members.aol.com/kamaeint/kamae.htm
UK online retailers of karate uniforms, equipment and training videos. They have put together all their products in catalogues to help your search. Everything is easily laid out and priced and you can order by mail, e-mail or telephone.
e-mail: KamaeInt@aol.com

Kitbag.com

www.kitbag.com
Probably the largest range of football merchandise on the web. Replica and retro shirts, shorts and socks, leisure wear, stadium plaques, footballs, souvenirs, accessories, textiles, flags, videos and prints featuring football history and some of the great players. Pay in the currency of your choice by credit card using the Datacash secure server payment gateway. They ship internationally, with UK delivery free.
e-mail: feedback@kitbag.com

Le Travel Store

www.letravelstore.com
Everything you need in travel gear and accessories from locks and tags to clocks and bags. Check the Travel Gear on Sale page for bargains.
e-mail: gear@letravelstore.com

Learn2.com

www.learn2.com/corporate
Before you buy your next pair of hiking boots be sure to read the instructions on this site. Apart from footwear there

is a large range of other travel and sports equipment. To start shopping click on the Buy it Here link, then follow the instructions until you are ready to check out.
e-mail: Learn2@Learn2.com

Leki USA

www.leki.com
US-based with hiking, trekking, skiing and fitness products. Click on the category on the navigation bar, use the search engine or the Find It index page. Fill out the online form, or e-mail for more info.
e-mail: service@leki.com

Lightweight Backpacker

www.backpacking.net/gearshop.html
Everything on this site has been designed to reduce the backpacker's load. Products from shelters to cutlery are manufactured in lightweight and ultra-light materials. Browse around the Gear shop and visit Gear Reviews for opinions.
e-mail: Associates@backpacking.net

Long Road Travel Supplies

www.longroad.com
Quality mosquito nets for travel, camping and home use designed for maximum possible protection against biting insects under almost any condition. See for yourself and order by e-mail or phone.
e-mail: sales@longroad.com

Luggage Land

www.luggageland.com.au
This Australian travel luggage store has online product information and an ordering facility. They offer international brands, fine quality Australian-made leather goods and a wide range of travel accessories. They also offer tax-free shopping, free delivery and other valuable services.
e-mail: luggage@luggageland.com.au

Macabi Skirt

www.macabiskirt.com
Original adventure travel skirts for cool comfort and an attractive alternative to shorts and pants. The quick drying fabric is durable and adjusts easily to changes in weather and activity. Prices are marked and you can order online or by mail.
e-mail: sales@macabiskirt.com

Maxtrack

www.maxtrack.com
Online UK suppliers of mountain boards. Either browse through their latest products, parts department or view the whole product list. Ordering is by e-mail within the UK and Europe.
e-mail: maxtrack@btinternet.com

MockBros.com

www.mockbros.com
US manufacturer and online supplier of rodeo accessories, equipment, clothing and protective gear. Products are placed in neat categories, displayed and described. Complete the order form with your billing details for delivery anywhere in the world.
e-mail: via online form

Moosejaw

www.moosejaw.com
Everything for the outdoors, equipment, clothes, sports gear, tents and more. All products are said to be up to 40% below real world store prices. Items are illustrated and the site is secure.
e-mail: moosejaw@voyager.net

Mountain Woman

www.mountainwoman.com
A wide selection of branded clothing
and equipment for adventurous women.
You can clad yourself from head to foot
and then some. Order online, e-mail
or call for advice or suggestions.
They ship world wide at cost.
e-mail: info@mountainwoman.com

MPI Outdoors

www.adventuresports.com
They manufacture and distribute a
range of unique comfort and protection
products for outdoor use specialising
in all-weather blankets. There are
online instructions on how to deal with
emergencies and develop survival
skills.
e-mail: outdoor@ix.netcom.com

Nomad Outdoor & Travel Equipment

www.nomad.nl/f-com.asp
Functional outdoor gear and wear from
tents to boots. For more details click
on the product picture. The site has an
expeditions page and a travel guide.
e-mail: not available

Northwest River Supplies

www.nrscatalog.com
One-stop shop for branded boating
equipment for men, women and
children. Other lines include boats,
kayaks and accessories and camping
equipment. All products are priced
and you can buy online.
e-mail: nrs@nrsweb.com

Online Sports

www.onlinesports.com
This is probably the Internet's largest
online sports equipment and
memorabilia catalogue. They offer
products from several stores covering
all the sports disciplines, teams, items,
suppliers and manufacturers. Browse
all you wish but with so much on offer
you're better off entering the keyword
into the search engine to find what you
need. Shipping is world wide.
e-mail: comments@onlinesports.com

Out in Style

**www.adventuresports.com/shops/
out-in-style/welcome.htm**
A large inventory of camping, hunting,
law enforcement supplies and military
surplus goods. When you're done
browsing you can order online, with
shipping generally within 48 hours.
e-mail: sales@outinstyle.com

Overtons.com

www.overtons.com
Online boating supplies, with everything
you might ever need for your water
craft. You can request a full catalogue
or place an order online, major credit
cards are accepted, deliveries possible
apparently world wide.
e-mail: service@overtons.com

Pareto

www.pareto-golf.co.uk
They claim they are leaders in the
business and Europe's largest suppliers
of range and course mats, practice
ground equipment and accessories,
range balls and golf course accessories.
All products are categorised and then
each is carefully detailed, displayed and
priced. You can order from anywhere
using a feedback form.
e-mail: Sales@pareto-golf.co.uk

Playwell Martial Arts

www.webworld.co.uk/playwell
Uniforms, protective wear and accessories for all martial arts listed by category and style. All products in this omnibus online store are displayed and priced. Add them to your shopping list and checkout. They accept major cards and deliver world wide from the UK.
e-mail: playwell1@aol.com

Premier Swap

www.premierswap.com
Online collectibles market for UK football fans. You can buy and sell tickets, programs, T-shirts and autographed memorabilia. They carry the latest news about matches and football clubs. If you want access become a member.
e-mail: not available

Proline Sports

proline-sports.co.uk
UK manufacturer and supplier of sportswear and protective clothing. Their products are categorised and displayed. All major credit cards are accepted and prices are lower than in high street retail stores. They give you advice on how to treat sports injuries and links to sports-related sites.
e-mail: empl-hp@proline-sports.co.uk

Quill Racing

www.quill-racing.co.uk
High quality silencers and exhausts for motor-racing bikes online direct from this UK manufacturer. All their products are catalogued and if you want further information or want to order, e-mail them.
e-mail: andy@quill-racing.co.uk

Raymond Sims Rowing Equipment

www.rowing.co.uk
Rowing boats, oars, equipment and strip from this UK manufacturer and retailer. The collection is divided for easy search and each product is detailed as to construction materials and performance testing. To order use the e-mail addresses provided.
e-mail: boats@rowinguk1.fsnet.co.uk

Robin Hood Watersports

www.roho.co.uk
The whole range of equipment for canoeing, windsurfing, diving and water-skiing. Each sport has its own online catalogue. They also offer special wear and protective clothing. Use the shopping basket to order online in the UK.
e-mail: sales@roho.co.uk

Scarpa UK

www.scarpa.co.uk
Italian manufacturer and retailer of mountain shoes. Full technical specifications and pictures support all their products. Clicking on a picture gives you details, sizes and styles.
e-mail: Info@scarpa.co.uk

Seattle Fabrics

www.seattlefabrics.com
Fabrics and hardware for outdoor and recreational activity. They have everything you need to make your own equipment down to the thread to put it all together. You can order in person, by phone, fax, e-mail, or post with payment by credit card, personal cheque or money order.
e-mail: Seatlefabrics@msn.com

Second Level Shop

www.secondlevelsport.com
This is a department of the UK's sole distributors of Kana mountain bikes, Burton snowboards and Gravis footwear. Each brand has a list of currently available products and which dealer stocks them. You can purchase from the nearest dealer. Their lists are updated weekly.
e-mail: via online form

ShopSports.com

www.shopsports.com
Online retailer of top US brand sports equipment. They are authorised dealers for most popular brands and have a collection of sports videos, books and software. Join as a member free before you purchase.
e-mail: not available

Ski Surf 2000

www.skisurf.co.uk
Windsurfing and winter sports equipment for all levels of competence. They stock most major brands, advise on equipment and run a mail order service. The Special Offers and Used Kit pages have some of the best bargains.
e-mail: howard@skisurf.co.uk

Slazenger Online

www.slazenger.com
As you would expect, this renowned manufacturer of tennis, squash, cricket and golf equipment has an excellent site. Products are catalogued by sport and then by item. Each category lists current products and clicking an item links up with detailed technical information, pictures and prices. Shop by placing items in a basket then submit your order. Deliveries are world wide as the company is represented in many countries.
e-mail: via online form

Snow + Rock

www.snowandrock.co.uk
General online sports store with gear for all sports disciplines. You have the choice of browsing online or getting a personal catalogue. They accept major credit cards and you get an account once you have registered. Each product has a picture you can enlarge for a closer look.
e-mail: webmastersnr@ hubinteractive.com

Soo Bahk Do

www.soobahkdo.co.uk
Soo Bahk Do is a Korean martial art. The philosophy and discipline of the art are discussed online supported by a picture gallery, calendar of events, classes in the UK and of course, sale of equipment. Belts, manuals, uniforms and other paraphernalia can be ordered online if you are a club member.
e-mail: webmaster@soobahkdo.co.uk

South African Spearfishing Supplies

www.spearfishing.co.za
They are distributors and exporters of South African products, particularly Rob Allan spear fishing and free diving equipment. The spear guns are regarded among the finest on the market and are exported around the world. For trade enquiries click the enquiry link.
e-mail: info@spearfishing.co.za

Sportif USA

www.sportif.com
Quality performance clothing for

outdoor activities from backcountry to beachfront and every place between. Check out the products by category or use the search engine if you know what are you looking for. You can order online.

e-mail: not available

SportOnLine

www.SportOnLine.uk.com

One-stop shop for all your sports books, videos and DVDs, established by a group of like-minded people dedicated to promoting sport on the Net. Their stock is sorted under Best Sellers, New Releases and Forthcoming Releases, so you're bound to find what you're looking for. Searching is as simple as you can get it and every item is either discounted or includes a special offer.

e-mail: contactus@sportonline.uk.com

Sports Connection

www.sportsconnection.co.uk

Huge UK online sports store offering the widest range of sports clothing, shoes and accessories. Products come in all sizes, are well displayed and shopping is simply putting your items into the basket and checking out. They accept major credit cards but deliver only within the UK.

e-mail: Info@sportsconnection.co.uk

Sports Elite

sportselite.com

This is the sports department of Shopping Universe, a large UK department store selling almost anything. Equipment is listed by gender. Each category has hot offers and a search engine to help you select by product, brand and price range. Fill your shopping bag and check out. All major credit cards are accepted and delivery is world wide.

e-mail: not available

Stagecoach Wrestling Products

www.wrestlingboots.com
Merchandising site with an online catalogue that lists all the products you can buy and a photo gallery to display them. You can buy a pair of their famous boots as worn by top wrestlers; T-shirts are a recent addition. The site itself is very basic and could do with a facelift.
e-mail: stagecoach@ala.net

Summit Sports

www.summitsports.com
Canadian site for online buying of wrestling gear with prices in US$. Shoes, singlets, kneepads, even scales to check your weight. It has an amateur wrestling forum link. Learn wrestling techniques and skills from Ken Chertow, a top US freestyle wrestler and coach. His 2-hour instructional videos are helping wrestlers throughout North America and can be bought from this site.
e-mail: info@summitsports.com

Surfstore

www.demon.co.uk/sdwsurf
Windsurfing equipment available online in the UK. Boards, sails, booms, fins, masts, wetsuits with all the accessories. Each category is separately catalogued. Order by e-mail and be sure to include your billing details. Major credit cards are accepted.
e-mail: sales@surfstore.co.uk

The Archery Centre

www.archery-centre.co.uk
UK archery store with a good range of equipment, video training courses and online professional advice. All their goods are displayed and fully described. Order by completing the form online or print and send it by mail. They ship world wide and quote freight rates on request.
e-mail: sales@archery-centre.co.uk

The Luggage Shop

www.the-luggage-shop.com
Good quality luggage, travel leather goods and accessories from top US manufacturers. You can browse by category or manufacturer. Ordering online is explained and shipping is world wide.
e-mail: inquiry@the-luggage-shop.com

The Queen Collection

www.queenconnection.com
US retailer of accessories and new and used clothing for rodeo enthusiasts. The site is well laid out with a colourful range of goods for sale. Complete the order form with your billing details. You can expect delivery world wide.
e-mail: ahedlund@queenconnection.com

Tilley Endurables

www.tilley.com
Manufacturers of adventure and travel clothing. The store locations finder will tell you where they are. Their web site has a testimonial board, clothing profile Q&A and more. Their products will cover you from top to toe and their accessories make welcome gifts.
e-mail: not available

Title Boxing

www.titleboxing.com
Boxing gear at discounted prices. To find what you are looking for either browse online or order an offline catalogue. There are books and videos about boxing and links to boxing-related sites. Purchasing is by secure form and delivery is world wide.
e-mail: info@titleboxing.com.

Totally Outdoors

www.adventuresports.com/shops/ totally/welcome.htm
Women's outdoor clothing and equipment made from hard wearing performance fabrics in flattering feminine fashions size XS - XXL. The online store departments have the products and educational resources to help women better enjoy the outdoors.
e-mail: info@totallyoutdoors.com

Tough Traveller

www.travelsource.com/travelstore/ toughtraveler/toughtraveler.html
Travel gear with the emphasis on toughness. The full range is displayed and if you want a complete catalogue, contact the agent. Order online by using the form.
e-mail: not available

Travel Products

www.travel-accessories.com
A wide range of practical, proven travel accessories for bikers and motorists from maps to meals on the go. All products are shipped within 48 hours with a one-year guarantee. The site has a search engine and useful travel links.
e-mail: delblau@msn.com

Travelsuppliers.com

www.travelsupplies.com
Travel luggage, organisers, outdoor accessories, guides, equipment and appliances for travellers. Browse by category, brand, or innovative items or use the search engine. Press the On Sale button for current bargains.
e-mail: not available

TST Leisure

www.tstleisure.co.uk
Online suppliers of equipment for home gyms, treadmills, exercise bikes, keep-fit accessories, sun beds and health supplements. Their catalogue has pictures of all products. Shopping basket and online credit card server facilities are provided.
e-mail: sales@tstleisure.co.uk

Typhoon Cyclone

www.typhoon-int.co.uk
Clothing for in or out of water and water sports products sold around the world. Products include diving dry suits and equipment, thermals, commercial and military dry suits, aviation immersion suits and more in an excellent range, all well illustrated.
e-mail: sales@typhoon-int.co.uk

Vee-Kay Sports

www.vks.com/product.htm

Online retailer of everything a cricketer would need. Gear is divided by category, age and skill to simplify search. Every product is described and illustrated and prices are compared with non-virtual retailers. Major credit cards are accepted but you can order only from eight specified countries.

e-mail: mail@vks.com

Walkabout Travel Gear

www.walkabouttravelgear.com

Online sports store and information centre for the independent traveller. Apart from a wide range of outdoor equipment you get travel tips, a newsletter and free catalogue sent to your door. Ordering is secure and goods will be delivered world wide.

e-mail: sales@walkabouttravelgear.com

WDP-Paintball

www.wdp-paintball.co.uk

UK manufacturer and retailer of paintball equipment. On site are lists of high street retailers, locations of paintball fields where you can indulge your warlike instincts and the latest news. The gear is categorised and products, as you might expect, come in a choice of colours. To shop, browse along the virtual aisles, add what you want to your shopping list and order. They ship world wide.

e-mail: not available

Whitlock Products

www.whit-prods.com

Nets to suit the type of fish you want to catch and how you want to catch them. They give you full details of all their products, accept major credit cards and deliver world wide from the UK.

e-mail: Fred@whit-prods.com

Wrestlingone.com

wrestlingone.com

They call themselves the largest and most complete distributors of wrestling products in the world. You can request or download a catalogue and shop online at this site for all the gear, of which there is a lot. Buy with a credit card. There is a bookstore, recruiting centre, a mailing list for coaches that you can join and links to associated sites.

e-mail: info@wrestlingone.com

Sports News

10 Tenths Motorsport

ten-tenths.accelerator.org

Motor racing fans will find all the news, views and information they want at this UK site. Top class presentation makes it a pleasure to use, especially since the news stories from F1, Touring Cars, Nascar and Rally are such good reading. There are circuit guides, TV guides and chat rooms and many of the links to other sites are well worth following up.
e-mail: Craig.Antill@Ten-Tenths.com

abcNews.com

abcnews.go.com/sections/sports

This almost exclusively US-oriented sports site features breaking news and information. The choice of sport and the quality of journalism are highly impressive, making for a very attractive site. Check out the selection of first class links to other sports sites.
e-mail: via online form

About.com

home.about.com/sports

While having its own though limited selection of news articles, the real force of this US site is its extensive list of links to other sports news and information sites. In addition to the major spectator sports there are loads of others to interest you, like figure skating, power boating and rodeo.
e-mail: reachus@about-inc.com

allAfrica.com - Sports

www.allafrica.com/sport

Using news articles from leading African newspapers as well as its own editorials, allAfrica.com is a good read. The sports section contains a generous selection of current reports from all over the continent with a large proportion on soccer.
e-mail: newsdesk@africanews.org

Amateur Golf

www.amateur-golf.com

News, views and information on the world of amateur golf with a selection of very readable articles. Emphasis is on the UK and Ireland with lists of courses and events but there is also information on golfing matters world wide.
e-mail: admin@amateur-golf.com

Arabia.com - Sports

www.arabia.com/sports
While concentrating on the Arab sports world, the site also pays a lot of attention to international sports. This is a simple yet effective site covering a wide spread of sport with chat rooms, bulletin boards and online shopping.
e-mail: info@arabia.com

Autosport

www.autosport.com
Autosport, as its name suggests, concerns itself with the latest news and information from the exciting world of motor car racing, from Formula 1 to Nascar and Rally to Cart. Keep up to date with the latest championship ranking, get profiles of all the top drivers or listen to race reports in the audio archive. The site also has regular competitions with prizes and the chance to drive a real F1 car up for grabs.
e-mail: via online form

BBC News Sport

news.bbc.co.uk/sport
The sports pages of the BBC online news site are very slick and professional, though possibly lacking the sharpness of other independent news services. As well as breaking news from the world of sport, the site displays a good selection of sporting photographs and audio clips.
e-mail: newsonline@bbc.co.uk

BikeMagic

www.bikemagic.com
Every form of competitive cycling is covered on this extensive UK site. You'll find news and information on road cycling, cross-country, down hill and BMX biking, useful sections on cycling holidays, personal fitness and bike maintenance. The news search engine could be less cumbersome.
e-mail: feedback@BIKEmagic.com

BowNet Archery

www.bownet.com
As the online version of the Bow International Magazine, the site has plenty to offer in the form of news and information from the UK and international world of archery. While the site could be slicker, it still has impressive features such as live video-streaming of archery events, a photo gallery, shopping links and a chat room.
e-mail: editor@bownet.com

Boxing Online

www.boxingonline.com
News, articles, schedules and interviews are neatly set out on this US boxing site which is hampered by slow loading. You can check out video and audio interviews, visit the photo gallery and even catch a live broadcast of a fight. Writing is of high standard and you can slug it out verbally with fellow fans in the chat rooms.
e-mail: not available

Britball

www.britball.com
The basketball scene in Britain and Ireland is adequately covered on this site. News, facts and figures for men's, women's and junior basketball are featured with Olympic news, player and coach profiles and a chat room.
e-mail: magazine@britball.com

CBS Sportsline

www.sportsline.com
Eminently good US site providing a diversity of news and features slanted mainly toward US sport. Photos, archives, a children's section, fantasy manager gamesand fans' forums add up to an almost endless list of quality items. Other sports covered include soccer, horseracing and wrestling. The merchandising section is of American proportions, holding stocks of an enormous selection of sporting goods.
e-mail: genqandc@sportsline.com

ChicagoSports.com

chicagotribune.com/sports
This section of the Chicago Tribune Internet Edition provides top quality sports news and features. It's not unexpected that the emphasis is firmly on US sport, particularly baseball, but if home-runs, free-throws and quarterbacks are your cup of low-fat de-caf, then this is something you will want to get into. To keep you there even longer they have added online shopping, games and fans' forums.
e-mail: eroth@tribune.com

CNN Sports Illustrated

www.cnnsi.com
While this site focuses on the US, its coverage of world wide sport is commendable for content and quality articles. There are some marvelous features including a very entertaining multi-media section packed with video and audio clips.
e-mail: cnnsi@cnnsi.com

Competition Results

www.terra.es/personal/jlpenag
Although small and basic, this site lists winners, scores and times from many branches of sport. Each section gives winners in all competitions, often dating back to the earliest records. The range covered is excellent, from sailing to football, gymnastics to water polo. Even triathlon statistics are entered. With scores, beaten finalists, times and years all lovingly presented, the site is a treasury of information.
e-mail: franpng@teleline.es

CricInfo

www-uk.cricket.org
The rather clumsy name of this site can't disguise the fact that it is a treasure trove of news and information for the cricket enthusiast. As well as news of the latest series and tours, the site has profiles of teams and players, along with nice features such as live audio reports, online shopping, a photograph database and chat rooms. It also has its own selection of online games including Fantasy Cricket and Cricket Trivia. And for those who don't know their silly mid-off from their square leg, there is an extensive explanation of the rules of the game.
e-mail: help@cricket.org

David Rawcliffe Sports Photography

drsp.merseyworld.com
Some great sports action shots. You can vote for your personal favourite Picture of the Year, or have a look at previous years selections. Then take part in their free competition for a chance at a prize.
e-mail: dave@shankly.u-net.com

Electronic Telegraph

www.telegraph.co.uk/sport

A wide range of sports news comes on this simple yet slick site. The journalism is high quality and the news stories are up-to-date. You can also check out the pools news. Some parts of the site are closed to non-members, so if you want to enter the inner sanctum, register online.

e-mail: etsport@telegraph.co.uk

ESPN.com

espn.go.com

News and information on domestic and international sports form only part of this major US site. The other part acts as an umbrella for several other top quality sports news sites. ESPN itself is well constructed and informative with a seemingly never-ending list of useful and entertaining features such as video and audio clips, photo galleries and games.

e-mail: comments@espn.go.com

European Hockey.net

www.eurohockey.net/news

Focusing not surprisingly on European ice hockey, this site is great for fans. News, match results and statistics come with information on players, teams and transfers. The stories and articles are a good read and you can use the chat rooms to take in what others have to say or lay it all down yourself.

e-mail: meha@limmat.ch

Eurosport

www.eurosport.com

This online site of the TV sports channel offers news and information on a wide range of European sports including Nordic and Alpine Skiing. The site has a video news service but overall is rather dull in its presentation. It offers a basic online shopping feature as well as information on sports holiday destinations and accommodation.

e-mail: enquiries@eurosport.co.uk

FinalWhistle.com

www.finalwhistle.com

Grand site with hearty helpings of news and stories from the world of football. Features, covering all major league and cup competitions, domestic and international, are presented for easy reading.

e-mail: infoA@finalwhistle.com

Football 365

www.football365.co.uk

A very fast breaking news service as well as loads of information, facts and figures on domestic and international football. Check out the opinions of the site's team of well-respected columnists, then have your say in the discussion forum. Other features worth a look include news flashes that pop up discreetly on your computer screen if you're at work, an interactive trivia game and some very good comedy stuff.

e-mail: themanager@football365.co.uk

Football Unlimited

www.footballunlimited.co.uk

This terrific site gives football fans everything they could want, with heaps of statistics, reports and breaking news. As part of the Guardian Newspaper Online, the site uses its own columnists, with some of the best football writing available on the

Internet. While you're at it, check out the range of very interesting bulletin boards.

e-mail: the.boss@guardian.co.uk

Footballed-Out.com

www.footballed-out.com

Very basic UK site featuring breaking news and information on English football. Other items include a trivia section, voting polls and some links. The limited scale of the site probably means that you won't leave even slightly Footballed-out.

e-mail: webmaster@footballed-out.com

FootballNews.co.uk

www.footballnews.co.uk

Bright and breezy UK site with stacks of news and reports on the most popular game on earth. It takes an even-handed approach, dividing coverage between the bigger clubs, non-league teams and women's football. World and European football are ably documented while other features include betting information, a photo gallery and some amusing online games.

e-mail: newsroom@footballnews.co.uk

Formula One Supporter's Association

www.fosa.org

The site for the fans with a treasure trove of news, information and feature articles on Formula One. The scope of the information is prodigious, with news, profiles, weather reports, technical information and press conferences all jostling for position. By using the links you can access some great stuff, from games to trivia and cartoons. Nice touches include live video feeds and a virtual cockpit, which gives you a taste of all the top racing tracks from behind the wheel of an F1 car.

e-mail: via online form

Fox Sports

www.foxsports.com

Big-hitting US site offering sports news with a distinctly American flavour. Major US sports events are covered in

meticulous detail with quality articles backed by the latest news and college reports. Very well-presented and easy to navigate, the site also takes in world wide sport. Nice features include video highlights which can be played on the site and an online shopping channel.
e-mail: sportscomments@foxsports.com

Golf Today

www.golftoday.co.uk
Golf Today delivers a slick online magazine full to the brim with the latest news, statistics and talking points from the game. The site provides a virtual clubhouse for members who can get advice from the professionals, check out the library and generally boast about how low their handicap is. Other useful features include an online shop and golf-related travel news.
e-mail: admin@golftoday.co.uk

Gone To The Dogs

www.thedogs.co.uk
The official site of the British Greyhound Racing Board gives you news, results and betting for the sport which has recently recovered its old popularity. Well designed and easy to use, the site has useful information, history and links to a large handful of related sites.
e-mail: via online form

Home News Now - Sports

www.newsnow.co.uk/-NewsFeed. Sport.htm
Clever and handy site with a section to take the work out of finding the latest sports news. Type in a sport or even your favourite team and it will scour the web's news sites to bring you the

very latest reports, listing the headlines. It searches from a good selection of sports news sites and updates info every five minutes.
e-mail: feedback@NewsNow.co.uk

iafrica.com

sport.iafrica.com
Bright and breezy, nice and easy and full of information, this sports site makes good reading. African and world sport are covered in fine detail and all the other features you'd expect of a top quality site including extensive statistics, chat rooms and online shopping.
e-mail: via online form

International Gymnast Online

www.intlgymnast.com
Online magazine with news, views and information from the supple world of gymnastics. The site is extensive and includes training tips, photos, an event calendar and gymnast profiles. Fans can also have their say in the discussion groups.
e-mail: ig@intlgymnast.com

Iskater.com

www.iskater.com
Flashy US site covers everything you could possibly want to know about the world of ice-skating. Aside from up-to-date news, you can check out the photo gallery, biographies and the list of forthcoming events and competitions.
e-mail: feedback@iskater.com

ITN Sport

www.itn.co.uk/sport.shtml
ITN provide a slightly limited online sports news service. With a strong

leaning towards football, the site transmits the latest news and articles on the world of sport with a lot of stories having audio or video clips. There is a small archive, fans' forum and a clutch of links to other sites.
e-mail: not available

Lycos Sports

sportshome.lycos.com
The US Lycos site has a well-presented package of US sports news and information. You'll also find a selection of top quality articles and columns. The range of sport covered is impressive even if somewhat US-oriented. Interesting features include an extreme sports section with video clips, a sports radio feature and online shopping.
e-mail: not available

MSN.Co.Uk

www.msn.co.uk/page/7.asp
Limited but impressive football news site. Individual club information is particularly worthwhile as a lot of news and information may relate to the club you support. An online shopping facility, competitions and excellent links to other sites world wide.
e-mail: via online form

NineMSN - Wide World Of Sports

sports.ninemsn.com.au
Australian sports news service focuses on the local staples of cricket, rugby and Australian Rules football. But not to be outdone, the site also provides good international sports services with the soccer section particularly appealing. Online shopping and chat rooms complete the site.
e-mail: via online form

OnRunning.com

www.onrunning.com
Invaluable site for athletics fans with breaking news, results and articles in a well structured and easy-to-use format with a strong UK bias. You can keep up to date with athletics events around the country including races such as the Great North Run. Former track star Peter Elliott runs a virtual training camp on the site. Other features offer health and fitness advice, chat rooms and video clips.
e-mail: not available

Planet Football

www.planetfootball.com
This superior football news site feeds the fan with red-hot news, lively reporting and superb columns. The site reports football world wide and has a number of useful features including an OPTA statistics section and a fans' forum. Taken as a whole this is a top of the league news site.
e-mail: via online form

Planet Rugby

www.planet-rugby.com
This quality site provides extensive news and detailed information from the world of rugby. Well presented and user-friendly, Planet Rugby features regular live online Q & A sessions with top players and an impressive archive featuring facts and figures going back as far as 1871. The shopping feature lets you buy match tickets online.
e-mail: via online form

Planet-F1.com

www.planet-f1.com
Hugely informative and enjoyable site

for cyber-F1 fans with everything you could want from your beloved sport. Breaking news, results, schedules and news archives are all provided with an array of interesting articles, a picture gallery, trivia games and an online shop. The vast library of information on every driver and team for the last 50 years will take a while to get through.
e-mail: via online form

Racenews

www.racenews.co.uk
UK site with up-to-date news, facts and figures on British horse racing. There are useful links to all major racecourses in the UK, the all-important betting news and information on forthcoming events.
e-mail: racenews@compuserve.com

RadioSport

www.radiosport.com
Fascinating and informative site with live radio broadcasts and audio clips of recent sports events and news stories. There are online links to an enormous number of sports radio stations, all accessible from the site. Links also take you to sports news sites that feature audio clips. The range of material is almost unbelievable as is the number of sports covered. The software required to put you in touch can be downloaded from the site.
e-mail: staff@radiosport.com

Rallycross Online

www.rallycross.de
Small German site with news, reports, facts and figures. Even though the set up is rather basic and a little awkward to use, the site does provide lots of

sound information on the Rally scene.
e-mail: aschrader@softcare.de

Rugby News

www.rugby.co.nz
New-Zealand magazine provides up-to-date reportage on the rugby scene in the home of the legendary All Blacks. In addition to results and talking points, the site has an online shopping facility, a fantasy rugby game and links to other sites.
e-mail: news@rugby.co.nz

SailSail.com

www.sailsail.com
To enjoy the site fully you have to register as a member. Registration is free and once you're in, you can check out the boatloads of information online, from sailing news to information on competitions like the America's Cup and the Olympics. Other features include tutorials, lists of sailing clubs and weather reports.
e-mail: info@sailsail.com

Scotland Online - Sport

www.sport.scotland.net
Keep up to date with all things sporting north of the border on this sports section of Scotland Online. Though stories are limited in scope several links to other Scottish sports sites are provided. There is some international sports news.
e-mail: editor@scotland.net

Sky Sports.com

www.sky.com/sports
Not surprisingly, this Sky sites focuses mainly on football with up-to-date news and lots of facts and figures. All the same, the site still gives good coverage

of other sport such as snooker, sailing and cricket. Exclusive video reports are available and occasional live chats with sporting stars may come your way. The quiz section with its lively choice of trivia games is worth a look.

e-mail: via online form

Slam Sports

www.canoe.ca/Slam

This Canadian site provides a remarkably detailed sports news service. As well as concentrating on Canadian issues, it brings you world wide sport in a well presented and user-friendly package. There are some entertaining games and a bunch of links worth exploring.

e-mail: slam@canoe.ca

SoccerAge.com

www.soccerage.com

SoccerAge is an impressive and easy-to-use site for the cyber fan, with news, features and information. The site covers everything going on in the game world wide, as well as useful archive material and a photo library. Discuss the major talking points of the day, or argue with fellow fans in the chat forum. You can also check live match reports or spend time in the online fantasy manager games. The choice is yours!

e-mail: info@soccerage.com

Soccernet

www.soccernet.com

Up-to-date and on the ball, this UK football site is a fantastic world wide service for football news. A member of the ESPN network, the site sets itself high journalistic standards with very readable articles on football past and present.

e-mail: via online form

Sportal

www.sportal.co.uk

A top quality sports news site, especially good for breaking news and views in several languages, with great extras such as photo galleries, video clips and statistics. While the site is limited to Football, Formula 1, Horseracing and Rugby Union, the quality and quantity of the information is staggering. Once registered as a member, you can enjoy the fans' forum, competitions and games.

e-mail: general-uk@sportal.net

Sportec

www.sportec.com

A major Spanish site with an English language version, it has an enormous range of sports news and information, with everything from handball to fencing, and to its credit, sport for the disabled gets good coverage. News is both domestic and international and online shopping rounds off a good site.

e-mail: websportec@ibm.net

SportingLife.com

www.sportinglife.com

SportingLife.com offers the cyber sports fan just about everything - a huge range of sport, breaking news and loads of information. Nice touches include betting information, regular competitions and a vidi-printer feature with as-it-happens sports news appearing directly on your screen. The writing is of a very high standard and the facts and figures should satisfy even the most demanding of sports junkies. You can even e-mail your views to the site's own fanzine.

e-mail: enquiries@sportinglife.com

SportLive

www.sportlive.net

This Express Newspapers online sports service offers user-friendly and highly-detailed news and information. All types of sport are covered in terrific detail and the site offers regular articles written by some of the top sports writers in the country. If all the facts and figures get too much, you can always play a few of the very funny online games, including Beat The Keeper, Leeds V Manchester United, You Be The Ref and a particular favourite, Dress Up Posh (or David), where you're given the earth-shattering opportunity to choose outfits for the glamorous Beckham couple. David looks particularly good in the string bikini.

e-mail: via online form

SportOnAir

www.sportonair.com

Excellent and lively sports news service with lots of audio reports, photographs and breaking stories. They cover a good range of sport with nice features like what the papers say, a trivia game and an hourly audio bulletin.

e-mail: andy.downie@datanetms.co.uk

Sports Central

www.sports-central.org

American in origin and focus, this site has an unimaginative news service that covers a limited range of sport. However, it is well put together and does have some interesting features, such as the Fan Press section, where budding sports journalists post their stories.

e-mail: via online form

Sports.Com

www.sports.com

Quite simply a superb site with a staggering amount of news and information on a wide range of sport. Football coverage is especially impressive with up to date news and information on everything from transfer rumours to individual players. Prepare to spend days rather than hours exploring the online sports shops, photo library and chat forums. Also check out the nifty Virtualive feature which gives you the chance to replay animated re-workings of recent football action in 3D.

e-mail: ukfeedback@sports.com

SportsFeed.com

www.sportsfeed.com

US sport with a lot of emphasis on the local staples - American football, basketball, ice hockey and baseball and a few others from volleyball to motor-racing. You get up-to-date news, betting odds and tips. There are short reviews of sports in the UK, Europe and Asia, which don't compare with the main body in scope, but they are no tail-pieces either.

e-mail: editor@sportsfeed.com

SportsForWomen.com

www.sportsforwomen.com

A welcome antidote to male-dominated sports sites on the web, this US entry is exclusively female. Slick and well-designed, it has news and stories from the world of women's sport and helpful features such as training schedules, expert advice and chat rooms. Regrettably it concentrates almost exclusively on US sport.

e-mail: info@sportsforwomen.com

SportsNews.com

www.sportsnews.com

Fascinating sports news site with chunks of interesting material from the entire world, including entertaining sections on Africa and Asia. If that's not enough, you get links to other sporting news sites around the globe directly accessed from here. Once on this site, you're not likely to leave in a hurry, so be warned.

e-mail: staff@wn.com

SportsPlaces.com

www.sportsplaces.com

Here you get lists of links to sports news and information sites. Though American in bias, it still manages to cover the wider world of sport enough to call it international.

e-mail: info@SportsPlaces.com

Sportzine.co.uk

www.sportszine.co.uk

Sports site almost without equal. It searches the Web for sports news and information to satisfy every taste. Search by keyword or by sport and let the engine find and list everything it has. It even gives its own top 5 choices in each category. The range is fantastic with specialist sport like martial arts, scuba-diving and snowboarding set alongside major spectator sports. If that's not enough, the site has its own sports news service.

e-mail: via online form

SwimNews Online

www.swimnews.com

While the form of this Canadian site may not have the finesse and style of other large sites, the content is of the highest standard. Breaking news is supplemented by information from the swimming world - ranking, times and placings from practically every recent major swimming event. An online magazine and shop come as part of the package.

e-mail: swimnews@ibm.net

Team Talk

www.teamtalk.com

An independent soccer and rugby news service covering all the top teams. Choose your team from the list and you get the latest news stories instantly. There are also links to quizzes, sports radio and online betting sites.

e-mail: via online form

Tennis.com

www.tennis.com

Loads of breaking news, information and statistics from the tennis world. The US site offers lots of training tips, equipment advice and information on how to get started in the game. A fitness section, online shopping and list of useful links complete this practical site.

e-mail: editors@tennis.com

The Irish Times - Sports Extra

www.ireland.com/sports
As well as a particularly impressive football section, this Irish site covers a wide range of sport including Gaelic football and hurling. A good mixture of domestic and international sports news and information comes with lots of interesting features, articles, chat rooms and an archive.
e-mail: sports@irish-times.com

The Sporting Press

sportingpress.rivals.com
US writers take a satirical look at sports news. Filled with spoof stories, headlines and cartoons, the site is entertaining even though it focuses totally on the US sports scene. There are video clips, competitions and a range of worthwhile links.
e-mail: sportingpress@hotmail.com

The Sports Network

www.sportsnetwork.com
Very good sections on American football, baseball and basketball are provided on this first-rate US site. News is up-to-date and statistics come in swarms. Sports coverage is both domestic and international, articles are well written, features and reports abound.
e-mail: kzajac@sportsnetwork.com

The Squash Player

www.squashplayer.co.uk
Squash fans can get all the news and information they need on this UK site. The news section is very comprehensive and the lists of events, ranking and reports complete the picture. In the online workshop you can learn more about the rules of the game and pick up some handy tips.
e-mail: post@squashplayer.co.uk

The Times - Sports

www.the-times.co.uk

All the sports news and writing from the columns of the Times newspaper appear online. Journalism is of the highest quality and reports cover lots of fixtures and results. A few fantasy sports games complete the pages.

e-mail: via online form

The Virtual Library Of Sport

www.sportsvl.com

Unsophisticated it may be, but this site supplies a worthwhile bundle of links to sporting resources on the Internet. An inclusive, if sometimes bizarre, range of sport is covered including the very popular past-time, uni-cycling! The links are generally of high standard.

e-mail: via online form

This Is London - Sport

www.thisislondon.co.uk/html/sport.html

The London Evening Standard's online news site has a sports section with a satisfying range of news items and well-written columns. Focusing, in descending order, on football, rugby and miscellaneous sports, the site provides intelligent analyses of the day's sports talking points.

e-mail: sportsdesk@thisislondon.com

TodaySports.com

www.todayssports.com

An enjoyable and comprehensive sports news site. The good selection of US and international sports stories and the range of articles by the site's columnists should keep everybody happy. A collection of interesting and fun features keep the site lively.

e-mail: info@todayssports.com

TotalSports.Net

www.totalsports.net

Stuffed full of lively features, this US site covers domestic sport in impressive detail as well as keeping up with the wider sports world. Lots of news, loads of facts and figures for your perusal, and when you're done there are online games, shopping and links to investigate.

e-mail: info@totalsports.net

World Soccer News

www.wldcup.com

Although quite basic, this football site covers a lot of ground with a lively selection of news from around the world. Unusual features include a vidi-printer style breaking news window and a truly impressive amount of detailed information on hundreds of top teams and players.

e-mail: ed@wldcup.com

www.fieldhockey.com

www.fieldhockey.com

Simple yet effective site that allows hockey fans to keep up with late news stories. Umpires have their own section with information on rule changes and talking points in the game, while coaches can download a virtual coaching program. Links take you to overseas hockey sites.

e-mail: george@fieldhockey.com

Stadiums & Arenas

Africa's Major Stadiums

www.soccer-africa.com/Stadiums.html
Links to the major stadiums and
arenas on the whole continent.
e-mail: stadiums@soccer-africa.com

Ajax

www.ajax.nl/eng/
Described as a football temple with a
unique mix of impressive architecture, the
site for this Dutch arena has a museum
page, online fan shop, supporters'
page, news and match information.
e-mail: not available

American Airlines Arena

www.aaarena.com
Scheduled to open during the 1999-
2000 NBA season, the arena was built
to provide superior acoustics and sight
lines from any one of its 20,000 seats.
When completed it will enhance the
experience and excitement of HEAT
games and every other event it hosts.
On the waterfront of beautiful Biscayne
Bay, it offers four premium seating
choices, enticing restaurants and exotic
retail stores.
e-mail: via online form

Amsterdam Arena

www.amsterdamarena.nl
A very modern football stadium is also
home to one of the most innovative
and dynamic clubs in the world – AFC
Ajax. Really stylish site whose opening
page offers a choice of four panels for
information, calendar, site map and the
arena itself.
e-mail: not available

Arrowhead Stadium

**www.kcchiefs.com/fanfair/v_arrow-
head.asp**
Take the field with the Chiefs by viewing
a video of the home of the Kansas City
Chiefs football team. There are statistics,
biographies, match schedules and
results, a page of what's in development
with players including new signings
and other news.
e-mail: not available

Astrodome

www.astros.com/dome.htm

Billed as the Eighth Wonder of the World by Astros' original owner, Judge Roy Hofheinz, the Houston Astrodome was the first ballpark to have a roof over the playing field. It boasts cushioned seats and is completely air-conditioned. New artificial turf for baseball and an enlarged seating capacity are two of the highlights of a $60 million expansion project completed in 1989. See it all online and enter the trivia quiz.

e-mail: via online form

B.C. Place Stadium

www.bcpavco.com/bcplacestadium/

They say in just a few hours they can convert the stadium from a football arena packed with cheering fans to a more intimate concert bowl where the crowd will hush to the strains of a solo violin. Home to the BC Lions football team, view the calendar of events, order tickets, connect to the Lions Team page or to Vancouver's tourist site.

e-mail: gramsay@bcpavco.com

Bank One Ballpark

www.azdiamondbacks.com/bob/

Regarded as the game's most innovative venue, it is the only sports facility in the world with a retractable roof, air conditioning and natural turf playing field. Ground was broken in 1995 and the project took 28 months and cost $354 million to complete. The Arizona Diamondbacks team site provides enjoyable reading with easy to use links and outstanding pictures of the retractable roof.

e-mail: via online form

Barcelona Stadium

www.fcbarcelona.es/stadium/default. sps?LanguageID=9

You can follow the site map, take a virtual tour, read the history of the club, visit the museum and shop at the online store. This very good site reflects the pride it takes in the impressive stadium it showcases.

e-mail: not available

Busch Stadium

www.stlcardinals.com

Home to the St Louis Cardinals baseball team, the site lists game notes, news, schedules, statistics, a photo gallery and a lot more. An innovative page shows the seating arrangement; click anywhere and you get the view from this position. Order your tickets online and plan your visit around some of the great giveaways of the season.

e-mail: not available

Chicago Bulls

www.nba.com/bulls/

You can order tickets and check your seats online at this site for the 21,000-seat basketball stadium, opened in 1994. Read the news, enjoy audio and video highlights of games and follow links to other sites. The Inside the Bulls page gives you a behind-the-scenes view of the team and their facilities.

e-mail: not available

Cinergy Field

www.cincinnatireds.com/redpages/ cinergy/index.shtml

Cincinnatti Reds baseball team live here in a 48-acre stadium called Cinergy Field with 53,000 seating capacity. Check out the stadium and other features.

e-mail: not available

Cleveland Brown Football Stadium

www.clevelandbrowns.com
An exciting looking site where you can get yourself an e-mail address. Information covers the club, seating arrangements, a video scoreboard and locker-room page.
e-mail: not available

Coors Field

www.blakestreet.com/coorsfield/
Win or lose, there's nothing like Colorado Rockies Baseball and there's no place like Coors Field. Paradise to a Denver baseball fan is a sunny day in left field at Coors. Now the Internet brings you baseball's greatest and most majestic facility. There's information on how to get there, with an A-Z guide to local facilities and restaurants thrown in as a bonus.
e-mail: not available

Enron Field

www.astros.com/newdome.htm
Houston's newest wonder opened in March 2000 when the Astros christened the Enron Field with an exhibition game against two-time defending world champion New York Yankees. This state-of-the-art 42,000-seat stadium is so new construction photos feature as much as sports info on the site. Videos show the retractable roof, you can check out the view from every section of the seating and a feature compares Enron Field to other fields. Buy your tickets online.
e-mail: ruggles@astrofan.net

Girondins de Bordeaux

www.fc-girondins-bordeaux.com/ girondins-html/us/Index.html
Information on the site is much the same as for other stadiums. You'll find a potted history of the club, a shop and links to other sites.
e-mail: via online form

Hong Kong Stadium

imspo07.netvigator.com/hkstadium/ oper/index.html
e-mail: via online form

HSBC Arena

www.marinemidlandarena.com
Multipurpose arena which hosts sports events and major concerts. It has its own search facility and links to the Buffalo Sabres basketball team. You can view photos of recent events and buy tickets online.
e-mail: not available

King Fahd Stadium

www.saudinf.com
e-mail: sair@saudinf.com

La Plata Stadium

www.wai.com/Structures/Fabric/ laplata.html
e-mail: not available

Liacuras Center

www.liacourascenter.com
10,000-seat, state-of-the-art arena, less than two miles from Philadelphia's City Hall.
e-mail: via online form

Metropolitan Football Stadium

www.mfsd.com
Denver, Colorado is where this new stadium is being built. You can use the outdoor web cam to capture stadium construction images live from the roof of Denver's Downtown Red Lion Inn. There is a photo gallery to view work in progress.
e-mail: jbroz@mfsd.com

Michigan Stadium

www.mgoblue.com/campusinfo/
michigan-stadium.html
Michigan Stadium, has seating for 107,501. The site takes you through links to ticket sales, merchandise and multimedia fun and games. Traffic and parking information and a seating plan complete the site.
e-mail: via online form

Nagoya Dome

nagoyadome.freeservers.com/
main.html
An American fan of Nagoya explains the Japanese baseball league with great enthusiasm on his web site.
e-mail: not available

New Comiskey Park

www.ballparks.com/baseball/
american/comis2.htm
The home of the Chicago White Sox has a capacity of 44,321 and cost $167 million to build in the 1990's. It is one of the most high-tech stadiums in the game if not the world and it's not in Texas.
e-mail: via online form

Neyland Stadium

www.utsports.com
The Tennessee football and baseball arena, known as Shields-Watkins field, has a capacity of 102,854. It is the largest football stadium in the South and second-largest college stadium in the country.
e-mail: not available

Olympic City

www.smh.com.au/2000/city/
stadiums/multi.html
Built for the 2000 Olympic Games the Millenium Park in Sydney, Australia has several arenas and stadiums. You can view the site as a whole and then use the links to other pages of interest, news, classifieds, Sydney city and a great deal more. The latest news from the Olympics has its place on this simple but colourful layout.
e-mail: via online form

Olympique de Marseille

www.babasse.com/marseille/
This stadium, built originally in 1938, started a rebuilding program in 1996. There are online links to European Cup information, fixtures and general news.
e-mail: not available

Osaka Dome

www.takenaka.co.jp/takenaka_e/
dome_e/map/osaka/osaka.html
This facility can hold up to 48,000 spectators for baseball games.
e-mail: not available

Pacific Bell Park

www.sfgiants.com/park/sfg_park-main.html

Home to the San Francisco Giants and one of the most intimate parks in baseball, but fans still don't get to see every nook and cranny of the new yard. Many areas are accessible only to the team and few outsiders ever got a peek, until now, when you get to see practically everything online, even the locker rooms. You can buy tickets online.
e-mail: via online form

Paris Saint Germain

www.psg.fr/en/stadium/0,2919,,00.html

Take a 360-degree virtual tour of the Parc des Princes stadium. Use the search facility to find things fast, get news about the matches, visit the supporters' club and online store where you can buy tickets.
e-mail: not available

Parker Sports Arena

parkersportsarena.com

An indoor sports arena for soccer and hockey in the USA with a 12,000 sq ft competition area. High ceilings make it suitable for air games.
e-mail: belthol2@aol.com

Phillips Stadium

www.psv.nl

Ten minutes from Eindhoven Airport, within walking distance of public transport and excellent parking facilities makes this a pretty extraordinary sports arena. The Stadium is home to PSV and the web site shows all the routes to get there. There's a picture of this impressive stadium to click and enlarge.
e-mail: not available

Pro Player Stadium

www.pro-player-stadium.com

Home to the Miami Dolphins and Florida Marlins. The lively blurb on the site previews events leading to another terrific season. This is a very high profile stadium with state of the art, multiple sport, open-air facilities and an outstanding history of hosting spectacular events.
e-mail: not available

Qualcomm Stadium

stadianet.vml.com/home.php3?stadium=qualcomm

One of America's finest multi-purpose facilities, Qualcomm Stadium opened in August 1967. Built to accommodate a wide variety of events, from baseball and football to concerts and off-road programs, the Stadium has become the centre of the San Diego sports scene.
e-mail: qualcomm@stadianet.com

RFK Memorial Stadium

www.dcunited.com

Fast-paced, action-packed soccer kicks off its fifth season at RFK Stadium. Join the excitement as D C United, the '96, '97 and '99 MLS Cup Champions, work towards their goal of winning their fourth MLS Cup title in 2000. Tickets are on sale online. You can view the stadium on the map and enter the fanzone, contests and promotions.
e-mail: mailto:info@dcunited.com

SAFECO Field

www.mariners.org/newpark/

The arena at Safeco Field was designed with fan comfort and convenience as top considerations. There's an online clubhouse, kid's room, multimedia features, views of the field as

spectators see it and of course ticket information.
e-mail: mariners@digital-sherpas.com

Saltlake Stadium

www.westbengal.nic.in/sports.html
e-mail: not available

Shanghai Stadium

www.wai.com/Structures/Fabric/ shanghai.html
e-mail: not available

Stade de France

www.stadefrance.com/ang/
An exceptional site that tells you how to get to the stadium, buy tickets, join an organised tour, check out the calendar of events and go shopping online. It's all there, it's French and it speaks English.
e-mail: via online form

Stadianet

stadianet.vml.com
Major world stadiums brought together onto one site. Become a member and you get access to a pros only page.
e-mail: not available

Texas Stadium

www.dallascowboys.com
Home of the Dallas Cowboys, where you can peek at the Cheerleaders page, view the seating plan, enter the fan club and learn the history of the stadium. Get the phone numbers for ticket purchasing and while you're at it, take advantage of special deals on offer.
e-mail: not available

Three Rivers Stadium

www.3riversstadium.com
The stadium is home to two of professional sports' most enduring franchises, the Pittsburgh Pirates and Steelers. Three Rivers also plays host to large festivals and world-class concerts by internationally acclaimed performers. Check out the special attractions lined up for the coming season.
e-mail: not available

Tokyo Ski Dome

www.ssaws.com
Nearly all in Japanese, there are some links in English on this interesting looking site. You can take a look through a live camera, check the site map and read the news.
e-mail: not available

Tropicana Field

www.stpete.org/dome.htm
Home to the Tampa Bay Devil Rays, the stadium is the centre of attention in St. Petersburg, FA. Having undergone major renovation, fan seating capacity has been increased to 45,200. The site has excellent links to other information about the Florida region.
e-mail: not available

Twickenham

www.rfu.com
A simple page of basic information about the home of English rugby. There's a site map and info about hosting corporate events.
e-mail: not available

USA Stadium

www.usabaseballstadium.org
Once known as Millington's Legion Field, this stadium has established itself as a unique sports facility in the USA. Twelve National Championships are decided at the stadium including Junior College, American Legion and AAU events.
e-mail: daigle@bigriver.net

Wembley Stadium

www.wembleynationalstadium.co.uk
Probably the most widely recognised stadium in the world. It has played host to some truly momentous events in sporting history. Pages are devoted to its history, events, news, facilities and how to book seats. A picture library and architectural plans show the proposed new stadium that will one day stand in its place. Sad to see it go.
e-mail: viv.taylor@wnsl.co.uk

World Stadiums by Munsey and Suppes

www.worldstadiums.com
A truly useful site with a huge database of stadiums world wide, lots of information and a bunch of links. There are pictures, statistics and a search engine.
e-mail: via online form

Wrigley Field

www.cubs.com/wrigley/history.htm
Claiming to be the most beautiful park in baseball, Wrigley Field is playing host in 2000 to major league baseball for the 87th season. Built in 1914, The Friendly Confines is the second-oldest ballpark in major leagues behind Boston's Fenway Park (1912). It prides itself on its excellent services for fans with disabilities.
e-mail: comments@mail.cubs.com

Yankee Stadium

www.yankees.com
Babe Ruth built the stadium in 1923 and it's now probably one the most famous in the world. You get an overview of the history of the stadium, access to the Fanzone, sports schedules and you can visit the Clubhouse online.
e-mail: dbernstein@yankees.com

Yokohama Stadium

city.yokohama.jp/me/isy/indexE.html
Opened in 1998, this arena is a magnificent setting for soccer, track and field, rugby and other sport and large-scale concerts. It's already the home field of both Yokohama teams in Japan's professional football league, the Marinos and the Flugels.
e-mail: not available

Tennis

1st Serve

www.1stserve.com

A good collection of photos of pro tennis stars, with tips and suggestions on how to increase your leg strength. Articles on the facts and fictions about strings and other subjects in the E-zine, plus statistical analyses of match records between great players fill most of the site pages. You can sign up to play 1st Serve Fantasy Tennis.
e-mail: nicevolley@aol.com

Asian Tennis Federation

www.asiantennis.com

Official site of the Hong Kong based Asian Tennis Federation. The ATF has 41 member associations, from Afghanistan to the Yemen, promoting tennis in their respective countries. You'll find complete and up-to-date coverage of the game in Asia and Asian players. A special feature is the Wheelchair Tennis Tour.
e-mail: atf.hkoffice@asiantennis.com

Australian Tennis Magazine

www.tennismag.com.au

The online companion to the Australian Tennis Magazine, much of the content of the printed version is reproduced on this site. It has a tennis calendar, subscription details and a list of Fan Club addresses for famous tennis stars.
e-mail: not available

Cross Court Tennis

www.crosscourt.com.au

Tennis news site with world wide and Grand Slam tournament news, an archive of news stories, a message board and forum to post news and views. There is an occasional interview with a top star.
e-mail: tennis@crosscourt.com.au

Go Tennis

www.gotennis.com

Extensive tennis coverage of both professional and amateur games. Tournament previews, match results,

schedules, scores and everything else builds into a first rate web site. Daily audio tennis news comes in RealPlayer or Windows Media Player format. Have fun playing tennis games online if you have Flash.
e-mail: not available

International Tennis Federation

www.itftennis.com
This is the official site of the governing body for the sport world wide. You get an overview of cups and competitions, including the Grand Slam and the Olympics, wheelchair and veteran tennis. Other sections include the Federation history and how it operates, rules and regulations of the sport, with facts and figures about the game at all levels.
e-mail: itf@itftennis.com

International Tennis Hall of Fame

www.tennisfame.org
Web site of the International Tennis Hall of Fame and Museum in the Newport Casino. There are details about the museum, its contents, who and what you are likely to see, opening hours and ticket information. You also get a bit about the Miller Lite Hall of Fame Tennis Championships, a tournament held in Newport.
e-mail: via online form

John Newcombe Tennis Center

www.newktennis.com
Head over to John Newcombe's Texas Tennis Ranch for information on courses and clinics to improve your game. Professionals provide training to juniors aged 8 to 18. The adults programme lasts a week and includes accommodation, meals and entertainment. Signing up form, training details and schedules are online.
e-mail: marketing@newktennis.com

Lawn Tennis Association

www.lta.org.uk/lta.htm
The governing body of UK tennis. This is its official web site and where you get all the latest on UK tournaments. The Coaching Zone explains how to go about becoming a tennis coach and provides a list of resources. Player profiles and photos are just as they should be and there are details of how to join the LTA and subscribe to Ace tennis magazine, all very worthwhile.
e-mail: not available

New Zealand Tennis

www.tennis.org.nz
The official New Zealand tennis web site talks about players and events in the country. Results and news cover senior, junior and schools levels. Player ranking and national team news are featured with up-to-date reports of significant matches.
e-mail: info@tennis.org.nz

Scott's Tennis Information Site

www.ascusc.org/judson321/scott/
Scott is a keen tennis fan who's put together a site to cover tennis news in general and recent developments in men's and women's professional tennis in the major tours. Talk all you want in the chat room, or contact the author with the online form.
e-mail: sparsons@usc.edu

Slam

www.canoe.ca/SlamTennis/
All the Tennis news stories and a day-by-day guide to major tournaments as they happen. Coverage includes schedules, seeds, draws, player profiles and a history of the event. Both ATP and WTA tours are covered. There are photo galleries of players including Anna Kournikova and Patrick Rafter. You can discuss the tennis news of the day in the interactive Sports Talk section.
e-mail: not available

sportonwheels.com

www.sportonwheels.com/home/
Leading independent multinational provider of wheelchair tennis and the Internet's only site dedicated exclusively to this sport. The site gives up-to-date results and news from tournaments around the globe with world ranking, a tournament calendar and match results, a photo gallery of matches in play and a Find a Player service.
e-mail: info@sportonwheels.com

Successful Doubles

successfuldoubles.com
The United States Professional Registry named Pete Collins as the 1994 Professional of the Year and he travels the USA teaching doubles tactics and strategies. Pick up tips and develop winning strategies online for successful doubles play. The program of the clinic run by Pete is given in detail.
e-mail: PeteColl@aol.com

Tennis Canada

www.tenniscanada.com
Official site of the Canadian Tennis Association with text in English and French. You get good coverage of Canadian tennis players, their ranking and the very latest news. Sign up to the Tennis Across Canada newsletter or read it online.
e-mail: commnctn@tenniscanada.com

Tennis Classic Forum Frigate

jollyroger.snap.com/zz/youtdoord/Tennishall/shakespeare1.html
Air your views on the subject of tennis whether you are an expert or not. There is a discussion forum and you can arrange times for live chat sessions with other enthusiasts.
e-mail: becket@jollyroger.com

Tennis.Com

www.tennis.com
Tennis news and features for professional, college, and junior level players. There are well-written weekly tips to improve your game and 101 other tips from seasoned professionals. A gear guide helps you choose the right equipment and fitness workouts should improve your form. You can post messages on the bulletin board and purchase tennis equipment in the online store.
e-mail: not available

Tennis for Africa

web.tiscalinet.it/tennisforafrica/
Non-profit organisation founded to assist the poorest populations of Africa. On their site you'll find details of their set up and the work they do. You can take part in charity auctions of tennis items donated by top stars and special tennis fundraising events such as the Shoot Out for Africa Tournaments.
e-mail: tafrica@tiscalinet.it

Tennis India

www.its.uci.edu/~jaykay/tenn-results/
index.html
R. Jayakrishnan has written and
dedicated this site to Indian tennis,
with news on the Indian tennis scene
posted daily, including schedules,
match results, comments and AITA
ranking. A few Indian players have
linked their home sites and there is a
chat facility.
e-mail: jaykay@translab.its.uci.edu

Tennis London

www.tennislondon.co.uk
Here's a way to avoid having to stay
in a hotel when in London for the
Wimbledon Championships. Rent a
flat or house in Wimbledon Village
and be fifteen minutes walk from the
courts. They are the only agents
recommended by the All England Lawn
Tennis Club. Prices, contact details
and a simple map of the area are
online.
e-mail: info@tennislondon.co.uk

Tennis Photo Archive

www.nando.net/newsroom/sports/oth/
1995/oth/ten/arts/pix.html
If every picture is worth a thousand words,
then this site must be worth an awful
lot of them. Check out the enormous
gallery of thumbnail photographs of
tennis players showing their skills.
e-mail: not available

TennisStation

www.tennisstation.com
As a resource for tennis fans, this site
takes some beating. It's probably the
most comprehensive on the Internet.
Tennis news on state and national level
comes daily with a searchable match
schedule database, audio updates,
results and player ranking. Junior and
college level tennis are given as much
coverage as is the pro game. Any news
or comments you have can be posted
on the discussion board or alternatively
feel free to write an article or player
profile; submit it using the online form
and they may publish it. This is a great
site and should not be missed.
e-mail: via online form

TennisWeek.com

tennisweek.rivals.com
First class tennis news site with daily
updates from around the world of tennis.
ATP and WTA tour info and schedules,
ranking and results. A message board
keeps you in touch with other fans and
tennis video clips can be found in
RealPlayer or Windows Media Player
format.
e-mail: info@rivals.com

The Tennis Server

www.tennisserver.com
The ever popular and longstanding -
online since 1994 - Tennis Server has
lots of news articles and stories worth
reading. Books and videos are previewed
and linked to Amazon.com for purchase.
Tennis clubs and organisations are listed
and the photo gallery is impressive.
e-mail: info@tennisserver.com

Tudor Tennis Court

www.calpoly.edu/~dlord/tennis.html
The game of Real Tennis is overshadowed
by its more popular cousin. This
indoor sport is now played at less than
thirty venues world wide. This page
looks at the rules of the game and its

history and has a fine photo of the main court in London's Hampton Court Palace.

e-mail: dlord@oboe.calpoly.edu

US Tennis Association

216.199.22.140/default.html

The official Internet home of the governing body of US tennis. Information covers every aspect of tennis nation wide and at all levels of the sport. Player ranking, news and all tournaments are featured. You can join the association online.

e-mail: not available

Wimbledon Information

www.geocities.com/Colosseum/ Stadium/8812/

Fan page for those who want to attend the Wimbledon Tennis Championships, with particularly useful tips on how to get tickets. The Art of Queuing is explained and directions to get to the venue via public transport are clearly set out, so you shouldn't get lost.

e-mail: j.brazier@wmin.ac.uk

World Tennis Center

www.worldtenniscenter.com

This is a resort in Florida with the focus on tennis, what else? Clay courts and hard courts, some of which are lit for night play, are available to paying guests. This site showcases all the facilities and what they cost. You can make reservations online.

e-mail: resort@worldtenniscenter.com

Worldwide Senior Tennis Circuit

www.seniortenniscircuit.com

Some of the players who made the legends and put the swing into tennis

continue to compete on the Senior Circuit. On court greats like Jimmy Conners and John McEnroe still entertain and thrill the crowds on this tour reserved for players no longer active on the ATP tour. With tournament and match results so ably reported on this site, you'll never miss out on the old masters.

e-mail: via online form

Youth Tennis Advantage

www.youthtennis.org

Non profit organisation that came about as a result of a merger between the Youth Tennis Foundation and Arthur Ashe's NJTL. Their programs, which target children from inner cites, combine tennis instruction, academic tutoring and mentoring. The aim is to help disadvantaged young people build character, self-esteem and community values. There is a lot to read about YTA, its history, youth programs and events and how you can support it.

e-mail: legacy@youthtennis.org

The Players

A dedication to Olga Barabanschikova

www.barabanschikova.com

A fan site dedicated to the rising star of Belorussian tennis, Olga Barabanschikova. Profile, personal details, up-to-date results and news take up several pages. A notable feature is the extensive photo gallery with over 300 pictures of Olga in action. The site has a guest-book posted by Olga, mailing list, discussion club and downloadable Windows wallpaper.

e-mail: jonathan@barabanschikova.com

Amanda Coetzer's LapDogs

www.angelfire.com/la/coetzer
Web site produced by a dedicated fan of the South African tennis player. Informal in style, it features a biography of the player and photo galleries of Amanda at press conferences and on and off the court. Bits and Pieces has snippets of information you won't find elsewhere.
e-mail: floggedlog@hotmail.com

Andrei Medvedev Fan Page

www.chez.com/benj/medvedev.html
The first fan page for Kiev born Andrei Medvedev has a collection of exclusive match reports and articles written by fans of the Ukrainian player. Over 100 photos, some of them exclusive, grace the site. The multimedia section contains audio and video clips requiring QuickTime and RealPlayer.
e-mail: ben_g@club-internet.fr

Anna Kournikova Site

kournikovasite.org
With text in English and Spanish, this site spotlights tennis sensation Anna Kournikova. News, match information and a detailed fact file accompany hundreds of photographs and video clips. Season results, free downloads of wallpaper, software skins and screensavers come online. You can use the message board and chat facility and sign the guest book. Full access to some sections requires membership, which is free.
e-mail: kournikovasite@egroups.com

AthletesDirect

www.athletesdirect.com
Scrapbook for fans of Martina Hingis, Anna Kournikova, Todd Martin, Jana Novotna and Mark Philippoussis. Their biographies and career records mix with personal snippets, anecdotes and the like. Some pages have feedback from the players themselves. An extensive collection of photos, video and audio clips, in addition to ShockWave Flash introductions make up an impressive site. Good place to start if you want to bone up on these players.
e-mail: not available

Azter 2000

www.azter.com
Profiles, biographical information, photo galleries, tournament news and career records of several top players. Anna Kournikova, Martina Hingis, Steffi Graf, Monica Seles, Mary Pierce, Andre Agassi, Marat Safin, and Yevgeny Kafelnikov are all included. Some RealVideo clips can be downloaded.
e-mail: mailto:webmaster@azter.com

Boris Becker

perso.club-internet.fr/olivepri/ En_Anglais.html
Fan site dedicated to the retired German tennis legend Boris Becker. Statistics include full career results, year-by-year from 1985 to 1999. Check the latest news section to see what Boris is up to now and the page of quotes from the man himself. His career highlights, photographs and press cuttings take up the remaining pages.
e-mail: borisbecker@post.club-internet.fr

Earth makes contact with Venus

www.geocities.com/emcwv/
A fan site for the American player Venus Williams dubbed the Ghetto Cinderella by her father. A photo gallery of Venus in action on court, details and pictures of head to head encounters with other top ladies professionals, a profile, latest news and results and a weekly quote from Venus make up the site.
e-mail: sterlingone@hotmail.com

Everything about Mary Pierce

marypierce.org/index.html
Dedicated to the millennium French Open Champion and French based Mary Pierce. There really is everything about Mary – the latest news, articles, match results and head to head records. There are Netcam photos and a Real Video interview. Some of the multimedia interviews on the list are onsite while others are linked elsewhere on the web. A biography and photo gallery complete the site.
e-mail: byilmaz@ug.bcc.bilkent.edu.tr

Future Stars Of Professional Tennis

www.geocities.com/Colosseum/Field/ 5819/
Attempting to look ahead and profile the tennis stars of tomorrow this site focuses on younger players who have won at least one professional title or had major success in junior matches. The fan site has assembled profiles, match results and photos of Martina Hingis, Anna Kournikova, Meilen Tu, Lindsay Lee, Olga Barabanschikova, Anne Miller, Corina Morariu, Amelie Mauresmo, Mirjana Lucic and Marlene Weingartner, Marcelo Rios, Mark Philippoussis, Tommy Haas, Justin Gimelstob and Daniel Elsner.
e-mail: tennis_fan@geocities.com

Gabriela Sabatini

www.geocities.com/Colosseum/7208/
Rula's fan site for the Argentine player Gabriela Sabatini. Come here for a biography, news, career details, ranking, titles won, Grand Slam and head to head records. The site also has a photo gallery with pictures from different stages in her career.
e-mail: w.y.azar@go.com.jo

Goran Ivanisevic

www.goranivanisevic.com
Judging by the counter, Goran's web site is very popular. It's packed with material about his life on and off the court, including an archive of press articles and highlights of his career. There's an excellent FAQ on tennis for any wannabe Ivanisevic. You can get his autographed picture and read his poetry or contribute to Goran's Children in Need Foundation through the site. There is a mailbox for your messages.
e-mail: via online form

Greg Rusedski

www.rusedski.co.uk
Fan site of Canadian born and
UK-based men's tennis player Greg
Rusedski features regularly updated
news archived back to January 1998.
Results include opponents and scores.
There's a thumbnail photo gallery,
tournament schedule of where Greg
is next expected to appear and a
message board.
e-mail: robin@british-tennis.
freeserve.co.uk

Gustavo Guga Kuerton

www.gugakuerten.com.br
The official web site of Gustavo Guga
Kuerton comes in English and
Portuguese, divided into two distinct
parts. One looks at his life, family and
personal matters, the other focuses on
his successful career as a tennis
professional. This includes news,
match results, ranking, archives and
playing schedule. Each section has its
own photo gallery. A forum lets you
talk to Guga himself.
e-mail: not available

Jana Novotna Online

www.crosswinds.net/~jnonline
Stylish and well-designed fan site for
former Wimbledon ladies champion
Jana Novotna with a full career history,
results page for doubles and singles,
links to an impressive collection of
transcribed interviews, some of which
are audible. There are pictures, career
highlights and details of head to head
encounters with other top professionals.
e-mail: novotna_fan@hotmail.com

Jennifer Capriati WebSite

capriati.com/contents.html
Dedicated to Florida-based ladies tennis
star Jennifer Capriati. The author has
written lengthy tournament reviews,
recorded her career with highlights,
ranking and up-to-date news. An
extensive photo gallery and fan club
contact details are available.
e-mail: mark.newman@bigfoot.com

La Casa De Arantxa

www.geocities.com/Colosseum/
Bleachers/7462/ArantxaMainPage.html
There is a real attempt to build a
community around Arantxa Sánchez-
Vicario by including a personal profile
and a facility to leave messages to be
passed to her before important games.
The home page keeps match schedules
and results up to date. An on-and-off
court photo gallery and biography will
satisfy most fans.
e-mail: caz@Casa_Arantxa.zzn.com

Lindsay Davenport

lindsaydavenport.virtualave.net
Dedicated to the former U.S. Open
and Wimbledon champion Lindsay
Davenport, the site has biographical
statistics, quick facts, personal details
and links to articles about her. Also
includes the 2000 Sanex WTA tour
schedule, photo gallery and a
message board.
e-mail: eertek@hotmail.com

MaliVai Washington

www.maltennis.com
An impressive site for 1996 Wimbledon
finalist MaliVai Washington. Media
reports on significant career events
have been transcribed on the site and

the player tells you about himself. The MaliVai Washington Kids Foundation gets a prominent place on the site with a section especially for children.
e-mail: aces@maltennis.com

Marc Goellner

www.marc-goellner.de
Official and regularly updated web site of Marc-Kevin Goellner welcomes you to an overview of his life in tennis. You can follow his career year by year with an illustrated biography, or keep up with Marc's progress on the Tournament schedule and results page. There are more pictures in the photo gallery. Leave a message for Marc in the guest book or join the mailing list.
e-mail: not available

Marc Rosset

www.marcrosset.com
The official Marc Rosset web site with lots about Switzerland's most successful tennis player, his match schedules, profile, photos and ranking history. You can contact Marc via an online form. The Olympic gold medallist has also launched the Marc Rosset Kids Foundation
e-mail: via online form

Marcelo Ríos - Web Site

www.marcelorios.cl
Official web site of Chilean born tennis pro Marcelo Ríos, loaded with biographical data, doubles and singles tournament summary, photos and drawings of Marcelo on court, latest news, ranking, match scores and an e-mail address to reach him.
e-mail: mrios@cmet.net

Martina's Home Page

ea.globalweb.it/martina/
Modern day tennis legend Martina Navratilova has her fan site. An illustrated biography of the player lists her record-breaking achievements with links to many interviews and press conference transcripts. The multimedia page has MPEG videos featuring key points in her career. Books about Martina and a photo gallery are featured.
e-mail: lisa@snipp.org

Michael Chang

www.mchang.com
Michael's biography takes you to the latest news about him and he even gives you a few tennis tips. There's a message board and you can e-mail him. Pictures in the gallery include one of the 2olb salmon he caught while out fishing.
e-mail: via online form

Monica Seles

www.monica-seles.com
With text in English and French, this site is all about Monica. News, a detailed biography, tournament schedule, gossip and rumours find their place on the site. You can download Windows wallpaper for your desktop featuring Monica and several other women players.
e-mail: not available

Natasha Zvereva Online

www.geocities.com/Colosseum/Court/ 3137/
Russian born Natasha Zvereva has a web site with her biography, match results, tournament news, an extensive photo gallery, interview transcripts and articles. Fans can interact by using the

message board, chat facility or the Yahoo club page.
e-mail: lindsey_ce@hotmail.com

Nicolas Kiefer

nicolaskiefer.tripod.com
News, match information and reviews, interview scripts and much more about Nicolas Kiefer. The site has a visual collection of Nicolas playing tennis with Netcam captures and a gallery with even more pictures and animated images of the tennis star. You can visit the guest book and e-mail Kiefer himself.
e-mail: not available

OnCourt

www.oncourt.com
Australian tennis player Patrick Rafter's web site has biographical information, statistics and career details. After visiting the photo gallery and reading the interview, you can leave messages that he promises to read, and buy his merchandise online. Some sections require membership.
e-mail: info@oncourt.com

Pete Sampras

petesampras.webjump.com
Two female fans of Pete Sampras have put together this fan site to tell the world that he's really not boring. News, a biography, match details and results accompany an archive of articles about Pete stretching back to the early eighties with quotes from the man himself. Of particular interest is the No Disrespect Intended section where you have irreverent thoughts, sly observations and gossip.
e-mail: champforages@yahoo.com

Richard Krajicek Fan Page

surf.to/krajicek
Grant's unofficial fan site for Richard Krajicek. Match results, a photo gallery of Richard on and off court and with his family, titles won by the former Wimbledon Singles Champion and biographical information make up the site of the Dutch star.
e-mail: oranjeman@bigfoot.com

Sabine Appelmans

www.esm.be
The left-handed Belgian ladies star Sabine Appelmans has up-to-date match results and tournament progress on her fan page. There are dozens of photographs, a breakdown of her prize money and some insights into the lady herself.
e-mail: kris@xylios.com

The Andre Agassi Web Site

www.andresite.com
High quality official web site for Andre Agassi. Lots of video clips of Andre in action and several interviews can be checked out online if you have QuickTime. There are up-to-date reports on his progress in tournaments and a look back at his recent and past record. A page of links to related books that can be purchased online via Amazon is another feature.
e-mail: not available

The Martina Interview Centre

www.hingis.co.uk
Unofficial fansite dedicated to top ladies professional Martina Hingis, with RealPlayer or Windows Media Player downloads of interviews. Some sections are unfinished but the bit on

the 1997 US Open is good and more is promised.
e-mail: jason@mhingis.com

The Ultimate Tribute To Stefan Edberg

www.geocities.com/Colosseum/Loge/8365/
Fan site dedicated to the former champion, with details of all the titles he has won in both singles and doubles matches. There's a biography with career highlights and photographs.
e-mail: e-mail: jhjehu@geocities.com

The Unofficial Álex Corretja Fan Page

www.geocities.com/Colosseum/Bleachers/8686/alex_home.html
Barcelona born tennis player, Álex Corretja has a bilingual web site with some very sharp photographs of himself both on and off the court. The biography covers his life and career, with quotes and news articles. You can contact Álex online and he promises to reply.
e-mail: pl8ennis@geocities.com

Thomas Enqvist

www.multimania.com/enqvist/uk/index.htm
Fan site with their hero's career, biography and some interviews. There are 80 pictures in the photo album including some from his youth, free to download. You can leave a message in the guest book or join the tennis discussion in the Enqvist Forum. Text is in English and French.
e-mail: enqvist@mygale.org

Tim Henman World

www.henmagic.freeserve.co.uk
Regularly updated fan site to Britain's current top player Tim Henman, with match results, news and schedules. Photos of Tim can be previewed online and prints purchased by printing the order form. A message board, shared with other players, is available for fan feedback and discussion.
e-mail: sara@henmagic.freeserve.co.uk

Wayne Ferreira

www.wayneferreira.com
South African born tennis player Wayne Ferreira's site. You can catch up on the latest news about his progress in current tournaments with results for the past two years archived online. A profile of the player includes some of his favourite players and personal details. A photo gallery will be added soon.
e-mail: not available

You cannot be serious! – John McEnroe

www.erols.co.uk/McEnroe.htm
The legendary player and bad boy of tennis, John McEnroe has his story told online. His career, with highlights and personal information accompany a gallery of photos of the great man. However the most intriguing excerpts are to be found in the section entitled Sounds. Listen to the often repeated – 'You cannot be serious!' and 'Can't you see anything, that cost me the damn set!' and many more. You'll need Windows Media Player or QuickTime to enjoy these little gems.
e-mail: erol@erols.co.uk

The Tournaments

2000 DuPont World Team Tennis

www.worldteamtennis.com
Billie Jean King founded the DuPont
World TeamTennis professional and
amateur co-ed tennis league. This is
its official Internet home. Membership
application forms and tournament
information come online.
e-mail: abrendel@imgworld.com

ATP Tour Rankings and Results Page

stevegtennis.com
Now here's a site for the train-spotter
tennis fan. Painstakingly detailed and
all embracing, this site lists ATP world
ranking, prize money and more
information of that sort, not just
current but week by week for singles
and doubles players. Archives go back
to 1997. You can download International
Tennis Weekly in PDF format. Clearly a
labour of love, the site reflects the hard
work that went into it.
e-mail: SD-Gocha@neiu.edu

Australian Open 2000

www.ausopen.org
If your browser is Java-enabled you'll
get a panoramic view of the Australian
Open venue. In addition to match
reports and feature articles, there are
some multimedia elements. Webcams
are online during the tournament and a
WinAmp skin can be downloaded.
e-mail: not available

Bausch & Lomb Championships

www.blchamps.com
This is where you go for coverage of
the annual Championships in Florida.
Order of play, match results and ticket
information are set out and you can
purchase tickets online. Player profiles
are featured and video clips of past
finals match points can be viewed with
RealPlayer.
e-mail: not available

College And Junior Tennis

www.collegeandjuniortennis.com
This site serves up some of the minor
tournaments, mainly college and junior
level competitions that don't otherwise
get widespread coverage. Results,
news, seeding, paths to the final and
photographs of winners. You can sign
up for the newsletter and get a personal
e-mail account.
e-mail: ClgAndJr@AOL.com

Copa Del Cafe

**members.aol.com/coffeebowl/COPACA
FE.html**
Costa Rican tournament for juniors.
The site gives a brief history of the
tournament, information on the
competition committee and full details
of the draws for girls and boys. Text is
in English and Spanish.
e-mail: coffeebowl@aol.com

Croatia Open Umag 2000

www.croatiaopen.hr
Home site on the Internet of the first
ATP Tour Tournament in Eastern and
Middle Europe. There is much general
news about the tournament and its
history, a photo gallery and information
on how to get tickets.
e-mail: Croatiaopen@croatiaopen.hr

Davis Cup

www.daviscup.org
The Davis Cup competition pits players

in national squads. There's a lot to read and learn on the site. Fixtures and match results are set out and players make their comments online. You'll find a brief history of the tournament and other articles to keep you interested.
e-mail: not available

Dubai Tennis Open

www.dubaitennisopen.com
The Dubai Tennis Open is an ATP Tour International Series tournament with a 32-player draw held in February each year. The site gives you a tournament history, match results and schedule of forthcoming events and fixtures.
e-mail: via online form

Dutch Open

www.m4.nl/grolsch-open
ATP tournament contested annually in Amsterdam. If you intend to be at the competition check out the ticket and travel information and directions on how to get there. Former winners and prize money are listed and the tournament is presented online during the competition.
e-mail: marcus@m4.nl

Ericsson Open 2000

www.ericsson-open.com
The competition takes place in March each year. This is a comprehensive site with information about the tournament, how to get your tickets and a grand collection of player biographies, photos and interviews.
e-mail: not available

Family Circle Cup

www.familycirclecup.com
Every year the Women's Tennis Association of the USA holds the Family Circle Cup tournament sponsored by Family Circle Magazine. The site tells you about the competition, gives a brief history, advises on how to buy your tickets and get there, where to stay and of course covers the event itself.
e-mail: familycup@aol.com

Hyundai Hopman Cup 2000

www.hopmancup.com.au
Named after the legendary Australian Davis Cup player, the Hopman Cup is a mixed event contested in Perth, Western Australia each year between the eight best national teams in the world. The web site relates the history of the competition from its origins, while Martina Hingis and Andrei Medvedev, among others, share their memories of the tournament. A photo gallery of the current year's play tells you who was there. To keep in touch, get onto the mailing list.
e-mail: via online form

Kroger St. Jude Tournament

krogerstjude.com
ATP Tennis Tournament held in Memphis annually. The competition is part of the charity and fundraiser program for St. Jude Children's Research Hospital to support their work combating cancer. The site contains tournament coverage, match schedules and results. Tickets can be bought online.
e-mail: via online form

Mercedes Benz Cup

www.mercedes-benzcup.com
Held annually since 1927, the Mercedes-Benz Cup is a World Series event on the ATP Tour. The site tells

you all about the tournament, gives the daily schedule, ticket information and travel directions to the Los Angeles venue. Player profiles come as a bonus.
e-mail: not available

Open Gaz de France

www.gazdefrance.com/open/
Site in English and French for the Gaz de France Open played in Paris. You can leave messages for tournament players or ask them questions, play addictive interactive tennis games online, read player profiles or view live snapshots from behind the scenes. Those seeking coverage of the tournament or ticket information and maps are well catered for. The games require ShockWave.
e-mail: not available

Pilot Pen Tennis 2000

www.pilotpentennis.com
Women's tournament held in Connecticut, USA. The site talls all about the competition including the draw, tournament schedule, ticket and travel details, TV schedule and special events. There are news items and player photos.
e-mail: via online form

RCA Championships

www.rcatennis.com
The RCA Championships are held annually in Indianapolis. The site details the competition and its history, sells tickets online and exhibits photos of players and the venue. If you want to work behind the scenes at the championship complete the online volunteer form and send it off. A bulletin board will soon be available.
e-mail: not available

River Oaks International Tennis Tournament

webshark.com/riveroaks
Played in Houston since 1931, this site represents the tournament's presence on the Internet. There are daily match recaps, schedules and results, messages from the president and press releases. A selection of player interviews can be watched in RealVideo format.
e-mail: not available

Roland Garros – French Open

www.rolandgarros.org
Official home of the Roland Garros Grand Slam Tournament has text in English and French. If you cannot get there in person try the Virtual Tour around the venue to see what you are missing; you can catch up with events on the courts by reading the lively coverage here. There is an online store.
e-mail: not available

Sanex WTA Tour

www.sanexwta.com
Official home on the web of the women's professional circuit which has more than fifty tournaments and an annual championship. The site features player biographies, ranking, results, news and schedules. You can post messages on a wide variety of topics on the very popular Sanex Wta Tour Web Board or join the conversation in the chat room.
e-mail: via online form

Sybase Open

www.sybaseopen.com
Great site dedicated to the Sybase Open Tennis Tournament with so impressive a content it received up to

four million hits per day during the event. If you have a Java-enabled browser you can download the scoreboard to sit on your desktop giving up-to-the-minute scores and tournament news. A web cam link gives images of games in progress. Download wallpaper and screensavers for your PC or view RealVideo content of player press conferences, match highlights and more.
e-mail: via online form

Tennis Masters Series Cincinnati

www.cincytennis.com
Part of the ATP Tour and one of the top 13 world tennis events. This is the official site where you can download an illustrated guide to tournament history and regular newsletters in PDF format. Hotels are recommended, ticketing details and a map for those planning to attend.
e-mail: info@cincytennis.com

The ATP Tour

www.atptour.com
First rate official web site of the ATP Tour. They have all the up-to-date news stories, features, history, archives, photos, player profiles, ranking and a good deal more. You get live coverage of current tour matches on centre court and live chat. In the Playground section you can play 3-D Open, an interactive game of tennis or follow your favourite star in the VIP Lounge. Text is in English and German.
e-mail: via online form

US Open

www.usopen.org
The US Open Tennis Championship site tells you the history of the competition and how to buy your tickets. Former champions are listed with finals scores going back over 100 years.
e-mail: not available

Welcome to The Queen's Club

www.queensclub.co.uk
This London tennis club was founded in 1886. Queen's is the venue for the annual Stella Artois Grass Court Championships and is also the national headquarters of Real Tennis and Rackets. Dial the telephone number for ticket information.
e-mail: not available

Wimbledon

www.wimbledon.com
The official site of the best known tennis club in the world. The site comes to life during Wimbledon fortnight with extensive coverage of the championship matches. That is not to say the other fifty weeks of the year are not also busy with player portraits, photo galleries and the moving international tennis scene. The online store will be happy to sell you Wimbledon and tennis-related goods.
e-mail: not available

Tickets

All Events Tickets

www.alleventstickets.com
Tickets for events around the world.
The sports pages list events, team
schedules and ordering information.
You can order tickets using the online
form.
e-mail: mail@alleventstickets.com

All Sold Out

www.allsoldout.com
They claim to be the world's largest
online tickets, auctions and classifieds
site. The ticket pages offer baseball,
golf, boxing, wrestling and other sport.
Click first on the sport and event, then
check out the bid price and closing
time. When the deal is closed, payment
by credit card is accepted. Feel free to
buy or sell your tickets on the site.
e-mail: via online form

Aloud.com

www.aloud.com
One of the most frequently visited
online ticket sites in the UK. Aside
from tickets you'll find the latest
entertainment news, press releases,
top records and nation wide venue
guide. Tickets are in categories and
you can search by city, venue, date or
event. Transactions are secure and
major credit cards accepted.
e-mail: via online form

Bass Tickets

www.basstickets.net
A division of Tickets.com offering much
the same as its parent - baseball, football,
basketball, hockey, tennis across the USA
and additionally tickets for arts events and
concerts. Use the online form to order.
e-mail: via online form

F1 Ticketshop

www.f1ticketshop.com
The official Formula 1 ticket agency.
The home page is continuously updated
with ticket status reports and links to
pages for each race, with an order
form. Each circuit page has seating
layouts and information on general
facilities. Use the virtual shopping cart
to collect your purchases then click on
Order to seal the deal by secure credit
card connection.
e-mail: service@f1ticketshop.com

First Call Tickets

www.firstcalltickets.com
Online ticket service for entertainment,
sports and travel events, categorised to
simplify search. If you specify where,
when and what, the search engine
comes up with suggestions. Choose,
then enter your billing details and
tickets will be sent to you.
e-mail: queries@firstcallgroup.co.uk

Front Row USA

www.frontrowusa.com
US nationwide ticket brokers for
entertainment of all types including
major league sports, concerts and
theatres. Browse through the categories
or make a direct request. You cannot
purchase in real time, so complete a
request form and wait for their response.
e-mail: via online form

Grand Prix Tickets

www.grandprix-tickets.com
Formula 1 tickets and how to get them.
Before buying tickets for each race of
the season, check out the online
information and details of the track,
clearly shown with diagrams. To order

your tickets, fill in the form online and
submit it with credit card details over a
secure connection. The full F1 calendar
and an information request form are
also available.
e-mail: sales@grandprix-tickets.com

Keith Prowse & Company

www.keithprowse.com
They arrange the tickets, accommodation
and travel for events all over the world.
The British Grand Prix, American NFL,
NBA and NHL, the Royal Shakespeare
Company, New York's spectacular
Radio City Christmas show are just
some of what's on offer. Offers for US
sports events are only available to
residents outside North America.
e-mail: via online form

NBA

www.nba.com/ticket
As the official site of the National
Basketball Association, they offer tickets
and information for all their matches.
Clicking on the region and match will
get you schedules, ticket prices, arena
seating plans and location guidance.
e-mail: not available

Paddock Tickets

www.paddocktickets.com
Only top of the range tickets to
Formula 1 races. These tickets don't
just cover a seat to watch the races, but
include full corporate entertainment,
lunch with the drivers and access to
private areas of the track facilities.
Prices are in US$ with a choice of 1,2
or 3 day passes. Get yourself on the
mailing list by submitting your e-mail
address.
e-mail: tickets@paddocktickets.com

Peel World

www.peelworld.com/sports
You'll find a good directory of tickets sites offering sports events around the world on the pages of this multi-functional site. Use the search engine to speed up operations.
e-mail: via online form

Premier League Tickets Limited

www.premierleaguetickets.com
Tickets for major football, rugby, golf, tennis and cricket events in the UK. Although the site does not have real time online purchase you can order tickets at any time and wait for a quick reply with instructions of what to do next.
e-mail: MCavell@premierleague tickets.com

Premium Tickets

www.premiumtix.com
User-friendly site with tickets for baseball, football and hockey in the USA. Their pages keep you informed about sports events, schedules and seating plans and tell you how to order and pay online.
e-mail: tickets@premiumtix.com

Sistic

www.sistic.com.sg
Leisure, entertainment and sports tickets for events in Singapore. You can either browse through the categories or choose from the hottest events in the calendar listed on the front page. Each event has details, seats, prices and discounts. Make your selection and proceed to the checkout page to complete the billing form and finalise your purchase.
e-mail: feedback@sistic.com.sg

Sport Ticket.com

www.sportticket.com
Major source of sports tickets in the USA including boxing, wrestling, college sports, golf, auto racing and others. By clicking on the event you want, you get prices and buying contacts online.
e-mail: adinfo@sportticket.com

Sports Tickets

www.tixx.com/sports.html
Tickets for almost every sports event in the USA. You can order using the online form and pay by credit card. Bear in mind that the ticket has a market price that may exceed its face value so it's a good idea to state your limit before ordering.
e-mail: via online form

Sports Travel Net

www.sportstravelnet.com
This online sports travel magazine welcomes you to the world of sports travel and tickets. On the ticket page

you will find world-class sports events and packages that can be purchased online using their form. There are several good links to other sports organisations that are worth a visit.
e-mail: via online form

SportTickets.com

www.sportticks.com
International sports ticket concessionaire specialising in annual premier events and other matches. Their network gives them access to tickets in most markets at short notice even when games are listed as sold-out. They may be able to help with events not currently listed on their home page. You can order with the online form.
e-mail: webmaster@sportticks.com

The Ticket Service

www.theticketservice.com
Independent, privately owned company engaged in providing tickets for admission to any and all sports events, concerts and theatre performances world wide. They accept cash, bank wire transfers, cheques, money orders and all major credit cards.
e-mail: webmaster@theticketservice.com

TicketBroker

www.thetticket.co.uk
Tickets to all kinds of London entertainment. Search by browsing the sports and cultural categories or the hottest events in town. The site does not provide real time selling, so send an enquiry first. If you change your mind after purchase they undertake to buy back the tickets.
e-mail: sales@TicketBroker.co.uk

Ticketmaster

www.ticketmaster.co.uk
This is the UK web site of international ticket agents. You can book for events in the UK and other participating countries. Search by browsing through the arts, concerts, family, leisure and sports sections or specify what you want. Tickets are available online and delivered to your address.
e-mail: customer.services@ ticketmaster.co.uk

TicketPro.com

www.ticketpro.com
They offer to find and provide tickets to any sports event, concert and theatre performance world wide. They are not affiliated with any box office, venue, theatre, stadium, sports team or association. They have access to the secondary market for tickets through their own sources and contacts. Tickets may cost more than their face value so check prices before ordering.
e-mail: via online form

Tickets.com

www.tickets.com
Hot tickets for Grand Prix, soccer, tennis, basketball, golf, hockey and other sport in the USA. They also arrange tickets for travel and entertainment. Tickets can be bought online and for convenience open an account if you intend to use them regularly.
e-mail: via online form

TicketWeb

www.ticketweb.co.uk
Tickets to any form of entertainment in the UK and abroad in real time. You can browse through categories or

search by country, venue and date, or choose from the list of forthcoming top events. When you find what you want you are directed to a secure credit card form where you enter billing and address details for delivery.
e-mail: info@ticketweb.co.uk

Web Tix Tickets Classifieds

www.tixs.com
Internet marketplace for sports tickets in the USA all year round. The package includes all major US sports, horse racing, auto racing, wrestling and college sports events. There are links to other ticket sites.
e-mail: ticketads@tixs.com

WebTickets

www.webtickets.com
A friendly site with US ticket information, seating charts, schedules and numerous great links to help you enjoy your leisure time. The sports tickets pages give you a choice of professional sport - baseball, tennis, basketball, college sport and major events. You can order tickets online even when events are sold-out. They also sell tickets for the arts, music and other events.
e-mail: not available

www.apextours.com

www.apextours.com
Tickets for all major sports. To book, use the telephone, fax or e-mail. You'll also find information on seating charts, an event calendar and sales policy.
e-mail: sports@apextours.com

Travel

1st Sports Tours

www.1stsportstours.com
Group tours for sports around the world arranged from the USA. Basketball, baseball, ice hockey, field hockey, football, horse riding, rugby and soccer are a few of those on offer. Click where you like on the home page to see their fabulous tour packages world wide. To book, use the telephone, fax or e-mail.
e-mail: 1st@1stsportstours.com

Ace Travel House

www.acetravel.com
If you are new to them click the New User button and get yourself a password. Then you can access the sports travel packages and tickets on offer. Other offers take you to Nashville for music and Jacksonville.
e-mail: not available

Alpine World

www.alpineworld.com.au
As the largest snow holiday operator in Australia, the company specialises in organising ski tours for families, groups, singles, couples and friends world wide. Check out what's on at the resorts this season, with great specials for the best events. The super saver provides economic ski trips for beginners.
e-mail:
reservations@alpineworld.com.au

APT Trentino

www.provincia.tn.it/apt/UK
This well-designed site from Trentino in northern Italy has links to winter sports, a calendar of events, accommodation and more, with lots of good pictures. Though most of the text is in Italian, enough is in English to make it useful.
e-mail: apt@provincia.tn.it

Aquatic Adventure Tours

www.divetours.com
Aquatic tours to the best diving destinations, combined with underwater fun, golf, kayaking, tennis and other sports. They operate more or less around the world so check the destinations online. Instructors will assist you and accompany the tours on request.
e-mail: not available

Australian Splash Down

www.ozsplashdown.com
Action galore in Australia. The range of activity and experience reflects Australia's sports culture. Services can be as inclusive as you like. Simply complete the information form and consultants will customise a holiday in Australia or Fiji.
e-mail: not available

Australian Sports Tours

www.astsports.com.au
Sports travel throughout Australia and world wide for the best in soccer, tennis, cricket and others listed online. For package tour information, click on the specific sport and all is revealed. There is a good display of snapshots to tempt you on your way.
e-mail: info@astsports.com.au

Benchwarmer Sports

www.benchwarmersports.com
They offer you the world of sport and expert services in putting together packages for individuals and corporations for such events as the Super Bowl, Kentucky Derby, Daytona 500, US Open Tennis Championships and golf tournaments anywhere on the globe. All arrangements can be made online.
e-mail: inquiries@ benchwarmersports.com

Blaney's Travel

www.blaneystravel.com
They package holidays with sporting events world wide. They also offer lively tours to exotic places like Bali, Petra, the Taj Mahal and the pyramids and camping holidays in Asia, Africa and America. Check out the discount travel by e-mail.
e-mail: blaneys@BlaneysTravel.com

C & B Sports Tours

www.skicbsports.com
This Canadian specialist organises ski trips including day trips to some popular ski resorts in New Hampshire and Vermont. You can book your trip with the online form.
e-mail: ski@SKICBSPORTS.com

Carlson Wagonlit Travel

www.goldenworldtravel.com/tours
Sports tours and tickets for fans of Super Bowl XXXV for the 2000-2001 game and the Kentucky Derby. Everything is organised by a US expert so you should be in good hands. To book, use the web reservation form and take advantage of packages going at discount prices.
e-mail: info@goldenworldtravel.com

Club Senior Sports

www.clubseniorsports.com
If you are a senior citizen and enjoy sport, the club has groups of like-minded who combine sport with their holidays all over the Americas. Bike through a rain forest, hike on a basalt beach,

kayak with spinner dolphins or snorkel with fish.

e-mail: Clubnews3@aol.com

Creative Travel Group

www.creativetravelgroup.com
Travel agents specialising in sports travel. The pages list and update all major sports events. You'll find schedules and packages currently being offered. To book, contact them by phone, fax or e-mail.

e-mail: creativetravel@ibm.net

CSTT - Sports Management International

www.sport-travel.com
They promote, develop and administer National and International sports travel. The web pages give you details of lots of international and North American sports tour packages, travel tips and newsletters to bring you up to speed on the tournaments that matter. You can book online and pay by credit card.

e-mail: sports@sport-travel.com

Dash Tours

www.dashtours.com
Mainly Canadian sports events and ice skating competitions neatly wrapped in tour packages. To book, use the reservation form. There are links to travel agents.

e-mail: via online form

E-golftravel.com

e-golftravel.com
Golf-travel site with European bias. Several pages are filled with courses and hotel lists and some help with planning a golfing tour. Some standard tours make choosing easy and can be booked online. Otherwise, a consultant will liase with you to help organise your holiday.

e-mail: info@e-golftravel.com

EF Sports Tours

www.efsportstours.com
Extraordinary opportunity to travel the world, following the best international competitions in swimming, soccer, football, baseball and basketball. The teams and competitors are among the best in the world. Tours are designed to fit into pre- and post-season training and can be customised for both professional and amateur athletes. If you lead a team tour, your own travel may be free.

e-mail: via online form

Esoteric Sports Tours

www.esotericsportstours.com
Package tours to the Super Bowl, Kentucky Derby, NBA finals and baseball series for sport fans around the world. You can find package tour information and make reservations

online. They accept credit card bookings.
e-mail: beth@esotericsportstours.com

Eurosports France International
www.eurosports-fr.com/indexGB.html
French travel experts who organise
sports tours to training camps and
tournaments in France and Europe.
Click on the pictures to uncover the
packages. All arrangements can be
made online. Text is in English and
French.
e-mail: sportin@club-internet.fr

Eurosports Promotions
www.eurosports.co.uk/tours.htm
Premier travel agents for good packages
to major sports competitions in the UK
and Europe with a peek behind the scenes
of clubs and events around the world.
Booking information is listed by sport.
e-mail: chris@eurosports.co.uk

Golden International
www.goldenint.com
They say they are your passport to
sport world wide. You can buy tickets
only or full-blown packages with
everything included. Their expertise is
mainly in football, hockey, horseracing,
basketball, baseball and tennis, but for
the full list check out the site.
e-mail: Steve@goldenint.com

Gullivers Sports Travel
www.gulliversports.co.uk
Regarded as the largest specialist
sports tour operators in the world
today, they run all manner of trips for
supporters and handle all aspects of
corporate and incentive travel.
Information is set out by group -
schools, universities or corporations

and also by sport - rugby, cricket, golf
and football. You can book online.
e-mail: gullivers@gulliversports.co.uk

Hoback Sports
www.hobacksports.com
This US based sport travel specialist
offers mountain bike trips in summer,
alpine skiing and snowboarding in
winter. Its service includes bike and ski
equipment rental, accommodation and
transportation.
e-mail: hobacksports@hobacksports.com

Info Hub
**www.infohub.com/TRAVEL/SIT/
sit_pages/Sports_Tours.html**
Based in California, they offer
comprehensive travel information to
the Internet community. The site is
essentially a list of over a hundred
sports tours for your choice. Under
each listing, you can find the time,
venue and booking information.
e-mail: agent@infohub.com

London Sport
www.londonsport.com
London Sport offers soccer lovers the
opportunity to watch Premier and
European matches live. Their holidays
include accommodation and
transportation. The site links take you
to the latest sports news and an online
sports bookstore. You get hotel details,
maps and a schedule of matches.
e-mail: sales@londonsport.com

Marvelous Tickets
www.marveloustickets.com
Tickets and travel for sports events
more or less world wide. They serve
individuals, groups, corporations,

arrange tickets, travel and tours. Their services include all aspects of travel as wholesalers, agents and brokers. You are bound to find something to suit. Use e-mail, telephone or fax to reach them.
e-mail: via online form

Network Cricket Tours

www.networkcrickettours.com.au
Australia's most experienced test cricket tour operator for supporters world wide. All details are listed on the site, including upcoming events. Contact them for more info and bookings.
e-mail: nntravel@networkcrickettours.com.au

Open Wing Tours

habitantes.elsitio.com/openwing/index.html
Argentinean organisation that puts sport first throughout South America. Their packages include transportation, accommodation and meals and of course the tickets. Tournaments are listed online with details of teams and athletes.
e-mail: openwings@ciudad.com.ar

Out There

www.out-there.com
Adventure sport in Canada is covered regionally in this guide. Each sport is identified with the best places to go, equipment rental companies, links to manufacturers' web pages, instructors and guides, accommodation, books, magazines and weather. A very good site.
e-mail: Info@out-there.com

Pengwern Sports Tours

www.pengwernsportstours.com
Fully inclusive package of activities for fun packed, energetic weekends including quad trekking, obstacle courses, Grand Prix carting, clay pigeon shooting or paintballing, among others. Contact them for bookings and more details.
e-mail: info@pengwernsportstours.com-

Player's Choice

www.pchoice.com
Golf vacations and golf travel. You'll find package tours to the United States, Canada and the International Gold Vacations. The deals include golf tee times, flights, hotel accommodation and car rental. You can arrange your trip online.
e-mail: info@pchoice.com

Premier Sports Tour

www.premiersportstours.com
Based in the USA, they guarantee reliable information and promise great tours to a range of major sports events anywhere in the world. As travel and entertainment specialists, they'll customise every detail to suit your requirements. Use the online form to book.
e-mail: thast1919@aol.com

Prime Travel

www.prime-travel.com
Broad-based assistance with travel planning, especially sports-related tours and services in Western Canada and packages to the finest ski towns and resorts in Switzerland, France and Austria.
e-mail: info@prime-travel.com

Pro Sports

www.pro-sports.net
Round the clock tickets and travel packages to major sporting events in the USA. They claim that they can arrange tickets to international sporting events even if they are sold out, with free delivery. The site is full of Pro-Sport chat and pages for hundreds of teams. Fan Central has news and photos for fans.
e-mail: Sales@pro-sports.net

Road Trips

www.roadtrips.com
They offer travel packages to sports events for fans and corporate groups. Check the site for current offers. Packages include tickets and accommodation for all major US sports. You can request a free brochure and newsletter for more information. The ticket exchange page is worth a visit.
e-mail: info@roadtrips.com

Snow Skiing

www.wildthings.com
Bored with conventional sports? Then visit this site and find out about some exciting sport adventures. There are links to adventure travel and extreme sports information, ski and snowboard tours and lessons in the German and Austrian Alps, comprehensive year round adventure sports camps, resorts and much more.
e-mail: via online form

South Africa Tours

www.capetours.co.uk
UK tour company with more than 25 years experience in South Africa. The easy to navigate site has sections on accommodation, safaris and sports holidays. You can customise your trip if you prefer.
e-mail: CapeTours@aol.com

Special Sports Tours

sports.travel.d9.com
If you love sport and travel check out this site. They combine the two in a range of packages for Australia, including group or individual travel.
e-mail: via online form

Sports American Tours

www.sportsamerica.com
An American ski expert providing trip information to over 20 ski resorts including Aspen, Breckenridge, Beaver Creek, Copper Mountain and many more. Book your trip by telephone, fax or e-mail.
e-mail: info@sportsamerica.com

Sports Car Tours

www.sportscartours.com
Classic sports car touring in the Virginia countryside. You'll find information about their sports car collection and tour packages. Book your trip by telephone or e-mail and enjoy scenic Virginia.
e-mail: info@sportscarrentals.com

Sports Tour Classics

www.sportstourclassics.com
All major spectator sports events including premier matches throughout the USA and the rest of the world. They offer packages that seem like dreams coming true - great accommodation, deluxe amenities, exciting theme parties, world famous celebrity guest speakers and service second to none. To book, use the

online reservation form.
e-mail: via online form

Sports Tours & Entertainment

www.sportstours.net
US company for sports travel with the focus on basketball, football and baseball. They cater for all age groups from school kids to senior citizens. Click on the icons left of the home page to find out more. You can book by phone, fax, e-mail or online and pay by credit card.
e-mail: emurzap@snet.net

Sports Tours International

www.sportstoursintl.com
Personalised tour services for young sports fans. Each summer they select a few teams and plan their tours, therefore early booking is a good idea. Tours are described online and are changed every season.
e-mail: info@sportstoursintl.com

Sports Travel

www.4sportstravel.com
Easy and affordable sports travel around the world for groups and individuals. Click on your chosen sport on the home page for touring packages that come with tickets, accommodation and transportation. Book using the online form.
e-mail: info@sportstravelandtours.com

Sports World Tours

www.sportsworldtours.com
Your sports connection for major league baseball and the NFL in Seattle, with 25 years experience in arranging travel packages for spectator sports. Click on the image buttons on the home page for service including tickets, transportation and hotel accommodation, all of which are set out for you in great detail.
e-mail: sportsworld@uswest.net

Taho Trips & Trials

www.tahoetrips.com
This American specialist offers first class active vacations for hiking, mountain biking, and multi-sport tours covering areas in Lake Tahoe, Southern Utah's Canyon Country, California's Wine Country, Teton National Park, and Hawaii. You'll find prices for each package, booking information and a photo gallery.
e-mail: tahoetrips@ltol.com

Thailand Golf

www.thailandgolf.com
Golf holidays, seminars and sports events in Thailand for a fun and memorable holiday on and off the golf course. Use the online form to book.
e-mail: info@thailandgolf.com

Trackside Entertainment

www.trackside-entertainment.co.uk
This small British company provides special services for the annual Le Mans 24-hour race. They arrange your tickets, travel, accommodation, food and additional entertainment, all listed individually with details and prices. There is a photo album to give newcomers an idea of what to expect and some links to other important motor racing sites. Book either by e-mail or telephone.
e-mail: stuart@trackside-entertaiment.co.uk

Travel USA

www.travelusa-mds.com
You get instant online pricing for air travel from most US cities to popular vacation destinations. Five major links on the home page deal with hot-spot destinations, casino cities, discount travel and special offers, corporate and group travel, speciality and sports tours, with tickets for the events included.
e-mail: bookings@travelusa-mds.com

Welton Sports

www.weltonsports.com
Golf vacations to play yourself or to watch the champions, including the US and UK Open and the Masters. The rest of the site tells you what they have to offer in customised golf vacations in Scotland, Ireland, Spain, Morocco and the USA. To book use the phone, fax or e-mail.
e-mail: via online form

Yahoo! Travel

**travel.yahoo.com/Destinations/
Activity/Sports_and_Outdoors**
Part of the Yahoo travel site dealing especially with sports. There are tours galore for sport and adventure and all the contacts are online.
e-mail: via online form

Trivia & Quizzes

Allstar Quiz

www.allstarquiz.com
If you want something to amuse
yourself during your coffee break, then
you could do worse than check out this
sports trivia quiz game. Most questions
have a US slant but if you prefer your
sports from this side of the Atlantic, try
the selection of home-made quizzes.
You can even make your own quiz if
you like, although you probably should
get back to work!
e-mail: info@coolquiz.net

Baseball Trivia Quiz

www.geocities.com/baseballtriviaquiz
As well as a baseball quiz, this site has
statistics, quotes, fun facts and handy
radio links that take you to live baseball
coverage in the USA. The trivia quiz
gives you one measly e-mailed question
a week with a leader board listing the
top baseball brains.
e-mail: baseballtriviaquiz@yahoo.com

Boxing By The Numbers

members.tripod.com/~fivedogs/misc.html
A very basic site, but if you want to
brush up on your boxing trivia get into
the thick of the facts files. For
instance, did you know that Jack
Dempsey vs. Jess Willard in 1919 was
the first fight to be broadcast over the
radio? You do now.
e-mail: not available

Cybergolf.com - trivia

www.cybergolf.com/contests
This simple but fun golf trivia quiz runs
from Monday to Sunday with a
leaderboard posted at the end of each
week. If you manage to top that very
board you'll win a golf-related prize.
The quiz tentatively follows a golf format
with questions answered in a hole-by-hole
system, with a par for a correct answer
and a triple bogey for a wrong one.
e-mail: via online form

E-online - Top Ten Sports Movies

eonline.com/Features/Topten/Sportsmovies

This nice little site gives you an intelligent run-down of its choice of the top ten sports films of all time. The movies are all American, yet the site still warrants a passing visit, especially as each film has a short video clip for you to download and play.

e-mail: support@eonline.com

Football Bastards

www.football-bastards.com

Not a site for the faint-hearted, Football Bastards lets football fans vent their dislike (and that's putting it mildly!) for an assortment of football stars. As well as a top ten chart of the most disliked players, you can submit a new object of hatred or pontificate with fellow bitter and twisted fans in the discussion forum. Honest and funny, this site deserves a visit from any self-respecting fan with an axe to grind over a star's diving antics, dirty play or tabloid shenanigans. Of course, jealousy at the fact that these players earn bundles every week for kicking a ball about has nothing to do with it!

e-mail: via online form

Forest Hills Rugby Football Club - Rugby Songs

www.fhrugby.org/songs.html

If you are partial to standing on tables in pubs and spilling drink on yourself while loudly singing expletive-ridden songs, then this is the site for you. There are links to rugby sites and songs from all over the world and many of the rather bawdy tunes are available as audio files for download. Rugby song heaven.

e-mail: fhrugbyfc@aol.com

FunTrivia.com

www.funtrivia.com

Apparently the world's largest trivia site, FunTrivia.com has an excellent sports section with literally hundreds of quizzes covering a wide range of sports including soccer, rugby and auto racing, with new quizzes being created daily. Your scores are analysed online and given a percentage so you can brag to your mates about how well you did.

e-mail: trivia@funtrivia.com

Graeme McLay - Sports Jokes Page

www.soton.ac.uk/~gdm/sport.htm

Simply one long page of sports jokes and quotes, this minimalist site is worth a look for its decent range of material. The jokes are up-to-date, sharp and credible and therefore ripe for entertaining your mates down the pub. The anti-Manchester United jokes will prove particularly entertaining to those bitter and jealous fans. Also check out the quotes - "I've plenty of bows to my string"? Vinny Jones, we salute you.

e-mail: not available

Great Sports Quotes

www.itsnet.com/home/getlost/quotes.html

If you're looking for sporting inspiration, then check out the motivational sporting quotes from the greats. Muhammed Ali to Carl Lewis share their wisdom with you; but what Vidal Sassoon, Van Morrison and Hannibal - the African general, not the A-team leader - are doing here, is a mystery.

e-mail: getlost@itsnet.com

Hockey Twins

www.hockeytwins.com
While the emphasis is mainly on US sporting stars, this look-a-like site is worth a visit. Nicely laid out and amusing, you'll have fun judging how good or bad the likenesses are, even if you don't know one star from the next.
e-mail: submit@hockeytwins.com

IIS Sports - Sports Trivia

www.iis-sports.com/trivia
Good quality American football, baseball and general sports trivia quizzes are on this US site. You can also peruse an archive of over 5,000 questions (with correct answers provided) and if that isn't trivial enough for you, you can chat with fellow fact fiends and even submit your own questions.
e-mail: comments@iis-sports.com

Infoplease.com - Sports

www.infoplease.com/sports.html
A handy place for chasing down an irritating unanswered sports trivia question from one of the quiz sites, this is an online encyclopaedia, dictionary and almanac all rolled into one. Stuffed full of facts and figures on pretty much anything and everything. The sports section delivers masses of material on most sports and the detail is terrific. Schedules, results, history and biographies are all there, as well as some good articles.
e-mail: support@chek.com

Kunal Ganju presents Cricket Trivia

www.geocities.com/Colosseum/Field/1613
Worth a browse for cricket fans needing to brush up on their trivia. Facts are divided into Miscellaneous, Batting, Bowling, Wicket-Keeping and Fielding categories. Presentation is very basic with an irritating bright red cricket-ball inspired background.
e-mail: kunalganju@bigfoot.com

Olympic and Soccer Logos and Mascots

www.geocities.com/Colosseum/2563
As the name says, you get to see posters, pins, logos and mascots from every major Olympic and Soccer tournament since the events began. Olympic bids are recorded and soccer tournaments take in the Copa America and, would you believe, the Under 17 World Championship! The site even grades them! You can check out logos for loads of other sports and a huge number of links to various sites. Have fun.
e-mail: vernik1@home.com

Rob's Homepage - Footy-net

www.linki.freeserve.co.uk
Concerned mainly with English and Scottish football jokes, this fairly average site will have a dodgy joke for you whatever team you support or rival team you hate! Other games get a mention along with more general funny stuff. You'll find a selection of mediocre quizzes and games and limited online shopping.
e-mail: via online form

Scatty.com - Sports Jokes

www.scatty.com/jokes/sports
What's the chilliest ground in the Premiership? Cold Trafford! And that's one of the better jokes on this site. The jokes are so bad, the trick is not to repeat them unless you're planning a very short career in stand-up comedy. So bad it's good. Sort of.
e-mail: via online form

Silly Sports

www.sillysports.com
If you're a fan of American Football, then you're sure to enjoy this US site. Full of humorous and relatively intelligent articles, the site takes digs at everything and everyone from the sports media to overrated players. You'll also find loads of links, news, columns and fantasy league information, all done in an entertaining tongue-in-cheek style.
e-mail: wildbill@sillysports.com

Snooker Heed

www.snookerheed.co.uk
Awarded the Nobel Prize for Failure and claiming to be the worst snooker site on the web, and we tend to agree. Very funny in parts, irreverant and sometimes just plain rude, it has a Q & A section called Thikki and an online shop full of joke items. It doesn't have the latest news on tournaments and competitions but it does have a load of miscellaneous garbage.
e-mail: snookerheed@bigfoot.com

Soccer Songs And Chants

home.wanadoo.nl/maarten.geluk
A site dedicated to the sweet music of the football terraces. You'll find chants and songs from club fans all over Europe, some of which can be downloaded. Funny, risqué and sometimes outdated, the selection of lyrics is fascinating. Taken out of context though, the chants often lose something in the translation - Bouncy, bouncy, bouncy, bouncy, na-na-na-na-na-na? Thank you Dundee United.
e-mail: ma.s.geluk@st.hanze.nl

Sports Jeopardy Online

www.station.sony.com/sportsjeopardy
Online version of the popular US TV game show, Sports Jeopardy is a fun way to test your sporting knowledge. However, unless you have a good grasp of all things sporting Stateside, you'll find it tough going. Presentation is very good with nice graphics and sound.
e-mail: not available

Sports Technology: An Introduction

www.wmin.ac.uk/media/cr98/jennyw
This very basic site offers those of you in pursuit of the trivial a mixed bag of facts and trivia on sports technology. Sections include tennis, athletics, aerodynamics and sports footwear, but the selection of information available is rather limited.
e-mail: not available

Strange Soccer Stories

www.royals.cx/story.html
Loads of bizarre and funny soccer stories that have been contributed by visitors to the site. The quality is varied but you're sure to find something that at least puts a smile on your face. Although the site hasn't been updated since 1996, it's still good for a giggle.
e-mail: SoccerStories@ patrol.i-way.co.uk

Tennis - Results & Head to Head Matches

gene.wins.uva.nl/~jellekok/tennis
With more statistics than you could shake a racquet at, this site will definitely appeal to tennis anoraks. In a very basic presentation, you'll find results for all the ATP tour tournaments

from 1993 to 1999, including every round, all the scores, seedings and so on. The head-to-head feature lets you input any two players and find out how they've performed against each other.
e-mail: jellekok@wins.uva.nl

The Famous Football Supporters Page

www.railwayinn.freeserve.co.uk/famous.htm
Disposable yet fascinating, this site lists the celebrity fans of football teams. It's as simple as that. While concentrating on British clubs, the site mentions a few foreign clubs and their star supporters. Not always accurate, it's still worth a look if only to learn that Uri Geller is a Reading supporter. This is stuff we all need to know. Well, maybe not.
e-mail: Mail@railwayinn.freeserve.co.uk

The Football Quotes Page

www.geocities.com/SouthBeach/Palms/6687/quotesmain.html
Making the most of the football fraternity's all-too-frequent habit of contracting foot-in-mouth disease, this hilarious site gives you loads of the most ridiculous quotes ever by players, managers, pundits and commentators. Kevin Keegan gets a particular roasting with some of his more famous outbursts played back in audio clips.
e-mail: s_tyers@yahoo.com

The Internet Football Ground Guide

www.footballgroundguide.co.uk
A must for obsessive football fans, this site piles in the details, photos and layouts of every Premier and Nationwide League ground, each club

and a bunch of useful links. Some non-league and foreign club grounds are also given the anorak treatment. If you share the site creator's passion for stadiums you can check out information on the 92 Club, the society for the select few who have watched a competitive match at every league ground in the country.
e-mail: duncanadams@dial.pipex.com

The Krysstal Website - Football Facts And Statistics

www.krysstal.com/football.html
We can safely assume that the creators of this site, Kryss and Talaat, have a lot of time on their hands. In the football section, you'll find list upon list of winners and runners-up in all major English and European club football competitions. Some of the more interesting lists include a table of Champions League wins by country and even a list of how long individual English clubs have gone without winning a trophy!
e-mail: not available

The Locker Room

hometown.aol.com/msdaizy/sports/
locker.html

A great site aimed at children, with loads of facts, hints and information on their favourite sports. Also included are sections on sports training and how to deal with your coach, team-mates or any problems you may be having while playing. Slightly twee in tone, The Locker Room is still a welcome site for kids interested in sports.
e-mail: via online form

The Murray Walker Quotes Page

www.worldmotorsport.com/murray/
index.shtml

Murray Walker's excitable tones are as much a part of Formula One as the drivers and cars themselves and this page pays homage to the king of the commentating blooper. Bask in the undeniable beauty of 'and I interrupt myself to bring you this....', 'He is shedding buckets of adrenalin in that car' and '...the lead is now 6.9 seconds, in fact it's just under 7 seconds' amongst myriad other gems.
e-mail: quotes@worldmotorsport.com

The Sports Cliché List

www.sportscliche.com5

If you follow US sport, then you'll enjoy this witty site which lays bare the age-old art of the sporting cliché. Be it players, coaches, commentators or journalists, their consistently unimaginative vocabulary is given a deserved dressing-down. Well worth a look.
e-mail: mph@SportsCliche.com

Totally Useless Facts - Sports

www.totallyuselessfacts.com/facts/
sports/sports0015.shtml

Here's your chance to stuff yourself on loads of useless sports facts on this funny US site. Worth a look if you're faced with a dinner party next week and nothing to say. Be sure though that the guests like sport and are American!
e-mail: via online form

Track and Field All-Time Performance Homepage

www.algonet.se/~pela2

This site gets straight to the point and gives you the all-time top times and scores for every track and field event there is. Men's and women's events are kept right up-to-date. Each list goes into the hundreds, so track trainspotters will be kept amused for hours on end. While little time has been spent on the presentation, who needs snazzy graphics when you can find out who holds the no. 260 position for the all time women's hammer throw? Olga Kuzenkova, but then you already knew that.
e-mail: pela2@algonet.se

Trivia Golf Country Club

www.triviagolf.com
With a mine of information, this US site lists just about everything to do with the game of golf. Statistics on all the majors, top ten trivia lists, profiles, history and quotes come by the number. Once you've learned everything off by heart you can try out the Trivia Golf 19 Hole Championship Course. But alas, all the statistics and records seem to stop at 1997.
e-mail: not available

Trivia365

trivia365.com
If you know it all or think you do, then Trivia 365 may have a surprise for you. The terrific sports section has general and individual sports quizzes. Trivia buffs can log on, play in live trivia quizzes, win prizes and probably never log off again.
e-mail: via online form

Uproar Trivia Blitz

www.cityweb.co.uk/quiz
With a weekly draw jackpot of a whopping £15, who wouldn't want to try out this simple but fun trivia site? Formula One and soccer get categories of their own and there's also a general sports quiz. You have a limited amount of time to answer each question and can play a new game whenever you want.
e-mail: not available

Useless Jokes.com - Sports

www.uselessjokes.com/Sports
The sporting section of Useless Jokes.com contains a good range of mainly American slanted material. So if you're looking for sophisticated wit, then this definitely isn't the site for you. However, if you're simply in need of a lowbrow chuckle, you'll find a few jokes to keep you happy.
e-mail: jokemeister@uselessjokes.com

Useless Knowledge.com

www.uselessknowledge.com/uk/Sports
Did you know that the official state sport of Alaska is dog-mushing? You'll find many more equally tasty, not to mention useless, morsels of sports trivia on this very entertaining site. A simple quiz is also available to test your knowledge.
e-mail: not available

We Love It!

cricket.toneware.com
Taking a look at the lighter side of cricket, We Love It! is a very entertaining site full of good features including trivia, quotes and photographs. Take a look around and you're sure to find something of interest, be it a useless cricket fact or an even more useless cricket joke.
e-mail: not available

Wembley Park

www.wembleypark.com
Very flashy and thoroughly enjoyable site, full of excellent football animations and games based around the much-maligned English national team. The South Park influenced cartoons, some with music, are well animated and very sharp, with the cast of characters including David Beckham, Vinny Jones and Michael Owen giving Cartman, Kenny and Co. a run for their money.
e-mail: info@hoddle.com

Winter Sports

Association of Ontario Snowboarders

www.snowboarders.on.ca
Find out how they do it in Ontario, with a celndar of events, results and a newsletter. A friendly Canadian site with a useful list of descriptions of the main snowboarding disciplines.
e-mail: aos@snowboarders.on.ca

Bobsleigh Canada

www.bobsleigh.ca
A complete guide to their competitive seasons to date. All events are listed with TV schedules, news and results, individual team members and coaches. A photo gallery pins up images you can download and a page of useful links takes you to other bobsleigh sites in the region. Recruitment information on the site is directed at Canadian nationals.
e-mail: webmaster@bobsleigh.ca

British Bobsleigh Association

www.british-bobsleigh.com
A history and guide to the sport, news on current competitions, including the Olympics, with a focus on the successes of the British team. Find out how to take part online. The results page comes courtesy of the official Bobsleigh Federation site.
e-mail: contact@british-bobsleigh.com

Canadian Freestyle Ski Association

www.freestyleski.com
If you are into acrobatic skiing then take a look here. The Canadian national team and coaches are profiled, all racing results are displayed with tables of world wide rankings. There are several fine articles on the big events and conferences, with info on how to become part of this sporting world. The aerial photos are stunning and text is in English and French.
e-mail: infor@freestyleski.ca

Canadian Luge Association

www.luge.ca
The Canadian national team and their participation in the Luge World Cup. You get all the news, results, schedules of training sessions and competition details. The media section includes a guide to luge and messages from the Association. Text is in English and French.
e-mail: via online form

Cross Country Ski World

www.xcskiworld.com
This site is incredibly informative about this skiing discipline, with tips on technique, equipment required and how to train effectively. An events list, news stories and a guide to where to go for the best cross-country skiing in the USA make good reading. If you are new to the sport, check out the beginners' page for an excellent introduction.
e-mail: info@xcskiworld.com

Freestyle Team

www.freestyleteam.de
Biographies of all team members and an overall guide to their results. Lots of news and media reports to read, some in German, with some good team photos. There is a guest book to sign and a mailing list to join.
e-mail: not available

Hahnenkamm Rennen - Kitzbuhel

www.hahnenkamm.com
The official online voice for the world cup downhill race and the resort. Details of racing programs, with lots of technical data about individual runs, take up several pages. There is travel and ticket information if you want to

attend. A history of the resort, an archive of results and several FAQ pages come in English and German.
e-mail: hahnenkamm@tirol.com

International Free Skiers Association

www.freeskiers.org
The official site for extreme skiing, where joining up is fully explained. The annual touring schedule is published with all results illustrated with spectacular photo galleries. A page is dedicated to competitors. You can either chalk up something on the message board or talk your way through the chat room.
e-mail: Lhotse@freeskiers.org

International Luge Federation

www.fil-luge.org
Extensive site of the governing body, covering all aspects of the sport including rules and regulations, competition results and world cup information. Tracks, athletes, the Olympic Winter Games in 2002, a calendar of events and a brief history of the sport take up several more pages. Contacts for national governing bodies around the world are listed on the NFS page. Text is in English and German.
e-mail: office@fil-luge.org

International Skating Union

www.isu.org
The four main styles – synchronised, figure skating, speed skating and short track, each with details of the current season of events and competition results. A message board and chat room complete the site and to keep in touch you can sign up for their newsletter.
e-mail: info@isu.org

International Ski Federation

www.fis-ski.com

All styles of skiing and snowboarding are covered on this official federation site, with competition result updates and championship standings, plus the official rules and regulations. There are guides to skiing in all its forms for the uninitiated and lots of links to other useful sites.

e-mail: not available

International Snowboard Federation

www.isf.ch

Everything for the snowboarding fan, with live action links and all the info about where, when and how races take place around the world. Rider profiles and separate calendars for national and international events fill several pages, with descriptions of all the styles involved.

e-mail: isa@isf.net

Jamaica Bobsleigh

www.cariboutpost.com/bobsleigh/

You've heard about them, seen the film, now check them out online. Team member profiles, competition schedules and results come with good pictures of them in action. A shopping page is under construction in case you want a copy of the video.

e-mail: cstokes@infochan.com

Kandahar

kandahar.chamonix.org

One of the world cup racing events in Chamonix, France. You get a map and photos of the run, a calendar of events, information on competitor registration and a picture gallery of great action shots. Text is in English and French.

e-mail: kandahar@chamonix.org

Palmer USA

www.palmerusa.com

A shopping site for snowboard gear manufactured by the company and a team site for their riders. You can check the hardware or go straight to the team area for a look at their achievements and awards, a photo gallery and a

techie section that discusses the finer points of snowboards.
e-mail: via online form

Richard Gravier

www.gravier.com
Simple site of a French ski team member. Personal details, a record of his achievements and aspirations for the forthcoming season, a guide to his sponsors and several photos complete the deal.
e-mail: richard@gravier.com

Salt Lake Olympic Winter Games

www.slc2002.org
Official site of the 2002 Winter Olympics, with all the info on where events will be held and how they will be organised. You can book tickets and purchase merchandise online. Check out details on how to volunteer your help with the competition.
e-mail: via online form

SnowBoard World Rankings

www.snowboardranking.com
As the name suggests, this site deals only with world ranking in this sport, divided into three categories with results from all competitions around the world. There are extensive links to official snowboard sites world wide.
e-mail: bill@snowboard ranking.com

Speed Skiing

www.speedski.com
Participants in this hair-raising sport are listed with a guide to where they race, with the top male and female racers profiled. A schedule of events and a page telling you how to get into the sport and the gear you need complete the site.
e-mail: via online form

The English Ski Council

www.bluedome.co.uk/interest/ski/index.htm
They tell you who they are, what they do and have good links to other organisations like the British Association of Ski Instructors. There are details on dry slope training in England and sponsorship opportunities from the council. The site is currently being expanded to cover all styles of snow sports.
e-mail: not available

The International Bobsleigh and Skeleton Federation

www.bobsleigh.com
Run by the official governing body for the sport, the site has a stack of information, including the rules and regulations. News items, a racing calendar and competition results for the current season blend in with details of competitors and their equipment and of course the tracks. There are TV listings and guides to each race.
e-mail: egarde@tin.it

The Luge

www.luge.com
An enormous resource put together by a great fan of the sport. A detailed history explores the beginnings of sledding and several guides take you to tracks and luge organisations around the world. News updates, results and a glossary are some of the other useful items. A fun page has luge sounds you can play back.
e-mail: webmaster@luge.com

The New Zealand Alpine Ski Racing site

www.skiracing.org.nz
Ski racing in New Zealand with a news and results service, a full calendar of events and a page of all championship tables. Interviews with competitors at recent events can be downloaded and heard with RealPlayer G2 software. There are lots of links to other skiing sites around New Zealand and the rest of the world.
e-mail: snowsports@iconz.co.nz

The Ski Directory

www.skidirectory.com
Top class site if you want to know more about winter sports and link up with related web sites. There are several channels with everything for winter sports - competition or holiday fun - and they are easy to navigate. The site has a ski club you can join, a ski chat room, lots of photos and good links to companies that either manufacture winter sports gear or arrange travel.
e-mail: not available

United States Luge Association

www.usaluge.org
Luge racing in the USA with news about the association, racing information, results and their tour. You can buy team strip from the online catalogue using the secure server. Their training complex and sponsors are on the home page.
e-mail: usaluge@usaluge.org

US Bobsled and Skeleton Federation

www.usabobsledandskeleton.org
Official online home to these sports in the USA with a focus on the national team. Pages are divided between team members, coaches and the history of the sport. Other sections deal with current results, photos and an online store still under construction.
e-mail: info@USAboblsed.org

US Ski Team

www.usskiteam.com
Every ski style including snowboarding is featured on this team site, each with its own area with news and articles, racing results and team line-ups. Major racing events have their own

pages as do media and TV coverage. There are brilliant action shots and you can buy merchandise from the online store.

e-mail: via online form

USA Snowboard Association

www.usasa.org
Snowboarding in the USA, with championships around the country listed with full details. You get weather reports for the next competition and guides to host resorts. An archive of all previous results, a history of the Association and a message board take up a few pages. Links connect you to related sites and information on scholarships awarded by the Association.

e-mail: Karen_office@usasa.org

World Extreme Skiing Championships

www.wesc.com
Sponsorship, competitors and the event itself with articles about the championships, results over the last ten years and lots of outstanding pictures and video clips. You'll find a guide to the competition venue in Valdez and a message board. If you want to take part, you can download an application form for the competition in several formats.

e-mail: wesc@alaska.net

Wrestling

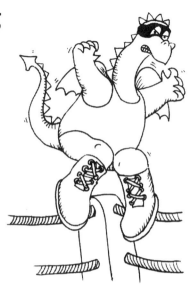

s1Wrestling.com

www.1wrestling.com
Bryan Wayne tells you about his Funking
Dojo experience! Vote in the Thunder
Poll, give it the thumbs up, thumbs
down or thumbs in the middle.
Otherwise nothing unusual at this site.
News, views and a few features.
e-mail: mailto:efortress.com

All Pro Wrestling

www.allprowrestling.com
Play the WWF theme song - Wrestling
is hardcore - visit the beginners or pro
sites, Boot Camp and Garage and get
an e-mail account at this site. It has a
chat room, message boards and job
openings as well as a diary of forthcoming
events in an easy to use layout.
e-mail: not available

Amateur Wrestling

amateurwrestle.about.com
This site calls itself the starting place
for amateur wrestlers so novices are
bound to find out what they need to
know. What, for instance, are the styles
of wrestling? What diet does a wrestler
need to maintain? There is information
about tournaments, products, publications
and the latest news and views.
e-mail: not available

Beaver Wrestling

wrestling.orst.edu
Their hotline can be accessed from
this site with up-to-date results and
information on all Oregon State
University wrestling events. There are
good photographs of wrestling action
and excellent coverage of news and views.
e-mail: not available

Berkshire Wrestling Online

www.berkshirewrestling.com
Quick Pins and Big Wins is the jazziest
title on this site which has information
about ranking, schedules, tournament
results and so on.
e-mail: not available

Canadian Amateur Wrestling Association

www.wrestling.ca
In French or English you will find a ring full of information about the sport internationally. Leipzig, Minsk, Faenza are all names with a place on their pages. There is a Tournament 2000 computer draw as well.
e-mail: via online form

Cathedral Prep

www.ramblerwrestling.com
A Pennsylvania high school site with its own unique style that screens videos through a media player. You'll find summer camps, photos and Coach O's Corner. Visit the Site of the Month.
e-mail: not available

ECW Wrestling

www.ecwwrestling.com
Enter the Danger Zone at the Lou E. Dangerously page with his 6/6 column and beware of Scrap Dog's Bytes. This is an exciting site, full of photos, pay-per-view, TV listings and a great deal more.
e-mail: not available

Flamingo Wrestling

www.flamingowrestling.com
The blurb says - Sexy female wrestling action at it's finest and the site is laid out in three sections. Flamingo boasts the hottest and best action pics in the world of female wrestling today. Black Falcon has sexy pics and stories. News and Chat gives you a news board and a chat room.
e-mail: not available

Freestyle Wrestling Home Page

www.dcs.shef.ac.uk
The aims of this soon-to-be re-designed site are to provide a contact address for wrestlers in Europe, particularly the UK and to focus on the conditioning aspect of this sport. It believes that freestyle wrestling is one of the most exciting sports in the Olympics because it combines strength, speed, willpower and technique. With this in focus, the site offers good, practical advice to wrestlers and lists club addresses world wide.
e-mail: M.Lee@dcs.shef.ac.uk

Gayscape

www.jwpublishing.com/gayscape/ wrest.html
Gay and Lesbian wrestling clubs, organisations and personal pages of people into wrestling and wrestling photography. Boxing, karate and other martial arts also feature. The index is said to hold 52,000 sites of similar interest.
e-mail: not available

Independent Wrestling Federation Web Ring

members.tripod.com/~dgpf25/ring.html
This Web Ring is dedicated to the small independent federations that run all across the country – sometimes to as few as 50 people and sometimes to as many as 500. It's also dedicated to the wrestlers in those organisations that work their butts off travelling to different States for only a few bucks or sometimes no money at all. Just to be seen - just to be in the ring. The site takes over from there.
e-mail: mailto:jdjz@efortress.com

Inside the Squared Circle

itscwrestling.com

The page giving the history of the ITSC starts - For over 7 years a counter-revolutionary force in Professional Wrestling... Inside The Squared Circle was born in June 1989 as a radio program on WMET-AM with Will Dunham, Fred Sternburg and Dirty Dick Daniel as co-hosts. The show steadily built an audience despite being the bane of station management, who could not understand why the program's hosts referred to listeners as humanoids. In news and views you can read Despicable Dave's diatribe or take an Intellectual Perspective by Theophileus Punivel.

e-mail: not available

Intermat Wrestling

www.intermatwrestle.com

Tom Owens is the founder of InterMat Inc. He started the company in July 1995 based on his love for wrestling. Tom wrestled at youth and high school levels while growing up in Moville, Iowa. That quote straight out of this fairly pedestrian looking site but it has all the necessary ingredients to hold your attention.

e-mail: info@intermat wrestle.com

John McAdams Wrestling Videotape Library

www.pconline.com/~sffl/john.htm

John McAdam bought his first VCR in 1985 and now publishes, online, the catalogue of his wrestling collection, some 500 in all, most available to buy. He updates the site around the beginning of every month.

e-mail: not available

Links2Go

www.links2go.com/topic/Wrestling

Chat in real time about wrestling or just post a message on the site. Here you'll find links to all areas of wrestling in a very simple screen layout - Sumo wrestling, world championship wrestling and a lot more.

e-mail: not available

Marshwood Wrestling

www.nh.ultranet.com

A small site with very much its own style. Mostly home news but with links to other wrestling sites. Worth a look if only for the curiosity.

e-mail: not available

New World Order

nwowrestling.com/now

The blurb on this site begins: In 1996, The Outsiders, Kevin Nash and Scott Hall along with Hulk Hogan, created a phenomenon that would change WCW as we knew it. The parallels were evident. Both groups enjoyed success and popularity on other fronts, but when they came together, it was like an explosion. Only this time, unlike the Beatles invasion of '64, the New World Order was out for blood and willing to take out anyone and anything in their

way. To find out what follows, visit the site.
e-mail: not available

Official Women of Wrestling

www.owow.com
As an independent site with no
affiliations, it presents pictures and
information about women in
professional wrestling. The photograph
album has lots of muscular women
posing in full colour.
e-mail: not available

Oklahoma Pro Wrestling

www.oklahomapro.com
A more bizarre bunch of wrestlers is
hard to find. The last few weeks have
been brutal for Body Count as they

have gone up against former two time
tag team champions, The Casualties Of
War. This feud is bound to continue.
Big Daddy Moore defeated Buck Few of
the Texas Outlaws and Grenade, the
newest member of the Casualties of
War and their entry in the Light
Heavyweight division of Oklahoma Pro,
will get his first title shot against
Ichiban Sense. To learn more, visit
the site.
e-mail: via online form

Ollie's Wrestling Resources

infoweb.magi.com/~ollie/wrestling.shtml
A very good and comprehensive site,
which has been going since 1995, with
a section dedicated to Japanese
wrestling. There are archives, the
Rumour Mill and Promotions. You can
download mp3s of the site's own Big
Papa Punk band.
e-mail: ollie@magi.com

Pennsylvania Wrestling

www.pawrsl.com/pa/
Fairly basic site with a link to the
magazine Wrestling USA. There are
links to other web sites, a useful section for coaching openings, a fan forum
and milestones of 1999-2000.
e-mail: via online form

Power Wrestling

www.powerwrestling.com
An elaborate site with personality.
At the King of the Ring section, you get
the latest on forthcoming pay-per-view
events as well as histories from past
King of the Ring Tournaments. Check
out the babe of the week picture.
e-mail: ogsucka@yahoo.com

Pro Wrestling Realm 2000

www.prowrestlingrealm.com
Win a custom car at this visually jazzy
US site. You'll find links to affiliated
sites and information pages.
e-mail: not available

Professional Wrestling Online Museum

www.wrestlingmuseum.com
Within the simple layout of this site
you'll find a little history of the sport,
biographies of the stars with some

fascinating insights into their backgrounds and links to related sites. The news board is active and you can tune into the sound clips archive.
e-mail: via online form

Scoops Wrestling

www.scoopswrestling.com
Stylish site with good links, exclusive interviews and columns where passionate words are exchanged. The photo gallery is very exciting. Make a booking for a match, visit the parody section, read an inside scoop; lost for a word? consult the online dictionary. It's all great stuff.
e-mail: via online form

Slam Wrestling

www.canoe.ca/SlamWrestling/
Canadian site dedicated to wrestling but with information and links to other types of sport. As well as headlines it has an extensive archive of stories, interviews and historical information.
e-mail: not available

Southern Region Wrestling Olympic Wrestling Association

www.pages.org/wrestle
A very basic site for the organisation that promotes amateur wrestling in the south of England. There is information on clubs, local wrstling news, competitions, tips and techniques and an address list. Links take you to other wrestling sites.
e-mail: sutherst@cadvision.com

The Law

www.liveaudiowrestling.com
This was the first radio show to make the transition from Internet-only broadcasts to mainstream radio. Go to The Edge and listen to uncut, unedited interviews. There is an online store, what's on, FAQ section, links and news. In all an excellent site.
e-mail: mailto:thelaw@ liveaudiowrestling.com

The Mat

www.themat.com
Describing itself as the home of amateur wrestling, the North Carolina site has a

wealth of information about the sport. Top stories deal with wrestling in all its aspects. There is a list of wrestling-related books reviewed online.
e-mail: info@themat.com

The Wrestling Lariat UK

www.spwrestling.com/uklariat/
For a mere £5 a year you can subscribe to this UK edition of the Lariat, filled with articles, interviews and cool stuff. Written by a team of wrestling fans from all over the world, the magazine gives you many points of view rather than a perspective from one pair of eyes. Up-to-date news, views and interviews take up the rest of the site.
e-mail: unclesam@aol.com

The Wrestling Spot

www.wrestlingspot.com
Fairly plain site about amateur wrestling which has recently passed the 100,000 visitors mark. It has news and links to other web sites and a photo gallery with some good pictures of wrestlers in action. It's updated only periodically.
e-mail: not available

Top-rope.com

www.top-rope.com
Check out the chick pic or move of the week, the top rope report or who's the baddest ass around on this full but slow site. You can contribute your stories if you want. There are links to stores, jobs, free mp3s, games and the weather among other bits and pieces, all of which add up to a colourful site.
e-mail: via online form

TWNP News

www.twnpnews.com
Soon to get a new design, this site has an easy-to-use search facility. The latest news, up-dates, games and an interactive page. Use the Prowler poll to air your views.
e-mail: not available

Ultimo Wrestling

www.ultimowrestling.com
Using the site's interactive database you can search for a location, promotion or show. Resident professor of Pro Wrestling, the Shooter, has returned with the infamous no-holds-barred commentary and Q & A Reverb. If you've got the questions, he's got the answers, whether you like them or not.
e-mail: editor@ultimowrestling.com

USA Wrestling

www.usawrestling.org
An official-looking, wide-ranging site containing live championship coverage, camps and clinics and a trivia section. If you have a question for a coach, submit it in the online panel. You can buy goods on the site. Links to other sports yield a host of rich pickings.
e-mail: mailto.USAW@concentric.net

Va Basic.Com

www.vabasic.com
They offer one of the most intensive wrestling training and physical conditioning programs in North Virginia. Experienced young wrestlers between 8 and 14 years old get the opportunity to practise together in an accelerated wrestling environment. The positive experience helps them to achieve greater skill while having fun.
e-mail: tinakdamon@aol.com

Webs Best of Amateur Wrestling

www.geocities.com
Tom Fortunato who runs this site claims 3063 links, 64 photo galleries; he adds a survey and feedback form, a slide show and a new movie clips page. Too big a handful to check the numbers, but you'll enjoy the site.
e-mail: not available

Whoo Wrestling

www.whoowrestling.com
Find out what happened in wrestling history on the anniversary of your log-in day, or take the link to the wrestling auction site where you can bid for all kinds of wrestling memorabilia. Additionally you get results of fights, upcoming events and links to other wrestling web sites.
e-mail: not available

William's Wrestling Tapes

www.angelfire.com/wrestling/barbwire/
You can vote for who you think is the True King of the Death Match and read a review of one of the Big Japan Death Matches. If you want to take an active role, write your own tape review for William. Updates are infrequent.
e-mail: gizmoo@oburg.net

World Wrestling Federation

www.wwf.com
Good layout and wide-ranging topics make this an interesting site. You'll find information about international events, news and profiles of wrestling superstars. Links to publications and live shows require a pay-per-view connection.
e-mail: via online form

Wrestleline.Com

www.wrestleline.com
The site may be a little flashy but the news coverage is extensive and in-depth. There are lively photographs, interviews and forums to pick up on and to finish off, an online store for wrestling related merchandise. Have some influence on the sport by voting in the poll.
e-mail: not available

Wrestling

microbiol.org/vl.martial.arts/wrestlin.htm
A page of martial arts topics including wrestling. There is information about the rules of the sport and refereeing and links to international sites, the UK included.
e-mail: not available

Wrestling History

www.garywill.com/wrestling/wresbook.htm
Wrestling Title Histories is the most complete record of professional wrestling titles and titleholders published. It is cited by wrestling publications around the world as the authority on the sport's champions and championships. This is just one of the books at this books only wrestling site. There are links to other sites maintained by the same author, such as Deceased Wrestlers.
e-mail: gary@garywill.com

Wrestling Holds Gallery

members.tripod.com/~Ungureanu/index-cats.html
Whether it's a Wedgie or a Sleeper you are looking for, an Anaconda or a Bodysplash, you'll find it here with a full description, technical specs and

pictures of female wrestlers demonstrating.
e-mail: not available

Wrestling Online

www.wrestlingonline.com
By the look on his face he's a difficult man to persuade but at this site, you can apply to join Duke's Wrestling Academy. Check out wrestlers' home pages, find a list of federations, buy merchandise or dive into the newsletters.
e-mail: info@wrestlingonline.com

Wrestling Planet

www.wrestlingplanet.com
Interactive site with lots of tasty gossip and the latest news. Information about recent events is up-to-date and there are exotic pictures of girls in threatening postures.
e-mail: via online form

Wrestling USA

www.wrestlingusa.com
This is a whole lot more than a magazine. Online you will find everything from the tourny of the week to every kind of accessory, even medical. You can check out back issues of the magazine and look for jobs in the sport.
e-mail: mailto:wrestling@montana.com

WrestlingInc.com

www.wrestlinginc.com
Busy site with an Internet search engine within its tabloid layout. Click a panel and you get to read an exclusive article or listen to live wrestling. The site offers a chance to win US$1 million through its scratch card lottery. Overall the site is colourful, easy on the eyes with quick access to topics.
e-mail: info@wrestling.com

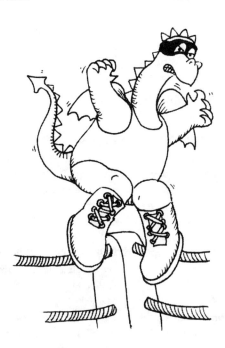

SUMO

Beginners Guide to Sumo

**www.wnn.or.jp/wnn-t/nyumon/
beginner/nyumon.html**
This is more than an introduction to
Sumo. The well laid out site site
explains the origins, rules and ranking
system then goes on to tell you about
the sport that fills Japanese stadiums
and fascinates the rest of the world.
Take a look at the plan of the Kokugaikan,
the famous arena of Sumo.
e-mail: not available

Bible Bell's Sumo Facts and Links

www.biblebell.org/sumo.html
Just as it says, this site gives in plain
language, all the basic information
about Sumo. If you don't know your
chanko from your kachikoshi or where
to put a mawashi, then don't look
further, it's all online.
e-mail: not available

Da Kine Sumo e-zine!

home.att.ne.jp/red/sumo/dakine.htm
Sumo news to fans all over the world.

Like cars, electronics and sushi this
Japanese export is finding international
favour. There is a link to Sportswear
With Humour and Kama'aina's
Restaurant and several more to Sumo
sites. You'll enjoy the Sumo pictures.
e-mail: via online form

Jcult

www.jcult.com/sumoindex.htm
The ever-amicable Konishiki was moved
to tears at his traditional danpatsushiki
hair cutting ceremony to bid farewell to
him from the ring. About 350 friends,
family and personalities participated in
the ceremony, each cutting a tiny piece
of the sumo's chonmage hair. The
best, as they say, is still to come.
e-mail: not available

Mainichi News online

www.mainichi.co.jp/sumo/
Online English version of the Japanese
Mainichi Daily News with a section on
Sumo tournament news, facts and figures
and rikishi profiles. Every issue features

some aspect of the sport and rise of one or other outstanding Sumo wrestler. The stories and pictures make good reading.
e-mail: not available

Okee the Otters WWWaterweb

home.uchicago.edu/~jacadden/sumo.html
The home page of this site calls it My Ma's Favorite Sport. There are links to other sites and newsgroups and a comprehensive book list for anyone wanting to read all about it. The site takes a serious look at Sumo despite some amusing pictures of Ma.
e-mail: mailto:ccadden@lycosmail.com

Sumo Archive

www.t3.rm.or.jp~sports/index.html
Here you get information about every Japanese tournament between 1996 and 2000. There is not much else except for some news.
e-mail: not available

Sumo Links

www.oz.net/~drc/sumolinks.html
The blurb says this is the official Sumo site. There are links to online Sumo-related games and contests, news, statistics, archives and a lot more. You can connect to Lynn Matsuoka's site for artwork, originals and prints. There are pages in English, Hungarian, Spanish and Hebrew.
e-mail: drc@oz.net

Sumo World

www.sumoworld.com
Within a very basic layout, there is an interesting page called Museum, where you will find old pictures of famous wrestlers of the past. Access the Gallery page to see quality photos of wrestlers in action and observe the final cut of a retiring wrestler – tome-basami.
e-mail: sumowrld@gol.com

Sumoweb

www.sumoweb.com/Sumoweb.html
Learn the rules and read up on the FAQ section of Sumo. Look up words and phrases in the glossary, get the numbers on Makuuchi rikishi and connect to other Sumo sites around the world.
e-mail: not available

The Sumo Mailing List

home.earthlink.net/~dgoddard2/
A group of people from around the globe with a common love for Sumo put together this web site. The List is a discussion conducted via e-mail on topics that include basho results, rikishi news, Sumo competitions and any other related subjects. The instant biographies and pictures of wrestlers world wide are excellent.
e-mail: sml@sumofans.com

Things Japanese

mothra.rerf.or.jp/ENG/Hiroshima/Things/72.html
The fundamentals of Sumo are said to be Oshi - hand push, Tsuki - thrust and Yori - body push. Unless these fundamentals are mastered, throwing and other techniques are of little value among top Sumo wrestlers. So says the introduction to this site, which contains tips and techniques both visual and textual.
e-mail: not available

Glossary

Acceptable Use Policy
The rules controlling the use of an **Access Provider, server** or shared area.

access account
Your personal account with an **Internet service provider.**

Access Provider
Any company that provides **Internet** connections.

Acrobat
Computer program used to read **PDF files.**

active content
Any part of a program that enhances the appearance and performance of a **web page.**

ActiveMovie
A Microsoft **applet** for displaying video from **MPEG, QuickTime** and **AVI** formats.

ActiveX
A program that is used to enhance the appearance and performance of a **web page**.

address book
A program used to keep details of contacts, names, **e-mail addresses** and so on.

ADSL
(Asymmetrical Digital Subscriber Line)
Digital technology for high speed data transfer over telephone lines.

anonymous FTP server
Any **FTP** site which accepts a **log-in** with a username of 'anonymous' and a password which matches the **user's e-mail address**.

anti-aliasing
A method of smoothing out the rough edges of irregularly shaped images on screen.

applet
A mini program which works together with other programs.

application
Any computer program.

ARPAnet
The precursor to the **Internet**.

ASCII
(American Standard Code for Information Interchange)
Computer coding system used to represent letters and numbers on computers.

attachment
A **file** sent together with an **e-mail** message.

auto-responder
A system that produces automatic replies to **e-mail** messages.

avatar
A character you choose to represent you in an **online virtual reality** environment.

AVI
A Microsoft format for audiovisual files.

backbone
A major **Internet** connection.

bandwidth
Gauge of the line available to transmit data. The greater the bandwidth, the more data can be sent at the same time.

banner ad
Small advertisements placed on **web pages** with direct **links** to the advertiser's own **web site**.

baud rate
Rate of change per second in the signal used by a **modem** to transmit data.

BBS
Bulletin Board System.

Bigfoot
A search system used to locate **e-mail addresses**.

binary file
A large unencoded **file attached** to a **newsgroup posting**.

BinHex
A method of encoding **binary** data **files** for transmission.

bookmark
A marked location within a **web page,** or the **Netscape Navigator** term for **user** designated **web addresses.**

boot up
To switch a computer on.

broadband
High speed **Internet** access.

browser or **web browser**
A program which allows you to search for and view **web pages** from the **Internet** on your computer. The most popular are **Netscape Navigator** and **Internet Explorer.**

cache
A temporary data store created by a computer program in order to speed up access to information.

capitals
To use capital letters when sending **online** messages, equivalent to SHOUTING.

CDF (Channel Definition File)
This holds the data for a **WWW** subscription **channel.**

CGI (Common Gateway Interface)
A programming system used on **web servers** to automate certain processes.

channel
A system for providing regularly updated data from a **web site** to a subscribing **browser.**

chat
Simultaneous **user** to **user** communication across the **Internet,** either with text or audio/video.

Chat room
A **web site** where members can communicate in real time.

click through
To click on a **banner ad** to visit the advertised **web site.**

client
Any program which accesses information across a **network.**

conferencing
Two or more computers connected to provide the sharing of information or resources.

cookie
A small data **file** stored on your computer by a **web server** in order to identify it.

crack
To circumvent a program's or a computer's security systems, or to fake a **user** ID.

crash
When a computer operating system or **program** ceases to function, or causes other programs to freak out.

cyberspace
The imaginary world created by the connection of computers, **modems** and telephones and the information they convey.

domain name
A unique name used to identify an organisation on the **Internet.**

download
To transfer a **file** from the **Internet** to your computer.

drill down
To go directly to the information you require, without going though intermediate pages of a **web site.**

dropout
Loss of signal on a data connection.

e-commerce
Commercial transactions carried out via the **Internet.**

e-mail
Electronic mail consisting of text, images and sound sent from one **user** directly to another via the **Internet.**

e-mail address
The unique address belonging to a **user**, used to direct **e-mail**.

emoticon
Icon used in text messages created with keyboard symbols to show an emotion when viewed from the side, for example: happiness :-) sadness :-(amazement :-o and so on.

encryption
The process of scrambling data in order to keep it confidential.

eye candy
Attractive graphic images used to enliven a **web page**.

e-zine
Online magazine.

FAQ (Frequently Asked Questions)
A list of commonly asked questions with answers.

Favourites
The way **Internet Explorer** notes your favourite **web sites**.

file
Any electronic document created by an **application** and stored on a computer.

firewall
A **network** security system for restricting internal and external access.

flame
To send abusive **e-mail** or **newsgroup** messages, often to a particular individual.

frag
To fragment or destroy, used in the world of **online** games.

freeware
Software available for free use.

FrontPage
Web authoring **software**.

FTP (File Transfer Protocol)
The normal method of **downloading files** or programs from a computer on the **Internet**.

GIF (Graphics Image Format)
A common format for graphic **files**.

GUI (Graphic User Interface)
The system of using **icons** to represent **applications** and **files** on a computer screen.

hacker
Someone who breaks into secure computer systems or programs.

hardware
The physical components making up a computer system, such as screen, processor, hard drive and so on.

history
A review of the past sequence of **web pages** visited by the **browser**.

home page
The main page of a **web site**, to which subsequent pages are **linked**.

host
A computer that offers information or services to network **users**.

HTML (HyperText Markup Language)
The computer programming language used to write **web pages**.

HTTP (HyperText Transport Protocol)
The system used to communicate on the **Internet**.

hyperlink
An area of a **web site** or portion of text which has been set up to take you directly to another **web page** when activated.

HyperText link
A text link from one **web page** to another, often shown underlined and in blue.

icon
A graphic device used to represent an **application** or **file** on a computer screen.

information superhighway
The media term for the **network** which provides access to the data and services on the **Internet**.

Internet
The sum of all the linked computers and the telephone **networks** which connect them around the world.

Internet Explorer
A popular web **browser**.

Internet Service Provider (ISP)
An ISP provides access to the **Internet**, using banks of computers connected by high speed data links to the **WWW**. Most **users** have an ISP account, which can be free or on subscription.

IP (Internet Protocol) address
A series of numbers allocated to each computer to identify it on the **Internet**.

IRC (Internet Relay Chat)
Simultaneous **user** to **user** communication across the **Internet**, either by text or audio/video.

ISDN (Integrated Subscriber Digital Network)
A standard for digital telephone communication.

Java
Programming language used to write programs to be used on all types of computer.

JPEG (Joint Photographic Experts Group)
A format for image **files**.

junk e-mail
Electronic junk mail.

Kbps
Kilobits per second, approximately one thousand bits per second.

LAN (Local Area Network)
An independent **network** of computers which in turn may be connected to the **Internet**.

link
A connection from one **web page** or **web site** to another.

log on/in
To connect to the **Internet**.

mail server
A **server** used to store and transmit **e-mail**.

MIDI (Musical Instrument Digital Interface)
Files containing music which can be played on a computer. Often used to play background music on **web sites**.

mirror site
A replica site set up at another location to permit easier access.

modem (MOdulator/DEModulator)
A device used to connect a computer to the telephone system in order to transmit and receive data.

metasearch engine
A **search engine** that uses other search engines in combination.

MP3
MPEG format for storing sound **files**.

MPEG/MPG
A format for audio visual **files**.

navigate
To find your way around a **web site**, or the whole **Internet**.

netiquette
How you should behave on the **Internet**.

Netscape Communicator
A popular program for sending and receiving **e-mail**.

Netscape Navigator
A popular **web browser**.

network
A system of computers connected to each other.

newbie
A new **Internet user**.

newsgroup
A system for posting messages for other **users** to read.

NNTP (Network News Transfer Protocol)
The standard used for **newsgroup** postings.

node
A specific point on a **network**.

offline
Not connected to the **Internet**.

offline browsing
Using your **browser** to view pages stored in the **cache** after disconnecting from the **Internet**.

online
Connected to the **Internet**.

online content provider
A company which provides information for **Internet users**.

Outlook Express
A popular program for sending and receiving **e-mail**.

patch
A temporary upgrade to a computer program.

parental control
Means of regulating the access to certain **web sites** from any **browser**.

PDF (Portable Document Format)
A format for **files** which can be read on many different computer systems.

plug-in
Small add-on program used to enhance the performance of another.

POP3 (Post Office Protocol)
A common format used by **e-mail servers**.

portal
A **web site** that acts as a **link** to other sites.

post
To put an electronic message on a **newsgroup** bulletin board.

PPP (Point to Point Protocol)
The system of allocating an address to your computer each time you **log on** to the **Internet**.

protocol
A recognised system used to permit communication of data between devices.

proxy server
A **server** used to store information before transmitting to the **user**.

QuickTime
A program used to play audiovisual **files**.

searchbot
A small search program which can be configured by the **user** to search for specific information.

search engine
A program used to search for information requested by a **user**.

server
A computer used to provide information or services to other connected computers.

shareware
Programs available for a small registration fee.

software
Any program or **file** stored on a computer.

spam
Junk **e-mail**. Beware.

surf
To use the **Internet**, going from **web site** to **web site**.

The Internet
The sum of all the computers and **servers** connected throughout the world.

thumbnail
A smaller version of an image **file**, usually linked to the full size image.

troll
Someone who thrives on causing controversy within a **newsgroup**.

upload
To transfer a **file** from your computer to the **Internet**.

URL (Uniform Resource Locator)
The address of a **web site**, usually prefixed by www.

user
Term for the person accessing information on the **Internet**.

UUencode
A method of encoding binary **files** for sending via **e-mail**.

V.90
Connection **protocol** used by many **modems**.

virtual reality
The imaginary world created using computer devices and **software** which mimics the real world.

virus
A mini program or string of code which attaches itself to your **software** with various results, usually bad.

WAP (Wireless Application Protocol)
Modified **web pages** for access by mobile telephones.

web address
The unique location identifying a particular **web site** or **web page**.

web authoring
Designing **web sites** and **web pages**.

webcam
A digital camera connected directly to the **Internet** and accessed via a **web site**.

web directory
Online database of **web sites** organised into categories.

web page
Single page of data published on the **World Wide Web**.

web site
A collection of electronic documents published on the **Internet**.

World Wide Web or WWW or the Web
The entire collection of electronic documents containing text, sound, graphics and video published on the **Internet**.

WYSIWYG
(What You See Is What You Get).
The way something appears on the screen is how it will appear if printed.

zip file
File compressed for transfer on the **Internet**.

Notes